COMMUNITY
ONONDAGA
COLLEGE
1962

0165 01 523392 01 1 (IC=0)

D1069204

FERTILITY DECLINE IN THE LESS DEVELOPED COUNTRIES

FERTILITY DECLINE IN THE LESS DEVELOPED COUNTRIES

Edited by
Nick Eberstadt

PRAEGER

PRAEGER SPECIAL STUDIES • PRAEGER SCIENTIFIC

Library of Congress Cataloging in Publication Data

Main entry under title:

Fertility decline in the less developed countries.

Includes index.
1. Underdeveloped areas--Fertility, Human--Addresses, essays, lectures. I. Eberstadt, Nick, 1955-
HB901.F47 304.6'3'091724 80-23528
ISBN 0-03-055271-0

Published in 1981 by Praeger Publishers
CBS Educational and Professional Publishing
A Division of CBS, Inc.
521 Fifth Avenue, New York, New York 10175 U.S.A.

123456789 145 987654321

Printed in the United States of America

ACKNOWLEDGMENTS

This volume emerged, piece by piece, from a symposium on fertility decline in the less developed countries that was sponsored by the American Association for the Advancement of Science; it was held, interestingly enough, on Valentine's Day 1978. We owe the AAAS our thanks. More specifically, we should like to thank Elisabeth Zeutschel, meetings manager for the AAAS, whose painstaking efforts were essential in the success of the symposium, and hence crucial in the evolution of the book.

Although their hands may not be immediately recognized, Nathan Keyfitz of Harvard's sociology department and Richard Tabors of MIT's Energy Laboratory made important contributions to this volume, first through the challenging ideas they presented at the symposium, then later with the many rigorous criticisms and useful comments they provided on the emerging manuscripts. Their help was greatly appreciated.

The Harvard Center for Population Studies and the Rockefeller Foundation have been gracious and generous sponsors for me as I attempted to assemble and edit this volume. Particular thanks are due to Ellen Hopkins of the Center for Population Studies, who served as my safety net during many of the acts of acrobatics that this volume necessitated, and to Henry Romney of the Rockefeller Foundation, who was not only unceasingly supportive but also exceptionally incisive in his advice.

If patience is a virtue, Lynda Sharp, our editor at Praeger, has proven herself to be a saint. Throughout the turbulent and often aggravating process of pulling this volume together, she has provided only support, encouragement, sound advice, and good cheer. Editors aren't supposed to be like that; it is a good thing Ms. Sharp hasn't found this out.

Finally, deep and very special thanks is due Professor Roger Revelle, who currently hangs his hat at the Revelle Campus of the University of California, La Jolla. In his 14 years as director of the Harvard Center for Population Studies, Roger Revelle brought demography new life. It was not just that his own vast and subtle understanding of the world permitted him to span that dangerous gap between science and art into which so many lesser students of population have fallen; as a mentor, colleague, and leader, he inspired all around him to strive for the pursuit of truth with the uncompromising rigor that he exemplified. Most of us associated with this volume were students or colleagues of Professor Revelle at one time; our debts to him, individual and collective, cannot easily be put into words. But this does not mean they should go unacknowledged. It is to Roger Revelle, and the example he has provided us, that this book is dedicated.

CONTENTS

ACKNOWLEDGMENTS v

INTRODUCTION
by Nick Eberstadt 1

Chapter

1 RECENT DECLINES IN FERTILITY IN LESS DEVELOPED COUNTRIES, AND WHAT POPULATION PLANNERS MAY LEARN FROM THEM 29
Nick Eberstadt

2 PATTERNS OF FERTILITY DECLINE IN DEVELOPING COUNTRIES, 1950-75 72
W. Parker Mauldin

3 FERTILITY IN AFRICA 97
John C. Caldwell

4 FERTILITY DECLINE IN CHINA 119
John S. Aird

5 THE FERTILITY DECLINE IN THE WEST AS A MODEL FOR DEVELOPING COUNTRIES TODAY: THE CASE OF NINETEENTH-CENTURY AMERICA 229
Maris A. Vinovskis

6 THE EFFECTS OF INCOME DISTRIBUTION ON FERTILITY IN DEVELOPING COUNTRIES 254
Robert Repetto

7 ECONOMIC VALUE AND COSTS OF CHILDREN IN RELATION TO HUMAN FERTILITY 274
Moni Nag

8 INFANT MORTALITY AND BEHAVIOR IN THE REGULATION OF FAMILY SIZE 295

Susan C. M. Scrimshaw

9 POPULATION, NUTRITION, AND FECUNDITY: SIGNIFICANCE FOR INTERPRETATION OF CHANGES IN FERTILITY 319

Rose E. Frisch

10 AMERICAN EFFORTS TO REDUCE THE FERTILITY OF LESS DEVELOPED COUNTRIES 337

William Petersen

INDEX 363

ABOUT THE EDITOR AND CONTRIBUTORS 371

FERTILITY DECLINE IN THE LESS DEVELOPED COUNTRIES

INTRODUCTION

Nick Eberstadt

In the quarter century following World War II, the most important shifts in the patterns of human fertility were thought to have occurred in the "developed nations."[1] First there was the baby boom, which peaked in the late 1950s, then later the "birth dearth," the rapid and in many respects puzzling decline that began in the 1960s, and has since swept nearly every advanced nation. Neither shift was anticipated by students of demography; in fact, neither was even recognized until it was already well under way.

In this same period demographers also devoted much of their time and energy to studying the less developed countries, whose populations now comprise about three-fourths of mankind. Here it seemed unlikely that scholars would be beset by unanticipated changes. The prevailing wisdom held that the poor nations of Asia, Latin America, and Africa were locked into a traditional regimen of high fertility.[2] Though the exact nature of this regimen was seldom explicitly confronted, the going assumptions were that it was of primeval origin (and therefore presumably both homogeneous and universal), that it was stable, if not unchanging, and that it would be extremely resistant to the best efforts of demographers, family planners, development experts, and other enlightened souls to alter it. There was little doubt among demography's more serious practitioners that the prolific societies could eventually be bent to a more reasonable will.[3] After all, the demographic transition, demography's own stab at a theory of historical inevitability, posited that all the nations of the world would eventually go the way of the small family in the face of pressures generated by what with convenient ambiguity was termed socioeconomic development.[4] But all this would take time, and most demographers did not expect any significant declines in the fertility of the peoples of the less developed countries before the 1980s, or maybe even the 1990s.[5]

Once again, however, events have taken demography by surprise. It now appears that tens of millions—and possible hundreds of millions—of couples in the poor world are deciding they will not have as many children as did their parents. As a result, fertility in the less developed countries is dropping; indeed, evidence is mounting to suggest that an important decline was already in progress by the mid-1960s, when demographers were arguing among themselves whether the incipient drop was 25 years away, or only 15.

The current decline is neither a universal nor a uniform experience; large areas of the poor world have yet to be affected. Nevertheless, it is widespread—and spreading wider, substantial in aggregate, and continuing at a rate that is extremely rapid in historical terms. It is undoubtedly affecting the quality of both material and emotional life in those countries caught up in it. Its size and speed speak to the importance of the changes those societies we so casually label "traditional" have already undergone, and to our seeming inability to recognize, or at least appreciate, these changes even years after they have become accepted facets of everyday life.

This book is a first attempt to map out and analyze the phenomenon of rapid fertility decline in the less developed countries. The caveats and disclaimers preceding some academic works owe more to their authors' sense of ritual than to their conviction that their studies are beset by limitations. Unfortunately for us, we are not in this happy position. Our readers should be aware of the difficulties under which we are laboring. The basic problem is this: population science is an extremely fragile discipline. It is still in its infancy. Admittedly, this is a peculiar and particularly drawn-out infancy, but an infancy it is nonetheless.

Observers of the more mature social sciences—I am thinking now of economics, sociology, political science—have been noting with alarm that while the forces of knowledge have been advancing rapidly on many fronts, they seem to be in disarray, even in retreat, on many others.[6] At the same time that ever more advanced and potentially powerful tools are being introduced to facilitate the analysis of collective behavior, they have remarked, social scientists are abandoning their allegiance to intellectual rigor, an allegiance that led to the growth of understanding in these fields in the first place. This paradoxical situation is nothing new to students of demography; their field has suffered from evolutionary regression for many long decades. In demography, the most imposing theoretical edifices and the most sophisticated applications of mathematics often build upon a base laid with false precision, doctrinaire argumentation, and careless universalization of limited experience. As a result, progress in demography has been slow. To be sure, there have been improvements in statistical technique. Neat new mathematical theorems have been propounded. Many perceptive observations about society and human behavior have been advanced. But for the most part, such contributions have been peripheral. The basic questions about the rhythms of motion in human populations remain unanswered. Whatever we demographers may sometimes tell ourselves, our data are still neither sufficiently accurate nor sufficiently comprehensive to allow us to undertake the sorts of analyses we might wish, and our framework for understanding events is still far from satisfactory.

The fact of the matter is that demography today can explain only a few of the demographic changes of the past unambiguously, and its ability to predict the demographic changes of the future in any meaningful way borders on the nonexistent.

Given the weaponry with which we must attack this new phenomenon, it would be unrealistic to expect us to come home with the pelt after a single outing. Our goal here, in fact, is much less ambitious. We are merely probing new territory, looking for tracks. Undertakings like this almost inevitably raise more questions than they answer; ours is no different. When we do come up with answers, moreover, we do not necessarily all end up in the same place. There are some important differences in interpretation in this volume: witness, for example, the range of conclusions about the effectiveness of family planning programs in contributing to fertility decline. That a question so basic remains to be answered to anything approaching general satisfaction suggests not only how much more work needs to be done on fertility decline in the less developed countries, but also how great the gaps in demographic knowledge more generally still are. It is our hope that this volume will stimulate curiosity about and controversy on some of demography's unanswered questions, and that it will encourage others to pursue these with the vigor and intellectual rigor that they deserve and require.

Often introductions summarize subsequent chapters; however, I am reluctant to do this, for these papers speak quite well enough for themselves. It is sometimes considered appropriate to synthesize the volume's findings into a workable whole; but given the diversity of our conclusions, I would run the risk of producing an elegant but sterile compromise. In the remainder of this introduction, therefore, I will use my editorial license to throw a little perspective on our chapters: to highlight the problems they raise, and to point out some of the promising paths for future research they open up.

MEASURING DEMOGRAPHIC CHANGE IN THE LESS DEVELOPED COUNTRIES

Underlying all other problems of interpreting data is the problem of the reliability of the data themselves. If we accept incorrect information, or impute to numbers an accuracy they do not merit, we will be led astray. How reliable, then, are our demographic figures for the less developed countries?

The grace with which Parker Mauldin discusses population and fertility figures in his masterful overview of demographic trends in the poor world in the third quarter of this century may suggest to the uninitiated that the information he is working with is clear-cut and unambiguous; it is not. Despite some salutary advances in both census coverage and enumerative techniques, our knowledge about population and its movement in the less developed countries is still far from precise.

By their very nature statistics carry with them margins of error. For our purposes we must have an idea of how large these margins are, and how systematic any biases embedded in them may be. Here the study of population ceases to be a science, and becomes instead an art. We must rely on experience and intuition in our attempts to give figures meaning.

Let us begin by examining the reliability of our figures for total populations. One measure by which we might judge our assessments of current populations is by the extent to which past estimates have required adjustment in the light of subsequent revelations. This measure, of course, has obvious limitations: on the one hand, such adjustments can occur only as errors are discovered, and the elimination of error is presumably a cumulative process that should lend our figures ever greater credibility over time; on the other hand, such adjustments can be made only after errors are recognized, and there is obviously no way to know exactly how many undetected errors remain to be found. Nevertheless, a comparison of past and present assessments of population numbers for some past data is instructive. In Table 1 we see a comparison of two sets of United Nations figures for representative LDCs for the year 1955. The first set was released in 1958, the second was issued in 1980.

Twenty-two years of hindsight have made for significant alterations: notice in particular how much the United Nations now thinks it erred in its earlier estimates for Africa. The U.N.'s demographers now believe that the principal failing of their past estimates was underestimation. It is easy enough to see how national or international agencies might have overlooked large numbers of people in societies where citizens did not generate readily collectible information about their lives, and where governments would have been in a poor position to process these even if they had existed. Perhaps more surprising is the fact that the United Nations now believes that its estimates for a not insignificant minority of less developed countries were overestimates. The origins of such mistakes of excess, as I explain in Chapter 1, are not always to be found in the limitations of enumerative techniques. Very real benefits may accrue to individuals, factions, or even entire nations from deliberate overrepresentation. A clan in China may wish to bolster its numbers in the year of ration-card reckoning; a tribe in a West African nation may find it expedient to exaggerate its size in hopes of wresting additional revenue or representation from the central government; an oil-rich Middle Eastern state like Saudi Arabia, fearing its own weakness,

TABLE I.1

United Nations Estimates of the Population of Representative LDCs for 1955, as Made in 1958 and 1980 (in millions)

	As Estimated in 1958	As Estimated in 1980	Percent Difference
Asia			
Burma	19.4	20.2	-4.1
China	600.0	614.5	-2.4
India	386.0	393.9	-2.0
Indonesia	81.9	82.8	-1.1
Iran	21.8	19.0	+14.7
Jordan	1.4	1.4	-1.2
Pakistan[a]	83.2	85.9	-3.2
Philippines	22.1	23.9	-8.1
Turkey	24.0	23.9	+1.8
Unweighted average of absolute differences: 3.9 percent			
Latin America and the Caribbean			
Argentina	19.3	18.9	+2.1
Bolivia	3.2	3.0	+7.3
Brazil	59.2	61.8	-4.5
Colombia	12.7	13.4	-6.1
Ecuador	3.6	3.8	-5.5
Guatemala	29.7	31.0	-4.2
Unweighted average of absolute differences: 5.0 percent			
Africa			
Algeria	9.5	9.7	-2.3
Congo[b]	12.6	16.7	-32.3
Egypt	23.0	23.0	—
Ethiopia	11.6	18.0	-55.2
Kenya	6.1	6.8	-12.1
Nigeria	31.3	37.3	-19.0
South Africa	13.7	15.4	-12.4
Tanzania[c]	8.6	9.1	-5.8
Unweighted average of absolute differences: 17.6 percent			

[a]Combined figure for West Pakistan and East Pakistan (Bangladesh).

[b]The former entity Belgian Congo is now two states, Zaire and People's Republic of the Congo.

[c]Tanzania was formed by the union of Zanzibar and Tanganyika.

Sources: Figures from column 1 taken from United Nations, The Future Growth of World Population (New York: United Nations, 1958). Figures from column 2 taken from United Nations, World Population and Its Age-Sex Composition by Country, 1950-2000 (New York: United Nations Population Division, January 2, 1980).

TABLE I.2

Possible Margins of Error in Current Regional Estimates of World Population

China	100 million
Japan	1 million
Other East Asia	35 million
Indo-Ganeatic Subcontinent	30 million
Southwest Asia	20 million
Latin America and the Caribbean	20 million
Arab Africa	5 million
Black Africa	40 million
USSR	5 million
Europe	5 million
North America	1 million
Oceania	under 1 million
Total	260+ million

Source: Compiled by the author.

may feel it necessary to inflate its population numbers in an attempt to mislead outsiders about its actual strength.

It is important to remember that unless all estimate errors are biased in the same direction, any aggregation of national figures will give a margin of error for a region or continent smaller than the sum of its parts, for over- and underestimates will appear to cancel each other out. This trick of arithmetic tends to make errors appear to be considerably smaller than they actually are—at least for most practical purposes.

How great are the margins of error today? We can only guess. In his chapter, Mauldin puts them in the 400 million range (that is, plus or minus 200 million). This is also the figure I settled upon, although both of our guesses were made before China, that vast demographic mystery, divulged new census figures last year. In light of China's revelations and the ongoing improvements in the statistical systems of other less developed countries, an updated guess should be considerably lower. I give one in Table I.2.

On a country-by-country basis, it is my guess that the absolute value of the errors in today's population estimates for the less developed countries would be about a quarter of a billion people. This is still distressingly large. It would be something like 7 or 8 percent of what we think to be the poor world total, and in areas like Africa and China it would be considerably more. Nevertheless, we can take heart from the fact that the margins of error have been narrowing continuously. Only 15 years ago relative margins of error might have been twice as high as today. Over the next 15 years, barring unforeseeable political difficulties, it might not be unreasonable to expect increases in administrative and technical skills in the poor countries to halve the relative margins of error once again.

If population levels can be approximated only with considerable difficulty, the situation with vital rates is even more arduous. On the face of it, a birth rate should be much easier to estimate than an aggregate population figure: with the first, at least theoretically, one can work with a limited sample, while for the second, one needs to take some measure of the whole. But as I explain in Chapter 1, vital rates have problems of their own.

We can get some idea of the difficulties demographers encounter when they attempt to measure birth rates by looking at the range of figures reputable organizations present for representative LDCs (see Table I.3). The cynics among us might try to explain away these differences as statistical manifestations of institutional bias: the Environmental Fund, which was chartered on a fear that mankind was overpopulating itself out of existence, comes out pretty consistently with high numbers; the Agency for International Development, whose good health depends on its success in convincing Congress that its family planning programs have made a difference, comes out just as consistently with low numbers. The fact of the matter, however, is that even the most objective observers are hard pressed to come up with accurate numbers on fertility in many areas of the poor world.

The societies where fertility is presumed to be high and stable, and hence in theory quite simple to measure, also happen to have the least developed technical and administrative superstructures with which to measure it. Look at the range of estimates for birth rates in Afghanistan! In societies where fertility is dropping, the technical capacity of the state is generally more advanced, but the difficulties inherent in approximating a rapidly changing birth rate more than nullify this advantage, as Chapter 1 explains. The data demographers must work with cannot always keep up with the changes in human life they are supposed to reflect; hence, for most LDCs with declining fertility, birth rate estimates will be biased high. The figures we present in this volume may indeed suffer from this affliction; in light of subsequent revelations, they will almost certainly need to be revised. We will have a much clearer impression of the fertility situation for the past decade in the 1990s than we could possibly have today. However, as the saying goes, you can only work with what you have.

TABLE I.3

Birth Rate Estimates in 1975 for Selected LDCs

	High Estimate		Low Estimate		Percent Difference
Asia					
Afghanistan	50-53	(CB)	43	(PRB)	16-23
Bangladesh	50	(UN)	42	(WB)	19
Iran	45	(UN)	41-42	(CB)	7-10
North Korea	44	(WB)	34	(UN)	29
Pakistan	47	(UN)	44	(PC)	7
Philippines	43	(UN)	32-35	(PC)	23-24
Sri Lanka	30	(EF)	26-27		11-15
Taiwan	26	(CB)	23	(PC)	13
Turkey	40	(EF)	34	(PRB)	18
India	40	(EF)	34	(PRB)	18
Latin America and the Caribbean					
Brazil	38-40	(CB)	36	(WB)	6-11
Chile	28	(UN)	22-23	(CB)	22-27
Colombia	41	(EF)	31	(AID)	21
Mexico	44	(EF)	39	(WB)	13
Africa					
Egypt	39	(CB)	35	(WB)	6-11
Ethiopia	52	(CB)	43	(CB)	21
Kenya	50	(WB)	48	(UN)	4
Nigeria	50	(CB)	48	(CB)	4
Zaire	47	(CB)	43	(CB)	9
China	36	(EF)	14	(AID)	157
Unweighted average of absolute differences: 22-24 percent					
Unweighted average of absolute differences, excluding China: 15-17 percent					

AID: U.S. Agency for International Development.
CB: U.S. Census Bureau.
EF: Environmental Fund.
PC: Population Council.
PRB: Population Reference Bureau.
UN: United Nations Population Division.
WB: World Bank.

Source: Adapted from Dudley Kirk, "World Population and Birth Rates: Agreements and Disagreements," Population and Development Review (September 1979).

REGIONS OF PARTICULAR DEMOGRAPHIC UNCERTAINTY

The two areas of the poor world in which demographic mysteries are greatest are Africa (more specifically, black Africa) and China. These regions are mysteries for rather different reasons: to oversimplify, Africa presents all the intriguing questions about high fertility and the onset of fertility decline, while providing very little of the information that might help answer them; China, to oversimplify again, has evidently been able to effect a substantial fertility decline over the past generation, but hosts a government too secretive to divulge the details of its experience.

Africa's statistical capabilities, as John C. Caldwell points out in Chapter 3, are minimal: there are few accurate overall records for today, and virtually none for the past. Geographically, Africa is an enormous expanse; socially and demographically, despite our tendency to think of it as homogeneous, it is very diverse. It is characterized by high fertility, but as Caldwell and others have shown, there are very important differences in fertility levels both among and within countries.[7] Some of this may be due to the prevalence of infertility, whose dimensions have yet to be plotted out fully, but it seems unlikely that all of it can be ascribed to biology.[8] As Caldwell points out, a great deal probably has to do with the workings of the African family.

Despite the steps Caldwell and others have taken to advance our understanding of family life in Africa, there is still an enormous range of questions that we cannot answer. I will mention just a few of these here. We have yet to map out the range of family arrangements within and among African societies, although the range seems to be quite large. To take just one example, mean household size of the LoWilli in West Africa was measured to be over 11 in the 1950s, while in East Africa in the 1960s the Bunyoro's mean household size was under four.[9] We need to know more about the evolution of African family structures. Surely these were not static over the past, and yet we have almost no information on the ways in which they might have changed.[10] We need to know much more about the role of women in African societies. Understanding their position [as childbearers (and often as principal family producers)] may help us to answer many of the questions about African fertility we wish most fervently to pin down. For example, it seems now that age at marriage in Africa is rising, and yet there are no indications of any corresponding drop in fertility. Can this be fully explained by the position of women in the structure of African societies? We need to know more about the economics of the African family. Caldwell has suggested that in high fertility societies children are a most productive asset. But does this turn out to be true in areas where land is scarce? Many such regions are now emerging in West Africa.[11] We need to know the effects that emerging class patterns are having on the family. Egypt has presented demographers with a puzzle they thought they would never see: a nation where fertility decline began, then stopped, and now seems to be in the process of reversing itself. Is this, as Caldwell suggests, a phenomenon related to class? If so, how exactly? And what does this augur for fertility decline in the nations that have yet to undergo it? If in fact the family turns out to be the key to understanding the mechanisms and timing of fertility decline, we have a great deal of work ahead of us, and not just in Africa.

The People's Republic of China, for all the statistical shortcomings John Aird points out in his superb chapter, is nevertheless relatively advanced in its enumerative capabilities, yet its demographic patterns remain inaccessible to us. The Peking regime does not believe in the free release of information, for in a controlled society uncontrolled information is at best an annoyance, at worst a very real threat to the ruling elite. Peking has successfully isolated its people; China's quarter of the human race is the least known to the outside world.

In recent years social critics and reformers claimed that the Chinese model of development offers many potential solutions to the problems of the less developed countries, including the demographic.[12] China's apparently rapid drop in fertility, and the presumed improvements in living standards that supposedly precipitated it, have been held out as cynosures for the rest of Asia, and sometimes even for Latin America and Africa.[13] Aird's chapter suggests that while a substantial fertility decline has indeed taken place in China, it was much less a response to improvements in standards of living than to China's third population campaign, an operation that was probably strongly coercive. If Aird is correct, the people of the less developed countries will have good reason to worry should their governments actually decide to learn from the Chinese model.

Two important questions about China's population control system should be asked. First, if the Chinese government has been successful in coercing parents into reducing family size against their will, how exactly has it been able to do so? Coercion in such a personal and vital area of one's life would arguably require a very strong and sophisticated state machine; yet from other sources there are ample indications that China's government has been in confusion, if not in chaos, for long portions of the past generation.[14] Can these apparently conflicting aspects of the Chinese experience be reconciled? Second, what have been the government's motives in promoting population control? Malthusian policies are surely inconsistent with Marxist doctrine, and Mao himself declared from time to time that population problems were an artifact of capitalist, not socialist, society. It is my suspicion that China's population control campaign has been a response to the disappointing performance of the planned economy, and in particular to collectivized agriculture. Work I have done elsewhere suggests there has been a significant drop in the efficiency of Chinese agriculture since land reform was completed in 1952.[15] It is difficult to identify the causes of this drop, but it may be presumed with some safety that many of the problems with Chinese agriculture today are inherent in the Communist system of organization, control, and reward. These are problems that seem to be shared by the agricultural systems of all Communist nations.[16] Faced with the prospects of having population growth outpace the increases in agricultural production, the ruling elite was, I suspect, faced in the extreme with two alternatives. It could relax its control over society in hopes of stimulating efficiency and production, but this road would be politically perilous, and ideologically distasteful to boot. Or it could attempt to stave off a production crisis by limiting the number of mouths to be fed. Although administratively far more imposing, this course would seem to be much safer politically. Such speculation is consistent with what little we know about Chinese policies and their results, but a great deal of work would need to be done to transform these musings into hard arguments.

SOCIAL FORCES AFFECTING THE FERTILITY DECLINE

What has precipitated the rapid and unexpected decline in the fertility of so many less developed countries? Except for the tiny fraction of couples whose fecundity was impaired by nutritional assault, the answer would seem to lie in social change. Five of our authors examine some of the factors that may help us come to terms with the phenomenon of fertility decline in the less developed countries, and with the complexity and diversity this phenomenon presents.

Fertility decline by its nature must take place over time, and yet for some reason students of population are shockingly ignorant of history. While no country today is an exact replica of another from the distant past, historical evidence provides a wealth of information on the variations and similarities between nations engaged in fertility decline. Maris Vinovskis does an excellent job of showing us the things we can learn about the present from an examination of the past. No single essay, of course, could do justice to the whole range of lessons demographers could learn from history; Vinovskis wisely has chosen to focus on the demographic experience of a single country, the United States. He covers his subject with a thoroughness and an eye for policy implications that other demographers could do well to learn from.

Some important lessons and questions concerning historical demography naturally fall outside the scope of Vinovskis's chapter. I will touch on only a few of these.

We often think of high fertility as an unchanging, age-old condition, but the evidence speaks differently. Stephen Polgar has pointed out that man's population grew only slowly until the modern era, and that even with the high mortality rates of the past, the fertility levels necessary to provide replacement would have been significantly lower than those prevailing in the poor world today.[17] By Polgar's estimate, replacement could have been achieved if mothers on average gave birth to four children. (For what it is worth, the total fertility rate of the bushmen of the Kalihari desert, one of the world's most primitive peoples, is believed to be about four today.[18]) Total fertility rates of six and seven, however, were common throughout the poor world only a generation ago, and still characterize most of Africa and the Middle East. Polgar's work suggests that a general and substantial fertility shift may have gripped the world once or more before the demographic transition of the twentieth century.

Jean-Noel Biraben has recently added support to Polgar's argument. He has shown that numbers have not increased steadily, but rather have advanced and receded in fits and spurts.[19] While population growth has usually been attributed to fluctuations in mortality, Biraben's essay suggests that variations in fertility may have been important as well.

Historical records suggest there may have been pronounced increases in fertility in the nineteenth century in such nations as Indonesia, Mexico, and Egypt.[20] Unfortunately, such evidence is too ambiguous to grant us firm conclusions. More recent records are not dogged by such severe problems of interpretation, however, and there is solid evidence that fertility rose significantly in many societies in the recent and relatively recent past. Table I.4 presents 19 cases in which fertility increases have been documented. While the limitations of the data may prevent us from placing our full faith in some of the more marginal cases (early twentieth-century Egypt, for instance), ten of the cases register increases of 20 percent or more—jumps too large to be easily written off to statistical ineptitude. It should be noted, furthermore, that most of the figures given are for birth rates, and since life expectancy was increasing rapidly during the years covered, age structure was changing in a way that would tend to depress birth rate numbers. The inherent bias in most of these figures, then, is toward understating the increases in fertility.

What social forces triggered these increases in fertility? If we can answer this question, we may be much nearer an understanding of the forces that trigger fertility declines.

TABLE I.4

Fertility Variation in High Fertility Societies: Estimates for Selected Countries

	Birth Rates		Percent
	Low Estimate	High Estimate	Difference
(1) Japan	23.1 (1871)	36.3 (1925)	+57
(2) Undivided India	46 (1891-1901)	49 (1901-11)	+7
(3) Egypt	41.6 (1913)	44.2 (1950)	+6
(4) Singapore	27.9 (1919-23)	43.4 (1950)	+56
(5) Taiwan	42 (1920-24)	46 (1950-54)	+10
(6) Pakistan	40 (1921-30)	47 (1951-60)	+18
(7) Malaysia	35.4 (1930-34)	44.0 (1955)	+24
(8) Mauritius	30.9 (1930-34)	49.7 (1950)	+61
(9) Reunion	42.4 (1946-49)	51.3 (1952)	+21
(10) Algeria	45.0 (1950)	52.1 (1963)	+16
(11) Costa Rica	42.9 (1950)	48.2 (1959)	+12
(12) Cuba	29.6 (1950)	36.3 (1960)	+23
(13) Jamaica	33.1 (1950)	42.0 (1960)	+27
(14) Panama	31.3 (1950)	40.0 (1960)	+28
(15) Surinam	39.0 (1950)	49.0 (1960)	+26
(16) Venezuela	42.6 (1950)	46.0 (1960)	+8
(17) Fiji	4.0 (1951)	4.4 (1964)	+10
(18) Albania	6.0 (1950-54)	6.8 (1960)	+13
(19) Dominican Republic	3.6 (1955)	7.7 (1965)	+114

Sources: Lines 1-3, 5: Peter H. Lindert, "Child Costs and Economic Development," in Population and Economic Change in Developing Countries, ed. Richard A. Easterlin (Chicago: University of Chicago Press, 1980); lines 4, 7-16: Moni Nag, "How Modernization Can Also Increase Fertility," Working Paper 49, Center for Policy Studies (Population Council, November 1979); line 6: Shahid Javed Burki, "Food and Fertility: Formulation of Public Policy in Pakistan," in ICP, Prologue to Development Policy and Population Policy—The Pakistan Experience (Washington, D.C.: Smithsonian Institution Interdisciplinary Communications Program, January 1975); lines 17-18: Kingsley Davis, "Population Policy: Will Current Programs Succeed?," Science (November 10, 1967); and line 19: Alice Henry and Phyllis Piotrow, "Age at Marriage and Fertility," Population Reports, November 1979.

One of the great advantages of historical data is that they permit us to work with time-series we cannot yet obtain from the less developed countries, and hence allow us to test hypotheses that otherwise would be forced to drift in the realm of conjecture. Much has been written, for example, about the role of socioeconomic development in promoting fertility decline; this is commonly held to be a necessary, and often also a sufficient factor to activate this process. Socioeconomic development is one of those wonderful words that can mean almost anything its user wants it to. If, however, we define it as having something to do with an improvement in standards of living, the history of nineteenth-century Europe is replete with examples of localities and even entire nations where fertility fell before living standards rose, and where they remained high long after a steady increase in human comfort began.[21] Then there is the intriguing case of Japan, where fertility was quite low during the Tokugawa era, and only rose to the levels we now associate with less developed countries after living standards began their now famous rise with the coming of the Meiji restoration. Alan Sweezy[22] and John Knodel and Etienne van de Walle[23] have shown that the conditions under which fertility decline in the countries now considered developed occurred werc tremendously diverse. This should come as no surprise: after all, we are all immersed in society as diving bells are immersed in water, staying where we are because forces pushing on us from a thousand different directions are canceling themselves out. If the pressure of one of these forces increases, or if another relents for whatever reason, things move. Just as there is more than one way to skin a cat, there should be more than one way to motivate parents to have smaller families. If we are to understand these better, we might be well advised to examine the changes in the forces affecting families over time, for in the final analysis it is parents, not societies, governments, or nations, who decide whether or not to have children.

An important question that historical investigation may help us answer concerns the role of contraception in promoting fertility decline. Almost 25 years ago the French demographer Louis Henry coined the term "natural fertility" to refer to the situation he saw in medieval Europe: a life-style in which women achieved their biological maximums for fertility, deterred only by such natural impediments as late marriage, postpartum amenorrhea, and nutritionally induced drops in fecundity.[24] There was a time when demographers generally assumed natural fertility to be the prevailing regimen in less developed societies; following this reasoning, they posited that the discovery and use of contraception would necessarily be associated with a decline in fertility. Today Henry's natural fertility hypothesis, to use Ronald Demos Lee's euphemism, is "controversial."[25]

Evidence from England,[26] Japan,[27] and elsewhere suggests that couples were indeed practicing contraception in various locales well before the modern age. Contrary to Knodel and van de Walle's assertion that the discovery and practice of family limitation is a one-way street leading to steady fertility decline, the experiences of Japan in the past[28] or Egypt and perhaps the Soviet Muslim republics today[29] would suggest that knowledge about contraception in no way forces parents to have ever fewer children; rather, contraception seems more to be a tool that can be used to attain a desired result. More research on patterns of contraceptive action in the past and its motivations may help us better understand the problems facing parents in the less developed countries today, as well as the family planning agencies that are supposed to serve them.

The process of economic growth is commonly linked with fertility decline in demographic theory,[30] but the relationship between economic growth and fertility is evidently more complicated than such casual theories would imply. In both Latin America and West Africa, the twentieth century has been a period of fairly rapid economic growth; aggregate rates of increase in both these regions compared favorably to England's when it was undergoing fertility decline in the middle of the nineteenth century. Yet fertility has not begun any measurable decline in West Africa, and in Latin America, where it is finally dropping, it seems first to have risen. By contrast, fertility has dropped rapidly and steadily in Sri Lanka, which has one of the lower growth rates among the poor countries.[31]

In his provocative chapter, Robert Repetto suggests that fertility decline may be related just as much to the distribution of the benefits from economic growth as to their aggregate magnitude. He points out that income distribution has improved markedly in such countries as Taiwan, South Korea, Costa Rica, the People's Republic of China, and in the Kerala province of India, and that despite relatively low average levels of economic output, fertility in these areas has fallen substantially. By contrast, in the regions of the poor world where income distribution is more highly skewed, such as most of Latin America and Africa, fertility is relatively high for the concomitant levels of average output. He also points out that income distribution may have played an important role in fertility declines in Hungary (and, one might add, Sweden) over the past century.

There is good reason to suspect that the distribution of benefits affects fertility in any society. Assuming this to be established, however, a number of important questions about economic growth, income distribution, and fertility would remain. Repetto points out that the relationship between income level and fertility in almost all societies is nonlinear; this, however, does not mean that the relationship is consistently inverse. In Indonesia and parts of Africa, wealth is positively associated with fertility;[32] in such areas, other things being equal, a redistribution of income to the poorest strata would presumably increase rather than reduce fertility. Why is wealth negatively associated with fertility in some societies and positively associated in others? Is it reasonable to expect other factors to remain equal if income is redistributed? Such questions remain to be answered.

It is easy enough to see how income distribution affects mortality: health is pretty clearly a function of wealth and the things it can buy, such as services and education.[33] The mechanisms through which income distribution affects fertility still need to be mapped out. The relationship is clearly complicated: think only of the recursive relationship between income distribution and economic growth. The complexity of the relationship has led some critics to question the validity of the fertility-income distribution hypothesis.[34] If we are to throw up our hands every time we are confronted by a complicated problem, however, we will not end up getting very far. Repetto's work with income distribution, naturally, has involved the analysis of intermediate variables; it challenges us to delve further into the relationships among family, society, and economic change.

One of the factors that may affect parents' decisions about numbers of offspring most directly is the economic costs and benefits their children are likely to present them. Perceived changes in the value of children may have an important impact on the number of children parents are willing to raise, even if the perceived economic worth of a child does not switch from being positive to negative.[35] In Chapter 7, Moni Nag skillfully reviews the historical and contemporary evidence on the value of children in poor societies.

Reading his chapter, one is struck by both the variations in the economic value of children among societies and over time, and by the difficulties facing an outside observer attempting to calculate the costs and benefits attendant with child-rearing. It is not only the diversity in economic rates of return from children, but also the difficulties involved in capturing these fully, that account for the tremendous discrepancies in the findings of modern scholars.[36] The methodology for reckoning the costs and benefits of children is in need of substantial improvement.

One question that needs more investigation is the relationship between the economic value of children and the structure of family bonds. It seems quite reasonable to suppose, for example, that the costs and benefits of children affect, and are affected by, such things as the age of women at marriage, the expectations families hold out for girls and women, and lateral and intergenerational kinship obligations. While Caldwell,[37] Ruzicka,[38] and others have dealt with some parts of this question, it is still largely unexplored territory, and merits much more attention than it has received.

Susan Scrimshaw's chapter on infant mortality in poor countries ties in with Nag's study on the value of children. Scrimshaw convincingly demonstrates that passive and active infanticide is prevalent in many parts of the poor world, and can be uncovered the world over in the past. The implications of this finding are that parents may use child death as a means of quality control over their brood, selecting out the disfavored (as girls turn out to be in so many societies) and the weak, and that infant mortality may be neither an accurate, consistent indicator of the value of children nor of the readiness of a community for other less tragic means of family limitation.

Infanticide is a relatively difficult phenomenon for an outside observer to document, and like all other forms of murder, it comes with many shades of justification, circumstantial as well as intellectual. The extent of neglect and active destruction of children has yet to be portrayed on a worldwide basis: this is work that anthropologists and demographers could profitably pursue in tandem. The Indian subcontinent will doubtless offer particular insights into the process of selective mortality: in this region, unlike many others in the poor world, death rates for females exceed death rates for males for every age cohort.[39] It is quite possible that further studies in selective mortality will bring us an understanding of poor societies extending far beyond the treatment of children in relation to fertility. To mention just one of the paths meriting pursuit, the study of feeding patterns within the family and the roles of primacy and denial in these may teach us a great deal about the true extent of world hunger, and the degree to which it is fomented unnecessarily by social custom.[40]

Although hunger may be caused by social forces,[41] its effects on the individual are unarguably biological. Among the other tolls malnutrition exacts is a reduction in the ability of parents to bear children. Since many people in the less developed countries are considered malnourished by international reference standards, it stands to reason that nutrition may play a role in changes of fertility. Rose Frisch explores the biological aspects of human fertility with rigor and insight in her chapter.

Frisch deals with her subject carefully and rigorously, but it is clear that she is treading dangerous ground. Demographers may take some perverse pleasure from learning that the basic questions about nutrition, presumably a "hard" science, have been answered even less satisfactorily than those in population studies.[42] Much remains to be done in nutrition as a whole, and in the relation between nutrition and fertility in particular. It is not yet known, for example, how genetic differences between populations affect the ability to remain fecund in the face of a curtailed diet, or how these genetic differences may have changed over time. Very little work has been done on the relation between diet and fertility in the past; this might serve as a useful check on current observations. Very little work has been done on the ability of the body to adjust to lower food levels over time by metabolizing what it does get more effectively; surely this sort of adjustment would impact on fecundability. Finally, it is extremely difficult to determine fecundity: it is an unobserved variable, the potential for fertility. As statisticians are well aware, the problems of dealing with unobserved variables are legion.[43]

Nutritionists investigating the relationship between food intake and fecundity clearly have their work cut out for them. Frisch has provided us with many answers about the mechanisms through which the body may curtail fertility, but the big questions about nutrition and fertility unfortunately still lie ahead of us.

Of all the chapters in this volume, William Petersen's is undoubtedly the most ambitious; it is also certain to be the most controversial. Petersen sets out to debunk the claims of family planning programs that they have contributed significantly to fertility decline in the less developed countries. In the process he critiques everything from interpretations of demographic history to the so-called Chicago school approach to the economics of fertility. Petersen's chapter is sure to draw both heated criticism and spirited acclaim; it will make every reader think more carefully about just what it is that family planning programs do.

In Eastern Europe and the Soviet Union, where fertility has been low and continues to decline, it has been explicit policy for many years to raise the birth rates.[44] The failure of pronatalist policy in such controlled and relatively affluent societies raises questions about what one can expect from antinatalist campaigns in poorer societies run by governments with many fewer means of influence at their disposal. (Indeed, it may also make us wonder about the extent to which coercion itself, rather than some associated change, may have depressed fertility in China.) The mechanisms through which antinatalist family planning programs might trigger a reduction in fertility beyond the elimination of accidental and unwanted pregnancy has yet to be convincingly detailed.

Even the most ardent believers in the power of family planning programs to encourage ongoing reductions in fertility admit there is difficulty in untangling the effects of family planning programs from those of the changes impacting on parents and their societies.[45] Some analyses of fertility decline in the poor countries have naively assumed that every person using a modern means of contraception represents a birth per year prevented;[46] besides the mathematical inadequacy betrayed by this assumption,[47] a fundamental misconception about the nature of contraception is also revealed. Virtually every exposed couple (this is family planning vernacular) in Sweden uses some form of contraception, and yet Swedish society continues to replace itself. The point is that contraceptives are not necessarily a means of eliminating and preventing fertility: they are far more likely to be used instead to regulate it. Studies that miss this simple distinction—and it is surprising how many do—have little to offer us.

Even the more sophisticated studies, alas, have difficulty estimating the actual effects of family planning programs on fertility.[48] There are simply too many unobservable variables, simultaneities, indeterminate lags, and intricate interactions at work for modellers to produce answers that can be considered meaningful. As our understanding of the interactions among fertility, family, society, and economy increases, however, we should be able to make tentative and reasonably precise steps in this direction.

When Petersen criticizes family planning programs and their more unscrupulous promoters, it should be emphasized that he is distinguishing between contraception and antinatalism. A couple contracepting is deciding how many children it wishes to have; a couple subject to antinatalist propaganda is being directed, with whatever good intentions, to have the number of children someone else wishes them to have. There are many salutary benefits to be had from contraception; these will be well known to the reader, and need not be run through here. Petersen's point is that antinatalist policies, like militantly pronatalist policies, are more than just aesthetically unappealing, and short of some very nasty measures, they are unlikely to produce much in the way of long-range results.

ISSUES FOR THE FUTURE

What are the prospects for the spread and continuation of fertility decline in the less developed countries? If the preceding pages are to be trusted, we might conclude that the progress of fertility decline in the poor world cannot be predicted with any certainty. One can always juggle numbers to see how low birth rates would have to be to achieve any given gross or net reproduction rate for a region by a certain date,[49] and then compute the speed at which birth rates would have to fall for this target to be attained. However, there are distinct limits to the utility of such exercises. At the present time we have no accurate means for predicting when the regions of the world that have not begun their fertility transition will enter into it, nor to judge the speed at which those countries currently engaged in fertility decline will continue with it. We cannot even tell how many countries, if any, will follow the "Egyptian model" and find their fertility slowly creeping upward after an initial drop. We can do little more than belabor the obvious: if present trends continue, birth rates in the poor world will continue to drop, and people in high fertility societies will come under increasing pressures to have smaller families. The answer is inadequate; unfortunately, the state of the art does not allow more precision.

While we cannot peer into the future, we can examine the past with greater care. Information on the fertility decline that so many poor nations are engaging in is becoming available in ever greater volumes, and the accuracy of such work is improving. As it filters in, we might begin to ask questions that previously could not be answered. I will list here only three of the topics that deserve pursuit.

The Status of Women

In Chapter 1 I suggest that a two-phased pattern of fertility decline seemed to be emerging in the less developed countries. In the first phase it was (principally) a decrease in the proportion of women married during their fertile years that powered the decline; by contrast, in the second phase, it was primarily drops in marital fertility rates that did the job. In the time since my chapter was written, much of the information from the World Fertility Survey has become available. The figures divulged thus far have been for South and East Asian countries; it would be imprudent to exaggerate their generality. Nevertheless, the patterns revealed are consistent with my earlier speculations. Fertility decline in its initial stages seems to be powered by changes in nuptuality patterns: in Indonesia, the Philippines, and Thailand, where birth rates have fallen from the low to mid forties to the low to mid thirties over the past ten or 15 years, changes in marital proportions have accounted for the largest part of the drop.[50] (On the other hand, in Sri Lanka, where birth rates have declined from the mid thirties to the mid twenties over the past 15 years, changes in marital fertility rates have been the engine of reduction.[51])

What sorts of changes in marriage patterns have made for this decline in fertility? Family breakups are on the increase, but their effect on fertility still seems to be very small. By far the largest portion of the change can be attributed to what appears to be a world-wide pattern of later marriages for women. To date there are no indications of any similar pattern for men. As a result, the difference in age at marriage between men and women is narrowing in the less developed countries.

The increase in age at marriage for women in the poor world has not yet been fully explained, but it would seem a safe bet that new job and educational opportunities, and a shift in obligations to the family, would have something to do with it. These would speak, albeit in a limited way, to changes in the status and position of women in poor societies.

It may seem surprising that demographers have paid so little attention to women's roles in poor societies; one does not have to be a population expert to recognize that they have a fairly important role in the childbearing process. Nevertheless, the fact is that students of population are still quite uninformed about the parts women play over the course of their lives in their families, their economies, and their societies, how these parts differ among peoples, and how these parts have been changing.

It is my hunch that fertility decline will not be terribly well understood until we have come to grips with the question of the status of women; if I am right, we have a long way to go.

The Influence of Values and Beliefs

In a recent article, Craig Bolton and J. William Leasure have related fertility decline in the West to changes in political consciousness.[52] This is an intriguing argument that deserves further examination, and it points to a problem that currently besets demography: most students of population are extremely reluctant to deal with any factor they cannot easily measure. The whole realm of values, attitudes, and beliefs clearly plays a major role in our decisions over children and family, and yet for the most part we ignore it. Not being able to measure something easily, however, is no guarantee that it is unimportant.

The changes in political and social ideology that have swept the world over the past 35 years have been profound; no less deep have been the changes in religious and secular values. As these change, so do the concept of happiness, the notion of duty, the standards of love, the degree of faith in or fear of the future, the belief in the importance of human life, and the idea of purpose, to name only a few. How can we fail to acknowledge the impact these have on the rich, subtle, and vastly intricate expanse of our emotional life? How, in turn, can we fail to acknowledge the impact of emotional life on one's decisions about the family? Future studies in demography might profit from excursions into this great unexplored territory.

The Effects of Fertility Decline on Family, Society, and Economy

This book deals almost exclusively with fertility decline and the forces that have contributed to it. Our work begs the question: How do these different declines affect the emotional lives and material prospects of the people living in the societies in which they occur?

A great deal of doctrinaire material has been published on the relationship between fertility decline and social or economic welfare, but very little work of substance in this area has seen the light of day. Most analyses of the effects of population growth blow with prevailing winds, and hence may be suspected of lacking serious foundation. During the Great Depression, when population growth rates in the Western world were declining, it was taken as a given that a healthy rate of natural increase was necessary for the maintenance of a healthy economy.[53] After World War II, when it became clear that the demographic growth rates of the peoples of the poor world had pulled ahead of those for Western societies for the first time in perhaps three centuries, population growth was suddenly a threat to economic security,[54] and perhaps even to national survival.[55]

A more dispassionate approach toward the effects of population growth and fertility decline is necessary. It should recognize the tremendous diversity in man's economic, social, and demographic experience, and should take account of the flexibility and resourcefulness he can show when faced with new problems or presented with new opportunities. At the same time, it should take account of limitations that political policies, social convention, and familial obligations can impose. It should be concerned with the conflicts between the interests of individuals and their families and their societies, and should make the distinction between gains or losses in the short and the long run. A few scholars are now attempting such an approach,[56] but their lead has yet to be followed.

NOTES

1. This rather imprecise term typically groups together the nations of Europe, the Soviet Union, Japan, the United States, Canada, Australia, New Zealand, and Israel. There is a certain fluidity, if not ambiguity, to the classification: over the last generation Japan and Israel were added to the club, for example, and Argentina and Uruguay dropped. All nations not termed developed in this taxonomy are automatically less developed. For a critique, see P. T. Bauer, _Dissent on Development_ (Cambridge, Mass.: Harvard University Press, 1972).

2. See for example the United Nations' authoritative Determinants and Consequences of Population Trends (New York: United Nations, 1973), chap. 4.

3. Ibid., chap. 15.

4. On this score, see John C. Caldwell's lengthy introductory essay on the demographic transition in John C. Caldwell, ed., The Persistence of High Fertility: Prospects for the Third World (Canberra: Australian National University, 1977).

5. Not all demographers were off the mark. Donald J. Bogue, for example, predicted the decline in poor world fertility fairly precisely. See his "The End of the Population Explosion," Public Interest (Spring 1967). Of course, the fact that one has made an accurate prediction does not necessarily mean that one has analyzed a situation correctly. See how Paul Demeny takes Bogue to task in his "On the End of the Population Explosion," Population and Development Review (Spring 1979).

6. See for example P. T. Bauer and A. A. Walters, "The State of Economics," Journal of Law and Economics (April 1975); Laurence E. Lynn, ed., Knowledge and Policy: The Uncertain Connection (Washington, D.C.: National Academy of Sciences, 1978); and in a slightly different vein, Ivan D. London and Warren Thorngate, "Divergent Amplification and Social Behavior: Some Methodological Considerations" (unpublished manuscript, 1980).

7. See for example O. Adegbola, "New Estimates of Fertility and Child Mortality in Africa, South of the Sahara," Population Studies (November 1977).

8. Here see Joseph A. McFalls, Jr., "Frustrated Fertility: A Population Paradox," Population Bulletin (May 1979).

9. Jack Goody, "The Evolution of the Family," in Household and Family in Past Time, ed. Peter Laslett (Cambridge: Cambridge University Press, 1972).

10. Ibid.

11. See note 2.

12. For an exposition and critique of the work of some of the more enthusiastic proponents of "the Chinese model," see Nick Eberstadt, Poverty in China (Bloomington, Ind.: IDI, 1979).

13. The names particularly associated with this viewpoint include P. C. Chen, Ruth and Victor Sidel, and Joe D. Wray.

14. See for example Stanley Karnow, Mao and China: From Revolution to Revolution (New York: Viking Press, 1972); Simon Leys, The Chairman's New Clothes: Mao and the Cultural Revolution (New York: St. Martin's Press, 1978); K. Ling, The Revenge of Heaven: Journal of a Young Chinese (New York: Putnam, 1972); Miriam London and Ivan D. London, "Great Leap Forward?," Barron's, January 1, 1979; and the December 31, 1977 issue of The Economist.

15. See Eberstadt, Poverty in China, and Nick Eberstadt, "Efficiency in Chinese Agriculture, 1952-75" (unpublished paper, 1977).

16. See for example Ronald A. Fransisco, Betty A. Laird, and Roy D. Laird, ed., The Political Economy of Collectivized Agriculture (Elmsford: Pergamon Press, 1979).

17. Stephen Polgar, "Population History and Population Policies from an Anthropological Perspective," Current Anthropology (April 1972).

18. See Richard B. Lee and Irven De Vore, eds., Kalahari Hunter Gatherers: Studies of the Kung San and Their Neighbors (Cambridge, Mass.: Harvard University Press, 1976).

19. Jean-Noel Biraben, "Essai sur l'Evolution du Nombre des Hommes," Population (January-February 1979).

20. See Polgar, "Population History"; see also Ben White, "Demand for Labor and Population Growth in Colonial Java," Human Ecology (Fall 1973), and the comments on this article, in the same issue, by Clifford Geertz and Etienne van de Walle.

21. See Chapter 1.

22. Alan Sweezy, "Recent Light on the Relation between Socioeconomic Development and Fertility Decline," Occasional Paper 1, Caltech Population Program, 1973.

23. John Knodel and Etienne van de Walle, "Lessons from the Past: Policy Implications of Historical Fertility Studies," Population and Development Review (June 1979).

24. The first important work on natural fertility was Henry's collaboration with Etienne Gautier, La Population de Crulai (Paris: Presses Universitaires de France, 1958).

25. See Ronald Demos Lee, ed., Population Patterns in the Past (New York: Academic Press, 1977).

26. E. A. Wrigley, "Family Limitation in Pre-Industrial England," Economic History Review (February 1966).

27. See for example Susan B. Hanley, "Fertility, Mortality, and Life Expectancy in Pre-modern Japan," Population Studies (March 1974).

28. See Irene B. Taeuber, The Population of Japan (Princeton: Princeton University Press, 1958).

29. See Ansley J. Coale, Barbara A. Anderson, and Erna Härm, Human Fertility in Russia Since the Nineteenth Century (Princeton: Princeton University Press, 1979).

30. See United Nations, Determinants and Consequences of Population Trends.

31. See Bauer, Dissent on Development; World Bank, World Development Report, 1979 (New York: Oxford University Press, 1979).

32. See T. H. Hull and V. J. Hull, "The Relation of Economic Class and Fertility: An Analysis of Some Indonesian Data," Population Studies (March 1977); Caldwell, The Persistence of High Fertility; Lado T. Ruzicka, ed., The Economic and Social Supports for High Fertility (Canberra: Australian National University, 1977).

33. See G. B. Rodgers, "Income and Inequality as Determinants of Mortality: An International Cross-Section Analysis," Population Studies (July 1979).

34. See for example A. T. Flegg, "The Role of Inequality of Income in the Determination of Birth Rates," Population Studies (November 1979); Nancy Birdsall, "Analytical Approaches to the Relation of Population Growth and Development," Population and Development Review (March-June 1977).

35. See Robert Repetto, "The Economic Value of Children: Some Methodological Questions," in Population and Development: The Search for Selective Interventions, ed. Ronald Ridker (Baltimore: Johns Hopkins University Press, 1976).

36. Contrast the approaches and findings of the following works: Teresa J. Ho, "Time Cost of Child Rearing in the Rural Philippines," Population and Development Review (December 1979); Mead T. Cain, "The Economic Activity of Children in a Village in Bangladesh," Population and Development Review (September 1977); M. Vlassoff, "Labour Demand and Economic Utility of Children: A Case Study in Rural India," Population Studies (November 1979); Helen Ware, "Economic Strategy and the Number of Children," in Caldwell, The Persistence of High Fertility; M. V. Nadkarni, "Overpopulation and the Rural Poor," Economic and Political Weekly (March 13, 1976); Mark R. Rosenzweig and Kenneth I. Wolpin, "An Economic Analysis of the Extended Family in a Less Developed Country: The Demand for the Elderly in an Uncertain Environment," Yale Economic Growth Center Discussion Paper 317, August 1979; A. Schnaiberg and D. Reed, "Risk, Uncertainty and Family Formation: The Social Context of Poverty Groups," Population Studies (July 1978); Ben White, "The Economic Importance of Children in a Javanese Village," in Population and Social Organization, ed. Moni Nag (The Hague: Mouton, 1976).

37. Caldwell, The Persistence of High Fertility.

38. Ruzicka, The Economic and Social Supports for High Fertility.

39. See Daniel D'Souza and Lincoln Chen, "Sex Differentials in Mortality in Rural Bangladesh," Population and Development Review (in press) for a review of this phenomenon.

40. Remarkably little has been written about this. See Nick Eberstadt, "Malthusians, Marxists, and Missionaries: Ideology in the New Literature on Hunger," Society/Transaction (in press).

41. See Nick Eberstadt, "Myths of the Food Crisis," New York Review of Books (February 19, 1976).

42. See Eberstadt, "Malthusians, Marxists, and Missionaries."

43. One gets some sense of the problems students of nutrition and fecundity are up against when one reads the following: John Bongarrts, "Does Malnutrition Affect Fertility? A Summary of Evidence," Science (May 9, 1980); John Bongaarts and Hernan Delgado, "Effects of Nutritional Status on Fertility," IUSSP Population Conference 1977; Jean Mayer and Johanna Dwyer, eds., Food and Nutrition Policy in a Changing World (New York: Oxford University Press, 1979); Emmanuel LeRoy Ladurie, "Famine Amenorrhea (Seventeenth-Twentieth Centuries)," in Biology of Man in History, ed. Robert Forster and Orest Ranum (Baltimore: Johns Hopkins University Press, 1975); Elborg Forster and Robert Forster, eds., European Diet from Pre-Industrial to Modern Times (New York: Harper & Row, 1976); Thomas McKeown, The Modern Rise of Population (New York: Academic Press, 1976); James Allman, "Natural Fertility and Associated Intermediate Variables in Some Arab Countries," Battelle PDP Working Paper 7, February 1979.

44. See Roland J. Fuchs and George J. Demko, "Population Distribution Policies in Developed Socialist and Western Countries," Population and Development Review (September 1979); Roland Pressat, "Mesures Natalistes au Relèvement de la Fecondite en Europe de l'Est," Population (May-June 1979), for some recent and perceptive reflections on the totalitarian experience.

45. See for example the introductory essay by W. Parker Mauldin and Gwendolyn Johnson-Acsadi in Measuring the Impact of Family Planning Programs on Fertility, ed. C. Chandrasekaran and A. Hermalin (Dolhain: IUSSP, 1976).

46. See for example Jay Teachman et al., The Impact of Family Planning Programs on Fertility Rates (Chicago: Community and Family Study Center, 1979).

47. Even among peoples who are well nourished and practice natural fertility, such as the Hutterites, the mean interval between births is over two years. Under the circumstances it would seem rather difficult to credit contraceptive users with preventing a birth for every year of protection. See John Bongaarts, "A Framework for Analyzing the Proximate Determinants of Fertility," Population and Development Review (March 1978). For the formal mathematics of the problem, see Nathan Keyfitz, Applied Mathematical Demography (New York: Wiley-Interscience, 1977).

48. Before approaching the literature, the reader would be well advised to look over William Petersen, "Some Postulates of Population Policy," Population Review (January-December 1971), and the four following pieces by Kingsley Davis: "Population Policies:

Will the Current Programs Succeed?" Science (November 10, 1967); "The Climax of Population Growth: Past and Future Perspectives," California Medicine (November 1970); "Population Policy and the Theory of Reproductive Motivation," Economic Development and Cultural Change, supplement (1977); "Testimony to the Select Committee on Population," in World Population: A Global Perspective, Hearings before the Select Committee on Population, U.S. Congress, February 7, 8, 9, 1978. With their methodological caveats in mind, the following studies, which represent some of the best literature on the impact of family planning programs on fertility, might be approached a little more skeptically: William Paul McGreevey and Barbara von Elm, "Socioeconomic Change and Family Planning: Their Impact on Fertility," Battelle PDP Working Paper 1, October 1978; K. S. Srikantan, The Family Planning Program in the Socioeconomic Context (New York: Population Council, 1977); J. T. Johnson et al., "Impact of the Malaysian Family Planning Programme on Births: A Comparison of Matched Acceptor and Non-Acceptor Birth Rates," Population Studies (July 1978); Ravi Gulhati, India's Population Policy: History and Future, World Bank Staff Working Paper 265, August 1977; P. S. Mohapatra, Measuring the Performance of Family Planning Programs, World Bank Staff Working Paper 257, June 1977; Susan H. Cochrane, The Population of Thailand: Its Growth and Welfare, World Bank Staff Working Paper 337, June 1979.

49. An unusually sensible analysis of this sort is Bernard Berelson's "Prospects and Programs for Fertility Reduction: What? Where?" Population and Development Review (December 1978).

50. World Fertility Survey, "The Indonesian Fertility Survey, 1975: A Summary of Findings" (London: World Fertility Survey, April 1979); World Fertility Survey, "Republic of the Philippines Fertility Survey, 1978: A Summary of Findings" (London: World Fertility Survey, November 1979); Sauvaluck Piambati and John Knodel, "Revised Estimates of Age-Specific Fertility Rates from the Survey of Fertility in Thailand" (Bangkok: World Fertility Survey, July 1978); World Fertility Survey, "The Survey of Fertility in Thailand 1975: A Summary of Findings" (London: World Fertility Survey, April 1978).

51. World Fertility Survey, "Sri Lanka Fertility Survey, 1975: A Summary of Findings" (London: World Fertility Survey, August 1978). A similar pattern seems to be showing itself now in Malaysia. See World Fertility Survey, "Malaysia Fertility and Family Survey 1974: A Summary of Findings" (London: World Fertility Survey, January 1978).

52. Craig Bolton and J. William Leasure, "Evolution Politique et Baisse de la Feconditie en Occident," Population (July-October 1979). In the same vein, see Gerardo Gonzalez-Cortes and Margarit-Maria Errazuriz, "The Marginal Family in Chile: Social Change and

Women's Contraceptive Behavior," in Population and Social Organization, ed. Moni Nag (The Hague: Mouton, 1976).

53. See Alvin H. Hansen, "Economic Progress and Declining Population Growth," American Economic Review (March 1939); John Maynard Keynes, "Some Economic Consequences of a Declining Population," Eugenics Review (April 1937); Gunnar Myrdal, Population: A Problem for Democracy (Gloucester: Peter Smith, 1962; originally published 1940).

54. See the most important of these works: Ansley J. Coale and Edgar M. Hoover, Population Growth and Economic Development in Low Income Countries: A Case Study of India's Economic Prospects (Princeton: Princeton University Press, 1958).

55. The most reasoned presentation of this view can be found in National Academy of Sciences, Rapid Population Growth, Volume I (Baltimore: Johns Hopkins University Press, 1971).

56. Among these are Harvey Leibenstein and Julian Simon. See Leibenstein, "Beyond Economic Man: Economics, Politics, and the Population Problem," Population and Development Review (September 1977); Simon, The Economics of Population Growth (Princeton: Princeton University Press, 1977).

1

RECENT DECLINES IN FERTILITY IN LESS DEVELOPED COUNTRIES, AND WHAT POPULATION PLANNERS MAY LEARN FROM THEM

Nick Eberstadt

Formulating effective policy to influence human behavior is difficult in many spheres, but probably nowhere do policymakers and planners encounter so many problems as when attempting to alter human fertility. There are several reasons why population planning turns out to be the most intractable of planning areas. First, population changes and their social ramifications are poorly understood. The clean numbers (sometimes calculated down to the very last digit) and the elegant theories that demography generates may suggest a certain precision, but this is an illusion. To use Kenneth Boulding's taxonomy, population studies are an "insecure" rather than a "secure" science, for its theoretical framework does not provide an adequate base either for explaining or predicting change within its field. To give two examples: population forecasts, even at their best, are accurate only about five years out,[1] which is not enough of a lead time even to plan accurately for primary school enrollment under the relaxed constraints of universal enrollment, and population studies are still at a loss over such basic issues as whether or not women fully replace children who die in infancy.[2]

Second, although population studies is poor at explaining or predicting population changes, such changes are known to have far-reaching social and economic effects. Fertility changes clearly have a far-reaching effect on human welfare, even if demographers cannot always quantify these effects, or even agree what they are. The

---

Reprinted with permission from World Development, January 1980.

complexity of demographic and social interactions is intuitively obvious. It is easy to imagine situations where second- and third-round effects of social change might outweigh and thereby reverse the direction of the first-round fertility effect. Such a situation is not always abstract. A good example of the unexpected complexity and strength of demographic-social interactions would be the inadvertent effect of raising the fertility of Puerto Rican women through improvements in education.[3] Although education usually has a depressing effect on fertility, it also tends to raise income levels, and in Puerto Rico the income effect associated with increased education evidently overpowered the fertility-depressing effect of increased aspirations. Likewise, many surveys show that families with larger numbers of children have the highest savings ratios, ostensibly because the prospect of having many mouths to feed pushes parents to work harder than they would otherwise.[4] Tailoring policy to anticipate these interrelationships is extremely difficult, if indeed it is possible.

Although changes in fertility may seem to affect nearly every aspect of human life, government policies explicitly aimed at affecting fertility have generally been unsuccessful. In the totalitarian states of Eastern Europe, where government control over the rhythm of life is complete (at least in theory), raising the birth rate has been explicit policy for a number of years, but birth rates have done little to respond.[5] The odds against influencing fertility through the very much more restricted policy instruments open to nontotalitarian societies should hardly be any better.

In less developed countries today, planners' concern for population manifests itself in two distinctly different types of policy.[6] The first set are "population responsive": their purpose is to accommodate the significantly greater numbers of citizens most poor world governments expect to see over the near and longer-term future. The second set are "population influencing": their purpose is to hasten the onset of the fertility transition, that part of the demographic transition when stable high birth rates become stable low birth rates, and where subsequently population growth declines dramatically. The first set of programs are not conceptually distinct from the normal activities of governments in the age of the welfare state. They include, for example, efforts to expand schooling, to increase and improve the stock of housing, and to stimulate agricultural output. The second set of programs are new—less than a generation old in most countries of the world—and conceptually quite distinct, involving as they do a direct attempt on the part of the state to intervene in and influence what is perhaps the most important decision most people in the world make in the course of their lives. In effect as well as concept, these sets of policies are radically different. Population-response policies, to oversimplify things, are a government's attempt to carry out the will of the nation; population-influencing policies, to oversimplify again, are a government's attempt to change the will of a nation. Sterilization bonuses, contraception dispensaries, village agents, maternal health clinics, and the like not only bring poor families into closer contact with the government than they may be used to, but also the government to which they are exposed has specific and predetermined ideas about the way they should have sex, the sorts of decisions the wife should make for the household, the way the family should be formed, and what it should look like. How modest the ambitions of reforming land tenure seen by comparison!

Attempting to influence or enforce changes in these personal and arguably vital areas of human life runs the risk of being not only ineffective or misguided, but actually hazardous for the government that undertakes them. The lesson of the downfall of Indira Gandhi and the largest popularly elected government in the world, mainly, if not principally, on the issue of semivoluntary population regulation, should not go unheeded by population planners.[7] It certainly will not be ignored by politicians.

The fertility transition which these population-influencing or antinatalist programs hope to encourage is a mysterious character: areas of uncertainty that surround it include what makes it begin, how long it lasts, and how far it continues.[8] The general consensus among demographers during the 1970s has been that government policies and other forces would start a generalized fertility transition in the less developed countries sometime in the 1980s.[9] One suspects that the date has been picked primarily because it is conveniently, yet not disparagingly, distant. Once again in demography, however, fact has proven stranger than prediction. As numbers from the early 1970s begin to trickle in (there is always a substantial delay in reporting population figures, as we shall see), it now seems that indeed by the mid-1970s, and perhaps even during the late 1960s, a substantial fertility transition was under way in Latin America, Asia, and a few outposts in Africa.

This chapter will analyze the nature of the recent fertility transition. Its first section will describe the magnitude and patterns of decline in the world as a whole, and in the less developed countries in particular. The second section will speculate on the contribution that antinatalist policy and those other factors to which demographers so frequently refer may have made to this transition. The third section will suggest what some of the policy implications of the decline may be, what governments and planners may learn from it, and how they can best coexist with it in the future.

RECENT DECLINES IN FERTILITY IN THE LDCs

The Limits of Demographic Knowledge

How accurate is our information on world population and fertility levels? Demographers reinforce the impression of precision that outsiders entertain about the science of population numbers by carrying their estimates for current population to the fifth, sixth, or sometimes even the seventh place. U.N. estimates from 1966, for example, had figures for world population in 1960 down to the last thousand.[10] In point of fact, enumerative techniques are simply not that good. In the United States, a land where proper enumeration has been an explicit policy concern for nearly 200 years (it is written into the constitution) and where, thanks to the availability of information in society, there are numerous trails through which to track down any given individual's existence (hospital births, school attendance, social security, drivers' licenses, telephone addresses, property deeds, income tax forms, and the like), something like five or six million people are missed at every census count. They are not missed randomly. The unrecorded tend to be the poor, the unemployed, the isolated, the drifters; 40 percent of them are guessed to be black, in a nation whose population is only about 12 percent black.[11] If the omission bias and enumeration problems are this great in the United States, the nation whose techniques are arguably the most sophisticated in the world, they are an order of magnitude greater in the less developed countries, which do not have comparable records, techniques, or resources. As late as 1970 about 200 million people in the less developed countries were totally, demographically uncovered; they lived in countries that had never had a census.[12] Many others lived in countries where censuses had been conducted, but with appalling inaccuracy. The U.N.'s 1958 estimate for total population in Ethiopia for 1950 was 12 million; by 1977, it had revised the 1950 figure to 19 million, a difference of more than 50 percent.[13] Likewise, estimates for Nigeria in 1950 varied by 20 percent due to problems of technical underenumeration and political overenumeration. (When state funds and political representation are at stake, there is an inherent incentive to inflate, just as there is an incentive to underestimate in tax polls.[14])

The margins of error in census counts have dropped in the past 25 years, but the magnitudes of inaccuracy are still high. On the one hand, statisticians and demographers are debating whether the population of Saudi Arabia is seven million or five million, while observers familiar with Saudi conditions suggest that the real population is probably closer to three million. On the other hand, the government of India, with what may be the most sophisticated census in the less developed world, admits that its figures may easily be off by 20 million people.[15] China, an enigma in so many ways to the outside world, is also a demographic mystery of staggering proportions. The Chinese have made no known attempt for 25 years to count their numbers,[16] and estimates of China's population today run from a low of 750 million to a high of over a billion.[17] In total, the absolute margin of error over the world's present population is probably somewhere near 400 million people![18]

Estimating vital rates is not quite so hazardous as estimating total populations, since one can extrapolate from relatively small samples to describe the behavior of entire nations. The problems involved, nevertheless, are considerable. Like censuses, samples tend to omit the isolated and the poor, and these people quite often have different patterns of life and death from the rest of the nation. Where total registration of births and deaths is relied upon, underregistration biases both birth rates and death rates downward. If one looks at India's apparent birth and death rates shortly after partition, for example, one gets a set of figures not terribly different from the United States' at the same time.[19] Finally, since large-scale samples or censuses are conducted at discrete points of time, the intervals between which are often as much as a decade and sometimes longer, demographers are left extrapolating from old rates while new conditions invalidate the premise of the exercise. U.N. demographers knew, for example, that life expectancy in India was rising, but they had no idea how fast it actually would rise. Therefore, their estimates for India's 1970 population, which they had made in 1960, were off by about 40 million.[20] Similarly, birth rates in Japan fell by 50 percent during the course of a decade (1946-55). If Japan had not been a statistically developed nation, the change would not have been picked up for years.[21]

Mexico is a nation whose vital statistics are among the best in the less developed world. Over the past few decades it has estimated its birth rate to be in the low or mid-forties. United Nations' demographers more or less rubber stamped the Mexican figures. Through the mid-1970s, U.N. numbers for the Mexican birth rate were over 40. Then, suddenly, information started to come in that suggested that the Mexican birth rate might have begun declining as early as 1965.[22] Mexican and U.N. estimates shot down. In a period of about two years, the U.N.'s estimate of Mexican birth rates went from the low forties to the mid-thirties. Fertility changes well under way were not picked up until 10 years later in Mexico. Evidently this has occurred in other countries as well. In fact, demographers are suddenly realizing that fertility in less developed countries has been plunging.

Dimensions of the Fertility Shift

Perhaps the easiest way to describe the fertility shift in less developed countries would be to explain the changes in world population patterns over the last generation, the magnitude of the LDC contribution to this shift, and the patterns within the LDC shift that have produced an effect of that magnitude.

Table 1.1 shows some (perhaps overly specified) estimates for changes in world vital statistics since 1950. Despite the fact that the world's population has grown by more than a billion people from 1950 to 1970, fewer people were dying ten years ago than 30 years ago. On the other hand, the number of people being born was rising continuously, from over 90 million a year to over 120 million a year. Since the absolute number of deaths was falling, the birth increase translated directly into population growth. Annual increments to the world's population rose from 43 million in 1950 to about 73 million in 1970. The increase in the size of the increments was much greater (about 70 percent) than the actual increase in population over the period (about 40 percent), or to put it another way, the rate of population growth was accelerating—a so-called population explosion was under way. From 1970 to 1977, however, a discernible change in the abso-

TABLE 1.1

Changes in World Vital Statistics, 1950-77

	1950	1960	1970	1977*
Population (millions)	2,501	2,986	3,675	4,165
Total Births (millions)	90.0	102.0	120.3	121.3
Total Deaths (millions)	50.0	46.4	48.3	49.5
Natural Increase (millions)	40.0	55.6	72.0	71.8

*Estimated.

Sources: Data are adjusted from United Nations, *World Population Prospects as Assessed in 1973* (New York: United Nations, 1977); Population Reference Bureau; USAID.

TABLE 1.2

Changes in World Vital Rates, by Region, 1950-77

	1950	1960	1970	1977
Birth Rates				
Developed Countries	23	21	18	16
China	40	37	30	26
Other LDCs	44	43	42	37
African LDCs	48	48	47	46
Other Asian LDCs	44	43	41	36
Latin American LDCs	42	41	39	34
Death Rates				
Developed Countries	10	9	9	9
China	23	16	11	10
Other LDCs	26	19	17	15
African LDCs	28	24	20	18
Other Asian LDCs	27	20	18	16
Latin American LDCs	15	12	10	8

Sources: W. Parker Mauldin, "Patterns of Fertility Decline in Developing Countries, 1950-75," Chapter 2; United Nations, World Population Prospects as Assessed in 1973 (New York: United Nations, 1977); Population Reference Bureau; USAID.

lute numbers has occurred. The absolute number of deaths has risen (though not because life is getting shorter, as we shall see in the next section), and although the absolute number of births has risen as well, the total increment to world population has fallen slightly. Since total numbers have been growing around 70 million a year over this span, the rate of population growth has not only peaked, but also has come down quite substantially. (Indeed, to judge from the trends, the rate, as distinct from the absolute level, of population increase may have peaked as early as the mid-1960s.) This turnabout in the rate of population growth is an historic moment for mankind, for it is the first slowdown in world population growth in the memory of modern man, and possibly in all of human history, that has not been related to disaster.

The different areas of the world have made varying contributions to the levels and rates of population growth, as is well known. The

TABLE 1.3

Components in World Fertility Decline, 1965-77

	DCs	China	Other LDCs	Total
Birth Rates, 1965	18	34	43	34
Birth Rates, 1977	16	26	37	29
World Population, 1977 (millions)	1,095	940	2,130	4,165
Total Births, 1977 (millions)	17.2	24.4	79.7	121.3
Total Births, 1977 Population, 1965 Birth Rates (hypothetical)	19.9	31.9	92.7	144.5
Difference (millions)	2.7	7.5	13.0	23.2
Difference (percent)	12	32	56	

Sources: Adjusted from United Nations, World Population Prospects as Assessed in 1977 (New York: United Nations, 1977); Population Reference Bureau; USAID.

differential effect on demographic increase can be seen in Tables 1.2 and 1.3. We begin by separating the so-called developed nations—all of Europe, Japan, Israel, and the areas of majority European settlement (United States, Canada, New Zealand, Australia)—from the rest of the world, which we call less developed. One may quibble about borderline cases, such as Argentina and Abu Dhabi arguably, but there are good reasons for excluding such countries, and in any event they constitute a marginal, if not negligible, proportion of humanity from the standpoint of our calculations. We may further split the less developed nations into two groupings: China and all the rest. There is good reason to do this. Size alone could justify this division. Whether China's population is 800 million or a billion (and the evidence points toward its being nearer the latter), it is nevertheless larger than Africa and Latin America combined, and nearly as large as all the developed countries taken together. But there are other reasons as well. The less developed countries, lumped together through the sleight of hand of negative definition (they are all "not developed countries"), have little in common but their heterogeneity. China stands out as the largest culturally, ethnically, and historically homogeneous patch in this crazy quilt of peoples. A facet of the uniqueness of the Chinese experience overall has been the uniqueness of its demographic trends; not to separate China from the other less developed countries would be to obscure trends for both. Finally, since Chinese vital statistics probably carry a higher margin of error than those of most other poor nations, compounding Chinese and non-Chinese errors will simply add to the haze through which we have to extract our patterns and trends. In demography it is not impossible for the margins of error to be greater than the changes we are trying to measure. Although margins of error are not strictly additive under a probabilistic framework, from a conceptual standpoint they are.

As we see from Table 1.2, and as is well known, birth rates in the developed countries have been consistently lower than in the less developed countries. (Birth rates, however, mask even greater differences in total fertility rates through differences in rich world and poor world age structures. Whereas the ratio of American to Indonesian birth rates around 1970 was 1:2.2, the ratio of American to Indonesian gross reproduction rates was 1:2.6.[23]) Chinese birth rates, as they have been reconstructed, declined through the 1950s and 1960s, but only began a rapid drop in the 1970s. Birth rates in the other less developed countries, taken as a whole, barely moved down at all during the 1950s and 1960s. Those changes in aggregate that did occur, in fact, were probably due as much to shifts in age structure (as life expectancy increases and the proportion of women in childbearing ages shrinks, the birth rate goes down even if age-specific fertility holds constant)[24] as to actual fertility reductions. By the 1970s, however, a significant drop was under way.

The fertility transition, which China and the (other) less developed countries currently appear to be engaged in, follows a familiar, if not entirely explainable or predictable, pattern. Figure 1.1 illustrates the progression. Birth rates start falling slowly, the drop speeds up, then slows down again as population growth stabilizes at new, lower levels. Given a relatively independent mortality schedule, it is then clearly the speed of the drop that determines the length of the fertility transition and the size of the post-transition population. Demographers have noted that over the past generation a new demographic transition seems to be in the making,[25] in which the rate of fertility decline has been markedly more rapid than in the past, though starting from ever higher levels. Recent information on aggregate fertility decline in the less developed countries and China is consistent with this description. Figure 1.2 illustrates the shift in pattern. The European nations that underwent fertility transition around the turn of the century or earlier, had relatively low preindustrial birth rates (generally in the mid-thirties) and took a comparatively long time to make the shift—over 100 years for England

FIGURE 1.1

Stylized Fertility Transition

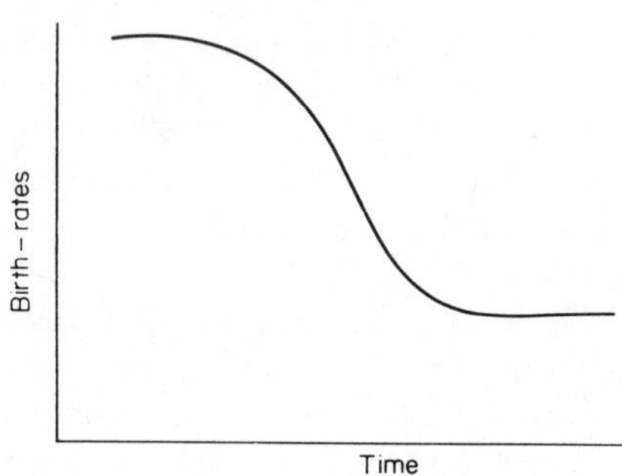

Source: Constructed by the author.

FIGURE 1.2

Fertility Transition in Different Regions

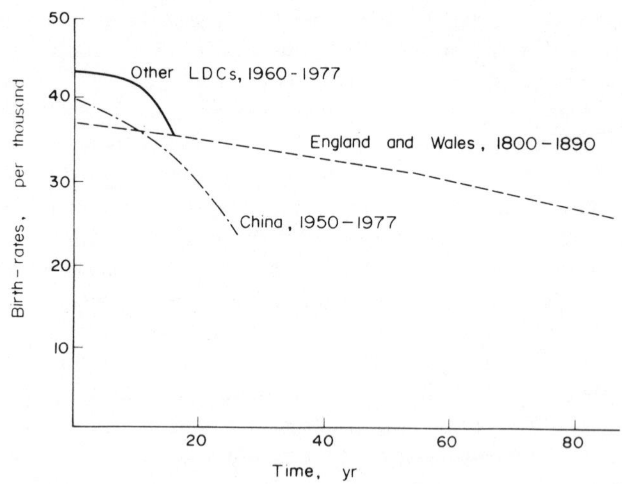

Source: Constructed by the author.

and France, 80 years for Germany, Sweden, and Italy, and so forth.[26] At no point in their demographic transitions did their birth rates fall more than about three points a decade. At the onset of China's fertility transition in the early 1950s, its birth rate was higher, probably close to 40.[27] Although demographers may debate whether China's birth rate is 28 or 22 or somewhere in between, the rate of decline in the birth rate has been about five points a decade since 1950, and more like six points a decade since 1970. Taken as a whole, the other less developed countries started their fertility transition from a still higher plateau (somewhere around 43 or 44 in 1960), and their rate of decline has been more rapid still (about seven points per decade for the 1970s thus far, with an annual rate for 1977 of over ten points a decade). These rapid rates of fertility decline mean (again assuming a relatively independent mortality schedule) that the fertility transition will take much less time, and that the projected population size upon stabilization will be considerably smaller than it would otherwise be.

Diversity

It would be a mistake to assume that fertility decline in the heterogeneous mass of less developed countries has been a homogeneous and even experience. Some LDCs began their fertility transition in the 1950s, and a great many others still do not yet appear to have gotten theirs under way. While there are differences in fertility within nations across geographical and class boundaries, the differences in fertility change among nations, and in fact among regions, are nonetheless rather pronounced. In Latin America and the Caribbean, birth rates in 1975 were around 36 per thousand, down from around 41 just a decade before. This is a 14 percent drop at the very least, since figures are now coming in, as for Mexico, to suggest that fertility in 1975 may have been substantially lower than registrations suggested. In Asia, excluding China, the drop in the birth rate was also about 14 percent, with a fall from about 44 to about 38. In Africa, however, the drop was minimal: 4 percent (from 48 to 46), almost all of it due to changes in Egypt and Tunisia. If we were to further decompose our regions, we would find that, east of Pakistan, Asia's fertility decline has been extremely pronounced since 1964, while the Islamic expanse stretching from Rawalpindi to Casablanca has been affected rather minimally. Likewise, in sub-Saharan Africa, only the colored population of South Africa has evidenced any real sign of reducing its birth rate,[28] and this is surely an atypical representation of the black African population.

TABLE 1.4

Birth Rate Declines in Selected LDCs, 1950-77

Country	1950	1960	1965	1970	1977
Algeria	51	51	50	49	47
Ethiopia	51	51	51	50	49
Kenya	48	48	49	50	49
Libya	48	48	47	47	47
Sudan	50	50	50	49	49
Tanzania	52	51	51	50	49
Zaire	47	47	47	46	44
Bolivia	47	45	44	44	43
Colombia	46	45	43	40	31
Costa Rica	48	47	41	36	27
Cuba	28	30	34	30	21
Jamaica	44	44	43	41	37
Venezuela	46	45	42	40	34
Afghanistan	49	49	49	49	49
Iran	48	47	46	46	45
Iraq	49	49	48	48	48
Jordan	45	47	48	48	47
Syria	47	47	48	47	46
Burma	44	43	41	40	39
Hong Kong	33	35	28	24	18
Kampuchea	49	49	47	47	47
Sri Lanka	39	36	33	30	25
Vietnam (North)	41	42	42	39	29

Sources: W. Parker Mauldin, "Patterns of Fertility Decline in Developing Countries, 1950-75," Chapter 2; Population Reference Bureau; USAID.

Although the fertility decline may not be a universal phenomenon, a birth rate drop of 14 percent in 12 years could not be enforced unless patterns were shifting rapidly in the population centers of the less developed countries. As Table 1.4 shows, such a shift has occurred. The dozen largest LDCs currently are home for about 1,400 million people: over a third of the world's residents, about two-thirds of the population of the less developed nations excluding

China. In accordance with the nature of the fertility transition, the incidence of the decline has been markedly uneven. Countries with the highest birth rates (Bangledesh, Nigeria, Pakistan) have shown few signs of fertility change, none of them substantial, while South Korea—the nation of the 12 with the lowest fertility rate in 1965—further cut its birth rate by 37 percent. A general shift, still, was taking place. Whether we use a weighted or an unweighted average of the birth rate decline, we find that birth rates in these 12 countries have dropped by about 18-20 percent in the past 12 years. This shift puts an interesting light on the despair and wrath that population activists in the Western world were levelling at the "tradition-bound peasants" who through their intransigence, the argument ran, were turning their nations into "demographic basket cases."

Who Is Having Fewer Children?

In the 1960s, the taxonomy of fertility decline in the less developed world was simple. With few exceptions, nations engaged were

TABLE 1.5

Birth Rate Declines in the Dozen Largest LDCs, 1965-77

Country	1965	1977E	Percentage Decline
Bangladesh	49	46	6
Brazil	42	36	14
Egypt	42	36	14
India	43	34	21
Indonesia	46	37	20
Mexico	44	33	25
Nigeria	50	49	2
Pakistan	48	44	9
Philippines	44	33	22
Korea (South)	35	23	34
Thailand	44	32	27
Turkey	41	31	24
Unweighted Average	44	36	18

Sources: 1965 figures from United Nations, World Population Prospects as Assessed in 1973 (New York: United Nations, 1977); 1977 figures adjusted from Population Reference Bureau and USAID.

TABLE 1.6

Selected Social Indicators for the Largest LDCs, 1977

Country	Birth Rate (E)	Per Capita GNP ($US)	Infant Mortality	Life Expectancy	Per Capita Calories	Literacy	Percentage University Students Women
Nigeria	49	403	162	41	2,085	25	26
Bangladesh	46	93	132	47	2,024	25	10
Pakistan	44	162	121	53	2,148	25	28
Indonesia	37	197	125	48	2,126	60	28
Brazil	36	1,008	82	61	2,516	68	47
Egypt	36	325	98	52	2,637	40	38
India	34	140	128	51	1,976	36	26
Mexico	33	1,304	61	63	2,727	82	25
Philippines	33	372	74	58	1,971	80	55
Thailand	32	339	78	58	2,382	82	43
Turkey	31	914	119	57	2,849	55	21
Korea (South)	23	552	47	65	2,630	88	26
Average, Highest Birth Rate Countries	41*	365	120	50	2,256	41*	29
Average, Lowest Birth Rate Countries	31*	603	85	59	2,422	71*	33

*Statistically significant at 0.05 level.

Source: Social indicators from Ruth Leger Sivard, World Social and Military Expenditures, 1978 (New York: Rockefeller Foundation, 1978).

TABLE 1.7

Annual Births per 1,000 Women by Age of Woman (mid-1960s)

Region	Countries	15-19	20-24	25-29	30-34	35-39	40-44	45-49	TFR
East and South-East Asia	9	124	275	280	223	154	64	22	5.71
India-Pakistan	2	158	277	(266)	(209)	(140)	(56)	24	5.65
Other Asia	7	62	268	305	248	179	78	19	5.80
Hong Kong-Singapore	2	(48)	(247)	315	237	148	58	(8)	5.31
Middle East	9	113	<u>305</u>	<u>352</u>	<u>290</u>	<u>199</u>	<u>82</u>	17	6.28
Black Africa	16	<u>183</u>	295	268	219	153	77	<u>32</u>	6.14
Latin America	16	121	296	308	243	181	74	22	6.23
Ratio, Highest to Lowest		3.8	1.23	1.31	1.32	1.42	1.41	4.0	1.18

Note: Summing the lowest fertility levels for each age-specific group (the circled figures) would give an overall TFR of 4.870. If, on the other hand, we were to aggregate the highest fertility figures for each age group (the underlined figures) we would get a TFR of 7.215—which is 48 percent higher. But the highest regional TFR is only 18 percent greater than the lowest, indicating the importance of spacing decisions over the course of the life cycle in the LDCs, even at a time of universally high fertility.

Source: Adjusted from Simon Kuznets, "Fertility Differentials between Developed and Less Developed Countries: Components and Implications," *Proceedings of the American Philosophical Society*, no. 5 (1975).

TABLE 1.8

Percentage of Birth Rate Decline Due to Specified Factors, Selected LDCs, 1953-75

Country	Period	Percentage of Change in Crude Birth Rate Due to Change in:			
		All Factors	Age Structure	Percentage Married	Marital Fertility
Sri Lanka	1953-63	100	57	43	0
	1963-68	100	-31	132	0
	1968-70	100	-21	30	89
Hong Kong	1961-65	100	79	10	11
	1965-67	100	13	0	87
Korea (South)	1957/1961-1962/1966	100	6	33	61
	1960-70	100	6	35	59
Taiwan	1960-70	100	13	60	119
Singapore	1957-66	100	0	63	37
	1957-70	100	-19	54	65
Malaysia	1957-64	100	-20	41	79
	1960-69	100	5	67	28

Source: W. Parker Mauldin, "Patterns of Fertility Decline in Developing Countries, 1950-75," Chapter 2.

islands, societies developing rapidly both socially and economically, countries with a large ethnic Chinese component to their population, or a combination of the three. When one looks at a list of the countries currently engaged in fertility decline, however, a simple taxonomy seems impossible. Looking at Table 1.5, one is struck more by the diversity than the similarity of the nine countries whose fertility is dropping significantly. The array of cultures, religions, ethnic groups, regions, economic structures, modes of government, and strategies and speeds of development is strikingly varied. The distinctive macro-level similarities and changes that demographers so often fish for are either remote or trivial when the comparison is made between India and Mexico, yet each of these large nations has almost mirrored the birth rate changes of the other over the past 12 years. The social indicators demographers frequently link to fertility change, moreover, correlate poorly with the birth rates, as an inspection of Table 1.6 will indicate. Even though there are evident differences between the higher and lower birth rate nations, most of these turn out not to be statistically significant. This suggests that macro theories of change and threshold hypotheses either underestimate the complexity of the current process of fertility decline in less developed countries, or else misexplain it by concentrating on phenomena at a national level when the mechanisms of change are working within families (nearer to the individual level).

Mechanism of Fertility Decline

The actual patterns of fertility decline within nations may offer us more of an insight into the sorts of linkages that have been depressing fertility in the less developed countries. As we can see from Table 1.7, the uniformly high completed family size figures from the different regions of the less developed world masked very different sorts of decisions about when one should have children in the course of one's life cycle. If we can analyze the patterns through which these age-specific fertility rates have declined, we will gain more of an impression of the links between fertility change and social change than we could by simply examining fertility change in the aggregate.

Unfortunately, the sort of information we need to make such an analysis is not yet available, and probably will not be available until after the 1980 world census. However, some preliminary work has been done on individual countries whose birth rates have dropped substantially. One general sort of pattern can be drawn from these admittedly limited studies.

There are three material, as opposed to social, means through which birth rates may decline (see Table 1.8). First, the age structure may change. A smaller proportion of women in childbearing ages, other things being equal, will push down the birth rate. Second, age-specific marital rates may change. If the proportion of women married declines, the birth rate will decline, other factors being equal. Finally, the age-specific intramarital fertility rates may change. If women have fewer children once married, birth rates fall, all other factors being equal. Although all these factors affect the birth rate, they are clearly quite different. What part do these three components play in lowering birth rates?

Breakdowns of the changing contribution of these three factors to lowering birth rates are presented in Table 1.8 for six countries in the less developed group. The sample is heavily biased: all are Asian, two of the six are island states, two are entirely ethnically Chinese, two more have large ethnic Chinese populations, and a fifth could be considered to be in the Sinitic cultural pattern. Whatever the shortcomings of this sample, however, it seems to show an interesting, though hardly rigid, pattern for birth rate decline. In the earlier stages of the fertility transition, age structure shifts account for a large proportion of the drop in the birth rate. As the decline continues, contributions from age structure become less important, or actually work against birth rate decline. Next, changes in marital proportions become significant, though their role in reducing the birth rates drops by the time that birth rates are down below about 30 per thousand. Over the final span of the fertility transition, it is declining rates of marital fertility that depress the birth rate.

Do these patterns have any relevance to other less developed countries? We may suspect that they do, although we have no direct evidence to prove it. What we do have, however, is a social trend that is consistent with the three-stage birth rate decline.[29] This is a general tendency toward rising age for women at marriage, and this is shown in Table 1.9. Changes in marital proportions are due primarily to changes in age at marriage, and as we can see here, throughout the less developed world there has been a trend toward increasing the age at marriage for women. (No such trend has been shown for men; we shall discuss the relevance of this disparity later.) We note that the continent with the lowest birth rate has the highest proportion of unmarried young women, and vice versa. We also see that age at marriage has been rising most rapidly in the high birth rate continent of Africa, and most slowly in Latin America, where birth rates have already dropped the furthest. This is consistent with the idea that changes in age at marriage have a larger impact on the birth rate at the higher levels, although it still leaves unexplained the question of why Africa has evidenced no signs of birth rate decline. Much more data will have to be generated before analyses of these possible patterns amount to anything more than gropings in the statistical dark.

TABLE 1.9

Percent of Females Aged 15-19 and 20-24 Never Married, Selected LDCs, by Region, around 1960 and 1970

Region	Number of Countries	1960	1970
	Females aged 15-19		
Africa	7	55.6	69.2
Asia	20	64.6	72.7
Latin America	13	80.8	81.7
	Females aged 20-24		
Africa	6	15.6	25.3
Asia	20	24.2	32.9
Latin America	13	42.6	47.4

Source: W. Parker Mauldin, "Patterns of Fertility Decline in Developing Countries, 1950-75," Chapter 2.

But our groping may give us some idea of how we should look at some of the social and policy factors so often associated with fertility change.

EXPLAINING RECENT FERTILITY DECLINES

As we know, fertility change affects almost every aspect of human life, and for this reason the game of associating social change with fertility change becomes both easy and misleading. Associations are not causes under the best of statistical circumstances, and when one is dealing with a world in which mechanisms of effect must be specified and lag times taken into account, they are on the face of things even less likely to explain what we observe. Furthermore, there is a tendency to think in terms of universal patterns, when from the experience in Europe, the European colonies, and Japan we might suspect that the causal mechanisms acting to depress the birth rate among countries may be specific to the nation involved.[30] In France, from what historical demographers can make out, inheritance laws played a primary role in powering national fertility decline;[31] in England, social aspiration may have been more important than on the continent;[32] in what is now Hungary, changes in land tenure seem to have been important;[33] with Australia, increasing educational costs may have been a decisive factor;[34] and Japan completed its fertility transition largely as a response to a national crisis of unprecedented proportion.[35] We may ask too much of nations by expecting them all to act the same when we know they are different in so many ways.

On the other hand, the variety of primary social factors in different nations' fertility decline patterns may be a reflection of the fact that nations are endowed with different assets, and saddled with different problems. Taking an extreme hypothetical, it may be that educational costs would, but for accidents of history and timing, have played very similar roles in Japan and Australia. In other words, it may have been the circumstances that were different among the countries, not the kinds of relations between social and demographic forces.

What sorts of social changes can be related to fertility change in the less developed world, either as a whole or in just some countries? It would be boring to run through the seemingly endless list of associations that might exist. We are better off if we examine the factors that have been associated with fertility change in the past with fairly widespread agreement, and some of the factors that promising new research is suggesting.

NONFACTORS IN THE DECLINE

We may start our examination by rejecting out of hand two frequently contended relationships between population growth and social forces, and qualifying a third. The first is the contention that fertility decline in poor countries does not occur in most poor countries where population growth is slowing down, but rather that increasing human suffering is pushing up the death rates.[36] This concept of the increasing immiserization of the masses of the world is dear to both Malthusians and Marxists, but fortunately there is little substance to it. As we see from Table 1.2, death rates in the poor world have been declining steadily over the past generation. There have been disasters that have pushed up death rates, as there probably always will be, but over the past generation these have been temporary in cause and effect, and increasingly infrequent. If we look at life expectancies, which are a less ambiguous measure of the relationship between death and the individual than are death rates, we see that length of life has been increasing everywhere, and most rapidly in the poor countries (see Table 1.10). One may still wish to argue that life in the poor world is brutish and nasty, but it is clearly no longer so short. In point of fact, the rate of population growth has slowed down despite, rather than because of, changes in poor world mortality.

TABLE 1.10

Life Expectancies in Different Regions of the World

Region	1950	1960	1970	1977E
Developed Countries	63.3	68.9	70.7	71.4
China	45	53	60	64
Other LDCs	40	44	49	52
African LDCs	35	39	44	47
Asian LDCs	39	44	50	53
Latin American LDCs	50	56	60	64

Source: United Nations, World Population Prospects as Assessed in 1973 (New York: United Nations, 1977).

Urbanization, unlike the decline in health, is a real phenomenon that has been documented. It occurs more rapidly now in poor nations than it did in the past.[37] Urbanized populations have lower fertility than rural populations in developed nations, and it was widely believed that urbanization would therefore depress fertility in the poor nations. There is little evidence to suggest that this occurred. Data for the 1960s show that although fertility is generally lower in urban than rural areas in poor countries, it is not that much lower—for all regions the average was about 5 percent, or about 2 birth rate points, which would account for less than a tenth of what was then the differential between poor world rural and rich world urban fertility.[38] In areas such as Central Africa, moreover, fertility seems to have been higher in cities than in the countryside (as indeed was once the case in England).[39] In other regions, such as Latin America, fertility differentials were declining because urban fertility was rising. Sociologists may argue that fertility has not been reduced in the poor world through the migration from the countryside because what has been labeled urbanization is instead merely urban growth, but the fact remains that the rise of cities, once viewed as a potential factor in easing so-called population constraints, has in this respect proven a false hope.

Nutrition

Still another factor whose relation to fertility decline can be contested is nutrition. In the 1950s Josue de Castro, a Marxist, suggested that the reason poor people had more children was that they were more fertile, and the reason they were more fertile was that they had less food, and specifically less protein to eat.[40] Although political sympathizers have for many years attempted to explain away this statement, or to reconstruct what he "really" meant, the fact of the matter is that this is nutritional idiocy, and it needs no further comment. In recent years work has been done to suggest that poor nutrition may have been a constraint on fertility that is now being eased. There seems to be no doubt that improving nutrition increases fecundability;[41] the question, however, is whether this is a relevant constraint. Under optimal nutritional conditions, women seem to be able to have about 15 children.[42] On diets currently available in poor countries, are they reduced to a biological maximum of five or six? Women in Russia in the nineteenth century lived on diets that apparently were less nutritious than those currently available in the LDCs, yet they had an average of eight children.[43] As we have already seen, age-specific fertility rates in different regions of the poor world vary dramatically. Even if we assume that the highest rate for each age group is the biologically set maximum, we find that total fecundability could not be less than seven. Nutritional levels, furthermore, have been rising slowly if not steadily in the less developed countries over the past generation. Even taking the good years of 1961/63 and the food crisis years of 1972/74 as endpoints, average caloric availability is up 4 percent,[44] and over this same period fertility has been falling in both the better nourished areas (Latin America, the Caribbean) and the more poorly fed areas (India, Indonesia, the Philippines). That fertility may not be constrained by nutrition in poor countries on the whole (in certain cases no doubt it is) obviously makes concern with hunger no less valid or pressing, but it seems misguided to expect nutritional changes to alter fertility. Fertility may be altered by the biological constraint of health, as we shall see in a moment, but declining fertility seems to be more a matter of choice than unexpected insults to the body.

Infant Mortality

Infant mortality has long been regarded as a factor bearing directly on fertility. The postulated relationship seems clear enough: if large proportions of children die, parents must have large numbers of children just to make sure a few survive. More than a decade ago, a computer simulation showed that with current age-specific death rates, Indian parents would have needed to bear an average of 6.5 children to be 95 percent sure they would have just one son surviving to adulthood.[45] Improvements in child health, therefore, were believed to be a precondition to fertility decline. Research since then makes the relationship between fertility reduction and reducing child death rates seem a little more tenuous.[46] There does not seem to be a specific level of infant mortality, for example, below which birth rates start to come down. Ecuador's infant mortality rate is about half as high as India's, yet it is India's birth rate that has been falling, not Ecuador's. To take two countries less culturally distant, it is Pakistan that has the lower infant mortality rate, but it is India whose fertility has been affected over the past decade.[47]

International comparisons, of course, are crude; their reference point is nations, rather than the individuals within them whose children are dying. But micro-studies do little to specify a connection between declining fertility and declining infant mortality. There is conflicting evidence, for example, over whether women attempt to compensate for lost children. In the studies that have found compensation in action, less than 50 percent of the losses are made back through extra births. The weak relationship between infant mortality and fertility may possibly be explained by the fact that parents use infant mortality as a method of quality control and retroactive abortion. The prevalence of what we might call passive infanticide doubtless varies from culture to culture, but if it is as common as new work suggests, it may be a sign that communities are ready for family planning.[48] Hence, fertility decline precedes rather than follows infant mortality reduction in many communities and perhaps even in nations as a whole. Again, this makes attempts to improve the health of children no less worthy or urgent; it simply means we should not rely on these improvements to depress fertility automatically.

Economic Growth and Income Distribution

In the early postwar period, economists assumed that development, by which they generally meant an increase in aggregate economic product, would bring down the birth rate. By now it is clear that both levels and rates of growth in economics have relatively little association with levels or rates of change in fertility. Some researchers have since suggested that the lack of association is due to the fact that income changes for the poor majority, who bear the large majority of children, are muffled out in national aggregates by income changes for the minority of the population with the majority of the purchasing power. Correlations between changes in income levels of the poorest 40 percent of a population and national fertility are reasonably close.[49]

This has suggested that the distribution of income within a

nation has a substantial effect on fertility. Early works concerned with income distribution and fertility showed that nations that had relatively low per capita GNPs, such as Sri Lanka, China, Taiwan, and South Korea, had been able to reduce fertility as income distribution became more equal, while nations like Mexico, Brazil, and the Philippines, which had relatively high income levels and growth rates and relatively unequal income distributions, showed little signs of fertility decline. Today we know that fertility has dropped significantly in those three countries, and against a background of increasing income differences. In other countries, such as Burma, income distribution has become more equal over the past generation, while fertility has moved down only slightly. Equalizing income distribution, therefore, is neither a necessary nor a sufficient condition for reducing fertility. It is possible, furthermore, that the association between income distribution and fertility is caused by other factors that affect them both. In the now developed nations, for example, economic growth at first skewed income distribution, and then equalized it, but it was in the second phase of development that fertility dropped dramatically in nations such as the United States, Germany, and Italy.[50] The danger of spurious correlation is clearly present, especially since the adjustment of fertility to income change is not likely to be instantaneous, and the lag times are neither known nor specified. A further problem exists in specifying the sort of income distribution we are to be measuring. Are we looking at changes in permanent income over the course of the life cycle for individuals of the same age? If so, measures like the Gini or Kuznets index will play tricks on us: even if age-specific income distribution is equalizing for every age cohort, income distribution will appear to skew if a large proportion of young people—who in every society earn less than their elders—is suddenly to be found in the labor force. This hypothetical shift in the labor force is not so far removed from what has actually occurred in many LDCs.

While these cautionary remarks indicate how difficult it is to establish a link between income distribution and fertility, careful work in the field shows that such a link may exist, at least in Puerto Rico, South Korea, and India.[51] A link may also have been at work in Hungary[52] and Sweden as they underwent fertility transition. But one may suspect that the method of redistribution could have as much to do with a fertility shift as the magnitude of redistribution. Child maintenance subsidies, for example, could have an effect on fertility different from the expansion of jobs for women, even if the statistical extent of redistribution were exactly equal. More work on the link between income distribution and fertility decline clearly needs to be done, but some connection does seem to be present; either through income or through side effects of the process of reducing them, fertility seems to decline more rapidly than it would otherwise.

FAMILY PLANNING

The effect of family planning efforts on fertility is a question of intense debate, and the parties involved are not disinterested. On the one hand, there would seem to be a high demand for improved contraceptive technology. In the United States something like one out of six children born were neither planned nor wanted,[53] and in countries where sophistication of contraception is pronouncedly lower, the demand could reasonably be expected to be high. Although problems such as post facto rationalization and attempts on the part of the interviewed to please their examiners should not be forgotten, surveys in less developed countries have indicated that anywhere from 16 to 35 percent of the children women bear are undesired.[54] Furthermore, it has been shown that significant fertility decline has not occurred in a single less developed country without an active family planning service.

On the other hand, there are reasons to question the influence such programs have had on fertility decline in the poor countries. The first questions one can raise are conceptual. If a family planning center is achieving its goal, it is allowing women to bear the number of children they choose. This does not necessarily imply that numbers will be reduced. Although nutritional constraints may prevent some mothers from having as many children as they wish, a far greater number are probably frustrated by health problems. In Central Africa, for example, birth rates in Gabon are in the low thirties, a full 15 points lower than its neighbors', and the main cause of this difference is the high rate of sterility induced by venereal diseases.[55] Even where entire societies are not afflicted with fertility-reducing health problems, large numbers of individuals within them may be affected. Throughout Africa surveys have typically found that 10 to 15 percent of the women of childbearing age are not able to have the children they desire.[56] (The personal tragedy of sterility exceeds the bounds of simple disappointment; the fate of a barren woman in a great many societies is not an enviable one.) We should expect, therefore, that an effective family planning service would <u>raise</u> fertility in many areas.

Where it lowered fertility, moreover, it would not be doing so through changing values, but through eliminating contraceptive inefficiency. Only a handful of societies, all of them extremely primitive and all of them representing a negligible fraction of humanity, do not recognize the connection between intercourse and pregnancy. Since this connection is generally recognized, most societies have developed methods of keeping fertility below the biological maximum. Enforced abstinence, abortion, and infanticide are no less effective methods of regulating population than IUDs; they are even more effective. They are just considerably more unpleasant. Coitus interruptus and the rhythm method are supposed to serve the same purpose as the pill and the condom; they are just less efficient at doing so. Every contraceptive method is a substitute for every other method; some just happen to be more attractive and effective. If a society switches from traditional to modern means of contraception, we may expect a decrease in the proportion of unwanted children born (perhaps concomitantly, as already suggested, a drop in infant mortality) and hence a drop in the fertility rate. But even if this were to occur, the number of children desired does not necessarily decrease. It may even increase, as sex becomes easier and less dangerous.

In any event, we should not make the mistake of confusing the numbers of modern contraceptive users with the numbers of births averted.[57] Parents using modern contraception are switching to a more efficient strategy of achieving whatever fertility target they may already have. If their modern contraceptives were suddenly taken away, they would devise other strategies for achieving their targets. These might not be entirely successful, but they would be unlikely to be total failures, either.

When we examine the interaction of family planning efforts and fertility decline, we run the risk of making spurious correlations. Is a family planning program successful in reducing fertility because it creates a demand for its service, or because a demand already exists that it then fills? The second case would seem more likely; it might also explain the correlation between weak family planning efforts in certain countries and the lack of fertility change.[58] Fertility was declining in most of the successful case study nations before they ever had family planning programs. What we would ideally like to measure would be the difference in fertility attributable simply to the introduction of family planning: in other words, how much higher would the birth rates have been if the program had not been implemented? Family planning programs unfortunately seldom build controls into their projects. The first one that did, the famous and enormous Khanna study, found that fertility at the end of the period was lower in the control region, perhaps largely for reasons we have discussed above.[59] Other studies with built-in controls have also frequently shown higher fertility in the family planning area than the control region.[60]

As we know, government efforts to raise fertility in certain countries have been conspicuously unsuccessful. Why should efforts to lower fertility be any more efficacious? If parents actually had no idea how many children they wanted or chose a target number irrationally, family planning efforts, heavily laced with antinatalist propaganda, might push down birth rates, but these are contrafactual conditions.[61] Furthermore, a great number of antinatalist family planning efforts have been insensitive to the needs of the people they were supposed to serve, and therefore may have slowed down any secular drop in fertility that might have been beginning.[62] In short, we need to have a great deal more information about family planning to evaluate its effect on fertility. There is no reason offhand, however, to assume that it has acted as a force to depress birth rates, aside from eliminating that fraction of births that was already unwanted. To doubt family planning's antinatal effect, however, is not to question its policy worth in other areas; it can be shown fairly conclusively that family planning increases the health of both mothers and children, and this is clearly a goal of every nation.

Family Level Variables: The Cost of Children

What demographers and statisticians sometimes seem to forget is that in the final analysis it is couples, not nations, that have children. We therefore may be better off looking at the sorts of changes that have occurred in the lives of the poor that could be pushing down the birth rate rather than burrowing through national-level variables.

The first and most obvious sort of change that might lead to a drop in fertility would be a decline in the economic value of children. This would not require children to have been a net economic asset in one period, and to turn into a financial drain in the next; the relative value of children could decrease even if they remained economic assets at the end, or even if they started off as a financial drain.[63] All that would be required, in economic parlance, is that the price ratio between children and other goods shift in favor of the other goods, as shown in Figure 1.3.

As a subject of research the economic value of children has been curiously neglected, and is only just beginning to be investigated. Preliminary results suggest that the long-standing assumption that children are a total drain on parental resources does not hold up in many communities in the poor world. Work done recently in a Bangladesh village shows that by age 12 the average boy is earning his caloric keep (that is, bringing in enough money to pay for his food, the major expense in the Bengali budget). By 15 he has paid for all past consumption, and by 21 he has paid for the consumption of a sister.[64] Since the age at marriage is in the mid-twenties, a surplus may accrue to the parents during this period, and more may come later since connection with the family is not severed. Studies

FIGURE 1.3

Stylized Changes in the Relative Cost of Children in a Neoclassical Framework

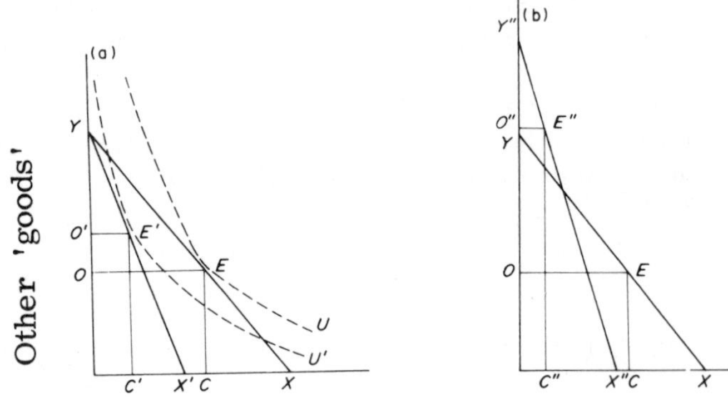

Children

Note: Let us simplify life and ignore the questions of child spacing and children's income. Let us say rather that parents in peasant societies purchase a certain number of children and a certain number of other goods with their income. Does a drop in the number of children chosen mean that the welfare of the parents has increased? Not necessarily. In Figure 1.3a, nominal prices of other goods remain constant, but the cost of children rises—say, through imposition of compulsory education laws. The number of children chosen falls from C to C', and the amount of other goods purchased rises from O to O', but indifference curve U' is below indifference curve U. Hence welfare of the parental decision unit has declined. Alternatively, and perhaps more realistically, a series of changes might make children more expensive as other goods became cheaper. This situation is represented in Figure 1.3b. Here again the number of children chosen declines, this time from C to C'', and the amount of other goods rises, this time from O to O''. But has welfare increased? We cannot tell; it depends entirely on the shape of the indifference curves. If there is a high marginal rate of substitution, that is, if parents place a relatively high personal value on their children as opposed to more material forms of consumption, they are now worse off. If on the other hand the MRS is relatively low, parents will be better off. The point should be clear, even in this simplistic exposition: merely documenting a decline in fertility does not prove that life has become better for parents, or even necessarily for children.

Source: Constructed by the author.

in Java and Nepal show that almost 80 percent of the old people in the villages were living with descendants and being supported at least partially by them.[65] These studies show that even by age five the average boy or girl was doing several hours of productive, and therefore presumably remunerative, work. In Nigeria surveys show that typically 60 percent of parents expect a net benefit financially from their next birth (although parents, it has been shown elsewhere, have a tendency to overestimate the benefits accruing from children, and to underestimate their costs).[66]

Whether children are actually a net economic benefit is in doubt. One would think that the U.S. slavery system might be the limiting situation for wringing a profit out of young labor, but work by Fogel and Engerman shows that the average slave did not pay for himself until age 27.[67] Subsequent work showed that slavery's competitive advantage over free agriculture came through the chain-gang system, by creating a factory in the fields.[68] Farms with under 15 slaves could not benefit from this, so their slaves presumably did not pay for themselves until even later. Very few families outside Africa (and few even there) have more than 15 in them, and the conditions under which their work is organized are presumably less rigorous than those a slavemaster might wish. For their children to be economic assets, peasants would have to have an extraordinarily high aversion to risk (that is, they would have to see their children as an expensive insurance policy for old age), and also an imperfect access to financial markets for alternative investments. It will take more research to tell whether these conditions hold up for people in the less developed countries.[69]

Evidence about changing values of children is largely impressionistic, but there are suggestions that the relative value of an additional birth is declining in many areas of the world. Education is a major instrument through which the shift is effected. Leaving all the aspiration-altering aspects of education aside, schooling is a very expensive proposition for poor parents; yet it is viewed as a clear avenue for the economic success of one's offspring, and the private returns from investment at all levels are high.[70] One loses not only the money that is invested in the education, but also the wage the children would have earned otherwise in the fields or around the community; foregone wages more than double the cost of education in both rich and poor countries. As the proportion of school-age population enrolled increases, the price ratio of children for more and more of the parents in poor nations swings against children. All other things being equal, this would tend to depress fertility. Similar arguments could be made for laws restricting child labor or promoting social security, for changes in agriculture, such as mechanization, which can decrease the demand for labor, or for declines in infant mortality that lead to a heavier investment in children. Note that changes in the relative price of children might reduce fertility without increasing benefits either to the parents (education in a system of family nuclearization) or even to the children (a simple decrease in the demand for child labor).

The Status of Women

Another factor that may be depressing fertility is a change in the status of women. Here again we have an area heavy in speculation and light in fact. Two definite trends, however, have been emerging over the past generation. The first is that women are becoming better educated. Literacy rates and enrollment rates are still lower for women than for men, but the gap is narrowing. Second, as women gain both absolutely and relatively in skills and abilities, their position in the labor force is shifting.[71] Labor force participation rates are notoriously poor for women from poor countries; household and field work are consistently underreported, for example.[72] Statistics from the relatively well-covered, high paying, modernized sector show, however, that the number of women involved is increasing both relatively and absolutely.[73] These may be the sort of out-of-home jobs that are difficult to integrate into a high fertility regime.

How would these changes affect fertility? Although parents may set targets for desired children, there is no reason to think offhand that these targets are the same for men and women. Most of the information gathered through fertility surveys suggests that women consistently desire smaller families than their husbands. A generation ago, average age at marriage for women was under 20, and almost all women were illiterate and had never lived outside their family before marriage. Husbands were on average almost a decade older (the average age difference in the developed countries was, and still is, three years), often at least partially educated, and more often than not skilled in some sort of profession, even if this was simple farming. A clear asymmetry in bargaining power existed. The women who are now at childbearing age are part of the first generation of women who have been through the educational system that expanded so rapidly after World War II. A rise in the average age at marriage is quite closely correlated with improvements in women's education. A change in the rhythm of life has occurred: instead of being married off, increasing numbers of women either stay at home and find work or go off to work in their early twenties and late teens. With greater education, work skills, experience outside the family, and a smaller age differential between herself and her husband (age at marriage has not been rising for the men), young brides are in a better position to bargain over family size. Experience outside the family unit, or the demonstration effect of friends' experiences, may also bring down women's desired family size. All this is consistent with changes in fertility patterns in the poor regions of the world; female education and job status shifts have been least pronounced in black Africa and the Moslem expanse, most rapid in East Asia and Latin America. Much more work needs to be done, however, before these hypotheses can be verified.

Intergenerational Wealth Flows

In a pathbreaking article, John Caldwell has suggested that the fertility transition is caused by a reversal of the intergenerational flow of wealth.[74] Caldwell hypothesizes that under circumstances where the flow of wealth runs from children to parents, the economically rational position is to have an infinite number. Social factors limit family size to a large, but biologically submaximal, number. Similarly, where the flow of wealth is from parents to children, the purely economically rational position would be to have no children, but social factors induce parents to have a few. Caldwell has extended his analysis to Nigeria and Australia, nations that have not yet begun and that have already finished their fertility transition, respectively. Caldwell's work for these two countries is compelling, but before the theory can be extended to other countries, a great deal more study must be done.

Inherently Immeasurable Factors

Other facts that may have changed the demand for children within the family are more generalized shifts in employment patterns, changes in communication and transportation, and demonstration effects from the lives of the middle-class elites that have developed over the last generation. Related to all of these, and more powerful than any of them, has undoubtedly been a change in attitudes, beliefs, aspirations, and values. Demographers have shied away from this nebulous and perhaps inherently immeasurable realm of population-influencing variables; just because these cannot be easily quantified, however, does not mean they are unimportant. Today we do not even have a beginning through which to trace the effects of change in psychological, social, and even political attitudes on fertility. Since tastes in rich countries appear to have much to do with variations in fertility both among countries and within countries over time, it may be reasonable to suspect that similar taste differences do exist in less developed countries, and it may be profitable to pursue research in this direction.

CONCLUSION

How can we relate fertility decline in certain countries—and the lack of fertility decline in other countries—to social change? We remember that a three-stage pattern of fertility decline emerged from the six countries examined earlier. We might do well to relate social changes causally to these stages. In the first stage, much of the reduction in the birth rate is not actually due to fertility changes, but rather to shrinkage in the proportion of women in childbearing ages. (We might also guess that some of the fertility change registered at this stage is due to a shift in the composition of the childbearing-age women toward the youngest and least fertile age groups.) The shrinkage is due largely to the postwar phenomenon of rising life expectancy in the poor world. While death rates in the over 50 cohorts have gone down, they have plummetted for children. This is likely a one-time phenomenon; presumably it has affected almost all countries, whether or not their fertility has declined. We may hypothesize then that the age-structure shift is a factor that is not directly causative, but one, which like so many other factors, will simply be associated with a drop in the birth rate in poor countries wherever it occurs.

The second phase of the fertility decline depends upon changing already established social patterns; the link between social change and fertility change here is clearly more causative. We would do well to have figures on age-specific shifts in the proportion of women married. Until we have these, however, we will go too far astray if we assume that the majority of the shift occurs at the early age groups through a postponement of marriage. Why is marriage postponed? To belabor the obvious, it must be because alternatives to early marriage now exist, and because these alternatives for whatever reason (in the final analysis) seem attractive to young women. We can see how improved education and new sorts of job opportunities may have played a significant role in pushing back ages at marriage. Other social factors involved are less obvious, and probably will not be properly specified without further research.

In the final stage of the fertility decline, marital fertility rates are the driving force behind fertility decline. Two factors seem especially important here. The first is the narrowing gap in ages, skills and extra-familial experiences between husbands and wives. The second is a decline in the relative values of children. (Associated with these may be a reversal in the flows of generational wealth, although this realm has been little explored.) Still another factor may be a shift in attitudes and values, although this too is hypothetical. There is simply a great deal about the relationship between fertility and social change which we not know and have not yet researched.

WHAT SHOULD "PLANNERS" LEARN FROM THE RECENT DECLINES IN FERTILITY?

Although fertility regulation programs were actively opposed by the leadership of a large number of the newly independent LDCs just a generation ago, a majority of people in the less developed world today live under governments with officially antinatalist population stances.[75] The tremendous spread of antinatalism has been facilitated by many factors; one of them has been the emergence of a consensus in academia and government over two issues.[76] The first concerns the effects of high fertility and rapid population growth on human well-being. Human well-being is supposed to be threatened socially, economically, perhaps even politically, by these phenomena. The second centers around the relationship between declining fertility and "development." Here the agreement is that development and declining fertility are mutually reinforcing, each being a causal factor in and a necessary condition for the other. It is easy to understand how consensus on these two issues helps justify and facilitate the construction of antinatalist population influencing policies. It is more difficult to understand how the consensus developed in the first place, however, since the evidence supporting these premises has always been anything but conclusive.

Let us examine the premise of a causal and necessary link between development and fertility reduction. Development is a nebulous concept whose definition can be altered to suit the needs of any immediate discussion, but if development is taken to mean an improvement in the standard of living for the majority of the populace, we know it is not a necessary condition for fertility decline. In England there was no clear evidence of an improvement in the lives of the working class until the end of the nineteenth century;[77] fertility began declining at the end of the eighteenth. In France fertility began its decline during the late eighteenth and early nineteenth centuries; during this period the French standard of living was almost definitely falling.[78] Japan's economic growth had been rapid from the 1880s on, but its birth rates did not fall until the 1940s, when the Japanese suffered a dramatic, if temporary, setback in their standard of living.[79] In the less developed countries, health has improved in all regions, but if we set aside this admittedly important, though exogenously induced, improvement, there is no evidence of a universal increase in living standards in areas of fertility decline. In India birth rates have dropped rapidly in Punjab and Kerala, states where the living standard is known to have improved dramatically. But birth rates have come down in Tamil Nadu and Uttar Pradesh as well, and if there is a shred of truth in the poverty studies the ILO conducted, living standards of the vast majority have not improved there.[80] Java is one of the few areas of the world for which historians have made a compelling argument that living standards may be worse today than a century and a half ago,[81] yet fertility has been declining rapidly in Java over the last decade. In Nigeria, on the other hand, a nation where living standards have unarguably improved over the past generation, the Biafran war notwithstanding, fertility has remained unaffected. Furthermore, there is as yet no evidence that the growth of per capita income has accelerated in the nations of Table 1.5 whose birth rates have dropped dramatically over the past decade.

Are high fertility levels and rapid rates of population growth unmitigated social evils? Space does not permit a full analysis of the enormous subject of demographic-societal interactions, which are hardly as simple as antinatalists suggest. It will suffice to make a few points here. First, the growth of population in the less developed world has been due primarily to an improvement in child mortality and a lengthening of the lives of the poor. Who among us will label these changes social evils? Second, unwanted births and improper child-spacing practices are unarguably social problems. We have fairly conclusive evidence that they threaten maternal and child health and decrease a child's chances of success in later life. But unwanted births occur even in West Germany, a nation with a negative rate of population growth, and it is still possible to have a seven-child family if one marries at 20 and spaces them three years apart. Third, surprising as it may seem, there is no economic evidence to show that rapid population growth stifles economic growth, or even per capita economic growth. Models built on incremental capital-output ratios and dependency rates have been used to do this instead, but as we know, these concepts generate meaningless numbers when one tries to use them for planning economic growth, and there is no reason for them to fare any better in demographic planning. If there is any international correlation between population growth and the rate of per capita economic growth in the less developed countries, and many are not convinced there is, it would be positive, not negative. There is a respectable case to be made for the proposition that rapid population growth increases per capita growth rates. Fourth, it is clear that coercing parents to have fewer children than they want is not only enormously undemocratic, but may also force parents to flirt with economic disaster either today or in their old age. To assume that rapid population growth is nothing but a social drain is to assume that parents who want to have large families, and at the same time strive to see their children survive, are incapable of controlling their fertility, irrational about or insensitive to changes in their standard of living, or unconcerned about the problems they will be bequeathing upon generations yet unborn. We know enough about peasant rationality and sensitivity to incentives and disincentives to close discussion on this question. There is evidence of varying quality to suggest that poor people—in aggregate—do indeed have more children than they would like to. But even reducing family size to desired levels would leave fertility high by Western standards, and the subject of intergenerational flows of costs and benefits has not been examined seriously despite the enormous amount of casual talk it has generated.

Two implications of these ill-advised consensuses are particularly disturbing. The first is that planners and policymakers are likely to perceive poverty and their difficulty in alleviating it as demographic rather than social problems. There are no good statistical indexes of overpopulation per se; what demographers use instead are signs of destitution. Destitution is a syndrome in which demographic effects are secondary. A change in land tenure arrangements can either create or eliminate symptoms by which demographers judge overpopulation, such as unemployment, hunger, and low incomes, even if the fertility level is totally unaffected. Although the elimination of poverty is not made inherently more difficult by high fertility or rapid population growth—every mouth, the saying goes, come with two hands—the elimination of poverty may indeed become more difficult if the government acts on the assumption that poverty is caused by irrational sexual proclivities on the part of the poor.

Second, if rapid population growth is postulated to be a social hazard, population rather than the people such numbers represent will tend to become the prime concern of policymakers. Preoccupation with numbers, acceptance quotas, and rates of growth is counterproductive. If we evaluate a program solely in these terms, we run the risk of diverting attention from, trivializing, and actually losing patience with the problems of parents who for some reason are having large families. A program biased toward numbers control is less likely to be used voluntarily by parents, and less likely to help them when it is used.

Even if these biases were eliminated, however, population planners would face a serious constraint toward the efficacy of their programs through the split between academic research and research needs for effective policy. Regardless of its quality, most research on demographic-social interactions has been academic. It has been geared toward answering general questions; policymakers need specific answers. Academic research should be painstaking, and as such will probably be slow; policymakers need information immediately. Academic research may be satisfied to point out associations; policy depends on getting causation straight. Academic research, when it traces causality, should attempt to uncover all mechanisms and pathways through which the variables in question interact; policy research should be concerned only with effects, and only those effects that can be brought about by the relatively limited policy instruments at the government's disposal. To give an example of the problem population policymakers face trying to use academic research: we have already seen that fertility changes in less developed countries seem to depend on changing the family structure, but this information is not necessarily of use, for the family of all social organizations has proven the most resistant to government penetration. Not only must more research on social and demographic interactions be undertaken, but also the proportion of policy research should probably be increased dramatically.

What can we do to improve the efficacy of population planning while we are waiting for the results of this research? First and foremost, if population planners are interested in improving a nation's welfare as well as reducing its fertility, they should seek our areas where the two goals are consistent with each other. Antinatalist ideology suggests that fertility decline and development reinforce each other; as we have seen, this is not always true. Fertility can decline independent of improvements in a population's well-being, and welfare can improve independent of fertility decline. Even after the fertility transition is in full swing, therefore, population planners should be sure that the programs they are pushing are consistent with the national welfare.

Population planners might do well for both themselves and their targets to work in areas where they share goals with the populace. In general, their work would be facilitated by affirming their belief that parents are the best judges of how many children they should have—recognizing, of course, that husbands and wives may have different ideas about what this ideal size is. Poor people, after all, are not interested in being eliminated; they are interested in improving their lives, and will respond more favorably toward programs that they see as helping them improve their lives. Parents uninterested in bringing down their nation's dangerously high rate of population growth may be interested in preventing unwanted births and seeing more of their children survive through safe spacing practices.

Population planners should realize that in the final analysis a good family planning program is population responsive, not population influencing. Family planning is a health policy instrument through which parents may safely achieve their fertility goals; it does not necessarily alter the demand for children. To influence demand, as we have seen, one must enter the family: by improving the status of women and decreasing the relative value of children, or perhaps by reversing the generational flows of wealth. The first two objectives cannot be achieved directly, and the third may be impossible to achieve even indirectly, but there are certain policies that are population influencing and consistent with the goal of improving national welfare as well.

To improve the status of women, governments are most likely to be successful if they concentrate on expanding opportunities for women in the educational system and the out-of-family labor force. Besides increasing family income and improving the life chances for half the population, one might expect these reforms to push up the age at marriage, reduce the proportion of women married at all ages, resolve the discrepancy between male and female family size ideals more equally, and perhaps alter women's family size ideals as well. To increase the relative price of children, governments might attempt to improve child health, increase school enrollments, implement effective social security or old-age insurance programs, and promote a reliable emergency relief system. Health improvements might be expected to encourage parents to increase their quality investment in children since risk involved, in this case their child's disability or death, would be reduced. The other reforms would all make children a less remunerative, or at least a less necessary, prospect.

A third set of policies concerning the equalization of incomes might also be attempted. By attacking the components of income inequality—low education for the mass of the population, unequal access to employment opportunities, unequal land tenure, overinvestment of government resources in urban areas, credit and pricing policies that transfer resources from agriculture to industry, and the like—certain deadweight efficiency losses in the system demonstrably will be eliminated and national welfare will arguably be promoted. In addition, some of the second-round effects are likely to depress fertility. The demographic results of these policies may not be significant in all countries, and some policies that narrow income differences may increase fertility: for example, a land reform that raises the demand for child labor rather than adult female or underemployed adult male labor. There is nevertheless a considerable area of potential overlap between the concerns of income equalization and fertility reduction.

The demographic effects of a host of policies—such as improving nutrition, increasing the quality of the housing stock, easing constraints to migration and mobility, and other ostensibly population-responsive programs—are not immediately clear or necessarily consistent internationally, since it is easy for second- and third-order effects to outweight first-order effects here. But, let us ask, what if improving the quality of these services could be proven conclusively to raise fertility? Should population planners rail against infant-feeding programs, the elimination of slums, or freedom of travel?

Planners tread an uncomfortably thin line between serving and controlling their subjects. In population planning the line is thinner than elsewhere. Controlling fertility and improving a people's welfare are not always synonymous goals. If population planners wish to serve rather than control, they must straighten out their confusion here. If they do, they may find that the difference, both conceptually and in policy terms, between population-responsible and population-influencing programs is smaller than they think.

NOTES

1. Nick Eberstadt, "Population Figures Are Misleading," New York Times, March 25, 1978.

2. See Chapter 8.

3. See McCabe and Rosenzweig's contribution in Ronald Ridker, ed., Population and Development: The Search for Selective Interventions (Baltimore: Johns Hopkins University Press, 1976).

4. See Simon Kuznets, "Population Change and Aggregate Output," in his Economic Growth and Structure (New York: Norton, 1965).

5. See the contributions on Eastern Europe in Bernard Berelson, ed., Population Policies in Developed Countries (New York: McGraw-Hill, 1974). Recently there has been a slight upswing in fertility in several Warsaw Pact nations. To what extent, however, has this been due to government policy? The answer seems to be: not much. In a brilliant article, Coelen and McIntyre attempt to assess the demographic impact of different components of population policy in Eastern Europe. They conclude that such instruments as child allowance payments do influence fertility, but only marginally. The cost of instituting major shifts in fertility through such means would be unfeasibly high. See Stephen P. Coelen and Robert J. McIntyre, "An Econometric Model of Pronatalist and Abortion Policies," Journal of Political Economy (December 1978). Eastern Europe's demographic resurgence, then, cannot be credited to its governments.

6. This taxonomy comes from Myron Weiner's essay "Political Demography," in Roger Revelle, ed., Rapid Population Growth, Volume II (Baltimore: Johns Hopkins University Press, 1971).

7. See Myron Weiner, India at the Polls (Washington, D.C.: American Enterprise Institute for Public Policy Research, 1978).

8. A good review of some of these issues is in Bernard Berelson, W. Parker Mauldin, and Sheldon J. Segal, "Population: Current Status

and Policy Options," which is currently available as Working Paper #44 from the Center for Policy Studies, Population Council, New York.

9. See, for example, the United Nations' World Population Prospects as Assessed in 1968 (New York: United Nations, 1973), and World Population Prospects as Assessed in 1973 (New York: United Nations, 1977).

10. United Nations, World Population Prospects as Assessed in 1963 (New York: United Nations, 1966).

11. See PHCE 4, Estimates of the Coverage of the Population of the United States by Age, Sex, and Race (Washington, D.C.: Bureau of Census, 1974).

12. United Nations Fund for Population Activities, The UNFPA and World Census Activity (New York: UNFPA, 1976). In the 1960s, of course, the situation was even worse: by 1965 only 3 percent of Africa, 4 percent of Asia, and 44 percent of Latin America had been covered by reliable counts. See Nathan Keyfitz and Wilhelm Flieger, World Population: An Analysis of Vital Data (Chicago: University of Chicago Press, 1968.)

13. See the U.N.'s The Future Growth of World Population (New York: United Nations, 1958) and its World Population Prospects as Assessed in 1973.

14. Nick Eberstadt, "The Politics of Enumeration: An Examination of Nigerian Census Data," unpublished paper, 1974.

15. Personal communication with P. N. Haksar, Deputy Minister of Planning, 1977.

16. See Judith Banister's 1977 dissertation at Stanford, "The Current Vital Rates and Population Size of the People's Republic of China and Its Provinces." Since this article was written China has released results for a 1979 census that put its population at 958 million. The margin of error imputed by Chinese demographers was 30 million in either direction. After discussing the Chinese methodology with a number of demographers who had been briefed by a Chinese delegation on a recent trip through the United States, however, it would seem to me that a margin of error of plus or minus 50 million might be a little nearer the mark.

17. The low estimate is Colin Clark's, from "Economic Development in Communist China," Journal of Political Economy (April 1976); the high is from John S. Aird, "Population Growth in the People's Republic of China," in the Joint Economic Committee's Chinese Economy Post-Mao (Washington, D.C.: GAO, November 9, 1978).

18. In light of the new data from China, the margin of error for the world today may be considerably lower. See my introduction in this volume.

19. United Nations, Demographic Handbook 1950 (New York: United Nations, 1951).

20. Eberstadt, "Population Figures Are Misleading."

21. Nick Eberstadt, "Fertility Decline in Japan: A Decomposition," unpublished paper, 1973.

22. Personal communication with Dudley Kirk, Stanford University.

23. Calculated from Sam Suharto and Lee-Jay Cho, "Preliminary Estimates of Indonesian Fertility Based on the 1976 Intercensal Population Survey" (Honolulu: East-West Center, 1978).

24. See Richard Anker, "An Analysis of Fertility Differentials in Developing Countries," Review of Economics and Statistics (February 1978).

25. For the earliest exposition on this subject, see Dudley Kirk, "A New Demographic Transition?," in Rapid Population Growth.

26. Ibid.

27. New work has suggested the birth rate might have been even higher in the early 1950s—one suspects as a result of having postponed births during the chaos of the 1940s. See Aird, "Population Growth in The People's Republic," and Leo A. Orleans, "China's Birth Rate, Death Rate, and Population Growth: Another Perspective" (Washington, D.C.: Library of Congress, September 1977).

28. See Chapter 3.

29. Ansley Coale was the first writer to notice a two-step break in the process of fertility decline, as fertility decline from decreasing the length of marital unions was superseded by decline from decreasing the intramarital fertility rate. See his "The Demographic Transition" in International Union for the Scientific Study of Population, International Population Conference, 1973 (Liege: IUSSP, 1973).

30. Two excellent volumes that bring together many of the similarities and differences in the experiences from the demographic transition are David Glass and David Eversley, eds., Population in History (Chicago: Aldine, 1967), and David Glass and Roger Revelle, eds., Population and Social Change (New York: Crane-Russak, 1972).

31. See Fernand Braudel, Capitalism and Material Life, 1400-1800 (New York: Harper & Row, 1973).

32. J. A. Banks, Prosperity and Parenthood (Atlantic Highlands: Humanities, 1954).

33. See Chapter 6.

34. John C. Caldwell and Lado T. Ruzicka, "The Australian Fertility Transition: An Analysis," Population and Development Review (March 1978).

35. Eberstadt, "Fertility Decline in Japan."

36. Typical of this immiserization approach is Lester R. Brown, "World Population Trends: Signs of Hope, Signs of Stress" (Washington, D.C.: Worldwatch Institute, 1976).

37. See Kingsley Davis, World Urbanization, 1950-70 (Berkeley: University of California Press, 1973).

38. Simon Kuznets, "Rural-Urban Fertility Differentials in Less Developed Countries," Proceedings of the American Philosophical Society, 1974.

39. Simon Kuznets, Modern Economic Growth (New Haven: Yale University Press, 1966).

40. His work has been reprinted under the title The Geopolitics of Hunger (New York: Monthly Review, 1977).

41. See Chapter 9.

42. John Bongaarts, "A Framework for Analyzing the Proximate Determinants of Fertility," Population and Development Review (March 1978).

43. Ansley Coale, Barbara Anderson, and Erna Härm, Human Fertility in Russia since the Nineteenth Century (Princeton: Princeton University Press, 1979).

44. Food and Agricultural Organization, Fourth World Food Survey (Rome: FAO, 1978).

45. David Heer and D. O. Smith, "Mortality Level, Desired Family Size, and Population Increase," Demography 5 (1968).

46. See Chapter 8.

47. Ruth Leger Sivard, World Social and Military Expenditures 1978 (New York: Rockefeller Foundation, 1978).

48. See Chapter 8.

49. See Robert G. Repetto's contribution in Timothy King et al., Population Policies and Economic Development (Baltimore: Johns Hopkins University Press, 1974).

50. See Simon Kuznets, Economic Growth of Nations: Total Output and Production Structure (Cambridge, Mass.: Harvard University Press, 1971).

51. Robert G. Repetto, Economic Equality and Fertility Decline in Developing Countries (Baltimore: Johns Hopkins University Press, 1979).

52. See Chapter 6.

53. Nick Eberstadt, "Questions and Answers about Population," Rockefeller Foundation Illustrated (January 1975).

54. Ibid.

55. See Chapter 3.

56. Pierre Pradervand, "Population Control, Family Planning, and Western Ideology," unpublished paper, 1974.

57. See Chapter 10.

58. See W. Parker Mauldin and Bernard Berelson, with Zenas Sykes, "Conditions of Fertility Decline in Developing Countries, 1950-75," Studies in Family Planning (May 1978). Mauldin, Berelson, and

Sykes recognize the correlation, but correlation, of course, does not imply causality.

59. Mamood Mamdani, The Myth of Population Control (New York: Monthly Review, 1972).

60. Anker, "An Analysis of Fertility," is one of the few authors whose statistical analysis of the contribution of family planning activity to intercountry fertility differentials is not clearly flawed methodologically. He found that the contribution was statistically insignificant under several different formulations of the effects.

61. See Mamdani, "Myth of Population Control," and Nick Eberstadt, "The Rich Get Richer and the Poor Have Children," Populi (Journal of the U.N. Fund for Population Activities), September 1976.

62. In the aftermath of the Gandhi government's sterilization debacle, for example, voluntary visits to family planning clinics were down by as much as 70 percent on a provincial basis.

63. Robert G. Repetto, "The Economic Value of Children: Some Methodological Questions," in Ridker, Population and Development. My understanding of this problem has benefited immensely from conversations with Professor Repetto.

64. Mead Cain, "The Economic Activities of Children in a Village in Bangladesh," Population and Development Review (September 1977).

65. Chapter 7.

66. See Thomas Espenshade's pamphlet on this subject for the Population Reference Bureau.

67. Robert Fogel and Stanley Engerman, Time on the Cross (Boston: Little, Brown, 1974).

68. Robert Fogel and Stanley Engerman, "Explaining Relative Efficiency of Slave Agriculture in the Antebellum South," American Economic Review (June 1977).

69. Demographers have given little thought to the effect of different sorts of family arrangements upon fertility or fertility decline. If, for example, parents are pensioned off by their children when they become old and weak, parents will have an economic incentive to bear as many children as will be necessary to produce the maximum pension, but, the benefit level being supposedly fixed, they will have no economic incentive to have any more than that number. In other societies the eldest man in the family may control the entire family's finances, in which case it may be to his advantage, at least from a purely economic standpoint, to father the largest possible number of children. Until we know more about the systems of family arrangements in the poor world, and the ways in which we are changing, we will be fundamentally in the dark about a most important factor influencing fertility and fertility change.

70. See George Psacharopoulos and Keith Hincliffe, Returns to Education: An International Comparison (New York: Elsevier, 1973).

71. Documenting such changes, however, has proven difficult. For a discussion of some of the issues, see Nick Eberstadt, Poverty in China (Bloomington: International Development Institute, 1979).

72. See Ester Boserup, Women's Role in Economic Development (New York: St. Martin's, 1974).

73. Elise Boulding et al., Handbook of International Data on Women (New York: Halsted, 1976).

74. John C. Caldwell, "Toward a Restatement of Demographic Transition Theory," Population and Development Review (June 1976).

75. Ronald Freedman and Bernard Berelson, "The Record of Family Planning Programs," Studies in Family Planning (January 1976).

76. Ibid.

77. For an overall presentation of the debate, see Arthur J. Taylor, ed., The Standard of Living in Britain in the Industrial Revolution (London: Methuen, 1975).

78. See Braudel, Capitalism and Material Life.

79. See Eberstadt, "Fertility Decline in Japan."

80. International Labor Office, Poverty and Landlessness in Rural Asia (Geneva: ILO, 1977).

81. See Clifford Geertz, Agricultural Involution (Berkeley: University of California Press, 1963). See also Keith Griffin, "Underdevelopment in History," in Charles K. Wilber, ed., The Political Economy of Development and Underdevelopment (New York: Random House, 1972). The argument about the decline in the standard of living, of course, does not take into account the impressive and terribly important increases in life expectancy that have occurred over the past generation. These cannot really be valued properly; in fact, when GNP per capita figures are calculated, the increase in health of the population actually lowers the apparent average wealth of the society.

2

PATTERNS OF FERTILITY DECLINE IN DEVELOPING COUNTRIES, 1950–75

W. Parker Maudlin

The population of the world increased by two-thirds, from 2.5 to almost 4.0 billion, during the past quarter century. In 1950 the population of the world was divided one-third in developed and two-thirds in developing countries. Both mortality and fertility were high in developing countries, with the expectation of life at birth being about 40 years, the crude death rate a little more than 23 per thousand population per year, and the crude birth rate about 42 per thousand population per year.

A revolution in mortality begun just after World War II, and mortality declined three to five times as rapidly as in previous decades. Life expectancy at birth increased from about 40 to more than 53 years by 1975, and the crude death rate dropped precipitously from 23 to 13-14. This remarkable revolution, which has yet to run its course, led to the enormous increase in population of 1.5 billion in just 25 years.

The purpose of this chapter is fourfold:

1. To establish when and where and by how much fertility has declined. For the most part I shall use two measures, crude birth rates (CBR) and gross reproduction rates;

2. To assess the effect of changes in age-sex structure on the numbers of births and on the crude birth rate;

3. To examine changes in age at marriage as a factor in fertility change; and

*Reprinted with permission from Studies in Family Planning, April 1978.

4. To determine the effects of changes in the patterns and levels of marital fertility on the CBR.

The proposed tasks are conceptually simple, but unfortunately these simple tasks become both complicated and to some extent speculative because of poor and missing data. The data I present come primarily from the United Nations and from the statistical offices of various countries, supplemented by analyses of statisticians and demographers from many countries.

The reader should be cautioned that there is much we do not know about the world's population size and growth. Our best estimate is that humankind numbers just over 4 billion, but that figure could easily be too high or too low by 200 million. Information about the numbers, rates, and trends of births and deaths is even less available and less reliable than population totals, particularly for the developing countries. Most registration systems are inadequate and inaccurate, and there are appreciable lags—sometimes of a few years—between the occurrence and recording of an event and the analysis and publication of the relevant numbers. Despite the lack of precise information, however, a great deal <u>is</u> known about population size and growth and about mortality and fertility trends.

FERTILITY TRENDS

Fertility remained high in most developing countries until about 1965 (see Table 2.1), but in the next ten years there were significant declines in fertility rates in Latin America and major changes in Asia. Changes in Africa were limited to a few countries, notably Egypt, Mauritius, and Tunisia.

Although fertility declined by only 2 percent in all of Asia from 1950 to 1965, there were appreciable declines during this period in several countries, including Fiji, Hong Kong, South Korea, Sri Lanka, and Taiwan. In each of those countries declines in CBRs accelerated during the next ten years, with declines ranging from more than 20 to 40 percent. For all of Asia the CBR decline for 1965 to 1975 is estimated at 17 percent.

In Latin America only, Barbados, Costa Rica, and Trinidad and Tobago reported significant declines in CBRs from 1950 to 1965, and for all developing countries in Latin America the difference between the 1950 and 1965 CBRs was trivial. The situation changed dramatically during the next ten years, with nine countries reporting declines of 20 to 40 percent—Barbados, Chile, Colombia, Costa Rica, Cuba, the Dominican Republic, Jamaica, Panama, and Trinidad and Tobago. Brazil, El Salvador, and Venezuela also reported declines

TABLE 2.1

Crude Birth Rates and Crude Birth Rate Declines, Developing Countries, 1950-75

Region and Country	Crude Birth Rates				Crude Birth Rate Declines (percent)	
	1950-55	1960	1965	1975	1950-55 to 1965	1965 to 1975
Africa						
Algeria	51	51	50	48	2	4
Angola	51	50	49	47	4	4
Burundi	48	48	48	48	1	1
Cameroon	44	43	42	41	4	3
Cen. African Rep.	46	46	45	43	2	5
Chad	46	45	45	44	3	2
Congo	45	44	44	45	1	-2
Dahomey/Benin	52	51	51	49	2	3
Egypt	45	44	42	35	6	17
Ethiopia	51	51	50	49	2	2
Ghana	51	50	50	49	2	2
Guinea	48	47	47	46	1	2
Ivory Coast	46	46	46	45	0	1
Kenya	48	49	50	50	-4	0
Lesotho	39	38	38	40	2	-4
Liberia	45	43	43	44	5	-3
Libyan Arab Rep.	48	48	47	47	3	-1

Madagascar	50	50	50	50	1	0
Malawi	49	49	49	47	-1	5
Mali	50	50	50	50	1	-1
Mauritania	45	45	45	45	0	0
Mauritius	46	40	36	26	22	29
Morocco	50	50	49	48	3	2
Mozambique	43	43	43	43	-2	2
Niger	52	52	52	52	0	1
Nigeria	49	50	50	49	-1	1
Rwanda	53	52	51	51	4	0
Senegal	48	48	48	47	1	0
Sierra Leone	45	45	45	45	0	0
Somalia	47	48	48	48	-1	0
Sudan	50	50	49	49	2	0
Tanzania	52	51	51	48	2	5
Togo	51	51	51	50	0	2
Tunisia	46	47	45	34	4	24
Uganda	47	46	46	47	4	-4
Upper Volta	50	50	50	49	0	1
Zaire	47	47	47	44	1	6
Zambia	50	49	50	50	0	-2
Subtotal	49	48	48	46	1	4
The Americas						
Barbados	33	31	27	19	17	31
Bolivia	47	45	44	44	6	1
Brazil	41	39	42	38	-2	10

(continued)

TABLE 2.1 (continued)

Region and Country	Crude Birth Rates				Crude Birth Rate Declines (percent)	
	1950-55	1960	1965	1975	1950-55 to 1965	1965 to 1975
Chile	35	37	33	23	7	29
Colombia	46	45	44	33	5	25
Costa Rica	48	47	41	29	14	29
Cuba	28	30	34	21	-21	40
Dominican Rep.	50	49	47	38	6	21
Ecuador	46	46	45	45	2	0
El Salvador	48	48	46	40	4	13
Guatemala	49	48	45	43	7	4
Haiti	40	39	38	36	7	4
Honduras	55	53	51	48	6	7
Jamaica	35	39	38	30	-11	21
Mexico	47	45	44	40	6	9
Nicaragua	53	51	49	46	8	7
Panama	41	41	40	31	2	22
Paraguay	45	43	42	39	8	6
Peru	44	44	43	42	3	2
Trinidad and Tobago	38	38	33	23	14	29
Venezuela	46	45	42	37	9	11
Subtotal	42	41	41	36	3	14

Asia and the Pacific						
Afghanistan	49	48	49	49	2	-2
Bangladesh	49	51	50	49	-2	2
Bhutan	46	45	45	43	4	3
Burma	44	43	41	40	5	3
China	37	31	34	26	9	24
Fiji	44	42	36	28	19	22
Hong Kong	33	35	28	18	15	36
India	42	44	43	36	-1	16
Indonesia	45	47	46	40	-2	13
Iran	48	47	46	45	4	2
Iraq	49	48	48	48	3	0
Jordan	45	47	48	47	-5	1
Khmer/Kampuchea	49	49	47	47	4	2
Korea, North	37	41	39	37	-6	5
Korea, South	37	41	35	24	5	32
Kuwait	45	44	46	44	-2	5
Laos	44	44	44	42	-1	5
Lebanon	41	43	41	40	0	2
Malaysia	45	45	42	31	7	26
Mongolia	40	41	42	38	-4	9
Nepal	46	46	45	45	3	-1
Pakistan	50	48	48	47	4	1
Papua New Guinea	44	44	43	41	3	5
Philippines	45	45	44	36	2	19
Saudi Arabia	51	51	50	50	1	0

(continued)

TABLE 2.1 (continued)

Region and Country	Crude Birth Rates 1950-55	1960	1965	1975	Crude Birth Rate Declines (percent) 1950-55 to 1965	1965 to 1975
Singapore	44	38	29	18	34	40
Sri Lanka	39	36	33	27	14	18
Syrian Arab Rep.	47	47	48	46	-2	4
Taiwan	46	39	32	23	28	30
Thailand	47	46	44	34	6	23
Turkey	45	43	41	34	10	16
Vietnam, North	41	42	42	32	0	23
Vietnam, South	41	42	42	41	0	0
Yemen	51	51	51	50	1	1
Yemen, P.D.R. of	51	51	50	49	1	3
Subtotal	41	39	40	33	4	17
Total	42	40	41	35	4	15

Note: All totals are weighted by population.

of more than 10 percent from 1965 to 1975. For all of Latin America, CBRs declined by slightly more than 12 percent from 1965 to 1975.

CBR DECLINES BY SIZE OF POPULATION

One frequently hears that fertility declines among developing countries have largely been confined to small countries, and particularly the islands. We have all heard about fertility declines in Hong Kong, Singapore, Taiwan, and in a number of the Caribbean islands, such as Barbados, Jamaica, and Trinidad and Tobago. There is increasing evidence, however, that fertility has begun to decline in many of the larger countries.

Thirteen developing countries had populations in excess of 35 million as of 1970. Three of these, South Korea, China, and Thailand, had fertility declines of more than 20 percent from 1965 to 1975 (see Table 2.2). Six had declines of 10-19 percent, namely, Brazil, Egypt, India, Indonesia, the Philippines, and Turkey. The remaining four, Bangladesh, Mexico, Nigeria, and Pakistan, had no declines in fertility or declines of less than 10 percent. Fertility declines in this group of 13 countries are very consequential because their combined population is more than 2.25 billion. Therefore, let us briefly consider the data on which these CBR declines are based.

China has not had a census since 1953, and even that census was of unknown quality. Thus, it is not surprising that estimates of China's population vary widely, usually in the range of 850 to 950 million. Similarly, there is very little information about vital statistics, although visitors to China have been given vital statistics for a few localities, mostly urban. Those data indicate that fertility levels are quite low and have fallen rapidly during the past two decades.

Statements by Chinese officials have made it clear that population planning is a national priority. In 1974, China's statement to the United Nations World Population Conference noted that: ". . . a policy of planned population growth is in the interest of the thorough emancipation of women and the proper bringing up of future generations as well as of national construction and prosperity" (Huang 1974, p. 9). And most recently, in his report on the work of the government delivered at the first session of the Fifth National People's Congress on February 26, 1978, Communist Party Chairman Hua Kuo-feng pointed out:

> Family planning is a very significant matter. Planned control of population growth is conducive to the planned development of the national economy and to the health of mother and child. It also benefits the people where

TABLE 2.2

Crude Birth Rate Declines, by Size of Population, Developing Countries, 1965-75
(percent)

35 Million or More		15-35 Million		5-15 Million		0.5-5 Million	
Country	Crude Birth Rate Decline	Country	Crude Birth Rate Decline	Country	Crude Birth Rate Decline	Country	Crude Birth Rate Decline
Bangladesh	2	Afghanistan	-2	Angola	4	Bhutan	3
Brazil	10	Algeria	4	Bolivia	1	Burundi	1
China	24	Burma	3	Cameroon	3	Cen. African Rep.	5
Egypt	17	Colombia	25	Chile	29	Chad	2
India	16	Ethiopia	2	Cuba	40	Congo	-2
Indonesia	13	Iran	2	Dominican Rep.	21	Costa Rica	29
Korea, South	32	Korea, North	5	Ecuador	0	Dahomey	3
Mexico	9	Morocco	2	Ghana	2	El Salvador	13
Nigeria	1	Peru	2	Guatemala	4	Fiji	22
Pakistan	1	Sudan	0	Iraq	0	Guinea	2
Philippines	19	Taiwan	30	Ivory Coast	1	Haiti	0
Thailand	23	Tanzania	5	Kenya	0	Honduras	7
Turkey	16	Vietnam, North	23	Khmer/Kampuchea	2	Hong Kong	36
		Vietnam, South	0	Madagascar	0	Jamaica	21
		Zaire	6	Malawi	5	Jordan	1
				Malaysia	26	Kuwait	5
				Mali	-1	Laos	5

				Mozambique	2	Lebanon	2
				Nepal	-1	Lesotho	-4
				Saudi Arabia	0	Liberia	0
				Senegal	0	Libya	-1
				Sri Lanka	18	Mauritania	0
				Syrian Arab Rep.	4	Mauritius	29
				Tunisia	24	Mongolia	9
				Uganda	-4	Nicaragua	7
				Upper Volta	1	Niger	1
				Venezuela	11	Panama	22
				Yemen	1	Papua-New Guinea	5
				Zambia	-2	Paraguay	6
						Rwanda	0
						Sierra Leone	0
						Singapore	40
						Somalia	0
						Togo	2
						Trinidad and Tobago	29
						Yemen, P.D.R. of	3
Total weighted by							
Unity[a]	14		7		7		9
Population[b]	13		7		6		6

[a]Each country is given a weight of one.
[b]Changes in CBRs are weighted by the population of each country.

> production, work and study are concerned. We must continue to give it serious attention and strive to lower the annual rate of growth of China's population to less than 1 per cent within three years. (Hua 1978, p. 38)

This perspective is reflected in the 1978 Constitution of the People's Republic of China, which stipulates that "The state advocates and encourages family planning" (Article 53).

It is clear that China has a strong family planning program that includes not only the widespread availability of a variety of contraceptive methods, plus sterilization and abortion services, but also a strong information and education program with substantial community involvement, including community pressure for birth planning.

I have used a CBR of 26 for China in 1975, which is consistent with the figures of Bannister (1977, pp. 26-30) and Orleans (1977, p. 27), and is somewhat below Aird's (1977, pp. 49-51) middle estimate (his range being 21 to 34, with a medium value of 28). My figure is well above the dramatic figure of Brown (1976) (CBR of 19) and the astonishing figure of Ravenholt (1976) (CBR of 14). Thus the figure I am using appears to be conservative. I am reasonably comfortable with the estimate that China's CBR has declined by about 25 percent since 1950, and with most of that decline having occurred since 1965.

India has a long history of population censuses, and thus its total population is known moderately accurately. However, the registration of births and deaths in India is incomplete. The estimated crude birth rate of 42.3 for 1950 is based on census data. The Registrar General's Office has created a sample registration scheme designed to provide accurate estimates of vital rates, and this system has been extended to much of India but not yet to all. Based on the information collected under this scheme, current official estimates indicate a crude birth rate of around 36 per thousand population and a crude death rate of 16 to 17 per thousand population, yielding an annual growth rate of around 2 percent. The evidence is unmistakable that fertility has fallen significantly in India during the past 15 years, even though the level of fertility is not known with precision. The 16 percent decline in fertility during the past quarter century, presented in Table 2.2, is a reasonable estimate.

Indonesia also has an inadequate statistical system, and hence annual data on births and deaths are not available. It is thought that fertility changed but little from 1950 until the late 1960s, but there are some harbingers of change since that date. In 1968 Indonesia embarked upon a large-scale family planning program, which has been well organized since 1970; indeed, it is commonly thought to be one of the most vigorous family planning programs in the world.

Gavin Jones (1977) analyzed the 1971 Indonesian census and the 1973 Indonesian Fertility-Mortality Survey conducted by the Demographic Institute of the University of Indonesia, and concluded that during the 1960s fertility altered very little. He also noted that the success of the family planning program to that date was encouraging, and "it should already be having a measurable impact on birth rates, especially in East Java." The Hulls and Singarimbun (1977), in a later article that included information from the 1976 World Fertility Survey, concluded that the total fertility rate for Java and Bali decreased by 15 percent from the late 1960s to 1976. Even if there were no fertility declines in the remainder of Indonesia, this would suggest a decline of about 10 percent for all of Indonesia, inasmuch as two-thirds of the population of Indonesia lives in Java and Bali. A later, unpublished analysis suggests that fertility may be somewhat lower than the figure of 40 that I have used for 1975. In any event there is ample evidence that fertility is declining in Indonesia, although the precise figures are still in question.

Among the other large countries, South Korea and Thailand had large fertility declines, and the data for both are reasonably firm. The figures for Brazil are less certain, although several different analyses indicate that fertility is declining. Egypt has a long history of moderately good birth registration, and, though there is some question as to the precise level of the crude birth rate, most observers agree that reported decreases in fertility are valid. The figures for Turkey are firmly based, and those for the Philippines at least moderately so. Among the countries having small or no decreases, Mexico has mounted a strong family planning program in urban areas, where one-half the population lives, and there is considerable evidence that fertility has begun to fall. Some observers report declines of fertility in Pakistan, but the evidence I have seen is not convincing to me.

In summarizing the data for the large countries, it is clear that fertility has declined appreciably in eight or nine of the thirteen, and has begun in at least one more (Mexico), but there probably have not been declines in Bangladesh, Pakistan, and Nigeria. These data suggest that the crude birth rate declined by about 13 percent from 1965 to 1975 for this group of countries, or about twice as much as in countires in the smaller categories of 15-35 million, 5-15 million, and 0.5-5 million.

QUALITATIVE FACTORS

Bernard Berelson and I (1977) have analyzed fertility changes in developing countries by socioeconomic status—high, upper middle,

TABLE 2.3

Mean Percentage of Crude Birth Rate Decline, by Socioeconomic Status and Qualitative Factors, Developing Countries, 1965-75

Socioeconomic Status	Qualitative Factors				
	By female status (percentage of women aged 20-24 never married, c. 1970)				
High	21 (15)		17 (6)		
Upper middle	12 (4)		12 (4)		2 (1)
Lower middle	0 (1)		5 (6)		4 (13)
Low	5 (1)				1 (5)
	By ethnic status				
	African	Muslim	Catholic	Chinese	Other
High		2 (4)	16 (9)	29 (5)	29 (6)
Upper middle	2 (4)	9 (8)	10 (7)	21 (4)	18 (1)
Lower middle	0 (12)	4 (4)	1 (2)	8 (3)	8 (3)
Low	2 (15)	0 (4)		5 (1)	1 (2)
	By island status				
	Islands		Quasi-islands		Other
High	31 (9)		23 (5)		7 (10)
Upper middle	17 (2)		13 (6)		4 (15)
Lower middle	9 (2)		8 (3)		2 (18)
Low					2 (24)
	By density*				
	High		Medium		Low
High	26 (10)		21 (5)		12 (9)
Upper middle	17 (3)		15 (11)		3 (10)
Lower middle	10 (4)		2 (7)		2 (12)
Low	1 (3)		1 (6)		2 (14)
	By pace of social change				
	Fast				Not fast
High	26 (15)				8 (9)
Upper middle	20 (5)				8 (19)
Lower middle	12 (3)				2 (20)
Low	5 (2)				1 (21)

*High density indicates 100 or more per sq. km., medium 26-99, and low, 25 or fewer.

Note: The number of countries is shown in parentheses.

lower middle, and low; by family planning program effort; and by a variety of other factors that here I call qualitative factors. The qualitative factors are: status of women within the society; ethnic status of the society; island or quasi-island character; density; and the pace of social change. In every case within the four socioeconomic categories, there are additional differentiations by these factors (see Table 2.3):

By female status as represented by the proportion aged 20-24 never married, which we rationalize as indicating the alternative economic and social roles for women;

By ethnic status, in which Muslim and black African average declines are uniformly low, Catholic averages are intermediate, and averages for all other groups, particularly the Chinese, are high;

By island or quasi-island status;

By density (closely related to island status, since islands have an average density of about 200 persons per square kilometer, omitting Hong Kong and Singapore as special cases with about 4,000 each, as against about 90 for quasi-islands and 38 for other countries), with a clear differentiation except for countries having low socioeconomic status, so perhaps "the psychology of crowdedness" does break through into conscious control of fertility; and

By social change, where a fast pace is associated with fertility decline.

AGE STRUCTURE

If the numbers of women who enter the reproductive age group annually, replacing those who move out of the reproductive span, raise the proportion of women aged 15-45 in relation to the total population, or if relatively larger numbers of the women aged 15-44 fall in the most fertile ages (typically 20-29), the result is a larger number of births and a higher crude birth rate, other factors remaining constant. In a population with a previous history of high fertility and with little immigration or emigration, the age structure changes but little until fertility begins to decline.

The age structure is primarily a function of past fertility rates rather than of mortality rates. In a country with a long history of high fertility and a low growth rate—say an expectation of life at birth of 40 years for females and a growth rate of 1 percent a year—about half of all females would be of reproductive age. But if the growth rate were 3 percent there would be a larger number of young people, and as a consequence somewhat fewer, say 45 percent, of all females would be in the reproductive ages.

TABLE 2.4

Index of Percent that Females Aged 15-49 Were of Total Population, by Region, 1950-75

Region	1950	1960	1970	1975
All LDCs	100	98.6	98.8	99.7
Africa	100	100.5	99.7	99.1
Latin America	100	96.4	95.7	96.8
East Asia	100	96.7	101.1	102.7
China	100	95.1	99.7	102.0
Other East Asia	100	99.9	101.2	106.9
South Asia	100	101.1	98.3	98.5

When fertility initially declines in a high-fertility country, the proportion of children decreases but the proportion of females in the reproductive ages increases because of the smaller proportion of youth, and also because of the increasing numbers of young women entering reproductive age. In Singapore, for example, it is estimated that the proportion of females in the reproductive ages will increase to 55 percent of all females within the next two decades. If low fertility is maintained over a long period, the proportion of females in the reproductive ages will again decrease to the mid-forties.

For all developing countries there has been very little change in age structure from 1950 to 1975. If we use an index of 100 as the proportion that females 15-49 years of age were of all females in 1950, the corresponding index for all developing countries is 99.7 in 1975—99.1 for Africa, 96.8 for Latin America, 102.7 for East Asia, and 98.5 for South Asia (see Table 2.4). These are relatively small differences, but as we shall see such summary statistics obscure more significant changes for some countries. Nonetheless, it is a reasonable generalization to say that, for most of the developing countries, changing age structure has had relatively little effect on crude birth rates and in general has not contributed significantly to observed decreases in crude birth rates.

The United Nations (1977) has computed indexes to reflect the effect of changes in age composition upon the crude birth rate for selected countries in Latin America for the period 1950-70, and those data are reproduced in Table 2.5. A figure above 100 indicates that changes in age composition were such as to increase the CBR, and a figure of less than 100 shows that age changes tended to decrease the

TABLE 2.5

Index of the Effect of Changes in Age Composition upon the Crude Birth Rate, Selected Countries of Latin America Having Relatively Good Statistics, 1950-70

Country	1950-55	1955-60	1960-65	1965-70
Caribbean				
Guadeloupe	92.6	97.0	95.6	94.5
Jamaica	92.6	95.9	91.4	90.3
Martinique	90.9	96.5	92.9	94.6
Puerto Rico	95.9	95.6	107.3	102.9
Trinidad and Tobago	u	99.0	102.3	98.8
Middle America				
Costa Rica	u	u	99.1	105.1
El Salvador	98.2	97.1	96.8	99.1
Guatemala	99.4	96.5	99.5	100.0
Mexico	u	98.5	97.3	100.2
Panama	97.7	97.6	99.2	101.6
Temperate South America				
Argentina	u	94.0[a]	96.0	u
Chile	100.3[b]	98.7[c]	98.4	102.5
Tropical South America				
Venezuela	u	88.5[d]	u	106.7[e]

u = data are unavailable or inadequate.

[a]For 1950-60.

[b]For 1952-56.

[c]For 1956-60.

[d]For 1950-61.

[e]For 1961-71.

Note: The figures represent the ratio, expressed in percents, of the proportions of the crude birth rate in each period to the corresponding proportions of the standardized crude birth rate. An index above 100 indicates a positive effect and an index below 100 a negative effect of changes in age composition upon the crude birth rate. For Chile, the relative change in the crude birth rates is compared with that in the gross reproduction rate.

Source: Calculated from method described by Berent (1970, p. 42).

CBR. The discussion of fertility trends in the UN volume notes that in Trinidad and Tobago the CBR decreased from 39.5 to 25.1 in the 12-year period 1960-72, and that this decline did not arise from changes in age composition of the population. In Jamaica, however, changes in age composition exerted an important, negative effect on the CBR, a reflection of sizable emigration of women in the reproductive ages. In Puerto Rico emigration tended to lower the CBR during the 1950s, but return migration worked in the opposite direction during the 1960s. Fertility also declined sharply in Cuba, but the effect of age on this decline was trivial.

AGE AT MARRIAGE

In most of the world almost all births are to married women, including women in common-law marriages, and, therefore, changes in age at marriage affect the number of births. We have information on the proportions of females 15-19 years of age never married for 1960 and for 1970 (Table 2.6) for 40 countries, and comparable information for females 20-24 years of age for 39 countries. These data

TABLE 2.6

Percent of Females Aged 15-19 and 20-24 Never Married, Selected Developing Countries, by Region, Around 1960 and 1970

Region	Number of Countries	1960	1970	Change: Absolute	Change: Percent
		Females aged 15-19			
Africa	7	55.6	69.2	13.5	24.3
The Americas	13	80.8	81.7	0.9	1.0
Asia and the Pacific	20	64.6	72.7	8.1	12.5
All regions	40	68.3	75.0	6.7	9.8
		Females aged 20-24			
Africa	6	15.6	25.3	9.7	62.2
The Americas	13	42.6	47.4	4.8	11.4
Asia and the Pacific	20	24.2	32.9	8.7	36.1
All regions	39	30.1	37.7	7.6	25.2

show that there are large differences in the proportions married and never married in different regions of the world, and there were significant increases in the proportions of young women not married during the decade of the 1960s, the latter being an important factor in fertility declines during the decade. Changes in proportions never married were least in the Americas, but the proportions never married were much higher in the Americas than in Asia and Africa. Increases in age at marriage of the magnitude shown in Table 2.6 would tend to decrease the crude birth rate by 5-6 percent in a high-fertility country. It should be noted that the countries for which data are available tend to be further along the continuum of development than countries for which data are not available, and thus these data cannot be considered representative of all developing countries. In 1975 the combined populations of the 40 countries in Table 2.6 totaled 1.4 billion, a significant number itself. Also, it is widely reported that age at marriage has increased appreciably in China, although there are no statistics to document this observation.

DECOMPOSITION OF CRUDE BIRTH RATES

Changes in crude birth rates can be accounted for by changes in four factors: the age-sex structure, the proportions married by age, marital age-specific fertility rates, and births to unmarried women. The data requirements for decomposing changes in crude birth rates into those component parts are conceptually simple, but relatively few developing countries have adequate statistical systems to provide the necessary information; hence, we are able to provide information for one or more of these factors for selected time periods for only nine countries (see Table 2.7). Where marital fertility rates are cited, they include all births to unmarried women.

An examination of Table 2.7 shows the relative contributions of changes in age structure, in age at marriage, and in marital fertility over various time periods for the countries listed. Changes in age structure had an impact on the CBR in Hong Kong, Singapore, and the Philippines, but not much impact in South Korea and Turkey. In Taiwan and Sri Lanka, changes in age structure affected the CBR both positively and negatively during different time periods since 1950.

Rising age at marriage was significant in each of the listed countries and was a dominant factor in explaining declines in fertility in Sri Lanka up until 1968, in Malaysia, and in the Philippines. But declines in marital fertility rates accounted for most of the declines in Hong Kong, South Korea, Singapore, Taiwan, and Turkey.

In Taiwan, the age distribution was favorable toward reduced fertility from 1961 to 1965 and from 1965 to 1970, but then relatively

TABLE 2.7

Crude Birth Rate Decline and Percent of Change Due to Specified Factors, Selected Developing Countries, Selected Years 1953-75

Country and Year of Data	Crude Birth Rate	Change in Crude Birth Rate (percent)	Percent of Change in Crude Birth Rate[a] Due to Change in:				Period of Change
			All Factors	Age Structure	Percent Married	Marital Fertility	
Sri Lanka							
1953	39.4						
1963	34.6	-12.2	100	57	43	0	1953-56
1968	32.1	-7.2	100	-31	132	0	1963-68
1970	29.4	-8.4	100	-21	30	89	1968-70
Hong Kong							
1961	35.5						
1965	28.8	-18.9	100	79	10	11	1961-65
1967	24.6	-4.7	100	13	0	87	1965-67
1970	19.4	-21.1					
Korea, South							
1958	44.8						
1960	42.9	1.8					
1961	42.2	-1.6					
1962	40.0	-5.2					
1966	32.0	-20.0	100	6	33	61	1957/61-1962/66
1970	30.0*	-6.2*	100	6	35	59	1960-70[b]

TABLE 2.7 (continued)

Malaysia, West							
1957	46.2						
1957-61	42.9	-7.1					
1962-66	38.6	-10.0	100	-20	41	79	1957-62/66
1970	37.0*	-4.1*	100	5	67	28	1960-69[b]
Singapore							
1957	42.7						
1966	28.6	-33.0	100	0	63	37	1957-66
1970	22.0*	-23.1*	100	-19	54	65	1957-70[c]
Taiwan							
1960	38.7						
1965	32.1						
1970	27.1	-30.0	100	13	23	63	1960-70[b]
1975[d]	23.0	-14.9	100	-90	60	119	1970-75
Tunisia							
1961	49.6						
1965	47.8	-3.6					
1966	47.0	-1.7					
1967	43.9	-6.6					
1968	43.0	-2.1	100	19	42	40	1967-68
1970	41/42	-2/-5					
Philippines[e]							
1960	40.4						
1968	38.6	-4.4	100	-67	102	65	1960-68
Turkey[f]							
1960	45.0						
1975	32.0	-29.0	100	8	23	69	1960-75

(continued)

TABLE 2.7 (continued)

---

*Estimated figure.

[a]Figures in subcategories may not add to 100 because of rounding. Where one of the three factors works against the decline, a minus sign is used. In such cases the other factors add to more than 100.

[b]The percent of change due to specified factors for this period are taken from Retherford and Cho (1974, p. 167). They are based on the following CBR declines: Korea, decline of 33.0 percent from 43.3 in 1960 to 29.0 in 1970; W. Malaysia, decline of 19.3 percent from 42.9 in 1960 to 34.6 in 1969; Taiwan, decline of 30.0 percent from 38.7 in 1960 to 27.1 in 1970.

[c]Chang (1974) reports a decline of 48.2 percent in the CBR during 1957-70 and in Table 3.11, p. 47, states that the net effects of change in age composition was 8.4 percent, of age at marriage, 23.4 percent, and of marital fertility, 28.3 percent. These figures imply an interaction effect of 4.9 percent.

[d]Data for 1970-75 were provided by Ronald Freedman, University of Michigan, January 1978. His figures indicate that, of the 4.2 point decline in CBR from 27.2 to 23.0 in 1970-75, changes in age structure were such as to increase the CBR by 3.8 points, the percent married to decrease the CBR by 2.5 points, marital fertility to decrease CBR by 5.0 points, and the interaction of these factors to decrease the CBR by 0.5 points.

[e]Data for the Philippines are from R. D. Retherford and L. V. Cho (1973).

[f]Ozboy, Shorter, and Yener (1977) estimate that the 13 point decline in the CBR can be assigned as follows: changes in age-sex structure, 1 point; decline in proportion married, 3 points; and all other factors, 9 points.

Source: The data are from Table 2 of John A. Ross et al. (1972), except as otherwise noted.

large numbers of young women entering the reproductive ages tended to raise the crude birth rate. During 1961-75 the CBR declined from 37.7 to 23, or by 14.7 points, a decline of almost 40 percent. The increase in females in the reproductive ages would have caused a rise in the CBR of about three points if age-specific fertility rates had remained constant. Increases in age at marriage caused a drop of 4.4 points in the CBR and decreases in marital fertility led to a further reduction of 11.7 points.

On the basis of information presented earlier, we know that changes in age structure were not very important for most of the countries in which there was substantial fertility decline, but we can only speculate about the relative contributions of increasing age at marriage and decreasing marital fertility. A reasonable guess is that in the early stages of fertility decline, a rise in age at marriage is a major factor, followed by larger and larger declines in marital fertility.

FERTILITY INCREASES

It is commonly assumed that once fertility begins to decline it is unlikely that it will rise again until low CBRs are attained, after which short-term fluctuations may result in temporary increases. The opposite tendency, of a persistent rise in recorded birth rates since World War II or the early 1950s, is observable in the statistics of several countries in the Caribbean and Middle American mainland areas (Byrne 1972; United Nations 1977). A real upward trend of fertility, however, is unequivocally established only for Guyana, Jamaica, and Trinidad and Tobago. For other countries in the areas mentioned, the rise in the recorded rates may be due merely to improving birth registration, although a real rise in fertility cannot be ruled out (United Nations 1977, pp. 5-6).

Migration has played an important part in the demographic history of several of these countries, and migratory movements have often had a decided impact on the CBR. Accordingly, data are presented for changes in both the CBR and the gross reproduction rate (the latter is not significantly affected by most migration patterns). The gross reproduction indexes show that fertility increased by 50 percent or more in Grenada, Guyana, Jamaica, St. Kitts, and Trinidad and Tobago. Less spectacular apparent increases were observed in a number of other countries.

Some but not all of the recorded increases may be due to faulty data. It should be noted that in each cited case, fertility fell, typically to the low thirties, and then increased again, typically to the low forties. The four most cited causes of the fertility increases are the removal of the causes of fecundity impairment—primarily venereal diseases and perhaps malaria—which led to decreased childlessness and fertility increases in older women; the reduction of widowhood, resulting in fertility increases in older women; a postwar recovery period similar to that of the developed countries, including prior "short-run" economic adversities that may have had the effect of decreasing fertility to a level that might not otherwise have been attained; and the theory that there is a relationship between family size and stability of unions. (The evidence relating to this last explanation is that there were increases in the percentage of legally married women among certain age groups, earlier entrance into stable unions, and declines in illegitimacy.)

The populations of most of the countries listed are quite small, although it is also possible that there were fertility increases in some of the larger countries. I cite these cases as an interesting departure from the more usual case of fertility continuing to decline to the low twenties or below once fertility begins to drop.

SUMMARY

From 1950 to 1965 fertility declines in developing countries were limited to a relatively few, and for the most part small, countries. The tempo of fertility decline increased during the next ten years, with 19 countries of half a million or more population having fertility declines in excess of 20 percent. An additional nine countries reported fertility declines of 10-19 percent. The combined populations of these countries was slightly in excess of 2 billion. Ten countries out of the 13 developing countries with a population of 35 million or more reported significant CBR declines, and the average decline of 13 percent for this size class was about twice as large as for smaller countries. Asian countries reported declines of 17 percent from 1965 to 1975, Latin American countries declines of about 12 percent, and African countries as a group experienced hardly any declines in fertility.

Changes in age-sex composition had little impact on CBR decline for most of the countries, but there were exceptions to this generalization for several of the smaller countries. There was a marked rise in the age at marriage in many countries, and this was a significant factor in the reported CBR declines. Marital fertility also fell appreciably in many countries, and was the principal factor in CBR declines in countries experiencing the largest percentage declines.

These changes are important both because they have led to a slight slowing in the overall rate of population growth and also because they suggest that more rapid changes may occur in the coming years. But current levels of fertility and rates of population growth remain high in developing countries, and the momentum of population growth is so strong that the world's population is likely to more than double in the decades ahead.

REFERENCES

Aird, John. 1977. Letter to People 4, no. 2: 49-51.

Bannister, Judith. 1977. "Implementing Fertility and Mortality Decline in the People's Republic of China—Recent Official Data." In The Current Vital Rates and Population Size of the People's Republic of China and Its Provinces. Ph.D. dissertation, Food Research Institute, Stanford University, 1977. Paper presented at the Annual Meeting of the Population Association of America, St. Louis, April 1977.

Berent, Jerzy. 1970. "Causes of Fertility Decline in Eastern Europe and the Soviet Union. Part 1. The Influence of Demographic Factors." Population Studies 24, no. 1 (March): 35-58.

Brown, Lester R. 1976. World Population Trends: Signs of Hope, Signs of Stress. World Watch Paper 8. Washington, D.C.: World Watch Institute.

Byrne, Joycelin. 1972. Levels of Fertility in Commonwealth Caribbean, 1921-1965. Kingston, Jamaica: Institute of Social and Economic Research, University of the West Indies.

Chang, Chen-Tung. 1974. Fertility Transition in Singapore. Singapore University Press.

Hua Kuo-feng. 1978. "Unite and Strive to Build a Modern, Powerful Socialist Country: Report on the Work of the Government Delivered at the First Session of the Fifth National People's Congress on February 26, 1978." New York: People's Republic of China Mission to the United Nations.

Huang Shu-tse. 1974. "China's Views on Major Issues of World Population." Peking Review, no. 35 (30 August): 6-9.

Hull, Terrence H., Valerie J. Hull, and Masri Singarimbun. 1977. "Indonesia's Family Planning Story: Success and Challenge." Population Bulletin 32, no. 6 (November).

Jones, G. W. 1977. "Fertility Levels and Trends in Indonesia." Population Studies 31, no. 1 (March): 29-41.

Mauldin, W. Parker, and Bernard Berelson. 1977. "Conditions of Fertility Decline in Developing Countries, 1965-1975." Draft manuscript. New York: The Population Council.

Orleans, Leo A. 1977. China's Birth Rate and Population Growth: Another Perspective. Report prepared for the Committee on

International Relations, U.S. House of Representatives, by the Congressional Research Service, Library of Congress.

Ozboy, Ferhunde, Frederic Shorter, and Samir Yener. 1977. "Accounting for the Trend of Fertility in Turkey." Paper presented at UN/UNFPA Expert Group Meeting on Demographic Transition and Socioeconomic Development, Istanbul, 27 April–4 May.

Ravenholt, R. T. 1976. Letter to _People_ 3, no. 4.

Retherford, R. D., and L. J. Cho. 1974. "Comparative Analysis of Recent Fertility Trends in East Asia." In _International Population Conference, Liege 1973_, vol. 2, IUSSP, pp. 163-81.

Ross, John A., et al. 1972. "Findings from Family Planning Research." _Reports on Population/Family Planning_, no. 12 (October).

United Nations. 1977. _Levels and Trends of Fertility throughout the World_. New York. ST/ESA/SER A/59.

3

FERTILITY IN AFRICA

John C. Caldwell

The largest area of persistently and largely homogeneously high fertility stretches from Africa across the Middle East to Pakistan. In continental terms Africa stands out conspicuously on any map of fertility levels.

About 14 countries in the world appear to exhibit crude birth rates over 50 per thousand, and all of them are to be found in the Africa-Middle East bloc.[1] It is doubtful whether many countries elsewhere have ever attained such levels. Nowhere else by the mid-1970s were total fertility rates exceeding seven to be found, yet a dozen countries in this area reached this level. Two-thirds of all African countries have crude birth rates over 45 per thousand, a similar fraction to that found in the Middle East, while this is now rare outside these two areas.

While Africa's fertility frontiers are blurred to its northeast, this is not so to the north. The few miles' width of the Strait of Gibraltar separates Morocco, with a crude birth rate of around 46 per thousand, from Spain and Portugal, with rates under 20. Indeed, The European northern shore and islands of the Mediterranean, with one exception, exhibit total fertility rates in the 2.0-2.9 range compared with 5.0-7.4 on the Mediterranean's southern coast (the one exception being Albania, Europe's only predominantly Moslem society, where the total fertility rate is still over five and where the trend has approximated that of Egypt).

It is this exceptional level of fertility, and the near absence of evidence that any early decline is likely, that led to the United Nations Population Division forecasting in the medium variant of its long-range projections[2] that Africa's population would rise before achieving low levels of growth from a little over 400 million now to more than

2,500 million a century hence, and that this great surge would carry it from 10 percent of the world's population in the mid-1970s to 21 percent in the stabilized global population of the second half of the twenty-first century. Recent fertility falls elsewhere have been somewhat steeper in certain areas than are incorporated in this projection, but this does nothing to lessen the likelihood of the latter proportion being reached.

THE PATTERN OF FERTILITY

Table 3.1 presents two measures of fertility, one of mortality and one of net reproduction for the mid-1970s, which is the most recent date for which information is generally available. The regions employed are widely accepted divisions in cultural and ecological terms. The estimates are often little more than educated guesses currently accepted by various international bodies, and sometimes conflict with each other.

The table shows that, with the exceptions about to be discussed, the crude birth rate is at least 45 per thousand almost everywhere. Indeed, the countries outside these two exceptional regions where that does not appear to be the case are more likely to be testimony to insufficient knowledge of fertility levels than to relatively low fertility.

The most conspicuous exceptions to high fertility are the oceanic islands, where fertility is in some cases almost as low as in industrialized countries. However, this is of little significance. One reason is their very small populations, with the possible exception of Mauritius, which is approaching one million. However, the main reason is that their experience is almost irrelevant to the continent itself. They are oceanic islands that are usually grouped with Africa in international classifications only because they are a smaller distance from it than from any other continent. In historical and cultural terms their closest real neighbors are some of the other oceanic islands such as the West Indies, Fiji, or even Sri Lanka, where fertility declines have also taken place. All but one of the island nations listed in the table were uninhabited at the time of European discovery, and it is significant that the exception, Comoros, exhibits typical African fertility. Only three, Cape Verde, Sao Tome, and Comoros, are of predominantly African ancestry, the latter two exhibiting high fertility. All but Comoros now share the religion of their European discoverers, and all have shared in the new life of maritime commerce.

A more significant feature of the table is the fertility shown for Middle Africa, where the crude birth rate exceeds 45 per thousand in only two countries, and where it falls as low as 32 per thousand in Gabon. This is not a artifact of poor data but neither is it evidence of

TABLE 3.1

Estimated Vital Rates and Population, Africa by Region and Country, around 1975

	Crude Birth Rate (per 1,000)	Total Fertility Rate (per 1,000)	Expectation of Life at Birth (both sexes, in years)	Net Reproduction Rate	Population (millions)
Oceanic Islands					
St. Helena	20	—	—	—	0.01
Mauritius	26	3.2	65	1.5	0.9
Reunion	28	4.6	63	1.9	0.5
Cape Verde Is.	29	4.2	50	1.5	0.3
Seychelles	33	5.6	65	2.5	0.1
Sao Tome and Principe	45	—	—	—	0.1
Comoros	47	4.8	—	1.9	0.3
North Africa					
Tunisia	37	5.1	54	1.9	6
Egypt	36	5.2	53	1.9	37
Mauritania	45	5.8	39	1.7	1
Libya	45	6.8	53	2.5	2
Morocco	46	7.4	53	2.6	17
Sudan	48	6.9	49	2.4	18
Algeria	48	6.9	53	2.7	17
Middle Africa					
Gabon	32	4.1	41	1.3	0.5
Equatorial Guinea	37	5.2	43	1.7	0.3

(continued)

TABLE 3.1 (continued)

	Crude Birth Rate (per 1,000)	Total Fertility Rate (per 1,000)	Expectation of Life at Birth (both sexes, in years)	Net Reproduction Rate	Population (millions)
Cameroon	40	5.7	41	1.7	6
Burundi	48	5.9	39	1.9	4
Central African Rep.	43	5.5	41	1.7	2
Chad	44	5.3	38	1.6	5
Congo	45	5.8	43	1.9	1
Zaire	45	6.0	43	1.9	25
Rwanda	50	7.0	41	2.1	4
Southern Africa					
Lesotho	39	5.1	45	1.7	1
South Africa	43	5.6	51	2.1	25
Mozambique	43	5.7	44	1.9	9
Botswana	46	6.5	43	1.9	0.7
Madagascar	46	6.7	43	1.9	7
Angola	47	6.7	38	1.9	6
Malawi	48	6.1	41	1.9	5
Southern Rhodesia	48	6.8	51	2.5	6
Swaziland	49	6.9	44	2.1	0.5
Zambia	52	6.9	44	2.3	5
East Africa					
Uganda	45	5.4	50	2.0	12

Somalia	47	—	41	1.9	3
Tanzania	47	7.2	44	2.2	15
Ethiopia	49	5.8	38	2.0	28
Kenya	49	7.4	50	2.4	13
West African Coast					
Guinea Bissau	40	6.1	38	1.6	0.5
Gambia	43	5.8	40	1.7	0.5
Sierra Leone	45	6.0	43	1.9	3
Ivory Coast	46	6.4	43	2.0	5
Guinea	47	6.3	41	1.9	4
Senegal	48	6.4	40	1.9	4
Nigeria	49	5.5	41	2.1	63
Ghana	49	5.9	45	2.2	10
Liberia	50	5.7	45	1.9	2
Benin	50	6.9	41	2.1	3
Togo	51	7.0	41	2.1	2
West African Savanna					
Upper Volta	49	6.7	37	1.9	6
Mali	50	7.4	38	2.0	6
Niger	52	7.1	39	2.1	5

recent fertility decline or of likely future falls. Indeed, this is the area of the world for which future rises in fertility can probably most confidently be predicted. The cause of the low fertility is not cultural but pathological and will be discussed further below. The difference between the low-fertility countries and the moderately low-fertility countries of this region, with the exception of Rwanda and Burundi, is that all of the former are to be found in this region of peculiar reproductive pathology, while only parts of the latter are.

Probably the most interesting data presented in the table are those for Egypt and Tunisia, where moderate fertility has been attained because segments of the population have over the past two decades indisputably controlled their reproduction. Indeed, the only other country where this is true in the case of indigenous populations in the whole Islamic belt stretching from Mauritania to Pakistan is Lebanon. A fourth area of demographic interest is South Africa, where fertility is modified in national terms by low fertility among the white and Asian populations and moderate fertility among the mixed or colored population. African fertility appears to be little below that found elsewhere in the continent in spite of a much higher level of industrialization.

Most of the continent has birth rates in the 45 to 52 range. No great store should be placed on differences within this range. Some are merely the product of distortion in data and others of the inadequacy of the crude birth rate as an exact measure. Those that are real are almost never the result of a deliberate decision to restrict family size, but are rather the unintended effects of differentials in the age of marriage, the period of postnatal sexual abstinence, the level of disease, or some other aspect of behavior not intended to influence lifetime fertility. It has been shown that fertility differences of this order are just as common and just as great between tribes in a single country as between nations across the continent.[3]

Finally, it should be noted that the net reproduction rates indicate that most African populations are increasing at a rate that implies a doubling every generation (that is, annual growth rates above 2.5 percent) and some might multiply by two-and-a-half in that period.

FERTILITY TRENDS

In the continent itself, we can speak about trends only in Egypt, Tunisia, and among racial subsections of the populations of South Africa and East Africa. Nearly nine-tenths of the population of the continent lies outside this discussion.

Egypt is an anomaly in the Arab world in that the evidence suggests that its fertility has been relatively low most of this century and perhaps for a longer time still.[4] There is no convincing evidence of its birth rate having been above 44 per thousand since the 1920s, a level it maintained until 1961. The reasons may lie in its density of population and in the settled nature of its society. One tends to draw parallels with the position of Java in Indonesia, although other parallels with premodern Japan and even northwestern Europe might be appropriate. During the 1960s, at a time when the provision of family planning services was being extended, the birth rate fell by one-sixth during the decade, ultimately stabilizing at around 35 per thousand, from which it may have risen one or two points during recent years. The halting of the Egyptian decline remains a major question to be examined by demographers of the region and a portent for the future.

The Tunisian experience closely paralleled that of Egypt both in the parameters and timing of the fall. The steepest fertility decline occurred slightly later than did that of Egypt and was concentrated in the latter 1960s, with the first check not occurring until about 1972. The major difference is that there is now some evidence of a continuing decline in Tunisia's birth rate during the mid-1970s, while all evidence from Egypt suggests no resurgence of a similar trend there.

In South Africa the fertility of the coloreds, who are about as numerous as the Afrikaners and share some ancestry with them, fell from about 45 per thousand at the beginning of the 1960s to around 35 per thousand in the early 1970s, thus reaching a level almost as low as that of the Asian population, which had exhibited no clear trend for almost two decades. In East Africa, with an Asian population of only about one-quarter of a million compared with over a half million in South Africa, Asian fertility has halved from typical African levels in the late 1940s to birth rates in the low twenties by the end of the 1960s. Postponed female age at marriage and a reduction in marital fertility contributed to the decline.[5]

A small decline in fertility has been claimed for Ghana,[6] but the evidence is far from certain. It may consist of nothing more than the chance variation between measurements by different investigators some years apart.

Beyond the shores of the continent, birth rates had fallen from around 45 per thousand to 25 per thousand in Mauritius and Reunion over the preceding 20 years, and from 40 to 30 per thousand in the Seychelles over 15 years. There has, however, recently been some rise in the Mauritian birth rates, perhaps at least partly attributable to some reduction in family planning services.

IS HIGH FERTILITY EXPLICABLE IN TERMS OF HIGH MORTALITY?

At first glance the question above looks to be a promising suggestion. In all but one of the low-fertility oceanic islands, the expectation of life at birth is 60 or more years. It is likely that fertility would be falling widely in Africa if such mortality levels were to be reached. However, the most recent United Nations population projections[7] assume that this level will not be attainable for the continent as a whole within the next hundred years. The point is not of critical significance as fertility decline began in Europe and elsewhere with expectations of life of under 50 years and below those now found generally in the countries of the North African coast, in Kenya, and probably in southern Ghana and other subnational regions. High mortality is an insufficient reason to explain the absence of fertility decline in Morocco, Algeria, Libya, Kenya, southern Ghana, and perhaps southwestern Nigeria and southern Ivory Coast.

It should be noted that in Middle Africa there is probably an association between some of the highest mortality in the contemporary world and relatively low fertility. The latter is apparently wholly explained by infecundity and subfecundity arising out of the same ill-health complex that is reflected in the low expectations of life at birth. In some areas such as northern Zaire[8] (and probably in all areas), improvements in health have already led to rising fertility, although it is not clear that this has been on a large enough scale to affect national trends.

IS HIGH FERTILITY EXPLICABLE IN PURELY SOCIOECONOMIC TERMS?

Africa is certainly poor. On the whole, its per capita incomes are among the lowest in the world, comparing only with south Asia, China, parts of Southeast Asia and Melanesia, and with scattered countries elsewhere, such as Bolivia. In 1970 the majority of African countries exhibited per capita GNP below US$200, and made up almost three-fifths of the countries in this category.[9] The continent was even more conspicuous in its low rates of economic growth, and contained a majority of the countries in the world that had been recording declining per capital income. Yet explanations of persistent high fertility based on economic indicators alone are worrying, if only because many countries elsewhere in the world have never been characterized by birth rates above 45 per thousand and certainly not by rates around 50. Some of the problems of socioeconomic explanation are brought out by Table 3.2, where selected countries are examined with some

TABLE 3.2

Some Socioeconomic Measures for Selected Countries Exhibiting Varying Fertility Patterns

	1970 Per Capita Income (US$)	1975 Percent Urban Population	1975 Percent in Cities with over 100,000 Inhabitants	1975 Percent Literate	1975 Percent Females Literate
Continental African Countries with Declining Fertility					
Egypt	210	48	33	35	21
Tunisia	250	49	19	40	23
Insular African Countries with Declining Fertility					
Mauritius	240	48	17	80	75
Reunion	800	—	—	63	65
Seychelles	70	26	—	58	60
Asian Countries with Substantial Fertility Decline					
Korea	250	41	33	91	87
Taiwan	390	63	35	86	80
Sri Lanka	110	24	7	78	71
Asian Countries with Slow Fertility Decline					
Malaysia (peninsular)	380	29	12	76	62
India	110	22	12	59	49

(continued)

TABLE 3.2 (continued)

	1970 Per Capita Income (US$)	1975 Percent Urban Population	1975 Percent in Cities with over 100,000 Inhabitants	1975 Percent Literate	1975 Percent Females Literate
Asian Countries with No Fertility Decline					
Iran	380	44	32	38	27
Afghanistan	80	12	6	7	—
Some Continental African Countries without Proven Fertility Decline					
Kenya	150	18	9	40	30
Ghana	310	32	15	43	34
Senegal	230	32	16	—	—
Ivory Coast	310	20	4	20	—
Zambia	400	—	39	47	35
Algeria	300	50	14	47	30
Morocco	230	38	34	60	13

Note: In some cases estimates have been made from trends and other data.

emphasis on the African countries most likely to achieve the first fertility declines.

If per capita incomes mean anything, many countries in Africa are not so poor that some fertility decline should not be occurring. This is the case on the Mediterranean coast and in a range of countries exporting minerals or tropical food crops, such as Zambia, Ghana, Senegal, Ivory Coast, and Kenya. It is possible that this index does not properly reflect the stage and pace of economic change, which seems to the visitor to be greater in parts of East and Southeast Asia. It is possible also that per capita incomes do not really reflect per capita living standards in mineral-exporting countries where foreign mining firms account for a considerable proportion of income generated. Nevertheless, the urbanization figures support the contention that considerable parts of Africa are no less economically changed and are no more largely rooted in the traditional subsistence economy than are countries of Asia were fertility transition is under way.

The real differences may lie in levels of literacy and education. Employing the simple index of literacy, which fairly accurately reflects the level of schooling, it is clear that sub-Saharan Africa exhibits unusually low levels in terms of total literacy, and North Africa in terms of female literacy. It is quite possible that the essential element in both is the low level of female education and hence the extent that this has allowed the retention of traditional social structures, particularly at the family level. The sub-Saharan African figure represents relatively low absolute investment in education (although the percentage of the budgets spent this way compares favorably with much of the world), and sometimes a low community demand for education. In North Africa, Islamic attitudes have meant that the educational expenditures are disproportionately concentrated on males and are relatively less effective in reducing fertility than the size of the overall budgets might at first suggest.

INDICATORS OF CHANGE: FERTILITY DIFFERENTIALS

The main reason that fertility declines do not seem to be imminent in most of Africa is the near absence of those kinds of fertility differentials that would suggest that some change is already at an early stage.

Even differentials by level of education are often small and insignificant in their national impact. It is likely that the pattern found among the Yoruba of Nigeria is widespread in sub-Saharan Africa. Here the fertility of women who have never been to school is significantly lower than that of those with primary education. With further increases in education, fertility falls moderately among women with completed secondary education and further among those who have been to university.[10] The explanation for the lower level of fertility among illiterates seems to be a greater incidence of sterilizing diseases together with a higher proportion of marriages split by death or separation, and perhaps longer periods of sexual abstinence. There may also be a lower level of persistent cohabitation and lesser sexual activity even in periods outside those of abstinence. An immediate effect of raising education levels might be some increase in fertility, although this is not certain because of such counteracting forces as the spread of contraception. More important may be the fact of community change resulting from a general rise in education levels of a type that cannot be predicted by examining differences between individuals at a given level of education.

In North Africa there is evidence of fertility differentials by education of mother in Algeria and Egypt.[11] The reduction in fertility becomes marked only among the relatively few women with at least some secondary education, and the evidence suggests that it is very largely explained by delayed marriage among the more educated.[12]

Even more surprising is the near absence in most African countries of urban-rural fertility differentials or of lower fertility in large cities. The existence of urban-rural fertility differentials in sub-Saharan Africa has been a matter of debate, but the most significant aspect of that debate has been that urban fertility has almost as frequently been cited as being above rural fertility as below it.[13] It is possible that greater infecundity and longer periods of sexual abstinence in rural areas obscure the fact that fertility in cities is lower than one might anticipate given the better health and greater sexual activity of the city residents. However, there is little evidence for this contention, and no evidence that such a balance of forces might lead to declining fertility in the near future.

In Ghana, one of the few sub-Saharan countries where there is clear evidence of both an urban-rural fertility differential and an urban socioeconomic class differential, one analysis concluded that in spite of the relatively high levels of urbanization, such differentials reduced the national crude birth rate in 1960 by only one point. These differentials were almost entirely explained by deferred female marriage arising from motives other than that of restricting ultimate family size.[14]

In North Africa there is evidence for Morocco that urban fertility is over 10 percent below that found in rural areas,[15] probably largely a product of a differential in age at marriage; but little evidence of any fertility differential in Algeria as late as 1970.[16] In Egypt urban-rural fertility differentials appear to be negligible,[17] but there has long been a socioeconomic class differential within urban areas.[18] Even the Moroccan differential would not reduce the crude birth rate by as much as two points.

Some of the fertility differentials that one might anticipate and seem to have been established elsewhere appear to be absent or much less certain in sub-Saharan Africa. One example is that between wives in monogamous and polygynous marriages.[19]

FORCES TENDING TO RAISE FERTILITY

There are two major reasons why fertility in sub-Saharan Africa might tend to rise. The first is the possibility of massive reductions of infecundity and subfecundity, and the second is the likelihood of substantial decreases in the practice of marital sexual abstinence.[20]

During the present century, relatively low fertility has existed over great areas of Middle Africa, notably in northern Zaire, the eastern Central African Republic, southwest Sudan, Gabon, mainland Equatorial Guinea or Rio Muni, southeast Cameroon, and parts of Chad.[21] The area is contiguous and much of it is found in low-lying equatorial areas with unusually high levels of disease. The low levels of fertility are not the result of widely accepted ceilings on family size but of a high incidence of childless women (the proportion being more than one-third of all women of completed reproduction in some districts of Zaire a quarter of a century ago).[22] That this is pathological in origin is shown by the intense concern felt in these areas over childlessness and low fertility, as is evidenced by the unusual number of indigenous specialists in treating such complaints. It has been argued that this phenomenon is the product of venereal disease and an unusual degree of sexual liberality,[23] but this view has been contested and the importance of other diseases, such as filariasis, has been suggested.[24] It may well be that there are a multiplicity of pathological causes and that behavioral patterns have also played a role. At least in northern Zaire the incidence of sterility appears to be declining.[25] It would appear certain that these problems will eventually be overcome with a resultant tendency for fertility to rise.

In much of sub-Saharan Africa, birth is followed by a period of postnatal sexual abstinence on the part of the mother, the duration of which varies by culture but may exceed three years.[26] Social change appears everywhere to be reducing the duration of such abstinence, and substantial reductions are associated with female education, the use of contraception, and urban residence. The practice of sexual abstinence appears to have been aimed largely at ensuring child survival rather than limiting family size, and the duration of abstinence is longest in areas most prone to infant and child protein malnutrition. Some abstinence is also practiced at other times, and grandmothers are likely to terminate all sexual activity.

The incidence of sexual abstinence will inevitably decline with social change and may occasion at least a temporary rise in fertility. This may well be the main explanation for relatively higher fertility in some urban areas than in their surrounding rural hinterlands. Certainly abstinence is a more effective form of fertility control than contraception, particularly as the latter is now practiced in those parts of Africa where family planning is relatively new. In Ibadan, Nigeria, average parity is higher among contraceptors than noncontraceptors and so may be marital fertility rates.[27]

It might be noted here that there is little evidence of other effective indigenous fertility restraint in Africa. In the anthropological literature there are many references to age-old contraceptive and abortifacient practices (particularly in the area in and around the Kalahari Desert), but the evidence seems to be that over most of the continent such methods have not been employed to control family size but only to prevent those conceptions that are socially condemned, such as incestuous ones. The age-specific fertility curves were all the convex ones identified as having characterized pretransitional populations,[28] and even now this fertility pattern has, on the mainland, been modified only in Tunisia and Egypt. Contraception is a very recent phenomenon and has largely been a feature of the age of the pill and IUD. However, there is evidence from parts of anglophone West Africa of its practice doubling well within a decade. Detailed evidence exists for one Nigerian city of contraceptive practice year by year that indicates a doubling period of only four years.[29]

CONTRACEPTIVE REVOLUTION AND FAMILY PLANNING PROGRAMS

South of the Sahara, family planning programs are found only in Ghana, Kenya, Botswana, and South Africa, although voluntary programs are given governmental encouragement and even support in a number of other countries such as Nigeria, Tanzania, Zambia, Lesotho, and southern Rhodesia. There is a comprehensive and effective program in Mauritius. In North Africa programs have existed for a considerable time in Egypt, Tunisia, and Morocco, while the government of Algeria has more recently added family planning facilities to its health services.[30]

In sub-Saharan Africa these programs have as yet had no measurable impact. Even where they are operating they may not reach as many people as the commercial sector, as has been shown in one city in Nigeria.[31] However, it is claimed that in 1970 three-quarters of contraceptives used in Egypt were obtained from the government program.[32] Projections have been attempted of the likely spread of contraception and family planning programs in West and Middle Africa for the decade 1970-80, which suggested that by the latter date one wife in 64 would be using modern contraceptives in the absence of massive crash programs (as has indeed been the experience), and that the effect on the birth rate would be less than half a point.[33] There seems at present to be little reason for varying that forecast. In North Africa it is almost certain that contraceptives, both as supplied by family planning programs and by the commercial sector, have played a major role in the Tunisian and Egyptian fertility declines. They have not been the sole cause of these declines because both countries have experienced some rise in the female age at marriage, which has been quite marked in the case of Tunisia, where the average age of female at marriage rose by over two years in the decade up to 1975. Indeed, Egyptian fertility may have risen somewhat recently as a result of a reversal of this trend following a substantial fall in the number of young men in the army after the 1973 war. Nevertheless, a Tunisian estimate claims for the government program responsibility for three-sevenths of the additional births averted between 1966 and 1973.[34]

Two questions arise from the North African experience. The first is the cause of the fertility decline in Egypt during the 1960s and its cessation during the 1970s, together with a somewhat similar experience in Tunisia. The truth seems to be that social change had produced a group, especially the urban middle class, who were somewhat motivated to reduce family size and found the means at their disposal during the 1960s. By the end of the decade this demand had largely been saturated. Social change appears to have been augmenting the proportion of persons in this group rather slowly, and hence, with regard to fertility restriction, Egypt and Tunisia remained divided societies, with only minority enclaves desiring and attempting to reduce their fertility.

The second question is why the provision of contraception did nothing to reduce fertility in Morocco and has not as yet had any measurable impact in Algeria. The question may be partly invalid, at least in the case of Morocco, where the family planning program may be so weak as not really to present most women with the possibility of contraception. Nevertheless, one might also look for significant differences between Egypt and Tunisia on the one hand and Morocco and Algeria on the other. One difference may lie in the position of women and hence in the nature of the family. Both Egypt and Tunisia have consistently assumed that their women should move toward greater equality with men. The movements have probably been slower in Morocco and Algeria, partly because of political conservatism in the former and of the nature of the left-wing ideology in the latter. Algeria has emphasized some of its traditional values in contrast to those brought in by the French, a situation heralded by Fanon defending even the veil on the grounds of nationalist resistance to imported culture.[35] South of the Sahara the little success that has been achieved by official and voluntary family planning programs has not all been a measure of attempts to reduce family size. The only attempt to analyze the nature of the contraceptive demand indicated that no more than one-ninth of female contraceptors were attempting to limit family size.[36] Contraceptives were primarily employed as a substitute for sexual abstinence after a birth or during grandmotherhood (so that the disgrace of pregnancy could be averted), or for premarital or extramarital sexual relations.

Perhaps for many years yet marriage changes will be more important than family planning programs in reducing fertility. Almost everywhere there is some rise in average age at female marriage, associated both with rising levels of female education and with the availability of employment for single females. In the more economically and educationally advanced areas north and south of the Sahara, the average age of female marriage has moved from around 15 years to close to 20, often over little more than a generation. Polygyny, or the possibility of it even in areas where its incidence was low, has widely encouraged either competitive fertility or a fear among wives of remaining too long at too low a parity. Polygyny is now yielding to legal changes to the north and is retreating before female education in parts of the south. Indeed, wide average age gaps between spouses, declining polygyny, and lesser discouragement of widow remarriage in the north may combine with declining mortality to produce a marriage squeeze and even a proportion of women who do not marry at all. This may well be already under way in North Africa.

THE UNCHANGING AFRICAN FAMILY

Africa is almost exclusively characterized by two types of family, the two that may well prove to be the most resistant to fertility decline. South of the Sahara the lineage is all-important and north of the Sahara the Islamic family is the mode.

Sub-Saharan Africa has been characterized by strong descent lineages and by weak conjugal bonds.[37] Land is most frequently communally owned, and hence power and fortune have been derived almost solely from the control of sufficient people. Children have by no means been brought up solely by the nuclear family, and fertility determines neither the number of economic dependents at any specific time nor the identity of the person meeting the costs of rearing a child. Traditionally the older generation has received much more from the younger generation than has the younger from the older. This is still true even among the majority of the urban middle class. Nowhere has it been shown that parents of large families have been economically disadvantaged compared with parents of small families. Even the extended education of children imposes few strains on parents because of traditions of help from other relatives and particularly a well-established pattern of siblings assisting each other. It is not even the case that the unit in which maximum economic welfare is desired by a man is the nuclear family he has created by marriage and reproduction. He often feels closer to his siblings and parents, a situation that is sustained by polygynous and arranged marriages (in many areas half of all women are polygynously married and most will be so married at some time before the end of their reproductive period). The search for all completed families where fertility had been deliberately controlled showed that in Ibadan City they numbered only around 1 percent and did not form a large fraction even of the educated, urban middle class.[38] Those that did exist were found to be in families of a nontraditional type, characterized by close relationships between monogamously married spouses and by a parental feeling of greater obligation toward their children than their children were expected to return. Wealth flows were predominantly from parents to children. Only among this group was high fertility clearly uneconomic, and only among them was family size deliberately restricted.

In the Islamic family of North Africa and the Middle East, marriages are also arranged and the extended family of economic obligation is also important. Yet it is possible that this check on the worthwhileness of fertility reduction is supplemented by more powerful blockages.

One of these is a confidence in the future that exceeds fatalism and probably exceeds the level of confidence generated by any other religion at the same economic level. Islam inspires a feeling not only that Allah will provide, but also that it would be impious to suspect that He might not.

However, the main block to change probably lies in the nature of the nuclear family itself. The husband-wife relationship is probably less equal than in any other culture. In one sense it has been reinforced during recent decades because it has led, during the spread of Western-type schooling, to a very marked differential in the education received by boys and girls. Clearly the Islamic family is less likely to suffer economically because high fertility prevents women from working outside the home. But the major structural differences in the Islamic families have much greater implications than this. The difference between the position of husband and wife, even if it is said to be based almost wholly on female modesty, means that women live more cheaply, as do their children, than their husbands. Arab society is publicly a culture of adult males who are responsible for a surprising fraction of all consumption. The economic burden of additional children is not great, especially when the chances are that the girls will not be educated. Early age of female marriage and male employment does much in many countries to reduce the burden of economic dependence. Wives have fewer reasons than women in other cultures for wishing to restrict family size, for the domestic life is the main thing they possess and the well-populated home is their castle. Even in rich, but traditional, urban commercial families, children may be an economic advantage in businesses that are largely an aspect of the family.[39]

FORECASTS AND PROJECTIONS

Fertility is sustained at a high level in most of Africa by the nature of its society and above all by the structure of its families, which renders the gains to be made by the restriction of family size small or even negative. Change is under way as can be shown in almost every society by the way of life of small minorities, almost microscopically small in some sub-Saharan African countries. Those families where high fertility is clearly uneconomic are invariably much closer to the Western family than is normal in the society. This may be partly the result of greater wealth, urban living, or employment in the modern sector of the society, but more important is the fact that the Western prototype is almost the only model for change and it is taught by the media, schools, and international expectations.

Education appears to cause the most changes. It challenges traditional authority, gives females an absolute criterion of value for comparison with males, teaches girls new aims and destinies that almost always include some move toward the more egalitarian Western family structure, and changes husbands' appreciation of their wives, wives' appreciation of themselves, and children's appreciation of their mothers. In families with educated women, wives become more expensive and so do children, partly because mothers appear to be more likely to stress the dependence of children and the primacy of the nuclear family. When spouses are more equal they are more likely to be able to challenge successfully each other's spending on relatives outside their own nuclear family of reproduction, and they are more likely to be able to agree to vary traditional reproductive patterns. Indeed, the major ingredients of fertility decline in sub-Saharan Africa may be a sexual revolution with the replacement of sexual abstinence by contraception and a concentration of sexual interests and activities within the home.

Family changes of this kind take time. In North Africa they are likely to be speeded up by the spread of Middle Eastern and Maghreb oil wealth. Such wealth is likely to be translated even into terms of female education in all Arab countries, probably with major implications for marriage and the family.

In sub-Saharan Africa, too, family change remains the key to fertility change. Female education is almost certainly the most powerful catalyst—a catalyst much more important than urbanization and rise in per capita income, although its rate of spread is obviously related to the latter.

It is likely that analyses of the Egyptian and Tunisian fertility declines will show that their chief parameters were the acceptance of family planning by families in which the wives had been educated. This will take time, although it should be noted that Nigeria's oil has meant that the country has now moved toward universal primary education.

There is nothing in this analysis to alter one's acceptance of the United Nations' long-range medium variant population projection suggesting that Africa will double its population between now and the end of the century to over 800 million, and will multiply again by three before all the family and fertility changes have run their course. However, it may well be that they have somewhat overestimated rates of growth in North Africa and underestimated them further south. The effects of the rise in oil prices in accelerating social change in the north could hardly have been foreseen. Further south the reduction of subfecundity and marital sexual abstinence may tend to raise or sustain fertility to a greater degree than had been supposed. If one had chosen demographic regions alone for this analysis, the Moslem bloc as far east as Pakistan might have been added. In terms of fertility, the whole area is largely homogeneous and will almost certainly form the world's last large expanse of high fertility and rapid population growth.

NOTES

1. Data from various sources, but the basic one is the United Nations Demographic Yearbook.

2. United Nations, Department of Social and Economic Affairs, Concise Report on the World Population Situation in 1970-75 and Its Long-Range Implications, Population Studies no. 56, ST/ESA/SER.A/56 (New York: 1974).

3. S. K. Gaisie, "Fertility Levels among the Ghanaian Tribes," in S. H. Ominde and C. N. Ejiogu, eds., Population Growth and Economic Development in Africa (London: Heinemann, 1972), pp. 84-92.

4. Pat Caldwell, "Egypt and the Arabic and Islamic Worlds," in John C. Caldwell, ed., The Persistence of High Fertility: Population Prospects in the Third World (Canberra: Australian National University, 1977), pp. 593-616.

5. Althea Hill, "The Fertility of the Asian Community of East Africa," Population Studies 29 (November 1975): 355-72; see also J. G. C. Blacker, "Fertility Trends of the Asian Population of Tanganyika," Population Studies 13 (July 1959): 46-60; and J. M. Boute, "Exploratory Analysis of Data concerning Indians and Pakistanis in Africa," in John C. Caldwell and Chukuka Okonjo, eds., The Population of Tropical Africa (New York: Columbia University

6. Office for Population, Agency for International Development, World Fertility Patterns: Age-specific Fertility Rates for Countries of the World, fact sheet (Washington, D.C.: 1977).

7. United Nations, Concise Report, op. cit.

8. Koni Bongoma, "Population Trends in Zaire" (Ph.D. dissertation, Department of Demography, Australian National University, Canberra, 1978), where relatively great rises in the rates of natural increase are shown for the areas previously most affected by infertility.

9. International Bank for Reconstruction and Development, World Bank Atlas of Population, Per Capita Product and Growth Rates, Washington, D.C., 1975.

10. Changing African Family Project, Survey 1 (Ibadan: 1973). Among women born before 1935, fertility (measured by live births, and taking those with no schooling as standard) was no schooling—100 percent, primary schooling only—104 percent, some secondary schooling—98 percent, completed secondary schooling—90 percent. See also Israel Sembajwe, "Fertility and Child Mortality Levels and Differentials among the Yoruba of Western Nigeria" (Ph.D. dissertation, Department of Demography, Australian National University, 1977).

11. G. Negadi, D. Tabutin, and J. Vallin, "Situation démographique de l'Algérie," in La Population de l'Algérie (Cairo: CICRED, 1974), pp. 40-41; M. A. El-Badry and Hanna Rizk, "Regional Fertility Differentials among Socio-economic groups in the United Arab Republic," in United Nations, Department of Economic and Social Affairs, Proceedings of the World Population Conference, Belgrade, 30 August-10 September 1965, New York, 1967, vol. 2, p. 140.

12. Negadi, Tabutin, and Vallin, op. cit., pp. 43-48.

13. John C. Caldwell, "Introduction," in John C. Caldwell et al., Population Growth and Socioeconomic Change in West Africa (New York: The Population Council and Columbia University Press, 1975), p. 11.

14. John C. Caldwell, "Fertility Differentials as Evidence of Incipient Fertility Decline in a Developing Country: The Case of Ghana," Population Studies 21 (July 1967): 5-21.

15. M. Rachidi, "La dimension de la famille marocaine musulmane," As-soukan, Centre de Recherches et d'Etudes Démographiques, Rabat, 1, 1973, pp. 67-81.

16. Jacques Vallin, "Influence de divers facteurs économiques et sociaux sur la fécondité de l'Algérie," Population 28 (July-October 1973): 817-42.

17. M. A. El Badry, "Some Aspects of Fertility in Egypt," Milbank Memorial Fund Quarterly 34 (1965): 22; M. A. El Badry, "Trends in the Components of Population Growth in the Arab Countries of the Middle East: A Survey of Present Information," Demography 2 (1965): 140-86; Atef M. Khalifa, The Population of the Arab Republic of Egypt (Cairo: CICRED, 1973), pp. 9-12.

18. H. Rizk, "Social and Psychological Factors Affecting Fertility in the U.A.R.," Journal of Marriage and Family Living 25 (1963).

19. P. O. Ohadike, "A Demographic Note on Marriage, Family and Family Growth in Lagos, Nigeria," in Caldwell and Okonjo, op. cit., pp. 386-89; Sembajwe, op. cit., pp. 210-12. But see Hilary Page, "Fertility Levels: Patterns and Trends," in Caldwell et al., op. cit., pp. 50-51.

20. Robert W. Morgan et al., New Perspectives on the Demographic Transition, Smithsonian ICP Occasional Monograph Series no. 4 (Washington, D.C.: 1976); P. O. Olusanya, "Modernisation and the Level of Fertility in Western Nigeria," Proceedings of the International Population Conference, London, 1969 (Liège: 1971), vol. 1, pp. 812-25.

21. Ansley J. Coale and Frank Lorimer, "Summary of Estimates of Fertility and Mortality," in William Brass et al., The Demography of Tropical Africa (Princeton: Princeton University Press, 1968), pp. 166-67; Anatole Romaniuk, "The Demography of the Democratic Republic of the Congo," in Brass et al., op. cit., pp. 319-34, 337; Page, op. cit., pp. 41-47.

22. Romaniuk, op. cit., p. 331.

23. A. Romaniuk, "Infertility in Tropical Africa," in Caldwell and Okonjo, op. cit., pp. 214-24.

24. B. Kwaku Adadevoh, ed., Sub-fertility and Infertility in Africa (Ibadan: Caxton Press, 1974).

25. Bongoma, op. cit.

26. John C. Caldwell and Pat Caldwell, "The Role of Marital Sexual Abstinence in Determining Fertility: A Study of the Yoruba in Nigeria," Population Studies 31 (July 1977): 193-217.

27. Ibid., pp. 208-10; Sembajwe, op. cit., p. 220.

28. John Knodel, "Family Limitation and the Fertility Transition: Evidence from the Age Patterns of Fertility in Europe and Asia," Population Studies 31 (July 1977): 219-49.

29. John C. Caldwell, "Fertility Control," in Caldwell et al., op. cit., pp. 91-92; John C. Caldwell and Helen Ware, "The Evolution of Family Planning in an African City: Ibadan, Nigeria," Population Studies 31 (November 1977): 492.

30. See generally Walter B. Watson, ed., Family Planning in the Developing World: A Review of Programs (New York: The Population Council, 1977).

31. Caldwell and Ware, op. cit., p. 497.

32. Khalifa, op. cit., p. 91.

33. John C. Caldwell, "Fertility Control," op. cit., pp. 58-97.

34. Mahmoud Seklani, La Population de la Tunisie (Tunis: CICRED, 1974), p. 54.

35. Frantz Fanon, A Dying Colonialism (Harmondsworth: Penguin, 1970), pp. 48-49.

36. Francis Olu Okediji, John Caldwell, Pat Caldwell, and Helen Ware, "The Changing African Family Project: A Report with Special Reference to the Nigerian Segment," Studies in Family Planning 7 (May 1976): 132. See also John C. Caldwell and Pat Caldwell, "Demographic and Contraceptive Innovators: A Study of Transitional African Society," Journal of Biosocial Science 8 (October 1976): 347-65.

37. This summary drew primarily on three papers by the author: "Fertility and the Household Economy in Nigeria," Journal of Comparative Family Studies, special issue (1976): 193-253; "The Economic Rationality of High Fertility," Population Studies 31 (March 1977): 5-27; and "Toward a Restatement of Demographic Transition Theory," Population and Development Review 2 (September/December 1976): 321-66.

38. John C. Caldwell and Pat Caldwell, "The Achieved Small Family: Early Fertility Transition in an African City," Studies in Family Planning 9, 1977, pp. 1-18.

39. Mohamed el Awad Galel el Din, "The Rationality of High Fertility in Urban Sudan," in Caldwell, The Persistence of High Fertility, op. cit., pp. 633-58.

4

FERTILITY DECLINE IN CHINA

John S. Aird

Generalizations about human fertility that do not include the experience of the 1 billion people of China are incomplete. The importance of China's contribution derives not merely from the size of its population but also from the uniqueness of its efforts to control fertility. No other country has committed itself so firmly to the reduction of population growth. No country has tried so hard to raise the age at which young people marry. No country has so effectively organized propaganda and programs to promote contraception, abortion, and sterilization and to insure the fulfillment of targets and quotas. No country has gone as far toward making family limitation compulsory.

There can be little doubt that the leaders of the PRC attach the highest importance to reducing the rate of population growth or that significant progress has been made during the 1970s. The critical questions are how much progress and by what means.

Despite extensive coverage in the Chinese mass media and many reports by foreign visitors to China, definitive data and information on the Chinese effort to control human fertility are lacking. The descriptions and the figures available indicate what is supposed to be happening but may not accurately reflect what is actually going on. Little is known about the methods used to collect data, except that they apparently are gathered by the same family planning workers and cadres whose effectiveness they are used to measure. Chinese press and radio dispatches are not intended to give objective accounts of the events they describe but to mold public opinion and secure popular conformity with official policies. Except in special situations, the Chinese media must give the impression that all facts confirm the correctness of present policies, that the population is substantially in agreement with what the government or the Party wants to do, and that nearly everybody is willingly if not enthusiastically cooperating. That some kinds of evidence are kept out of the channels to which foreigners and the Chinese public have access is apparent from the revelations of previously withheld information that take place during the infrequent periods when past mistakes are exposed.

The analyst's judgment is also affected by his own biases, which reflect his philosophical inclinations and the political and social currents of his milieu. In the continuing debate among Western social scientists over the effectiveness of family planning programs in developing countries, advocates of birth control who use the Chinese example to support their case are inclined to accept uncritically the progress reports from China and occasionally claim more success for the Chinese program than do the Chinese themselves. In some quarters China is now idealized, as was the Soviet Union in former times, as the place where all things go well that go badly elsewhere, and contrary evidence from China is ignored. On the other hand, some observers tend to distrust anything the Chinese say and dismiss their statistical data as worthless. Hence there is a persistent danger that foreign analysts, including China specialists, may accept either too much or too little. Maintaining the skepticism appropriate to the circumstances creates a vacuum of uncertainty that it is in many people's nature to abhor. Yet a proper regard for the uncertainty of the evidence is essential in analyzing developments in contemporary China.

Given the nature of the source materials, this chapter cannot claim to be definitive, but it attempts to weigh all of the available evidence, drawing on the data collection experience of the recent past in China. The purpose is not to provide new estimates of the national birth rate or to assess the effectiveness of China's planned birth efforts, but to point out the limitations of the evidence, and particularly of the data on fertility and natural increase, and the questions that remain to be answered before firm conclusions can be reached.

FERTILITY DATA PRIOR TO 1949

Almost from the beginning of the twentieth century, and particularly from the 1920s onward, there was considerable interest in Chinese government circles and among both Chinese and foreign scholars in gathering data on the size, structure, and vital rates of the population of China. A number of attempts were made by government agencies and by private academic and research institutions to conduct censuses and surveys and to establish vital registration systems in the hope of collecting data that would throw some light on China's perennial demographic mysteries. These efforts were, on the whole, not very successful.

Beginning in the 1920s a series of experimental censuses and population surveys were conducted in various parts of China under various auspices, in some cases with financial support from foreign research institutions and the active participation of foreign social scientists. Among the first of the sophisticated large-scale investigations, and certainly the most famous, was a series conducted by Ch'iao Ch'i-ming and John Lossing Buck in 1924-25 and 1929-31. The work was carried out in several stages, ultimately reaching families in 191 localities in 22 provinces. Some of the original survey reports were considered inadequate and were rejected. The records that have survived to the present time are from 119 localities in 16 provinces; they include data on 46,601 families with a total of 202,617 members.[1] By design the study covered only farm families living in agricultural communities, but even within this universe the selection of units was not random. The choices were determined in part by political conditions, by the cooperativeness of local authorities, and by whether or not there was a University of Nanking student among the residents of the locality. Presumably the communities and the families surveyed tended to be more prosperous and more stable than those not included in the study.

The initial stage of the study covered over 12,000 families in eight provinces and yielded a crude birth rate of 35.7 per thousand population.[2] The second stage covered over 4,000 families in four provinces and produced a birth rate of over 42.2.[3] Subsequent efforts further enlarged the scope of the study. By the time Buck published his major report on the project in 1937, he had population data for over 38,000 families in 101 localities in 22 provinces, from which he derived a crude birth rate of 38.3 and a crude death rate of 27.1. The two lowest birth rates were 10.2 and 9.7.

Another famous study during the years before the Communist revolution was that conducted in the Kunming Lake Region of Yunnan Province by the American-trained demographer Ch'en Ta and the Tsinghua University Institute of Census Research.[4] The study included experimental vital registration that began in 1939 in the 27 villages adjacent to the city of Cheng Kung on the edge of the Kunming Lake Region and, after some initial success, was extended to the rest of the country in 1940 and to the entire Kunming Lake Region in 1942. Ch'en's report includes birth rates for Cheng Kung for a span of five years, 1940-44, but the rates vary greatly from year to year, and the overall average is only 24.9. Ch'en explains the low figures as due in part to the departure of males for military service in 1942, a drought and famine in 1943, and the imposition of a large number of "government tasks" in the latter year, which, he says, caused the population to become increasingly uncooperative with the registration.[5] The low level of the rates even in the earliest years suggests that underregistration was the principal cause.

The most carefully conducted of the experiments in vital registration during these years was one undertaken by Ch'iao Ch'i-ming, Warren Thompson, and D. T. Chen in a rural district of Kiangyin County, Kiangsu Province, in 1932-35. The district, Hsiao Chi, was chosen because it was thought to be fairly typical of the rural areas in the lower Yangtse delta, a region believed to be representative of conditions in East Central China in general. Vital reports from the 221 villages in Hsiao Chi were obtained on a monthly basis by Chen, who personally visited each of the 202 local reporters he was able to recruit for the purpose. The reporters were usually community leaders or persons recommended by them. Each reporter was responsible for keeping track of births and deaths among not more than 200 persons, or about 20 families.[6]

The birth rates for Hsiao Chi calculated for the four years from midyear 1931 to midyear 1935 were 48.3, 44.1, 40.0, and 48.0, respectively. The decline between 1931 and 1934 was explained as due to an economic depression, which caused a drop in marriages and an accelerated outmigration of young people, and to a severe epidemic of malaria in 1933. Some further complications were added by a flood in 1931, a cholera epidemic in 1932, and droughts in 1932 and 1934. It was assumed that in the absence of these misfortunes the level of fertility would have been higher still.

The authors also describe at some length the difficulties encountered in winning the confidence of the local population so that they would willingly provide information about births and deaths to the reporters. Initially there had been some concern that the reporting of this kind of information would invite various misfortunes, and Chen himself was asked to leave one village for this reason. In one of his reports he expressed doubts about the completeness of the data, and at the beginning of their report the authors concede that the demographic profile of Hsiao Chi they have been able to obtain is "not absolutely accurate."[7]

On the basis of such evidence, foreign demographers who discussed China's birth rate during the 1940s and 1950s were generally of the opinion that it was over 40 per thousand, that it was sustained by basic elements of traditional Chinese culture, and that it would prove highly resistant to change.[8] The consensus among knowledgeable persons was that culture and society in China tended to maximize fertility and that, despite recurrent catastrophes, the national birth rates were fairly stable.

The prevailing views about Chinese fertility and about the validity of the population data collected in China before 1949 have been challenged in the past few years by new research. Early in the 1970s Irene Taeuber began a series of analyses in which she reexamined the data from the 1930s and 1940s using new methods of estimating fertility and mortality levels from defective age-sex distributions.[9] The techniques corrected for omissions of infants and children under 5 years of age, for differential omissions of female children, and for sex-selective infanticide. Fertility levels in the Manchurian provinces estimated from the 1940 census data under varying assumptions about mortality yielded provincial birth rates ranging from the middle thirties to the middle fifties, but mainly in the forties. Birth rates estimated for the Kunming Lake Region were mostly in the upper forties when the female population was adjusted for a sex ratio at birth of 105 and the ratio of the female population aged 0 to 4 to the female population aged 15 to 44 was used. The data for Yunnan Province from the Buck survey tended to confirm the high birth rates for the province suggested by the Kunming Lake survey data. Taking the Buck data for all of the 101 localities in 22 provinces, the analysis indicated a birth rate of 43.8 instead of the 38.3 obtained by Buck from the unadjusted data.

The analysis of the Buck data begun by Taeuber was carried further after her death in 1974 by several of her colleagues at the Princeton Office of Population Research, and some of the findings were published in October 1976.[10] When all the adjustments were made and mortality levels and patterns were estimated, the implied overall birth rate was 41.2 per thousand.

Two other interesting findings emerged from the analysis. One was that there were significant regional differences in vital rates. The birth rate for the northern regions was at an intermediate level—38.7; that for the southern regions was distinctly higher—43.4. The level of fertility in both regions was well below what might have been expected on the basis of the widely held presumption that birth rates in China tended toward the biological maximum. The second finding throws additional light on this discovery. Marital fertility at all ages is roughly 35 percent below the natural maximum levels of fertility found in other countries that place no limitations on family size. Why this is so is not clear. The level of fertility may have been determined by health, nutrition, social disorders, and other constraining circumstances that began to be moderated after 1949. However, in the absence of corroborating evidence, such hypotheses are little more than speculation.

The demographic investigations in China before 1949 illustrate the difficulties of obtaining accurate population statistics from a largely nonliterate people without sophisticated technical supervision, a well-organized force of trained enumerators, recordkeepers, and reporters, and a fund of practical experience in the collection of mass data. All of the population surveys and registration efforts in the years before 1949 were defective in varying degrees, and the data reflect their limitations. The birth and death rates reported were, in almost all cases, well below what the most knowledgeable observers, and in some cases the investigators themselves, believed to be the actual levels. Although modern analytical techniques permit the extraction of more meaning from the data compiled in these investigations than was formerly thought possible, it is not clear that all of the deficiencies can be overcome by retrospective adjustments.

FERTILITY LEVELS IN THE 1950s

It is generally assumed that conditions in the areas covered by the Buck surveys favored high fertility at the time when the surveys took place. Presumably they became much less favorable in a large part of the country during the next decade because of the war with Japan and the subsequent revolutionary struggle, the consequences of which must have been felt in regions far removed from the locus of armed conflict. Not only the disruption of families and delay of marriages caused by military service and the displacement of population in the areas of military activity, but also the political uncertainties and economic crises brought on by the wars probably would have had a depressing effect on marriage and fertility rates.

Local catastrophes of indeterminate scope continued into the early years of the PRC. Throughout the first half of the 1950s, famines were reported over large areas every spring, and considerable attention was devoted in the press to problems and progress in famine relief. The land reform movement also caused political and economic dislocations in many parts of China, and purges that may have cost millions of lives undoubtedly created acute anxieties at least among some segments of the population.[11] The Marriage Law of 1950 had, as one of its immediate consequences, the effect of dissolving a number of parent-arranged marriages and precipitating marital and family conflicts over the new freedoms it authorized, which led to thousands of suicides and murders, mainly of women.[12]

But on the whole the period seems to have been marked by a gradual establishment of social order and an increase in economic security, at least in comparison with the war years. People dislocated by military actions in the final stages of the revolution returned home, and the industrial plants in the cities, also ravaged by the war and by retiring Soviet forces, were being restored to production as fast as possible. The peasants who had received land and farm equipment as a result of the land reform redistributions were enjoying a prosperity many of them had not known previously. According to Chinese sources, marriage and birth rates were rising and infant mortality rates were falling sharply.[13]

To the extent that the increase in marriage and first birth rates reflected the restoration of civil order and postwar economic recovery, it was probably of brief duration. By the late 1950s the wave of marriages delayed by the war years should have been over, and even in the absence of other depressants, fertility probably would have declined again. But other factors also played a part. In 1955 and 1956 the collectivization drive was completed, depriving the peasants of their land, livestock, and implements, and reducing them to the status of agricultural laborers within the cooperatives. In 1958 the mass labor projects of the Big Leap Forward and the absorption of the cooperatives into the communes brought further dislocations in the rural economy and the living arrangements of the peasants. Local grain shortages were again reported from various parts of China in 1957 and, after a year of good harvests, three bad crop years ensued in 1959, 1960, and 1961. All of these developments probably contributed in varying degrees to a decline in fertility rates.

Official Birth Rates During the 1950s

Trends in fertility during this period cannot be traced through official vital data because the figures available are too incomplete and too defective to reflect clearly the actual changes in fertility. The vital rates of the 1950s are distinguished from those made available in more recent years mainly by the fact that the 1950s data more often appeared in sets covering a number of areas or a span of years or both, which makes possible assessments of internal consistency and plausibility that are impossible with highly fragmented data.

Vital rates for seven important municipalities for the years 1952-56 were given by officials of the State Statistical Bureau to a French demographer, Roland Pressat, during a visit to China in 1958 (see Table 4.1). As Pressat observed, there are some strange irregularities in the data that seem to imply changes in completeness or registration and perhaps changes in municipal boundaries during the period they cover.[14] The rates for 1952 are in some cases much too low to be taken as a reflection of postwar recovery and must therefore indicate that registration was still comparatively incomplete in that year. The urban registers had been established in major cities in 1949 and 1950, but there were many reports that the system was in difficulties in its earliest years, and new field counts had to be taken repeatedly to update the faltering records.[15] For six of the seven cities, the peak year for the birth rate was 1954, the year that a national food grain and cloth rationing system was instituted. Undoubtedly birth registration was more complete during this year than

TABLE 4.1

Birth and Death Rates for Selected Cities in the People's Republic of China, 1952-56

City	Birth Rates					Death Rates				
	1952	1953	1954	1955	1956	1952	1953	1954	1955	1956
Peking	35.0	39.6	43.1	43.2	39.3	9.3	9.3	7.7	8.1	6.7
Tientsin	27.1	39.5	44.9	43.9	40.2	6.0	8.6	7.6	8.4	6.6
Shanghai	38.0	40.4	52.6	41.4	40.3	12.4	9.9	7.6	8.1	6.7
Harbin	47.0	48.1	53.1	47.3	41.3	14.8	15.9	9.7	10.6	8.5
Sian	33.3	41.2	49.9	45.3	47.7	9.5	7.4	6.9	7.4	7.4
Hangchow	40.1	40.6	45.4	39.6	36.8	12.4	9.7	9.0	9.6	8.5
Canton	36.7	41.8	43.7	39.5	39.0	9.2	7.9	7.2	7.0	6.8

<u>Source</u>: Roland Pressat, "La Population de la Chine et son Economie," <u>Population</u> (October-December 1958): 572-73.

in previous years; in fact, the 1954 birth rates were probably inflated somewhat by the belated registration of some births that had occurred before 1954. The premature drop in the death rate in 1954 also testifies to the distortion of population registration because of rationing. The central authorities were aware to some degree of these problems. In 1957 the State Statistical Bureau, noting "unusual phenomena" in many localities in connection with the vital data for 1954 and 1955, undertook an analysis of birth statistics in Shanghai, on the basis of which it was concluded that in 1954 there were about 20,000 late registrations in the city, or 5 percent of all births registered in that year.

The urban vital rates given to Pressat were presumably processed by the State Statistical Bureau prior to their release, which may have included adjustments to eliminate even more conspicuous anomalies. As it happens, absolute data on births and deaths in Peking for the years 1950 through 1956 were published in the Peking People's Daily in November 1957 that are obviously inconsistent with Pressat's vital rates for Peking (Table 4.2). Not one of the ratios between birth and death rates even approximates the ratios between the corresponding absolute figures for births and deaths. The two series are simply not compatible. Moreover, the numbers of births, which were increasing by from 1 to 8 percent per year between 1950 and 1953, suddenly jumped 45 percent in 1954, and deaths, which had declined in the two preceding years, increased 27 percent in 1954, indicating a major discontinuity in that year.[16]

Experimental vital registration work was conducted by the Ministry of Health between 1950 and 1954 in a sample of urban and rural registration areas that by spring 1953 numbered 77 and included a total population of 7,660,000. Only 19 of the 77 areas were rural. In October 1953 the number of areas was reduced, and in November 1954 the State Statistical Bureau directed the Ministry of Health to terminate its experiments in vital registration and thereafter to obtain vital data from "the departments which are responsible for household control," which at that time were the Public Security departments for urban areas and the Internal Affairs departments for rural areas.[17]

When the final census results were announced in 1954, the news releases also gave the results of surveys of vital data for areas containing a total population of 30,180,000. The components were described as "29 large and medium cities, the whole province of Ningsia, 10 counties of other provinces, as well as 1 representative municipal district [ch'ü], 2 representative towns, 58 representative villages, [and] 7 representative hamlets of 35 counties." Neither the dates of the surveys nor the agencies that gathered the data are identified, nor is there any indication of how it was determined that the reporting areas were really representative. The resulting birth rate was 37,

TABLE 4.2

Births, Deaths, and Natural Increase in Peking, 1950-56

Year	Births	Deaths	Natural Increase
1950	72,712	29,190	43,522
1951	78,801	32,578	46,223
1952	79,917	25,274	54,643
1953	83,456	21,823	61,633
1954	121,057	27,722	93,335
1955	128,275	30,302	97,973
1956	131,232	25,034	106,198

Source: Sun Kuang, "Urban Population Must Be Controlled," JMJP, November 27, 1957; translated in SCMP, no. 1668, December 10, 1957, p. 4.

death rate 17, and natural increase rate 20 per thousand population.[18] The rates were cited as though they were believed to be the vital rates for the country as a whole as of 1953. But if the 29 cities included the seven for which Pressat was given vital data, which had a total population of just under 16 million according to the 1953 census, and if the remaining 22 "large and medium" cities had an average size no larger than the average size for all cities of 100,000 population or more at the time of the census (less the figures for Pressat's seven), then the urban components of the sample of 30,180,000 would have accounted for almost 80 percent without counting the population in the smaller cities.[19] The 1953 census results indicated that the population was only 13.3 percent urban in 1953. Hence, no matter how the sample components were distributed by region or province, they could not have been representative of vital conditions throughout the country. There is no indication that any attempt was made to weight the rural and urban components according to the national proportions of rural and urban, or otherwise to adjust the data to compensate for underregistration or lack of representativeness.

Apparently the results of these investigations were used as the base for a series of vital rates reported or estimated for subsequent years, presumably by the State Statistical Bureau, and evidently regarded as national vital rates. They were never officially released but were given to two foreign demographers who visited China in

1958. Vital data for 1952, 1954, and 1957 were provided to Pressat by bureau officials in August, and six sets of vital rates were obtained from an unspecified source by Sripati Chandrasekhar in December (Table 4.3). Pressat's figures include absolute totals of births, deaths, and natural increase, the magnitude of which shows that they were meant to be national figures. Pressat's 1952 vital rates are identical with those released in 1954 as the results of the investigation of areas with a combined population of 30,180,000, but dated 1953. Pressat surmised that the figures were not based on national registration but involved extrapolations from data received from areas that the State Statistical Bureau believed were doing a satisfactory job of keeping vital records.[20] The 1952 and 1954 figures could not have been based on national registration because registration was not instituted in the rural areas of China until late in 1954, and did not become complete until either late 1955 or 1956. Chandrasekhar was told that national registration was almost 100 percent complete as of December 1958,[21] but it does not seem likely that even the 1957 figures he and Pressat were given were based on local vital data from the whole country. Evidence strongly suggests that the 1957 rates, and perhaps all the rates after 1953, were obtained by extrapolating an arbitrary series of absolute births and deaths and dividing by the official national population totals. Obviously such a procedure would explain the continuity of the rates despite major changes in registration area. It would also explain why the national series shows little or no increase in the birth rate for 1954, the year that grain and cloth rationings were instituted, in spite of the jump of almost 20 percent in the weighted mean birth rate for Pressat's seven municipalities.

The vital data of the 1950s show that the problems of data collection and the deficiencies in the data collected before 1949 continued in spite of the efforts of the new government to establish full demographic accountability. Often the local authorities were evidently inclined to accept manifestly defective data and to pass them on to higher levels. The central authorities accepted figures from small and atypical samples as representative of the whole and cited sample figures as the results of national reporting, but avoided revealing much about the origins of the figures and released them only through unofficial channels. Hence neither the levels nor the trends of the local and national vital rates issued during the 1950s can be taken as reliable measures of vital phenomena.

Factors Affecting Fertility in the Late 1950s

However defective the figures, the somewhat hesitant downward trend in the national birth rate in the latter half of the 1950s is not

TABLE 4.3

Vital Rates Obtained from Chinese Sources by Foreign Demographers Who Visited China during 1958

Year	Birth Rate	Death Rate	Natural Increase Rate	Births	Deaths	Natural Increase
Pressat's figures						
1953	37	17	20	21,510,000	9,880,000	11,630,000
1954	37	13	24	21,560,000	7,790,000	13,770,000
1957	34	11	23	21,660,000	6,890,000	14,770,000
Chandrasekhar's figures						
1952	37	18	19	—	—	—
1953	37	17	20	—	—	—
1954	38	13	24	—	—	—
1955	35	12.4	22.6	—	—	—
1956	32	11.4	20.6	—	—	—
1957	34	11	23	—	—	—

Sources: Roland Pressat, "La Population de la Chine et son Economie," Population (October-December 1958): 570; Sripati Chandrasekhar, China's Population: Census and Vital Statistics (Hong Kong: Hong Kong University Press, 1959), p. 50.

implausible in view of what was happening in China during those years. The rapid growth of the urban population and the efforts from 1955 onward to expel unauthorized rural migrants from the cities brought more of the population under the influence of the urban environment and encouraged more spatial mobility, circumstances that probably tended to reduce fertility at least slightly. There were also efforts on a limited scale to relocate population from the more densely inhabited areas to sparsely settled frontier regions. Some of the latter were not adequately prepared to receive the new residents, with the result that living conditions were adverse and backflow was considerable. Within urban areas, the work assignments for young workers of both sexes often separated families, and in some cases spouses, so that family formation probably was delayed. The forced completion of cooperativization in 1955 and 1956 that drove many peasants into the cities also created considerable social upheaval among those who remained in the rural areas. Even where they were relatively successful, the cooperatives afforded greater insurance against economic catastrophe at the cost of individual economic incentives, and thus damaged the productivity of the most productive peasant families. The net effect of these changes on the fertility of rural families cannot be demonstrated, but it is unlikely that it would have been positive. During 1958 and 1959, the exhaustive mass labor projects of the Big Leap Forward and the unhealthful conditions in the commune dormitories and mess halls also may have depressed fertility somewhat. It may be conjectured that a gradual downward trend in intrinsic fertility levels was taking place in both urban and rural areas during the latter part of the 1950s.

Of all the social policies of the period, the birth control campaign of the 1950s was the one that should have had the most direct impact on the birth rate. However, there are many reasons for believing that the campaign had little immediate demographic significance.

The intensive phase of the campaign had lasted only a little more than a year. There were problems in maintaining adequate supplies of contraceptives, the propaganda efforts often were inept and offensive, and there was much popular resistance, even from administrative cadres and health personnel, who in many cases were opposed to the objectives and methods of the campaign. Promotional efforts were largely confined to the cities, and even in some of these the work was delayed as long as possible and done in a perfunctory manner.[22] There were some claims of success from local units and much talk of planning and target setting, but what was actually accomplished is questionable. In 1957 a spokesman for the Ministry of Health attributed the decline in the Peking birth rate from 43 in 1954 to 39 in 1956 to the success of the birth control effort, ignoring the temporary inflation of the birth rate in 1954 that other authorities had already conceded.[23] Chunking reported a lower birth rate for the first six months of 1957 than for the corresponding period in 1956,[24] and Sian claimed a drop in the birth rate between January and June of 1957.[25] Other smaller jurisdictions—a cotton mill, an urban neighborhood, a rural cooperative—also reported falling birth rates. But some reports indicated no progress or even rising fertility. If the quantitative measures of the results of the campaign even in urban areas were equivocal, the impact in the country as a whole must have been negligible.

THE FERTILITY DATA OF THE 1960s

Demographic data for the PRC for the 1960s are fewer than are available either for the 1950s or the 1970s. A second national population count was taken in summer 1964. No mention was made of this effort in Chinese press and radio dispatches at the time, and the results have never been officially released in a statistical communique, as were the results of the 1953 census. From the middle 1960s onward, a number of provincial population totals in round millions appeared in local news items, but in many cases the figures were markedly inconsistent with the provincial data from the 1953 census and those obtained from the population registers at the end of 1957. Beginning in 1972, a series of Chinese atlases began to repeat a set of provincial population figures given in units of 10,000 that were generally consistent with the round figures of the middle 1960s and seemed, from all indications, to be the long unpublished 1964 figures. More recently, Chinese officials have indicated that the atlas figures are in fact from the 1964 census.[26]

No national or local vital rates were released during the 1960s, but some vital rates for the 1960s have been released during the 1970s, including two surprisingly high national natural increase rates. Why the rates ascribed to the 1960s were not made public at the time is not clear. Some may have been withheld because they indicated little or no progress in birth control work, but others imply significant declines, which should have been cause for celebration. Was their validity in doubt, or have the rates only recently been computed from old population records? For the present, these questions cannot be answered.

Rural Birth Rates

A look at the rates raises other questions. Considering first the birth rates reported for rural units, most of those reported thus far are not very high for communities that are not practicing contraception. Of the seven communes for which there are figures, most fall in a range of 20 to 34 per thousand. Four of the seven are within Shanghai's municipal boundaries and two are within the municipal area of Peking. The one rural commune that is not in a municipal area is Cheng-kung, Lin County, Honan Province, which reported that its birth rate began to decline in 1964 and reached 30 per thousand by 1966 and 20 by 1971.[27] Its 1971 death rate was reported as 4 per thousand, which means that vital registration in that commune was incomplete in the 1970s; it is not likely to have been more complete in 1966, during the Cultural Revolution.

Among the municipal communes reporting 1960s birth rates, the most complete set is for Ton-wan Commune in Shanghai Municipality. One series was obtained from a photograph of a graph on display at the commune clinic taken by David Berliner, from which the following values were read:[28]

Year	Birth rate	Year	Birth rate
1963	45	1968	21
1964	35	1969	20
1965	23	1970	15
1966	20	1971	13
1967	17	1972	10.4

Different figures for three of the years had been given several years earlier to another foreign visitor: 1963—46, 1970—11, 1971—13.6.[29] The discrepancies are slight and easily may have arisen because of inaccuracies in reading from the graph or because the graph was drawn so as to minimize the rates. However, more serious discrepancies appear in the rates obtained for Ton-wan by a third visitor, Margaret Wolfson, who copied another birth rate graph from a wall during her visit to the commune in 1975 and reproduced it in her report. The values are as follows:[30]

Year	Birth rate	Year	Birth rate
1963	42	1969	20
1964	28	1970	14
1965	26	1971	12
1966	24	1972	11
1967	27	1973	10.5
1968	25	1974	10

The Wolfson graph obviously is not the one photographed by Berliner. It covers two additional years and the values differ—by as much as ten points per thousand in one instance. Most curious is that the Berliner graph shows a dip for 1967 whereas the Wolfson graph shows a peak. Moreover, the contour of the trend line in the Wolfson graph indicates that specific values were plotted for the first four years, a single value was used for 1967-68, and a freehand curve was drawn in for the remaining six years, apparently in lieu of plotting data. It is difficult to believe that a model unit chosen as a showplace for foreigners would lack current birth rates. Even more significant is the implication that old data are subject to rather extensive retrospective revision.

Urban Birth Rates

Urban vital rates for the 1960s are as rare as those for rural areas, and the reporting units are at least equally atypical. Only Shanghai has reported separate figures for the central city and the "suburbs," a term that refers to the municipal counties outside the central city and therefore embraces an indeterminate proportion of nonurban population. For Shanghai Municipality as a whole, the birth rate was reported as 30 per thousand in 1963, the rate for the central city was 23, and that for the suburbs was 41.[31] Birth rates of 43.4 in 1963 and 23 in 1965 were reported for Peking Municipality[32] and a birth rate of "about 23" for Nanking "around 1966."[33] Nanking Municipality claimed a birth rate of 41 per thousand in 1963.[34] In three of these four cases, the 1960s birth rates were cited in the 1970s to show subsequent progress in lowering birth rates.

No other birth rates are available for entire cities of municipalities during the 1960s. However, Sian Municipality reported a natural increase rate of 40.5 in 1963 and 17.4 in 1966, which, if the registered death rate were around 7 per thousand, as in the late 1950s, would imply that the city's birth rate fell from the upper forties to the middle twenties in a three-year period.[35]

An interesting series of urban birth rates for the 1960s is reported by the Shih-jen-chang coal mine in northern Kwangtung Province:[36]

1964	59
1969	12
1970	10.9
1971	6
1972	6

How large a population is involved is not indicated, but the mine area apparently includes at least 16 different residential communities. The source also implies that the 1964 birth rate was a peak figure and the actions that brought about the decline in fertility began in 1968. The timing is strange. The peak coincides with the year of the 1964 investigation, when other urban units were showing declines, hence the peak cannot be explained as the result of belated birth registration prompted by the investigation. If the almost 80 percent reduction in the birth rate during the 1960s was a response to the resumption of birth control work in 1968, which would mean that the demographic consequences would have been largely confined to 1969, this could be the most spectacular planned fertility decline on record. How was it accomplished?

The source, which dates from the middle of 1973, also a year of intensified birth control efforts, is not altogether explicit about the tactics used. It does say that the "leading bodies" of the mine "placed family planning work on the order of the day" and made sure that it was treated as "an important item when studying, arranging, checking up, and summing up work." Leaders had "heart-to-heart talks" with those reluctant to accept family planning, and population plans and measures for their implementation were drawn up each year.[37] The methods and the phrases used to describe them were not adopted until several years after the beginning of the third birth control campaign. They are not those in vogue during the 1960s. The story therefore has a rather anachronistic sound. This does not necessarily mean it is fabricated, but it is a reminder that the purpose of news items reporting on birth control work is to support current family planning efforts, not to provide an accurate historical account.

Provincial and National Vital Rates

From the fragmentary rural and urban vital data for the 1960s, it might be inferred that no data were available for larger units or that the data available did not indicate progress in health and family planning work or were otherwise unsuitable for public dissemination. However, in July 1978 the most complete series of provincial vital rates thus far released in the PRC was obtained in Kwangtung Province by Pi-chao Chen.[38] The series includes figures for 1962 and 1965, for which years the birth rate declined from 43.3 per thousand to 36.28 and the natural increase rate from 36.8 to 29.6. The natural increase rates reported for Kwangtung in the 1960s are somewhat higher than the only other provincial rates available for the 1960s, a rate of 25 for Hopeh and 27.5 for Kiangsu, both for 1965.[39]

At various times during the 1960s and early 1970s, foreign visitors to China were given national population growth rates that could be taken as approximations of the national natural increase rate and an indication of the level of fertility reflected in official data. The rates for the 1960s range from just under 2 percent to 2.5 percent, the high point reportedly being reached in 1962 or 1963.[40] However, recently there have been several indications that new estimates of the level of natural increase during the 1960s have been prepared that are much higher than those used previously.[41]

The Second Birth Control Campaign

Contemporary descriptive materials do not offer much basis for judging the effectiveness of the second birth control campaign. Much of the press coverage at the time consisted of direct appeals to the population to practice late marriage and contraception and efforts to allay anxieties about the side effects of chemical contraceptives, the intrauterine ring, and sterilization. Many of the appeals were in the form of testimonials from men and women who had accepted late marriage, contraception, or sterilization and were reaping the happy rewards. Often the testimonials indicated that much community and familial opposition had been encountered and that conforming to birth control policy required exceptional courage and persistence. The fact that progress reports were few and equivocal suggests that birth control had not made much headway even in the most favorable situations, otherwise the exceptions would have been held up for emulation as with other popular campaigns before and since.

Significance of the 1960s Data

What then is to be inferred from the few data released during the 1970s indicating falling birth rates during the 1960s? Certainly they do not support a conclusion that there were substantial reductions in fertility in the country as a whole during the decade. It is virtually certain that birth control achieved no significant penetration in rural China. Less certainty can be attached to conclusions about possible successes in selected urban areas, but the absence of success stories in news accounts of the 1960s is curious, particularly in view of the magnitude and abruptness of the declines indicated by some of the recently issued figures. If such data were available at the time, surely some local administrator would have cited them in order to claim credit for the achievements.

Actually, a gradual decline in the national birth rate during the middle 1960s is not altogether implausible. Changing age composition would have had a depressing effect on the birth rate from the early 1950s through the next 20 to 25 years. Social, economic, and political factors also may have had some effect, particularly in urban areas, but their significance is easily overestimated. The birth control campaign probably contributed little to the trend, and the trend itself may have been reversed temporarily by a rebound in fertility after the food crisis of 1960-61, and again around 1970 following the rise in marriage rates at the end of the Cultural Revolution. In the absence of empirical corroboration, however, neither the belatedly cited vital rates for the 1960s nor the alternative speculations can be regarded with much confidence. For the present, no firm conclusions can be drawn about either the level or the trend of the birth rate in the PRC during the 1960s.

THE FERTILITY DATA OF THE 1970s

The scarcity of population data eased somewhat during the 1970s. Beginning in 1972, foreign visitors to the PRC were occasionally given local vital rates, data on age at marriage, and numbers of acceptors of contraception, sterilization, and abortion. By 1973 such data also began to appear in press and radio news items on birth control and public health. Other items contained local population totals, usually rounded and undated. In fall 1976 and for more than a year thereafter, provincial population totals in millions or tens of millions were cited frequently in news dispatches. These figures also were undated. Since 1976 birth and natural increase rates have been released for about one-third of China's provinces, often to three or four significant digits and almost always precisely dated. Until 1979 national data were limited to population totals in hundreds of millions that were usually imprecise and undated. In 1979 the State Statistical Bureau once again began to release national population totals and rates of growth, and other Chinese sources began to cite current national vital rates. Chinese statisticians traveling abroad during that year indicated that the bureau had complete national series of population totals and vital rates from the 1950s to the present, except for a gap during the Cultural Revolution years for which estimates had had to be made in lieu of reported figures. They expected the figures would be released in due course, and a few have already appeared.

As of the present writing, only about 100 mortality rates of various kinds have been released for the 1970s, but there are around 175 birth rates and around 300 natural increase rates. Up to this point, the birth and death rates have come mainly from reports by foreign visitors; news items from China seldom cite these rates. Moreover, of the units for which the news items provide rates, less than one-third are urban, whereas of the units for which the sources are visitor reports, about two-thirds are urban or suburban. Chinese sources indicate that in 1978 the urban population was "over 110 million" in a total population of about 958 million, or over 11.5 percent.[42] The vital rates come from about 200 reporting units of varying size, from the country as a whole down to rural brigades and urban factories and neighborhoods. The numbers of rates and reporting units increase year by year, especially in the spring.

Rural Vital Rates

Most of the reported 1970s vital rates for small rural units indicate very low levels of fertility, mortality, and natural increase, and, where figures are provided for two or more years, very sharp declines in birth and natural increase rates. Among the rural units for which birth rates for the 1970s are available, a brigade in Hopeh Province claims to have reduced its birth rate to "around 10" per thousand during 1974-76, and one in Kwangtung Province reports a rate of 12 to 13 for the five-year period from 1968 through 1972.[43] Several other brigades report rates in the teens and twenties. Some other rural units report much lower birth rates. Among the 10 rural units visited by the Wheat Studies Delegation in 1976, for which 1975 birth rates were reported, one was as low as 10 per thousand, another 9, another 8, and still another 5.5. But the death rates for the same units were also extremely low, and the units with the lowest birth rates tended to be the ones with the lowest death rates. If the same situation holds in the rest of the country, a part of China's apparently high achievements in birth control and health work may be due to low achievements in vital registration.

The rural natural increase rates thus far reported include quite a number of very low figures. Among the lowest are a rate of less than 5 per thousand for a brigade in Hopeh Province in 1975, a rate of under 4 for a commune in Shantung Province in 1974, a rate of under 3 during "the past seven consecutive years" for a commune in Chekiang Province, a figure of 2.2 for another brigade in Hopeh in 1975, and a figure of 1 per thousand for a commune in Hunan Province in 1977.[44] These are all relatively small units, but among the 40 or so Chinese counties for which natural increase rates are available as of the present writing, about two-thirds claimed rates as low as 10 per thousand or less by 1978, among them Hei-shan County, Liaoning Province, with a rate of 5.1 in 1974, Nan-kung County, Hopeh Province, with a rate of 2.64 in 1978, and Chiang-chin County, Szechwan, with a rate of less than 2 per thousand in 1977 and 1978.[45] The lowest rates for rural units available thus far are those implied by a recent report that in "one county, 4 districts, 56 communes and towns and two neighborhood offices" in Kewichow Province, presumably as of the end of 1978, there was "no population growth for the last two years."[46]

Urban Vital Rates

The birth rates and natural increase rates reported for urban areas are generally below those for rural areas. The highest birth rates cited for the 1970s range from the low twenties to almost 30 per thousand, but all of the figures are for years prior to 1973.[47] Some other municipalities claimed much lower rates. Shanghai reported a birth rate for the municipality as a whole of 12 per thousand in 1971, around 10 in 1972, and 9.19 in 1974, and a central city rate of between 6 and 7 per thousand during the same years. Nanking claimed a rate of 11 for the municipality and 8 for the central city in 1975.[48] Wuhsi claimed a birth rate of "about 10" for its rural components and "under 10" for the city proper in 1975.[49] Smaller components of cities boasted even lower rates. It may be significant that, unlike some of the advanced rural units, most of the urban units were cited only once, early in the 1970s; few have provided recent figures.

Most of the natural increase rates given for urban populations are quite low. Taking first the rates for whole municipalities, which sometimes include significant rural populations, Suchow reported a rate of 5.4 per thousand for 1972, Peking a rate of "less than 5" for 1977, Yangchow 4 per thousand for 1973, and Shanghai 3.36 for 1975.[50] Other municipalities claimed less progress in reducing natural increase. Canton reported a natural increase rate of 14 per thousand, Loyang, 18, and Anyang 21.7 for 1972.[51] In the few cases for which both central city and rural hinterland figures are available, the central city figures are lower. The lowest figures are for parts of cities; for example, Tientsin's Ho-p'ing District, with a natural increase rate of 3.66 per thousand in 1978, Shanghai's T'ien-shan Street, with 2.86 in 1978, and Nanking's Wu-la Street, with 0.7 in 1972.[52]

Vital Rates for Larger Units

Natural increase rates are available for 18 of China's 26 provinces, but of these 18 only Kwangtung provides birth and death rates. By 1977 six provinces claimed to have reduced natural increase to less than 10 per thousand, and by 1978 there were eight making the same claim, led by Szechwan, China's most populous province, with a rate of 6.06.[53] The list is curious in several respects. It does not include several provinces that have claimed relatively rapid progress in birth control work, but it does include Jupeh Province (and Tientsin Municipality), which had previously said little or nothing about progress in birth control work. The provinces of Hopeh and Kiangsu, cited earlier as leaders in birth control work, seem to have been hard pressed to sustain the decline in their natural increase rates. Kiangsu apparently had to exert major efforts to get its rate down from 10.02 in 1976 to 9.97 in 1977, and no precise figure has been released for 1978. Yet Szechwan, a late starter and in some respects a rather backward province not too easily controlled from Peking, is now reported to have snatched the lead.

Other provinces have given much higher rates of increase, particularly several that have admittedly encountered difficulty in family planning work. One of the most laggard, Kiangsi, reported a rate of 21.58 for 1977 and 19.7 in 1978.[54] Two other notoriously backward provinces, Fukien and Yunnan, have yet to provide natural increase rates.

From 1958 until 1978, no national vital rates were released through any channel, public or private. Chinese officials occasionally cited population growth rates, sometimes for specified years, and some of the citations were contradictory. There were numerous references to an average annual population growth rate of 2 percent over a span of many years. But late in 1978 a news dispatch from Kweichow Province noted that one of its counties had attained a natural increase rate of 12 per thousand in 1977, thus "reaching the average level for the whole country."[55] Since this almost inadvertent disclosure of the national natural increase rate for 1977, the director of the State Statistical Bureau, Ch'en Hsien, revealed to Courtenay Slater, chief economist of the U.S. Department of Commerce, during her visit to China in May 1979, that the 1977 population growth rate was 1.212 percent, which is almost exactly equivalent to a natural increase rate of 12 per thousand.[56] Still more recently, on June 27, 1979, the State Statistical Bureau included in its statistical communique on the 1978 national economic plan (the first such communique issued by the bureau in 20 years) a natural increase rate of 12 per thousand for 1978, which a later source gave as 12.05 per thousand.[57] The second source also gave the 1978 birth rate as 18.34 per thousand, which implies a death rate of 6.29. Other recent sources have provided a 1977 death rate of 6.9,[58] a 1971 natural increase rate of 23.4,[59] and a 1963 natural increase rate of 33.5 and birth rate of 43.6, implying a death rate of 10.1 per thousand.[60]

Even the most recent of the figures now available for the country as a whole seem to pose some anomalies. The 1978 natural increase rate is not quite consistent with the 1978 population growth rate that can be derived from the national population totals for yearend 1977 and yearend 1978 also released recently by official sources, which is about 1.36 percent.[61] To rationalize away the inconsistency would require the assumption that net in-migration into China amounted to 1.4 million persons during 1978, but this is impossible. Chinese sources have indicated that the influx of Chinese refugees from Vietnam during the year was only 200,000,[62] and this influx was partly offset by an accelerated exodus into Hong Kong during the year. The Chinese authorities are aware of the discrepancy and explain it as due to the fact that the national vital rates are estimated based on incomplete vital reporting.

Changes in Vital Rates

The local, provincial, and national birth and natural increase rates now being reported are quite low and, if reasonably accurate, would indicate a major change in the level of fertility in China. The figures are, in some cases, roughly consistent with other data for the same units on increasing compliance with the stipulations on age at marriage and increasing use of contraception, but this is not a sufficient basis for judging the plausibility of the vital rates. The only other basis of judgment is the rapidity of the changes in vital rates in units for which figures for two or more years are given.

Among the units for which a series of figures extending over several years is provided, a common phenomenon is a sharp drop in the birth or natural increase rate followed by a much slower rate of decline or, in some cases, even a rise. The initial decline is often so sharp that it cannot be satisfactorily explained as a result of a change in popular values about family formation, even assuming an aggressive program of mass indoctrination. Ironically, the most spectacular declines are not those for cities and municipalities, even though Chinese officials say that the urban areas have responded more readily to the family planning campaigns than the rural areas (see Table 4.4). The reason seems to be that among the urban units the decline in fertility began earlier and covered a longer time span, whereas many of the rural units did not do much about reducing fertility until recently, when they were suddenly brought under extreme pressure from higher authorities.

Chinese news dispatches almost never cite birth rates for the exemplary rural units, but the changes in natural increase in these units are very sudden. For example, the natural increase rate of Lai-hsi County in Shantung Province reportedly went from 28.61 per thousand in 1970 to 8.62 in 1974, a decrease of 70 percent in four years, while the rate for Nan-kung County in Hopeh went from "over 15" in 1972 to 3.83 in 1974, a decline of 75 percent in two years. The

TABLE 4.4

Vital Rates for Kwangtung Province, Two Counties, a Rural Commune, and Sian Municipality, 1970-77 (per thousand population)

Year	Kwangtung Province			Tao-yuan County, Honan Province			Heng County, Kwangsi Chuang Autonomous Region			Wan-t'ou Commune Han-chiang County, Kiangsu Province			Sian Municipality, Shensi Province		
	BR	DR	NIR	BR	DR	NIR	BR	DR	NIR	BR	DR	NIR	BR	DR	NIR
1970	29.24	5.78	23.46							30.9	6.5	24.4			
1971	29.02	5.52	23.50							24.3	8.4	15.9	24.45	5.46	18.99*
1972	28.55	5.97	22.58	28.97	9.73	19.74				18.4	7.3	11.1	21.11	5.49	15.62
1973	27.21	5.95	21.26				34.1	7.7	26.1	14.9	7.0	7.9	17.67	4.95	12.72
1974	23.91	6.30	17.61				31.1	7.3	23.8	15.2	7.7	7.5	16.20	5.32	10.88
1975	21.01	6.06	14.95	21.88	9.01	12.87	27.9	6.4	21.4	18.9			15.45	6.12	9.32
1976	18.85	6.25	12.60	18.48	8.82	9.66	21.1	6.4	17.7	17.8	6.4	11.4	14.88	6.23	8.65
1977	18.58	5.97	12.61	15.30	9.08	6.22	20.2	5.7	14.5	16.4			15.88	5.87	10.01

*Derived figure. The originally reported figure seems to be in error.

Sources: Wan-t'ou Commune figures: Table dated November 7, 1978 provided by Nicholas R. Lardy, based on data obtained during a visit in May-June 1978. Other figures obtained by Pi-chao Chen during a visit in June-July 1978.

rate for Tu-shan County in Kweichow went from 21.8 in 1975 to 9.7 in 1976, a drop of over 55 percent in one year. Yen-tai Prefecture in Shantung reported a natural increase rate of 23.4 in 1970 and 11 in 1974, a drop of more than 50 percent in four years, and Chiang-chin Prefecture in Szechwan reported rates of 22.65 in 1974 and 3.07 in 1978, a drop of 86 percent in four years.[63] Given the size of these units (the two prefectures have reported populations of 9 and 7 million, respectively) and the fact that they are predominantly rural areas, such radical changes are in need of further explanation.

Although the units cited in birth control progress reports are undoubtedly those considered to be exceptionally successful in birth control work, the declines in natural increase reported by a number of provinces suggest that most other local units have not been far behind the leaders in reporting falling fertility during the 1970s. Hopeh and Kiangsu were reportedly the most successful among the provinces in the middle 1970s. Hopeh reported a natural increase rate of 20.24 in 1970 and 8.75 in 1977.[64] Kiangsu reported 15.09 for 1972 and 9.97 for 1977.[65] Szechwan, China's most populous province, was one of the highest among the provinces in 1970 but was the lowest in 1978. The Szechwan figures are given as follows:[66]

Year	Natural Increase Rate
1970	31.21
1971	28.96
1972	—
1973	26.92
1974	22.91
1975	—
1976	12.25
1977	8.67
1978	6.06

According to these figures, the natural increase rate declined by 47 percent between 1974 and 1976 and by about 30 percent in each of the next two years. Other provinces made less startling claims. The unweighted averages of the available provincial natural increase rates for 1970-71 and 1977-78 come surprisingly close to the national natural increase rates for 1971 and 1978, respectively, and the percentage decline over the seven-year period is the same—49 percent.[67]

Not all units have been able to sustain their progress toward lower fertility levels. Some of the urban natural increase rates that declined during the early 1970s have recently shown signs of rising again,[68] and several provinces have recently reported rising increase rates. Liaoning gave its natural increase rate as 8.87 in 1977 and 12.5 in 1978, and said it was still rising in 1979. Hunan's rate rose from 10.82 in 1977 to 13.9 in 1978. Kwangtung reported a low point of 12.60 in 1976, after which the rate rose to 14.75 in 1978, and fears were expressed in the middle of 1979 that it could go as high as 16 by the end of the year. Honan reported, without giving figures, that its natural increase rate rose in 1977 and 1978 and was still rising in the first months of 1979.[69] The failure of the national natural increase rate to decline between 1977 and 1978 suggests that, in computing national averages, the rising rates reported by some provinces were sufficient to offset the falling rates reported by provinces like Szechwan.

The Credibility of the Data

Whatever the difficulties of the moment, the local and national vital rates, taken at face value, indicate a revolutionary change in the level of fertility and the rate of population growth in China within the short span of seven or eight years. Are the figures to be believed?

The reactions of foreign observers to the Chinese data range from utter incredulity to a willingness to impute to the Chinese more success than they themselves claim. The truth undoubtedly lies somewhere in between, but where?

Several Chinese social scientists who have recently visited the United States have insisted that vital registration in China is complete and accurate because registration records are used to allocate food and cloth rations and for other purposes that require personal documentation. But, with a few exceptions, the Chinese authorities have always assumed that demographic data systems work as they are supposed to work and seldom question anomalies in the data. During the 1950s, Hsüeh Mu-ch'iao, the first director of the State Statistical Bureau, rated population statistics among the more defective categories of data compiled by the bureau, but little was said in the statistical journals of that time as to the extent and direction of the biases.[70] There are also indications that Chinese statisticians recognize a need to examine critically the population data reported by the provinces and that they are checking past population data before issuing a national series. They also plan to investigate the completeness of vital registration at the time of the next census, now scheduled for June 1981. Meanwhile, until there is a careful analysis of China's population data, there is an inevitable tendency on the part of both Chinese officials and foreign observers to treat the data as essentially accurate.

There are, however, several good reasons to resist that tendency. One is the almost universal bias of vital registration systems toward the understatement of vital events. Even in countries where there are as many needs for registration records as in China and where the registration system is not used to impose unwelcome social controls, not all births, deaths, and other vital events are registered. Some degree of underregistration is virtually inevitable. Chinese spokesmen, including Mao himself, have noted that some families fail to report deaths so that they can retain the rations of the deceased.[71] If deaths can be concealed, so (presumably) can births.

A second reason is that vital rates are used as a means of measuring the effectiveness with which health and family planning policies are being implemented at the provincial and local levels. The provincial and local Party leaders are responsible for seeing to it that the target birth and natural increase rates and other quotas relating to family planning assigned by higher levels are achieved on schedule. Some sources seem to indicate that the vital rates cited in the provincial and national family planning conferences do not come from the registration records maintained in the local public security police dispatch stations, but are instead obtained from records maintained by the local family planning committees. If this is the case, the rates are compiled and reported by the very people whose work they are used to evaluate. Whatever the actual arrangement, it is evidently not wholly corruptible, otherwise there would be no reports of backsliding provinces and the national natural increase rate for 1978 would not have failed to meet the target. But one cannot assume that because some bad news is reported, all good news is true and the bad is no worse than it appears.

Thus far there have been no reports from China of falsification of vital rates or fabrication of "typical examples" of high achievement in birth control work. However, other reports, though less explicit, make it clear that falsification is not unusual. A Peking newspaper accused Chiang Ch'ing of insisting that "data must be obtained with the needs of the struggle in mind and not for their own sake,"[72] an idea closely akin to some of those advanced during the "Hopeh reform" of statistics in 1958 that led directly to the statistical exaggerations of the Big Leap Forward.[73] Another report suggested that the falsification of data was sometimes due to efforts to meet reporting deadlines for data not yet collected and sometimes due to the fear of criticism, presumably in case the actual figures did not measure up to expectations.[74]

Media personnel sometimes invent news to support current campaigns, presumably at the instigation of higher authorities. A dispatch from Kwangsi asserted that reporters would "supply you with what you wanted," including making up stores about "things which are nonexistent," exaggerating, "voicing empty words," and fabricating "typical examples." The account concluded, "These practices must be eliminated . . . before we can restore the honesty of the Party newspapers."[75]

The same pressures that cause production cadres to exaggerate, falsify, and fabricate are brought to bear on family planning cadres and on their superiors in local Party and government units. The family planning program has its quotas to be filled and targets to be met, and the same superiors who look for good news in the economic sphere want good news about birth control. Hence it is very likely that some falsification and fabrication takes place in birth control progress reports. Local cadres who hesitate to engage in outright deception of higher authorities may nevertheless be little inclined to improve on the completeness of vital registration, which would only detract from their apparent success. Therefore, the reported birth, death, and natural increase rates for all large units are probably below the actual levels. How much below and what the cumulative effect on the national rates may be cannot be determined until independent, well-designed, and well-executed surveys are taken to measure the direction and magnitude of the errors.

Nevertheless, even if the actual vital rates are somewhat higher than those now reported, there seems little reason to doubt the general conclusion shared by foreign analysts and the Chinese authorities that an unprecedented reduction in fertility has taken place in China during the 1970s. The magnitude of the deception required to produce the current national vital rates in the absence of a real vital revolution would be equivalent to that perpetrated in agricultural statistics during the Big Leap Forward of 1958, when a modest bumper crop was turned into a doubling of food grain output in one year.[76] But in about four months the illusions conjured up by the Leap collapsed, and the agricultural miracle of 1958 was scaled down to the more modest exaggeration of a 35 percent increase over 1957.[77] Presumably the current claims about progress in reducing fertility and population growth rates could not be sustained for as long as they have been already unless they were at least broadly consistent with popular knowledge. Moreover, there are enough corroborative details about contraceptive usage, numbers of abortions and sterilizations, and locally declining school enrollments to lend strength to the statistical evidence that the Chinese birth rate has taken a marked turn downward.

CAUSES OF THE DECLINE IN FERTILITY

If fertility has in fact declined sharply in China during the 1970s, what factors are responsible for the trend? Three general explanations have been put forward, and they are not mutually exclusive. One is that fundamental social and economic changes have taken place in China since 1949 that have eroded traditional values supporting large families. A second is that the family planning campaigns have succeeded in convincing a majority of the population in the childbearing ages that a smaller family size is in the best interests of individual couples, the local communities, and the country as a whole. The third explanation is that, by a combination of indoctrination, incentives, pressures, and outright coercion, many Chinese families have been induced to limit their childbearing. The first explanation implies that the decline is spontaneous, the second that it is at least voluntary, the third implies that it is in large measure involuntary.

Social and Economic Changes

The idea that since 1949 China has undergone a profound social and economic transformation that has reoriented values and restructured basic human relationships was widely accepted among foreign observers until very recently. Even cautious China specialists found it difficult to avoid being influenced in some degree by the claims of social and economic progress that were standard fare in the Chinese media in good times and in bad during most of the first three decades of the People's Republic. In 1978, however, much more pessimistic assessments of China's domestic developments during the preceding 20 years began to appear in press and radio dispatches in response to Teng Hsiao-p'ing's new policy of "learn truth from facts," which called for greater objectivity and candor (at least in reviewing the past). As a result of the new revelations, it now seems questionable whether the changes in those parameters that are thought to be related to the level of human fertility have been enough to bring about a spontaneous decline in the birth rate.

Living Standards

One of the most pervasive ideas among foreign observers is that living standards have steadily improved in China since the 1950s, not only in the cities but also in the countryside, and that the net gain has been substantial. This perception led many observers to suppose that an incipient consumerism may have already begun to provide China's masses with incentives to control family size. But recent new dispatches seem to indicate that the rise in living standards has been confined for the most part to urban centers and a few rural areas and has not been very great. Highly placed Chinese officials have complained that the misguided policies of the previous leadership have cost China at least ten years of economic stagnation. Some of the assessments seem to imply no significant economic progress since the Leap Forward. In September 1978 the New China News

Agency said that the level of production in China "is still very backward," that the gap between Chinese and foreign technology was large, and that at one point the nation's economy was "on the brink of collapse."[78] Subsequent sources indicated that the economy had been "stagnant for a long period of time,"[79] its agricultural foundation is very weak,[80] the countryside had faced a shortage of grain "for a number of years,"[81] and "100 million people throughout the country do not have enough food."[82]

The problem of low living standards is most acute in the rural areas, in spite of longstanding policies designed to erase rural-urban differences.[83] Hsueh Mu-ch'iao, who, since his recent rehabilitation, has been an authoritative spokesman on economic matters, told a symposium in Peking in fall 1978 that income differentials were greater in rural than in urban areas and that while a few rural areas developed rapidly, many more developed slowly or not at all. He noted that, in spite of considerable investment in agriculture in the two decades since collectivization, "agricultural production has not developed correspondingly."[84]

The reasons for the slow development of China's agriculture were discussed extensively in the media during the second half of 1978. In an editorial, the People's Daily asked, "What is the main obstacle to rapid development in agriculture?" The answer given was that "irrational burdens" on the peasants had dampened their "enthusiasm" for production. The specific nature of the burdens was revealed in this and subsequent sources: increases in production that do not result in increases in the peasants' income, promised income distributions that are not made, levies of labor, money, and materials are imposed on the peasants without remuneration, and the prices paid to the peasants for agricultural products are deliberately held down while the prices of the industrial products they purchase are inflated even though the products are often of poor quality and deliveries shortweighted.[85]

Any notion that China's peasants might have been motivated during the 1970s to limit family size because of rising living standards, then, is obviously unfounded.

Although they are generally better off than the peasants, China's urban workers are also far from prosperous. The PRC has been following a policy of "lower wages, wider employment" since its founding, with the expectation of "gradually improving the people's livelihood on the basis of increased production."[86] But due to the economic stagnation of recent years, there have been long periods with no wage increases. The first in many years was granted as of October 1, 1977 to some 60 percent of state-employed wageworkers. The raise amounted to about 10 percent, but the People's Daily explained that the increase was "not a large one because the country is poor."[87]

Despite a policy of overhiring, China's unemployed are presently estimated at 20 to 40 million, rural surplus labor is again being discharged into the cities, jobs are being sought for some 7 million unemployed young people in urban areas, and urban youth must be resettled in the countryside because of the lack of employment.[88]

The increase in urban wages also brings its problems because the supply of consumer goods is limited. Not only food, cloth, and cooking oil, but also furniture, sewing machines, bicycles, watches, television sets, pottery, and even soap require ration coupons or other authorization to purchase.[89] In such circumstances, wage increases do not necessarily lead at once to the kind of consumerism that is believed to have contributed to declining fertility in Western countries.

Urbanization

The urbanization of the population, which in other settings is thought to produce major cultural and social dislocations that free individuals and households to pursue their own self-interest without regard to traditional imperatives of family and community, has probably had only a limited impact on overall fertility levels in China. Chinese officials believe, and the available evidence tends to confirm, that family planning is more readily disseminated in urban than in rural areas, but the data thus far released are confined to a few large metropolitan centers. Also, it is not clear at this point whether or not there has actually been an increase or a decrease in the proportion urban among the population in the 26 years since the 1953 census, when it was reportedly found to be 13.26 percent.[90]

Aside from the question of whether the urban population has grown or declined in recent years, it is questionable whether either the large or the small cities in China are comparable to cities in the West or in other parts of Asia in the amount of social mobility, economic opportunity, and personal freedom they afford. Hence the significance of urbanization in China for value change in respect to childbearing and family size is dubious. The more rapid adoption of family planning by large city populations in China may be due not so much to value change as to the greater effectiveness of policy enforcement in urban than in rural communities.

Emancipation of Women

Much has been made of the emancipation of women in Chinese publications for foreign consumption and in Western analyses of the changing role of Chinese women. Some foreign analysts have inferred that in China the liberation of women has been completed and Chinese women now enjoy equality with men. However, much evidence from China indicates that this is not the case. In both urban and rural areas there have been marked increases in labor force participation by women since 1949, but the trend has not been steady, and the changes are difficult to measure because of statistical anomalies. Data are few and fragmentary. Often no indication is given whether the numbers cited represent full-time or part-time employment. Nevertheless, working with the available data, one analyst has estimated that the total number of women between the ages of 15 and 59 who were employed in rural China ranged from 40 to 75 million in 1953-54, from 75 to 100 million in 1965, and from 135 to 155 million in 1978.[91] It was recently reported that the numbers of women workers in industry, communications, transport, finance, and trade has increased "from some 3 million in 1957 to nearly 30 million now."[92] If these figures refer to urban women, they imply a rise in the proportion of urban women in the labor force from about 11 percent in 1957 to about 95 percent at present, but the latter figure seems too high and should not be accepted without confirmation. The urban population totals for 1957 and 1978 may not be comparable, or the 30 million figure may include some rural women.

Not only the change in proportions but also the socioeconomic significance of employment may be greater for urban than for rural women. Rural Chinese women have always made an important contribution to agricultural work, and the incompatibility between childbearing and work outside the household is probably not as great in rural as in urban communities in China and throughout the world. But Chinese women are still discouraged somewhat from seeking employment by unequal treatment on the job. Chinese sources indicate the wage differentials by sex and other forms of discrimination against women workers continue and that women in both rural and urban areas still have a way to go to achieve comparable status with men. The principle of equality was laid down by the Party leaders before 1949, was reaffirmed in the Common Program of 1949 and the Marriage Law of 1950, and was the subject of a Party directive in December 1971.[93] However, in September 1978 K'ang K'o-ch'ing, president of the National Women's Federation, was still calling for implementation of the policy that "men and women are equal" and the principle of "equal pay for equal work."[94]

One reason progress has been slow is that the position of the Party leaders on employment of women has not been constant. At the Third National Women's Congress in September 1957, the main theme was the importance of women's work in household management. Employment for women was discussed largely in terms of auxiliary production within the family as a contribution to family income.[95] At that time maintaining full employment for men was regarded as enough of a problem without taking women into the labor force in large numbers. A year later, during the Leap Forward, masses of women were drawn into production, and large numbers of mess halls and child care facilities were hastily organized to facilitate their emancipation. With the collapse of the Leap, women were returned to domestic occupations.

Within the Party leadership there seem to have been differences of opinion about the desirability of going much beyond the token stage in the emancipation of women. After the Third National Congress, 21 years elapsed before the next congress was convened; within the interval, it is now alleged, the National Women's Federation was "forcibly disbanded," its work was "interrupted for 11 years," and "to varying degrees women's federations at various levels were forced to suspend operations."[96] The fault is now ascribed, like all other faults, to Lin Piao and the gang of four, but as the _People's Daily_ noted in a 1978 editorial, their "pernicious influence" on employment of women remains "quite profound" more than two years after their downfall.[97] Under these circumstances, the significance of the figures on employment of women as an indicator of changing attitudes toward family planning can easily be exaggerated.

Collectivization

The aspect of the Chinese revolution that has presumably had the greatest impact on the lives of workers and peasants is collectivization. Despite the assurances given during the land reform movement of 1950-53 that peasant ownership of land would be allowed to continue for at least 15 years, the collectivization of agriculture proceeded at an accelerated pace under direct orders from Mao in 1955 and 1956. The nationalization of urban enterprises was completed at about the same time, virtually eliminating private ownership of the means of production throughout the country. But the transformation of human motivation from individual selfishness to collective altruism that was supposed to ensue has not yet been realized. Individual economic incentives apparently have been dampened by the practice of allocating work points and distributing agricultural income to peasants on an equal basis without regard to individual differences in "the quality of labor."[98] These practices are now denounced as egalitarian and blamed on the gang of four, but Hsüeh Mu-ch'iao thinks they have their roots in some unsolved problems in "the relations of production," which, after two decades of collectivization, "many people" still allegedly "do not understand."[99] This is probably as close as one can come in China at present to an open admission that collectivization has not worked very well.

If the effects of collectivization on incentives for production have been minimal, it is unlikely that the effects on attitudes toward childbearing would have been profound. In fact, there were reports that some families were less inclined to limit fertility immediately after collectivization because they expected the collective to come to their aid if they encountered hardships in the future.[100]

There are some indications that the dependency of urban youth lasts longer now than it did in the early 1950s, particularly with the increasing problem of unemployment in the cities, the lack of self-sufficiency of urban young people resettled in rural areas, and the apparently considerable numbers of rural transferees who return without authorization and live off their families because they are unregistered and hence not eligible for employment in urban enterprises. But in the rural areas some of the remuneration systems still favor families with a large number of working members. The usefulness of child labor in private subsidiary production has probably helped to maintain the economic advantage of large families.[101] In both rural and urban areas, children are still perceived as a source of economic security in old age, because most rural communities have not yet established retirement systems for their members. A recent source says that "at present only a few well-to-do communes and brigades" can afford retirement systems. Of those that could, many have not set them up because their leaders view retirement as a family concern.[102] All in all, collectivization has probably not had much direct effect on attitudes toward childbearing in China.

Literacy

Increasing literacy and educational attainment in China are sometimes cited by foreign analysts as factors favoring fertility decline, again on the assumption of analogy to Western experience. The analogy is not very appropriate. There has undoubtedly been a considerable increase both in marginal literacy and in the average level of formal schooling in China since 1949, but the significance of these trends as indicators of cultural change is questionable.

The amount of progress is itself subject to much ambiguity, in part because both literacy and education have had an up-and-down history throughout the last 30 years. It has often been alleged in Chinese sources that the Chinese people were 80 percent illiterate at the time of liberation in 1949. The new leaders immediately undertook a commitment to raise the level of education among China's workers and peasants. In 1953 they launched what turned out to be an ill-conceived mass campaign to provide literacy training for the children of peasants, which was later criticized as a case of "blind adventurism" that resulted in the "early loss of knowledge hastily learned."[103] Concern about a repetition of this misadventure was expressed in 1955, when the central authorities called for a new drive aimed at "basically" eliminating illiteracy among young people within seven years, or by the end of the Second Five-Year Plan period. It was estimated at the time that there were some 100 million youth in rural China, of whom 70 million were illiterate or semiliterate.[104] By the end of 1956, with some 62 million peasants in literacy classes, it was discovered that "adventurism" and "commandism" were rampant, "objective conditions" were disregarded, and plans were being set at "excessively high levels," with the result that some of those who had completed the literacy courses had lapsed once more into illiteracy.[105] On the other hand, many areas had relaxed their efforts and were failing to meet their targets. The goals of the campaign were modified to make them easier to attain, and by September 1957 it was claimed that the number of former illiterates in China who had learned to read since 1949 had reached 22 million.[106]

The Leap Forward of 1958 pervaded the literacy program as it did all other aspects of domestic policy in China at that time. At first only a minor acceleration of literacy work was called for, but by May 1958 the leadership had become impatient with gradual progress. At the rate at which literacy work had advanced during the previous eight years, in which an average of 3 million persons reportedly became literate each year, it was anticipated that it would take another 50 years to bring literacy to the estimated 150 million rural illiterates between the ages of 14 and 40. Instead, the task was to be accomplished within the next five to ten years, which would have meant that 30 to 40 million persons must acquire literacy each year beginning in 1958.[107] At once, various provinces announced crash programs; within a few months, some proclaimed that they had "basically" wiped out illiteracy. Although between 1949 and 1957 only 27,970,000 persons had become literate, the total of new literates between January and September 1958 was put at 100 million.[108]

Like many other Leap Forward claims, this one seems to have been largely a statistical fiction. From 1958 onward the citation of national literacy figures was discontinued. How much progress was made in Leap literacy classes may be judged from the fact that in subsequent years new literacy campaigns were mounted, even in provinces that had claimed at the height of the Leap to have eliminated illiteracy.

In a Peking suburb that had boasted that 90 percent of its people were literate in September 1958, a 1960 investigation found that "large groups of new literates had already relapsed into illiteracy."

By early 1960 the numbers of illiterates and semiliterates in the area amount to 34.6 percent of the population. In one dictation test, only 28.4 percent of those tested were able to write correctly 60 or more of the 100 characters in the test.[109] During the rest of the 1960s, little was said about illiteracy work.

In the 1970s reports from the provinces again referred to the problem of having to deal with large numbers of illiterates. In July 1978 Li Chi, vice-minister of Education, said that "owing to the sabotage of Lin Piao and the gang of four in education, China still had a fair amount of illiteracy, mainly among the peasants." In October 1979 another source stated that "China still has 100 million young and able-bodied adults who are illiterate or semi-literate."[110] There has undoubtedly been some improvement in overall literacy as a result of these efforts, and certainly the rising proportion of the population with at least an elementary education should have had some effect. But the extent of literacy in China is probably much less than foreign observers and the Chinese public have been given to understand. Furthermore, it is not clear that literacy in China means that the masses are made much more susceptible to a change of values, even where the reading material consists largely of propaganda intended to bring about such change.

Educational Attainment

The development of public school education in China since 1949 has followed a course that is similar, though not quite parallel, to that of the literacy program. The central authorities attached great importance to education initially, and in 1951 there was a marked increase in the numbers of primary schools and in primary enrollments in China. But from 1952 through 1955 enrollment figures almost leveled off at about 51 to 53 million. In June 1954 the Second National Education Conference was told that primary and secondary education would not be developed further and that young people should be directed toward work in the fields and factories.[111] At the beginning of 1956, there were still only 51 million children in primary school in China. During the year another policy shift took place and enrollments rose again, reaching 63 million.[112]

The Leap Forward increased primary school enrollment still more sharply to 86 million, an expansion achieved without a commensurate investment of resources by a policy of "letting the masses run their own schools." How much education went on in these or in any other schools in China during the Leap is uncertain. The qualifications of the newly recruited teachers, some of whom were parents pressed into service as instructors, could not have been very high. It was asserted that the standards in the people-run schools often equaled those in the government-run schools, but they were not expected to meet those standards and most probably did not.[113] The curriculum in some cases was reduced to reading and how to use the abacus, and even these studies apparently took second place to production activities. Although reported primary enrollment peaked in 1964 at 130 million, the educational significance of this figure is dubious.

During the 1960s and the first half of the 1970s, populist ideas about education dominated the thinking of the central leadership. At the start of the Cultural Revolution in 1966, schools at all levels were closed throughout the country so that students could rampage through the cities and the countryside in the name of the revolution and Chairman Mao. In 1967 and 1968 efforts were made to reopen the schools and get the students to go back to their studies, but there was much resistance. Many sources indicate that the students preferred to go on "wandering about, free and unrestrained" and that the teachers, whom the Cultural Revolution had subjected to "mass criticism and repudiation," "re-education and remolding," and "ideological revolutionization" were afraid to teach. Many students were convinced that "study is useless" and many teachers that it was "no good being a teacher." Schools were supposed, while educating, to run farms and factories and supply labor needed to maintain production.

Not much serious learning took place under these circumstances. Looking back on that experience, Education Minister Liu Hsi-yao said that "because of sabotage of the gang of four, schools were for years in a state of chaos and their general mood was not sound."[114] In any case, the chaos attributed to the gang lasted until after Mao's death and the succession of Hua Kuo-feng in fall 1976.

In 1978 it was reported that enrollment in the primary schools had reached 146,164,200 in 1977, which was said to be 95.5 percent of those in the eligible ages.[115] But in view of the anti-intellectual philosophy that dominated Chinese education between 1958 and 1976, the attainment of virtually universal primary education does not signify the kind of liberal enlightenment that has elsewhere been associated with the erosion of traditional values supporting high fertility.

Familism

Over the years, many of the domestic policies of the PRC seem to have been aimed at weakening the traditional ascendancy of family and kinship over the individual, the community, and the state. The Marriage Law of 1950, the implementation of which was promoted vigorously in mass campaigns in 1951 and 1953 and less strongly in later years, was concerned primarily with instituting freedom of marriage and equal rights for women, prohibiting bigamy, concubinage, and child betrothal, and permitting the remarriage of widows. In pursuing these objectives the campaigns also sought to "eliminate the influence of reactionary social customs within the consciousness of the people."[116] However, the most conspicuous immediate consequence of the Marriage Law was a sharp increase in litigations over divorce and other domestic quarrels and a rash of divorces, murders, and suicides.[117]

Other government policies put new strains on marriage and family relationships. One was the practice of assigning husbands and wives to work in different parts of the country, which separated them for long periods. Only recently the Shanghai Municipal Party Committee decided to arrange for the return to the city of husbands and wives of Shanghai residents who had been assigned elsewhere.[118]

In the 1960s women were advised to break away from the narrow sphere of traditional domesticity and find happiness in work, careers, and political action. The small family of husband, home, and children was said to be inferior to the big family of the collective.[119]

Most of the problems discussed in the journals for women and youth were those of young urban Party cadres and were probably not widely shared among the rest of the urban, let alone the rural, population. But the institution of the people's communes in 1958, with the induction of both men and women into vast manual labor projects, the placement of preschool children in child care facilities and school age children in boarding schools, the substitution of mess halls for home cooking, and the consignment of the aged to "happiness homes," was perceived for a time as a major revolution in both urban and rural family life. The popular reaction was strong and negative. Critics charged that these arrangements meant the segregation of husbands from wives and parents from children, the dissolution and destruction of the family, and the "end of natural and kindred relationships of man." The Party spokesmen replied that they were not trying to destroy the family but to bring an end to the patriarchal system. When that was accomplished, "the only difference between men and women . . . [would be] a physiological one," and the net result would be to make family life "more salubrious and blissful."[120] With the collapse of the Leap Forward and the retrenchment of the communes, the attainment of the promised bliss was postponed a while longer.

From many recent news items it is apparent that the fire has not yet gone out of the ashes. Matchmakers still ply their trade, wedding feasts and exchanges of gifts continue, and some marriages are still arranged by parents.[121] The efforts to eradicate these influences have probably made some progress, but the power of family ties has not been broken. Even among leading Party cadres, instances are reported periodically of the use of political position on behalf of family members and the use of family affiliations to enhance political power. Party leaders have attempted to have their children exempted from mandatory rural assignments and to get them into the universities outside the normal admissions route. If the family still counts in the circles where political principles supposedly rule supreme, it can hardly have crumbled away in peasant and worker circles.

Declining Infant Mortality

One change affecting family relationships that the PRC sought deliberately and quite successfully to bring about was the reduction of infant mortality. During the 1950s considerable progress was made in improving famine relief, in mass immunization against infectious diseases, and in diffusing modern methods of child delivery and maternal care, which probably caused a sharp decline not only in infant and maternal but also in general mortality. Statistical support for this conclusion is limited to infant mortality rates for a few cities, some sample rates for rural and urban areas, and several national rates of dubious origin, all of which have probably been affected in varying degrees by underregistration and tend to understate the actual levels of infant mortality. An American medical delegation to China in summer 1973 was given an infant mortality rate of 8 per thousand live births for the city of Shanghai, but when they asked Vice-Premier Li Hsien-nien about this ridiculously low figure, he told them not to believe it. He thought it probably applied only to a small section of the city.[122] During the Cultural Revolution Mao charged that the Ministry of Health had failed to provide health services for rural areas, contradicting the impression given earlier by the Chinese press. However, even allowing for statistical deficiencies and other impediments, it is likely that infant mortality has declined markedly from the extremely high levels that prevailed in the past.

The effects of declining infant mortality on attitudes toward family formation are also indeterminate in the absence of reliable data. Current birth control propaganda argues that, because of higher survival rates for infants, it is not necessary now to have as many births as were formerly required in order to assure the continuity of family lines. However reasonable, the effectiveness of this argument in persuading people to have smaller families depends upon whether Chinese parents think in terms of an ideal number of surviving children and are prepared to stop having children when that number is reached.

This attitude would not be consistent with the traditional view that happiness means numerous descendants, which implies no upper limit. It is also in conflict with the views of many families, especially in rural areas, who see economic advantages in enlarging the family labor force.[123] Besides, it is doubtful whether many of the families that could accept the notion of a family size limit would be willing to set it as low as the officially established quotas of one or two children per couple.

Increasing Population Pressure

It is conceivable that an awareness of population pressure and some of its adverse consequences may have contributed at least to a greater understanding of the need to control population growth and therefore to increased acceptance of family planning during the 1970s. The economic problems caused by rising population densities and declining ratios of arable land per capita have been discussed extensively in the Chinese media during the past two years, but to what extent they have entered the consciousness of the masses is not clear. There have been a number of complaints recently about food shortages, some of which have taken the form of protest marches that appear to be wholly spontaneous.[124] However, given the fact that some of the local shortages have been caused by excessive mandatory sales of crops to the government, some peasants may not be easily persuaded that population growth is the underlying cause. Even if some of the hungry recognize that their numbers may have something to do with their distress, it is quite another matter to translate that awareness into a desire for smaller families.

Urban residents may have a somewhat clearer understanding of the connection between population growth and the already acute shortages of food, clothing, housing, other consumer goods, and employment in their communities. Many of them must have recognized years ago that the long-standing policies on the transfer of urban youth to rural areas were being pushed, in spite of considerable resistance from the young people and their parents, because of the lack of employment opportunities for youth in the cities. In January 1978 a New China News Agency dispatch said that, "in the past 10 years and more," the transferees numbered "well over 16 million."[125] The connection between the "rustication" program and city population growth was recently made more explicit in some cities by the institution of a policy of guaranteeing to parents who agree to have only one child that their child will never be sent down to the rural areas.[126] The discussions of the problems of surplus labor in rural and urban areas, which have become numerous in the Chinese media since early 1979, may also in time affect popular values relating to family size, but they are too recent to have affected the birth rates reported to date.

In summary, it appears that socioeconomic change in China has not been as rapid or as profound as the Chinese media seemed to claim prior to 1978. Some of the changes in China since 1949 may have contributed to a small extent to popular motivation to limit childbearing, particularly the increasing employment of women, the decline in infant mortality, and the mounting population pressures. But these factors are insufficient to account for the sudden marked decline in the birth rate that has occurred during the 1970s. That phenomenon must be in large measure a direct result of the third birth control campaign.

The Third Birth Control Campaign

Why has the current birth control campaign been so much more successful than its predecessors? Has public education, propaganda, and indoctrination succeeded in altering traditional values supporting high fertility even in the absence of significant economic incentives for family limitation? Or is the decline in fertility due instead to a combination of rewards, penalties, pressures, and coercion? Within the mix of administrative expedients, which has contributed most to the restriction of childbearing? Is the change essentially voluntary, or are a majority of the Chinese people being obliged to limit their families against their will?

To understand the greater effectiveness of the current birth control campaign, it is important to note the ways in which it is unlike its predecessors. There are five significant differences: the current campaign has been assigned a much higher priority than the earlier ones; the official rationale for reducing birth and natural increase rates is more plausible and conveys a greater sense of urgency; organization and control have been tightened; the promotional tactics are much more aggressive; and the campaign has been sustained without significant interruptions for a longer period.

Higher Priority

When the third birth control campaign began in 1968, the storm of the Cultural Revolution had not yet subsided, the Maoist youth gangs were still on the rampage, and the administrative apparatus, which had been under constant attack during the struggle, had not had time to recover. Initially, the new campaign seemed hesitant and lacking in conviction. During 1968 and 1969 it consisted mainly of appeals to young people not to succumb to Confucian notions about filial piety reportedly being spread by some cadres, or to be swept away by the "wave of getting married now" that was surging through

Shanghai and other cities.[127] In 1970 and 1971 birth control propaganda was resumed in some areas, but the campaign did not gather momentum until late 1972 or early 1973.

Already, however, there were signs that the leadership intended to attach higher priority to birth control than in the past. One was the fact that Mao was for the first time personally identified as a strong supporter. At first what Mao had actually said about birth control was not revealed. His injunction to "be prepared against war, be prepared against natural disasters, and do everything for the people" was sometimes cited as an endorsement of birth control, although the connection was less than obvious.[128] However, in 1977 and 1978 several explicit statements in support of birth control made by Mao during the 1950s were published for the first time. In his "National Program on Agricultural Development" in 1956, he had said that "except for sparsely populated areas inhabited by people of minority nationalities, it is necessary to publicize and promote birth control, and planned parenthood in all densely populated areas," and had directed that population growth plans be included in the five-year plans in subsequent years.[129] In his speech to the Eighth Central Committee of the Chinese Communist Party in October 1957, Mao had recognized a long-term need for birth control and called for a ten-year family planning program, including "open education" for the masses and gradual dissemination until the practice became universal. This speech contained the assertion, often quoted without attribution early in the 1970s, that population growth was in a state of "anarchy."[130] Of course, Mao had also made other statements in 1949, 1957, and 1958 in which he scornfully rejected the idea that China might need to control population growth,[131] but these have not been quoted in domestic media since the third campaign began.

Although in April 1956 Chou En-lai had told foreign visitors that China needed population and therefore did not need birth control, and had expressed only lukewarm support for birth control in his report on the Second Five-Year Plan in September 1956,[132] his remarks to foreign visitors on the subject of birth control during the 1960s and the early 1970s were much more positive. Still, during his lifetime, he, like Mao, was not identified with the birth control program through direct and unequivocal declarations.[133]

Hua Kuo-feng's involvement in birth control was much more recent than that of Mao and Chou, but in his case also the details were not revealed until late in 1976. At that time it was reported that at some unspecified earlier time Hua had "acted as a leader of the birth control leadership group of the State Council, . . . personally worked out the annual plans for birth control work, personally attended every report meeting . . . , listened soberly to the reports made by representatives from various places, and made notes."[134] In February

1978 Hua told the Fifth National People's Congress that "family planning is a very significant matter" and issued a call to reduce population growth to less than 1 percent within three years, a target subsequently adopted by the State Council as a national objective.[135]

Teng Hsiao-p'ing has not yet publicly committed himself to the birth control program, but it has certainly been greatly accelerated and intensified since his reemergence as a central figure in the Chinese leadership. Moreover, both the State Council and the Party Central Committee were linked with birth control when they issued a joint directive on the subject in 1971.[136] The prominence given in recent news items to pronouncements by Ch'en Mu-hua, a vice-premier and chairman of the State Council's family planning group, and Vice-Premier Li Hsien-nien, a senior member of the top leadership, clearly attests to the strength of high level support for family planning work.[137]

Lest there be any doubt about the permanence of the priority assigned to birth control, which has had its ups and downs in the past, some Chinese sources emphasized that planned population growth was an "established" policy of the Chinese government.[138] Any remaining uncertainty was removed in March 1978 by the inclusion in Article 53 of China's new constitution of a statement that "the state advocates and encourages family planning."[139]

The Official Rationale

As the third campaign unfolded, the official rationale justifying the family planning effort became much more forceful and the argument more fully developed. At first the explanations were stereotyped and superficial, and sometimes bordered on sophistry. The current rationale seems to be essentially Malthusian, despite the continuing denunciations of Malthus.

From 1968 to 1971 a number of sources, mainly from Shanghai, put forward a composite rationale that included the protection of maternal and child health, revolutionizing the thinking of young people, boosting public morale, and consolidating the "dictatorship of the proletariat," and the dubious proposition that in a planned economy population growth must also be planned—hardly the kind of message that could stir the multitudes. Early in 1973 several sources said that family planning was needed to improve "the people's welfare," that a large population in little land made double-cropping essential to increased rice production, and that birth control could help to raise living standards.[140] But these reasons do not suffice to explain the marked intensification of the birth control effort in 1973.

Apparently the central authorities were not ready at that point to acknowledge openly the real basis for their rising concern about population growth. In international meetings in 1973 and 1974, the Chinese representatives emphatically denied that population growth posed serious problems. At the Twenty-ninth ECAFE session in Tokyo in April 1973, the Chinese delegate, Chi Lung, reaffirmed Mao's old claim that people are a positive resource for national development because they tend to produce more than they consume. He argued that the fundamental cause of backwardness in Asia and the Far East was not population growth but imperialism, colonialism, and neocolonialism, that in China's case population had increased during the previous 24 years by an average rate of only 2 percent per year, whereas the rate of increase in grain production had been 4 percent, and that the Western notion that population growth posed insoluble food problems was "nonsense."[141] At the United Nations World Population Conference in Bucharest in August 1974, China's experience once again was cited to show that population growth is no deterrent to economic progress. Although living standards in China were still admittedly low, they were "steadily improving."[142]

Even after the fall of the gang of four in September 1976, there was no immediate change in the arguments advanced by the authorities, but here and there a few more pessimistic notes began to be sounded. At a Ta-ching conference in May 1977, Vice-Chairman of the Party Central Committee Yeh Chien-ying said "only if agriculture is run well can the problem of feeding our 800 million people be solved. . . ." He quoted an earlier statement by Mao about the importance of agriculture that concluded with the warning:

> Take heed, for it is very dangerous not to grasp grain production. If this is ignored, there will be widespread disorder some day.[143]

In retrospect it is obvious that the Party leaders, regardless of faction, were much less optimistic about China's population problems than they chose to appear.

Early in the 1970s the provincial and central authorities already had in their possession data and information that indicated serious problems, some of which were made public in 1978. In February 1978 the first secretary of the Kirin provincial Party committee charged that the former "principal person" in the committee had ignored birth control and "caused disastrous results" in agriculture; in 1976 Kirin's grain output was only 63.8 percent greater than in 1949, but the population was 119 percent greater.[144] In April a Kwangtun Party leader mentioned a provincial conference in 1972 that concluded that the province was making little progress in agriculture, the increase in grain production was below the national average, and in some places the level of the peasants' grain rations was low.[145] In July the Kiangsu

Party secretary said Kiangsu was a "small, heavily populated province" with an average of "less than one mou of arable land per capita."[146] In September the Szechwan Daily said the level of grain production and distribution in the province was so low that after selling grain to the state, some production teams had to buy back grain in order to feed their people.[147] The Fukien first secretary said that in his province "the speed of increase in grain production does not match the speed of population growth,"[148] and the first secretary of the Kwangsi Region said that because of population growth "the average area of farmland . . . per person has decreased."[149]

By May 1978 the somber note had begun to be sounded by the national media also. An article in a Peking newspaper stated that

> The problem of food is after all the basic problem of economic life, particularly in our country, where the production force is backward. The problem of feeding hundreds of millions of people has not yet found a solution.[150]

In June a Red Flag article said that because China's population was growing fairly rapidly and the country was technically and economically backward, the available capital and consumer goods were limited and the country lagged behind others in labor productivity and economic development. Therefore, the writer argued,

> China must control the growth of its population while striving to increase the national income rapidly. Only in this way will it be possible for the country to accumulate more funds for its construction and improve its people's life.[151]

During the remainder of 1978 and throughout 1979, a grim realism pervaded most discussions of the relationship between population growth and economic development. The problem of food supplies emerged as a matter of grave concern. In October Hu Ch'iao-mu, president of the Chinese Academy of Social Sciences, made the startling revelation that the average per capita grain for distribution in 1977 "only matched that of 1955," which, he said, "shows that grain increases were only sufficient to compensate for increases in consumption caused by population growth and industrial use."[152] In February 1979 a Peking University professor disclosed that the amount of food grain per capita in 1977 was actually lower than that for 1957. In the interval, he said, the population had grown by 300 million, but the amount of arable land in China had decreased by 100 million mou.[153] The newly available figures not only discredited the previously cited figures on the relative rates of increase in population and food grain, which were based on the depressed and probably incomplete grain totals for 1949 and therefore exaggerated the increase in grain, but they also showed that 22 years of collectivization in China's agriculture had failed to increase the per capita availability of food grain.

During 1979 concern about declining ratios of food grain and arable land per capita became recurrent themes in both national and local discussions of the need to control population growth. National sources said that solving the problem of feeding "a population of 800 million" was "a momentous question," the national average grain allotment of a little over 600 catties per person was "far insufficient" to meet consumption needs, the rate of growth of marketable grain was "even less encouraging," and China's grain rations were among the lowest in the world.[154] While national sources were calling attention to the fact that per capita food grain in the country as a whole had not increased, provincial sources reported significant declines.[155] A critical factor in the food situation was the fact that with an absolute decline of 6 or 7 percent in the amount of arable land, the figures on arable land per capita were falling sharply.[156] One source indicates that arable land per capita amounted to about 3 mou in 1949 but had since dropped to about 1.5 mou,[157] and another adds that per capita arable land would fall to 1.28 mou by the end of the century if population growth continued at 1 percent per year, or to 0.96 mou if population grew at 2 percent.[158] Ch'en Mu-hua and other leaders pointed out that the land under cultivation was not enough for a population as large as China's, reclamation of wasteland was too expensive to afford much relief, and the level of output on the existing cultivable land could not be raised significantly within a short period of time.[159]

Uncontrolled population growth had other adverse consequences. A writer in a Shanghai newspaper pointed out that

> Housing is one of the most important things in the life of the masses. It is also closely related to population growth. From 1956 to 1977 the state invested over 35 billion *yuan* in urban housing, five hundred million square meters of new residential space were added. According to statistics as of the end of 1977, per capita living space in the cities was 3.6 square meters, which is 0.9 square meters less than the 4.5 square meters at the beginning of liberation. This shows that even though the state spends a large sum of money annually to solve the housing problems of the masses, the critical situation in housing has not been relaxed. An important factor is that the population has been increasing too rapidly.[160]

Several sources related population growth to excess labor supply in both urban and rural areas, which caused serious problems of unemployment, especially in the cities, and low levels of labor productivity, especially in the rural areas. A writer in the People's Daily said that "the cities are now over-populated," the task of finding employment for the 2 million urban young people who reach working age each year was "extremely difficult," the labor resources available in the cities were more than sufficient already, and it was "imperative" that urban population growth be controlled.[161] A New China News Agency reporter said that "generally speaking, China's labor force on the agricultural front is too large" and "the overly large labor force is one of the important factors that have retarded China's agricultural mechanization."[162]

The low standard of living in most of the country was also attributed to the excessive population growth.[163] Two writers in a Peking paper listed the very low living standards of the people among China's serious population problems.[164] Ch'en Mu-hua warned that if population growth were uncontrolled, the "four modernizations" would be hampered, the scientific and cultural level of the nation could not rise, and the people's living standards would decline.[165]

Many sources spoke in more general terms of the need to control population growth either to hasten national economic development or to assure that it would occur at all. Some suggested that "unrestrained" population growth would put the national economic plan out of balance.[166] Several sources cited calculations of the cost of child-rearing to the state. One of these noted that, "according to calculations by relevant units," each child costs the state 500 yuan by the time it reaches school age.[167] Other sources said that by a "rough estimate," raising a child to age 16, when it can take part in manual labor, costs 1,600 yuan in rural areas, 4,800 yuan in towns, and 6,900 yuan in cities, including the costs of primary and middle schooling.[168]

However, it is doubtful whether or to what extent couples in the rural areas or even in the cities of China can be persuaded to limit childbearing voluntarily by arguments that relate to the general development of the economy or to the financial burden children impose on the state. One writer pointed out that in the matter of population growth, "there exists a contradiction between the private interests of the family and the public interest of society and between the immediate interests of the individual and the long-term interests of society." In the past, he continued, not enough attention was paid to the development of policies that would bring the disadvantages of population growth to bear directly on individual families.[169]

The specific nature of the contradiction is made clear by several sources. A journalist who interviewed cadres and commune members in a suburban area of Peking reported that the majority of retired commune members rely on their children for economic support, and that under present economic conditions, peasants with only one child would have a difficult time once they stopped working. This, he said, was the reason why many commune members still believe they need children to have security in their old age.[170] A Honan commune that had made initial progress in birth control work, and later experienced a rising natural increase rate, conducted an investigation that found the reason was that the burden of household chores was greater for families with few children. When they got sick there was no one to help care for them, hence many commune members came to the conclusion that "life is difficult without children."[171] A writer in a Shanghai paper said the standard argument in Chinese birth control propaganda that popular notions about the desirability of having many children was merely a feudal conception inherited from the "old society" was, in truth, a "one-sided view." It was "unrealistic," he said, to demand that families ignore their own economic interests in deciding how many children to have. The problem for birth control, he added, is that "in our cities, and especially in our rural areas, there are some economic advantages to the family in varying degrees in having a large number of children, and especially of having a large number of sons." He then pointed out that, because of the low level of productivity in rural areas and the fact that children became economically productive at an early age, they actually do increase the family income, and thus there is some basis for the feeling that the cost to individual families of raising many children is well repaid by the added security in later years.[172] At least until 1979, many areas were still allowing full adult grain rations for infants and children.

Given the marginal economic circumstances in which many Chinese live in both rural and urban areas, they may understandably be reluctant to risk their future by having fewer births on the chance that the four modernizations may bring them a degree of economic security other national economic policies during the past 30 years have often promised but never delivered.

Improved Organization and Control

One of the serious shortcomings of the first two birth control campaigns was the lack of effective organization in birth control work due to an inadequate chain of command from the central to the local levels. National policy declarations were not followed by firm administration actions at the provincial level, let alone in the factories and communes across the land. Local guidance committees were set up in some areas during the first campaign, but these quickly vanished during the Big Leap Forward of 1958. They were reestablished after the start of the second campaign, and there was some effort to get local Party leaders to play a more active role in them. However, up to the start of the Cultural Revolution, central exhortations could not be transmitted to the local units without a considerable loss of force.

The basic organizational apparatus for birth control work used during the current campaign does not seem to differ greatly in form from the models that were supposed to be followed in the earlier campaigns. The "leading groups" at all levels correspond approximately to the "guidance committees" of previous years. The linkages between the local planned parenthood organs and local health, labor, women's, and production organizations, and the use of birth control "detachments," propaganda teams, surgical teams, and activists are not new, nor are the efforts to combine birth control drives with other campaigns and programs, such as the elimination of the "four pests," the environmental sanitation drives, the checkups on women's diseases, antischistosomiasis work, the campaigns to learn from Ta-chai and Ta-ching, the campaign against the gang of four, and the campaign for the four modernizations. However, the involvement of local Party cadres and Party leaders at all levels has become much more extensive and direct. There seems to be a much more effective system of inspection and reporting, so that local cadres are held accountable for what happens or fails to happen in the units under their control.

During the first years of the third campaign, the organization of the work was evidently not regarded as very satisfactory. But as the campaign unfolded, Party leaders at all levels began to play an increasingly important role in the work. By 1978 birth control was the "task of the whole Party," requiring the full mobilization of the Party cadres. By 1979 local Party cadres were supervising, reviewing, and doing field work at the "grassroots" level.[173] The direct and extensive involvement of the Party in planned parenthood work at all levels is undoubtedly a major factor in the comparatively greater success of the third birth control campaign.

Aside from direct Party involvement, two features of current administration seem to have contributed to the effectiveness of the work, at least as judged from official progress reports. One is the demand that local efforts be inspected by higher level authorities, and the other is that regular progress reports be submitted to higher levels for comparison with the reported achievements of other units.

The practice of holding regular conferences and report meetings at national, provincial, and lower levels became well established in 1978 and 1979. On these occasions, outstanding units and their leaders were commended and laggard units brought under increasing pressure to catch up with the rest. Shensi Province called upon its Party committees to "search out the leadership responsible" for units that did poorly in birth control work, and Hunan Province ordered that backward units be criticized and excluded from consideration as model units. Individual cadres who were negligent of family planning work or failed to set examples themselves were to be subjected to severe disciplinary action, and several specific cases have recently been cited in the media as a warning to others. How effective the increased pressures on the cadres may be in actually securing more conformity among the masses with the objectives of the birth control campaign cannot be judged only on the basis of exhortations and punitive actions. Deception of higher levels by those below is still possible, and the imposition of penalties for poor performance may add to the incentives for concealment and falsification as well as to incentives for conscientious work. But clearly a much greater effort has gone into organizational work in the late 1970s than in either of the two previous campaigns.

More Effective Tactics

Because the Party leaders are more deeply involved and organization is tighter, propaganda tactics that were unsuccessful in the previous campaigns may be more effective in the present campaign, and some that could not be attempted earlier can now be implemented. All of the promotional means that were employed before are in use again, including films, lectures, dramatizations, study sessions, exhibitions, posters, newspaper and magazine articles, and mass meetings. Young people registering for marriage are lectured on the appropriate ages for marriage and the need for birth control. Women in the childbearing ages are reached through maternal and child health clinics. Activists and cadres visit people in their homes, especially those reluctant to limit their childbearing or pregnant out of turn, and have "heart-to-heart talks" with them until their resistance collapses.[174] Old ideas about marriage and childbearing, the importance of having many children, the advantages of sons over daughters, and the reliance on children as a source of security in old age are systematically and repeatedly attacked and ridiculed in birth control propaganda. All of these approaches were tried in the earlier campaigns.

Among the new tactics developed during the present campaign, one is the very prominent use of what are called "typical examples"—units or individuals considered outstandingly successful in birth control work who are held up for emulation by other units. Their use was mandated in one province as follows:

> It is imperative to grasp typical examples and use the experience gained in one place to guide the work of other places. Each municipality or region must assign a county

as a typical unit for the rest of the counties to follow, and each unit must have its own typical example.[175]

The most celebrated of the county level typical examples is Ju-tung County in Kiangsu Province, which has been given national attention for its progress in lowering birth and natural increase rates. In March 1978 a provincial telephone conference on birth control work directed planned parenthood leaders throughout the province to "launch an emulation drive for catching up with and overtaking Ju-tung County." Subsequently, its exploits were even serialized for foreign consumption in the Peking Review.[176] During 1979 Szechwan emerged as the leading province in birth control work, and other provinces are now urged to follow its example. Whatever else the typical examples in birth control work may be, they are certainly atypical. The reports of their accomplishments tend to convey an exaggerated impression of actual or potential progress. However, the extensive use of model units for emulation in planned parenthood and other mass campaigns shows that this is still regarded as an effective tactic.

Another new approach in the third birth control campaign is the setting of target figures for late marriage, contraceptive use, sterilizations, birth rates, and natural increase rates and the mobilization of the masses to meet or exceed the target figures. This tactic is combined with the formulation of collective and individual family birth plans at the local unit level and efforts to hold people to their commitments. The idea of obliging individual families to prepare birth plans and making these plans a public matter was tried out toward the close of the first birth control campaign, when it was reported that women with two or more children were promising to have no more during the Second Five-Year Plan period, women with one to have only one more, and women with none to have not more than one.[177] Nothing was said about birth plans and public pledges in the media during the second campaign, but the idea was revived early in the third campaign and has now become the principal means of bringing direct pressure to bear on individual couples to prevent unauthorized births.

In the first half of the 1970s, the birth plans were linked to recommended family size limits for individual couples, which seem to have varied somewhat from place to place. Primary sources said little about ideal family size, but visitors to China were told that urban families were supposed to have not more than two children and rural families three, or, in some cases, four.[178] By the end of 1977, Chinese sources began to call for a universal limit of two children per couple.[179] By the end of 1978 the precept was "one child, two at most."[180] When birth quotas were allocated to local units on the basis of the target increase rates, the allocation was distributed among the eligible couples on a priority basis, first priority going to couples with no children, second to couples with one child born several years earlier, and third to couples with one child born recently.

The system of target setting was elaborated over the years until by now it is supposed to reach from the central to the grassroots level and to govern all individual birth plans. The national targets are established by the State Council. According to one probably idealized description, the government makes preliminary proposals on the basis of "investigation and research" that local levels review in the light of their own conditions. Their suggestions are supposedly sent back up the line and are taken into account in the determination of the final target figures. These figures come down once more to the local levels as their assigned "tasks" under the state plan. This method is supposed to "coordinate" the "demands of the state" with local conditions, thus assuring that the targets are realistic and attainable.[181]

However, there are indications that in practice the suggestions from local units do not confront the demands from the higher levels on an equal footing. A Kiangsi provincial birth control conference in 1978, for example, was given instructions that leave little room for doubt as to where the basic decisions on plans and targets are made: "All places should work out population plans according to state plans and implement them in every production team, workshop, and street residents' committee."[182] Although provincial and local units frequently fail to fulfill their assigned targets and probably complain to the higher authorities that the targets are unreasonable, the fact remains that the instructions come from above, and the lower levels are under considerable pressure to carry them out.

The pressures presumably intensified in spring 1978 when Hua Kuo-feng called for the reduction of the national natural increase rate to less than 1 percent within three years, a goal that the central authorities insisted was entirely feasible. Several provinces promptly adopted this target as their own, and some that had already reported natural increase rates as low as 10 per thousand set targets well below the national figure.[183] Within a year, a number of provinces had run into difficulties. Fukien found that it was "very far from hitting the targets laid down by the state," and Kwangtung, Liaoning, Honan, Tientsin, Shanghai, Peking, and Canton were experiencing rising increase rates.[184] Nevertheless, the national targets were not greatly modified. Probably the national and the provincial targets are deliberately set at impossibly low levels simply to sustain the pressure on local units.

The tactics used at the subprovincial level to encourage local cadres to keep up their family planning efforts include public recognition and commendations for leaders of advanced units, and the awarding of "red banners," "typical example" status, and even television sets, which are usually conferred at special planned parenthood rallies or "congresses of progressive collectives."[185] Local units are encouraged to emulate the more advanced units, and periodic inspections are made by higher levels, on the basis of which the backward are compared with the progressive and then help up to public criticism.[186] In one province it was stipulated that any unit that failed to reduce its natural increase rate below 8.5 per thousand or did not achieve a 90 percent utilization rate for birth control among eligible couples would not qualify as a "learn from Ta-chai" unit.[187]

The local leaders in turn bring pressures to bear on the people in their units to adhere to their birth plans. With the first intensification of the third birth control campaign in 1973, mass mobilizations and public criticism were used to secure compliance in units that took the lead in birth control work. One such unit described how it "mobilized the masses to revise their next year's birth control plans," applied "mass criticism" to "shatter" their old-fashioned ideas about the value of children, and "strengthened solidarity" among a group of 21 women members of a production brigade "who should have controlled their childbearing but did not."[188] Often pressure is focused directly on resistive individuals. In 1975 the Party secretary and other cadres of a brigade in Kwangtung Province visited the home of a commune member who had had four daughters and refused to be sterilized. There they had "heart-to-heart talks" with him until he gave in.[189] In 1979 a Shanghai woman commune member discovered "not acting according to the demands of planned parenthood" was visited repeatedly by the team leader, who had "heart-to-heart talks" with her until she adopted birth control measures.[190] In another case, a women who was "not complying with the demands of planned birth" was visited more than 20 times before she was "convinced."[191] There have been reports by foreign visitors of individual childbearing records and birth plans posted by name on factory walls, with the apparent intent of placing women under collective surveillance to assure the observance of birth plans. Although most of these tactics have their antecedents early in the third birth control campaign, they have apparently been carried further and disseminated more widely within the past few years.

Since the beginning of 1979, two important new developments have taken place in birth control promotional tactics. The first is the sharply increased efforts to persuade more couples to limit themselves to a single child and to restrict the third and higher birth orders. The second is the adoption of regulations at the provincial level throughout the country that establish rewards for one-child families and punishments for couples who have three or more children.

The new policy on family size was announced by Ch'en Mu-hua at a national family planning conference held in Peking from January 4 to 18, 1979. At that time Ch'en stated that families should be encouraged to "have only one child or two at most" and that "restrictions should be placed on those who had too many children."[192] Soon afterward, provincial spokesmen were upholding the one-child family as the ideal and urging that it be "promoted with great effort."[193] Some units went further still. Shanghai issued regulations calling on each couple to have only one child; Heilungkiang declared that "from now on . . . a married couple should give birth to only one child"; Kansu's regulations stated that "a married couple may have only one child"; Tientsin told family planning workers in suburban counties that as of the fourth quarter of the year they "should see that the practice of bearing more than one child is stopped in the main," and Kweichow issued a "new requirement" that "we had better have only one child."[194]

Meanwhile, special attention was also directed at eliminating third births. In February 1979 Shensi announced as a target that no married couple should give birth to a third child, and Anhwei warned that "to produce a third child is to violate the state regulations."[195] In July Ch'en, in a lecture to the CCP Central Committee Party School in Peking, said that "resolute action should be taken to prohibit the birth of a third baby," and even suggested that, according to a new planned parenthood law still in preparation, "strict measures will be enforced to control the birth of two or more babies."[196] Thereafter, calls for action against those having third children acquired a flinty hardness.

Both the one-child ideal and the prohibition against third children have been reinforced by elaborate systems of rewards and punishments that have been established under regulations adopted at the provincial level during 1979. The regulations vary somewhat from place to place, but they bear enough similarity to each other to show that they followed a common model provided by the central authorities. During the first half of the year, the provincial regulations were usually described as "trial" regulations, and they apparently required prior approval by Ch'en Mu-hua before they could be regarded as fully in effect.[197]

The first reference to provincial regulations appeared in a January 1979 news dispatch describing new trial regulations in Kwangtung that promised preferential housing allocations for couples who married late and limited themselves to two children; immunity from transfer to rural areas or early return if already transferred for the children of urban families with only one or two children; preference in job assignments for the children of parents with only one child or two daughters; waiver of schooling fees from nursery through secondary school for one-child families; and the allocation of an adult's grain ration for only children in rural areas.[198]

In February Szechwan Province also announced that it had drafted trial regulations.[199] However, the first of the provincial regulations to be described in detail in a source available outside China were those "initially formulated" at a planned parenthood congress in Anhwei in mid-March and described at length in a radio broadcast on April 18.[200]

The Anhwei regulations and the comments of the "responsible person" quoted in the broadcast reflected a strongly punitive attitude toward families that have three or more births, which was rationalized on the grounds that, given "the country's actual conditions," such families were adding to the burdens the state has to bear. Therefore it was "reasonable and just" that they should themselves be made to carry a greater burden. The 12 regulations stated, among other things, that each one-child family is to be given:

1) A planned parenthood "glory" coupon.
2) Priority in getting the child admitted to nurseries and kindergarten.
3) Priority in medical treatment and hospitalization for the child.
4) Health expenses for the child from age 4 to 14, the rate of 5 Yuan a month for only sons and 6 Yuan for only daughters in urban areas and 30 health expense supplementary workpoints for only sons and 40 points for only daughters in rural areas.
5) The same housing space as is allowed for two-child families [for urban families].
6) An adult's grain ration for the child [for rural families].
7) Priority in labor recruitment and school enrollment as among equally qualified children. [This provision also applies to families with two daughters.]

Families who have a second child after having been rewarded for their single-child status must surrender their planned parenthood glory coupons and pay back all of the other financial and workpoint benefits they have received.

Parents who have a third or additional child within six months after the promulgation of the regulations are to be subject to the following sanctions:

1) A 5 percent reduction in their total income in urban areas and 5 percent reduction in total workpoints in

rural areas from the time the child is two weeks old up to age 14. For a fourth child the deduction is 6 percent, for a fifth 7 percent, and so on.

2) Their third and later children are not allowed to take part in the comprehensive medical systems or labor insurance treatments provided by urban enterprises.
3) Their third and later children are not to be allowed to obtain food grain at special prices after they reach the age of 14.
4) No ration coupons are to be issued to their children before the age of 14 for supplementary foodstuffs or commodities except for cloth.
5) No financial assistance is to be allowed these families in case of future economic hardships, and they are to receive no extra housing space or private plots.

In addition to these penalties, disciplinary action is to be taken against "individual cadres, staff, and workers who insist on practicing anarchism in parenthood, cause a bad influence among the masses, and commit relatively serious offenses," and those who fail to practice planned parenthood are not only to suffer the specified economic penalties but also be "denounced by public opinion."[201]

How effective the new system of rewards and punishments will turn out to be it is too early to tell. It cannot account for much of the general decline in fertility in China during the 1970s because most of that decline took place before the new regulations were instituted. During 1979 when the new tactics were being tried out, birth and natural increase rates in many areas were rising again, as has already been noted. The decision to institute the system, with its evident potential for increasing the pressure for popular conformity, may, in fact, have been inspired in part by the reports of rising population growth rates in many areas. Not all of the rewards or, for that matter, the punishments, may be equally persuasive. In August 1979 an investigation in Shanghai found that "many families" would rather have two children than receive "even several hundred Yuan" as a reward for having only one, but that the housing shortage was a significant constraint.[202] Besides, promulgation of regulations is seldom followed by prompt and uniform enforcement, particularly where their effective application involves complicated records and financial transactions and preferential treatment for various categories of the population. An example of the kinds of problems that may be encountered was given by a teacher who wrote to a Shanghai newspaper to complain that, because he had had himself sterilized after the birth of one child, the commune administration denied his wife more remunerative employment on the grounds that since the family had only one child they did not need the extra income. His wife now holds him to blame for their economic disadvantage because he accepted sterilization too readily.[203] If such local deviations from policy can occur in Shanghai Municipality, they can occur throughout China. It therefore may be some time before the results of the rewards and punishments system can be assessed.

One important change in tactics during the third birth control campaign, about which little is said in dispatches from China, is the much more aggressive promotion of what are now referred to as the "four family planning operations"—abortions, tubal ligations, vasectomies, and insertions of IUDs.

At the start of the first birth control campaign, abortion was allowed only in cases where continuation of the pregnancy created complications for the woman, and even there approval of a medical organization and the woman's place of work was a prerequisite. Sterilizations were restricted to women with health and other problems who already had six or more surviving children. The restrictions on abortion were relaxed in 1957 over the objections of the Chinese Medical Association, but official policy still regarded abortion as dangerous and not a suitable substitute for contraception. The easing of restrictions on sterilization, which also occurred in 1957, encountered less resistance from the medical profession. Sterilization was generally unpopular with the public and was opposed by some Chinese scholars. Official policy urged sterilization of males rather than females because of the greater ease and safety of performing vasectomies, but those requesting sterilization were also to be warned that the operation was essentially irreversible. Few abortions and sterilizations were performed during the first birth control campaign.[204]

Early in the second birth control campaign, the suction method of abortion began to see widespread use in China. The risk to the health of women was said to be much less than with conventional methods. Although abortion was now available on the request of the woman, it was not allowed after the second month of pregnancy, and a woman was not permitted more than one abortion a year. Contraception was still the preferred method for preventing births, but the number of abortions began to increase somewhat. Sterilization was more openly encouraged, with the emphasis once again on vasectomy, but popular fears kept the numbers down. The IUD, which had seen only experimental use during the first campaign, was more widely advertised during the second campaign, but its use seems to have been confined mainly to the cities and was probably not extensive even there.[205]

Early in the third campaign the official attitudes toward abortion and sterilization were not noticeably different from those during the second campaign. However, by 1973 it was apparent that the former cautions relating to these measures had been set aside, and that abortion, sterilization, and IUDs were being promoted on a mass scale. The main emphasis in published accounts was on increasing the numbers of cases of "family planning operations." On January 27, 1980, the New China News Agency reported that in the eight-year period from 1971 through 1978 over 170 million "operations for sterilization or emplacement of birth control devices" were performed in China, reducing the number of births during the period by 54.6 million.[206]

How such startling numbers were achieved is not indicated in the dispatches that present them. Certainly they suggest a national requirement that the provinces report the numbers of operations performed. At least one province had instituted quotas for sterilizations as early as 1978: in December 1978 Kweichow Province congratulated its Tung-jen Prefecture for having "overfulfilled by 10 percent" by the end of September "the sterilization operation quota assigned by the province."[207]

In some areas, planned parenthood surgical teams dispatched to the countryside were credited with the high numbers of operations reported.[208] The qualifications of the medical personnel providing these services were not indicated directly, but there were many indirect indications that they were not the best. In some cases the barefoot doctors played a prominent part, some of them actually performing sterilizations on women.[209] The use of paramedicals in China was widely hailed by Western doctors during the 1970s as an example from which the West had much to learn; but where birth control surgery was concerned, they seemed to be a source of constant anxiety to the Chinese authorities. Except for occasional statements that some thousands of operations had been carried out "without mishaps," "without a single incident," or "without any major accidents,"[210] there was no indication of what the human costs of acquiring skills on the job may have been, but some of the oblique references to the problems encountered sound a little ominous. A Kwangtung county "took warm care of those commune members who experienced difficulties after operation and properly handled and settled certain special cases," and a national health magazine editorialized that "if a problem arises from a birth control operation, it must be handled seriously and solved earnestly to help the patient recover rapidly."[211]

Recently Chinese sources have announced the development of new chemical sterilizants for males and females that are said to be both safe and effective and much simpler than surgery. In February 1979 the New China News Agency described a drug called gossypol made from cotton seeds, stems, and roots, which reportedly proved "up to 99.89 percent" effective in producing infertility in a group of "over 10,000 healthy men."[212] In August and September 1979, several Chinese sources described a new nonsurgical permanent sterilizant for men that involved injection of a "phenol mixture" into the spermatic duct. The method, which had been under experimentation since May 1972, had been tested on some 50,000 men, was said to be 90.95 percent effective, required only 10 minutes, and had two-thirds fewer adverse effects than does vasectomy.[213] Whether these new techniques will prove on fuller application to be free of the drawbacks that have been a deterrent to popular acceptance of surgical sterilization in the past remains to be seen.

Chinese sources scarcely mentioned abortions during the current campaign until 1979, but their numbers have also undoubtedly increased greatly during the third campaign, and especially in the last few years. In August 1979 a Fukien dispatch said that the numbers of abortions in May and June had doubled, and Honan claimed a 30.6 percent increase in the first half of 1979 compared with the respective period in 1978.[214] The reason for the sharp increases during 1979 was that women who got pregnant without authorization were being put under direct and rather insistent pressure to take what were euphemistically called "remedial measures."

The drive for remedial measures must have gotten out of hand: in an August 11 speech, Ch'en advised that they should be "avoided as much as possible."[215] But this advice lacked the force of a prohibition, and in November Kwangtung officials were still telling the local authorities to study the experiences of other localities and "get a good grasp of artificially terminating pregnancies outside the scope of the plan."[216]

The effectiveness of sterilization in assuring compliance with family size limits and the convenience of abortion in holding to target growth rates are both obvious. That these two measures have contributed in major degree to the recent decline in fertility in China is also beyond question. What is not as clear is how so many people have been induced to accept or at least to tolerate these measures in spite of contrary values that are evidently still widely shared. We will return to this question a little later.

Longer Duration

The last of the major differences between the present birth control campaign and the others is its much greater duration. The first campaign continued for less than four years, from September 1954 to about May 1958, and did not really start until August 1956. The second campaign also had a span of less than four years, from about April 1962 until June 1966. The present campaign has continued for more than ten years and, despite occasional lapses, with mounting intensity. It has survived a change in leadership that resulted in the radical reorientation and in some cases virtual reversal of other important domestic policies. If continuity is important in the development of organizations and personnel, in the accumulation of program experience, and in the gradual accretion of public acceptance, the sustained promotion of birth control work over so many years must also be a factor in the greater success of the third campaign.

In summary, the higher priority assigned to birth control during the current campaign has resulted in much greater attention to birth control by political leaders at all levels, and therefore in more action on the part of local officials and functionaries. The more plausible rationale and the greater sense of urgency it conveys have at least provided administrators and family planning personnel with more effective ideological weapons with which to combat local resistance. The strengthening of organization and control have added to the overall effectiveness of policy implementation and presumably to increased compliance throughout the chain of command. The more aggressive tactics at the grass-roots level have undoubtedly made passive resistance more difficult and active resistance more dangerous, increasing the amount of involuntary compliance. The duration of the campaign may also have undermined whatever hopes people may have held that, as with some other unpopular domestic policies in the past, birth control efforts would presently be abandoned and the attention of the authorities shifted to other concerns.

Among these factors, the most significant are undoubtedly those that bear directly on the attitudes and behavior of young and middle-aged couples in the childbearing ages. They are obviously not having as many children as did previous cohorts. Why not? Have they been won over by the official argument, have they succumbed to the persistent pressures of officials and peers, or are they really being coerced into limiting their childbearing against their will?

Persuasion, Pressure, and Coercion

No accurate measure can be taken of public opinion in China in the absence of systematic and objective investigation. News dispatches over the years have regularly reported the sentiments of the masses on various subjects and have quoted testimonials from individual workers and peasants, almost invariably to show that official policies and actions have the virtually unanimous support of the people. Dissent has seldom been registered in a medium that reaches the outside world, except for the brief months of the Hundred Flowers movement in spring 1957 and the much more profuse flowering of critical opinion in the dissident newspapers and the democracy wall posters of the past two years. The official press and radio have rarely mentioned deviant points of view except to argue against them or denounce them. Some indication of popular attitudes not otherwise publicized has been obtained over the years from interviews with refugees from China, but these were at best uncertain measures of popular thinking. Although they served to show that public opinion was by no means as unanimous as the official media claimed, there was no way to gauge the pervasiveness of the undercurrents among the general population.

Demonstrations and riots occurred that went unrecorded unless, like the outcry against the premature termination of mourning for Chou En-lai in April 1976, they occurred in the few cities where foreign newsmen and diplomatic personnel could observe them directly, or, in a few other instances, where they were mentioned in the official news channels many years later after a change in political climate. During the dominion of the gang of four, abuses of Party members, officials, and ordinary citizens were tolerated without any demur in the mass media. Even in cases in which people were "falsely accused" or "died as a result of their persecution," their "family, relatives, and friends still had to show a 'correct attitude.'"[217] The extent to which public opinion can be misrepresented when it conflicts with what the authorities want is exemplified in a rather interesting account in the People's Daily in October 1979. One brigade in a commune in Hopeh Province insisted that its members had agreed to collective management of private plots and had a file of signed documents from the peasants to prove the claim. When a reporter from the Hopeh Daily went door-to-door and interviewed the peasants, however, he found that more than 90 percent were opposed to collective management. Why, he asked, had they put their thumbprints on the documents? Some replied that they were compelled to do so by the cadres.[218]

Many current sources indicate that until recently there were some subjects, such as population theory, which were "forbidden areas," which meant that no one was allowed to talk about them publicly. A similar inhibition may prevent open expression of opposition to birth control at the present time, even though opposing ideas are still widely shared. In any case, the absence of outspoken dissent against the family planning effort may not be taken as an indication that it has gained acceptance among a majority of the population.

Persuasion and Popular Acceptance

On the contrary, a careful reading of the relevant evidence in Chinese sources suggests that truly voluntary cooperation with the birth control effort is relatively uncommon. The evidence speaks with two contradictory voices, but the affirmations of success in the struggle for the hearts and minds of the people seem to be overwhelmed by the indications that ideological work is less successful in securing compliance than are other, more forceful tactics.

From the earliest years of the third birth control campaign, there were some assertions that Mao's call to practice birth control had become "increasingly popular with the masses" and had "gone deeper and deeper into the hearts of the people";[219] opposing early marriage had become a "fad"; a new "vogue" of taking pride in planned parenthood was "beginning to take shape"; a new custom or a new trend had been established;[220] and women in various places had undergone a "profound transformation" in outlook, considered planned parenthood "good for them," and wanted to limit family size.[221] A few sources claimed that the numbers of those who subscribed to late marriage and planned parenthood were increasing, the practices were becoming a "spontaneous" action, the "masses' spontaneity was rising all the time," and even "wherever you go, you can hear people saying that planned parenthood is good."[222]

However, most of these confident assertions were probably either exaggerations or fictions conjured up for propaganda purposes. Often the same dispatches that boasted of the growing popularity of birth control also inveighed vehemently against the persistence of old ideas and customs and the "sabotage" carried out by various alleged enemies of birth control. By 1978 the claims of progress in reducing birth rates seldom attributed the gains to success in changing people's minds; usually the reason given was the determined initiatives and firm control on the part of leaders and functionaries of the Party and government at all levels. An American reporter visiting a commune in the outskirts of Chengtu, capital of Szechwan Province, the pacesetter in birth control work, was told in January 1980 that peasants must apply for permission to have a second or third child. The requirement was necessary, as the director of the commune explained, because

> Liberalism cannot be practiced here. If we let the masses discuss and decide for themselves, we could not do our family planning work.[223]

The main impression conveyed by the evidence is that popular opposition was and still is deep seated and compliance with the requirements of the birth control program is in large measure involuntary. From the beginning of the third campaign, news items on birth control have indicated that the influence of old habits and customs is difficult to extinguish, and to instill the required new attitudes calls for a "deepgoing ideological revolution."[224] In her article in the People's Daily in August 1979, Ch'en Mu-hua conceded that the old idea that it was "unfilial" to be without posterity "still exists stubbornly among the masses, especially among the rural masses."[225] Continuing popular resistance was undoubtedly the reason why it was widely conceded in 1978 that the demands of the birth control program were "an extremely arduous" task that would require unrelenting efforts by the local cadres.[226]

The persistence of traditional attitudes was sometimes recognized as a natural and inevitable tendency, but until 1979 it was also frequently attributed to the connivance of "enemies" both ancient and contemporary. The idea that rearing many sons was an act of filial piety and a key to personal happiness, and many other "reactionary fallacies," were traced to the pervasive influence of Confucius and Mencius until the late 1970s.[227] Early in the third campaign, Liu Shao-ch'i, who had been vilified during the Cultural Revolution, was accused of encouraging early marriage and spreading other forms of "venomous poison" to corrupt young people.[228] Later Lin Piao, after his downfall and death, was linked with Liu in charges that they conspired to obstruct birth control work. For a brief time between the death of Chou En-lai and the fall of the gang of four, there was an attempt to identify Teng Hsiao-p'ing with the opponents of birth control.[229] But from December 1976 at least until July 1977, the gang and their agents were designated as the principal saboteurs of birth control, sometimes in collusion with Liu and Lin.[230] Besides these, in various parts of the country there were other nameless opponents, described only as "capitalist roaders," "class enemies," or "bad elements," who were alleged to have undermined and sabotaged birth control work.[231] Who these persons were was not clearly indicated, but apparently they were local residents who openly disagreed with birth control policies and attempted to arouse others to resist also.

Much of the opposition probably is simply an affirmation of traditional values about having many children. At the First National Symposium on Population Theory held in Peking in November 1978, some speakers noted that "there is still resistance to the work of planned births, especially in rural areas," where traditional attitudes continue to be strong.[232] In the cities, some of the opposition stems apparently from resentment at the planned parenthood program's encroachments on individual freedom, even among young people who recognize the need to control population growth.[233] Some civil rights dissidents demanded that the program be abolished in the name of civil rights.[234] Other arguments glimpsed fleetingly now and then in various sources include: the traditional Chinese Marxist views to the effect that the rationale for birth control ignores the fact that people have hands as well as mouths;[235] enforcing the one-child rule will result in a population of elderly people and a shortage of labor;[236]

the rewards paid to one-child families would increase the economic burdens on the state and slow the "four modernizations";[237] and economic sanctions against families that have too many births will cause undue hardship.[238] No doubt there are other arguments that have not yet found expression in the mass media.

There is also opposition from some Party and government cadres who register their disagreement in various ways, from simply neglecting planned parenthood work to actively resisting. Many reportedly do not attach much importance to it. Others, especially during the latter half of 1978, became complacent and relaxed their efforts.[239] Some cadres were under the impression that family planning was a "soft" (low priority) task[240] or felt that it did not matter as much as meeting production targets.[241] In Nanking, some comrades who neglected planned parenthood said, "If you cannot increase output, you have to quit as secretary; if you cannot promote planned parenthood, you can still be secretary."[242] Recently the authorities have tried to establish the idea that failure in family planning work is to be considered just as serious as failure in production work.[243]

Some cadres have not obeyed the instruction to set a good example for the masses by practicing planned parenthood themselves.[244] Because of the importance of cadre compliance of masses, cadres who have more children than are authorized have been subjected since about the middle of 1979 to severe disciplinary actions. In July a Party branch member and director of a brick factory in Liaoning was dismissed from all posts for having nine children; in September a Party standing committee member in a Kewichlow county was denied an appointment as deputy Party secretary for having a sixth child; in November a deputy district leader in charge of planned parenthood work in Chekiang county was dismissed from all posts for having a sixth child; in December a deputy director of a county armed forces department in Hunan was dismissed and downgraded for having a fourth child after seven attempts by military and planned parenthood officials to "mobilize" his wife to have an abortion; and in the same month a commune Party official in Kwangtung who was chief of the family planning leadership group was dismissed from all posts for refusing "remedial measures" for his fourth child.[245] What these cases reveal is not just that the authorities take a serious view of cadre deviance, but that the masses readily take advantage of any laxness on the part of their local Party leaders to have additional children.

In short, one must conclude from the evidence available that there is a great deal of popular resistance to the family planning campaign among both the general population and Party and government officials at the local levels. While many people may be ready to accept some of the arguments about the adverse effects of population pressure on national development and community welfare, their personal inclinations are still very strongly toward having more children than current targets would allow.

Pressures for Compliance

It is not easy to draw a clear distinction between pressure and coercion even in the abstract, let alone in respect to the tactics applied in a government program assessed only at a distance using mainly the evidence in the mass media. However, it is certainly clear that the central authorities in China are putting very strong pressure on Party and government leaders at provincial and local levels to get results immediately, and that they expect these pressures to be transmitted down the chain of command until they land with compelling force on young people of marriageable age and couples in the childbearing years. There is also abundant evidence that, with several short lapses, the pressures have been mounting since at least 1973.

Within the past two years, instructions relating to family planning are frequently presented as the "demand" of higher levels and are characterized as "urgent" or "imperative." Local leaders are called upon to show their "determination," take "resolute action," and "guarantee" or "insure" that certain results are achieved. So far as the public record is concerned, the central authorities said very little about means, but they made clear what results they wanted.

To lend the force of law to the birth control campaign, the rather bland provision about family planning that had been written into the new constitution was interpreted to mean that family planning was mandatory. The *People's Daily* July 1978 editorial on birth control explained that the statement that "the state advocates and promotes" family planning signified that the practice of birth control was every citizen's "basic right and obligation." Therefore, the editorial reasoned,

> We must resolutely implement the series of important instructions of Chairman Mao, Premier Chou, and Chairman Hua, strictly abide by stipulation of the new constitution, and fulfill within the prescribed time limit the planned parenthood task for the new period laid down by Chairman Hua.[246]

In September 1978, Women's Federation leader K'ang K'o-ch'ing said women's organizations must act according to the provisions of the constitution and "encourage and promote family planning,"[247] a relatively mild suggestion. But in 1979 other sources said the constitution had "decreed" that planned parenthood was one of the fundamental rights and duties of citizenship, and that "every one of us should conscientiously carry it out."[248] Ch'en Mu-hua said the constitutional provision was the "legal basis for our control of population growth."[249] It served to legitimize the national and provincial family planning laws and the punishment of people who opposed the program or had unauthorized children.

How far local authorities in some areas were willing to go in exercising the new authority is illustrated by the actions of Kwangtung Province, which was embarrassed in recent years by rising population growth rates. At the beginning of 1978, the provincial authorities were confident they had "effectively controlled" the provincial natural increase rate and that planned parenthood was taking root among the population.[250] But by July 1978 they were aware population growth rate in some localities was increasing, due, they said, to lack of attention by local leaders and to interference and sabotage by the gang of four.[251] By September they had discovered that the rising rates applied to the province as a whole,[252] and in December they estimated that the number of "unplanned" births was likely to exceed 100,000 by the end of the year, because "many localities" had relaxed their efforts and some local cadres had "set bad examples."[253]

In January 1979 Kwangtung's new planned parenthood regulations were announced. Figures showing declining arable land per capita in the province were cited as justification for the increased urgency of controlling population growth.[254] By May the authorities noted with satisfaction that units in which rising growth rates had appeared were "gradually correcting the situation."[255] By June, however, they conceded that despite great efforts and some success, population growth was increasing in 28 counties and municipalities, and that the provincial population growth rate would continue its rise in 1979.[256] In July it was estimated that if the trend of the first six months of the year continued, the growth rate would reach 16 per thousand for 1979, well above the figure of 14.75 per thousand for 1978, when Kwangtung ranked twenty-first among the provinces in reducing growth rates.[257] In a telephone conference on July 1, all areas were called upon to take remedial measures, especially during July, August, and September, to terminate all third and higher birth order pregnancies and as many second pregnancies as possible, so as to "reduce pressures on us next year and the year after."[258] The provincial Party committee issued an "urgent notice" at the same time demanding that the "whole Party and people take immediate action to get the populations growth rate down to 10 per thousand in 1979." Remedial measures were again recommended and local leaders were told that "any policy that is advantageous to planned parenthood work must be carried out." The notice further demanded that

> . . . Party committees at all levels take quick action and have tight control over implementation. At present, the thinking that the population increase rate for this year is already a foregone conclusion must be changed. The idea must be made clear that if the whole Party takes urgent action and makes immediate arrangements to do the work well, there is still hope that the population growth rate in our province will be lowered to 10 per thousand this year.[259]

This was a rather reckless proposal. If the birth rate for the first six months of the year indicated a prospective natural increase rate of 16 per thousand for 1979, the expected net increase for the year would have been about 900,000. To bring the natural increase rate down to 10 per thousand would have required cutting the net increase by about 340,000, all to be accomplished in the second half of the year and all through abortions to women who as of July 1 had been pregnant for more than three months, who presumably numbered about 600,000. This would have meant aborting more than 55 percent of the pregnant women in Kwangtung Province who were due to deliver in the second half of the year![260] Of course, the provincial authorities probably did not seriously intend that the local cadres should meet this target regardless of costs, which would have endangered the lives of many of the 340,000 women. But in their public exhortations, the provincial authorities did not warn the local cadres about the hazards of late term abortions, nor did they indicate any concern about the risks.

By late August the provincial authorities had scaled down their demands. They suggested that the local family planning efforts could at least insure that the provincial growth rate would not rise again in 1979, a more modest goal requiring only about 70,000 late term abortions.[261] Even that goal seemed in doubt in November, when it was disclosed that in the period from January to September the provincial birth rate had risen by 1.53 per thousand over the rate for the same period in 1978. If the trend continued to the end of the year, it would have meant a natural increase rate somewhat over 16 per thousand. The pressure to reduce the numbers of births continued, however, and various localities were being congratulated for having "taken remedial actions as requested by the province and [having] overfulfilled the task."[262] At a meeting called by the provincial Party committee in December, planned parenthood workers were told that they "must resolutely accomplish the target of controlling population growth" and "insure that each couple has only one child if possible."[263]

Given the mounting pressures exerted by the central on the provincial authorities, which they in turn passed on to the local authorities, and the directives about fulfilling and overfulfilling targets and quotas, the emphasis on remedial measures and other family planning operations, and the legally authorized sanctions against those who did not conform to the local birth plans, it was perhaps inevitable that local cadres seeking to win approval from their superiors would cross the undefined boundary between pressure and coercion. As shall be seen, presently, some did.

Coercion

The official position in regard to coercion in family planning work has been consistent and unequivocal: it is not allowed. This position was stated during the first birth control campaign and has been repeated during the current campaign. However, the recent reiterations have not been frequent, and there is an implicit inconsistency between the official policy on coercion and the demands for plan fulfillment in birth control work.

During the first birth control campaign it was made clear from the outset that the adoption of birth control was to be a voluntary matter. The decision would be left "entirely up to individuals," and "nobody is at liberty to interfere with or coerce" couples into accepting birth control.[264] The media also claimed that the policy on birth control was in response to "the demand of the masses," it was "welcomed by the broad masses," "parents generally are putting forth a demand for birth control," and it had "become the universal demand of the masses today."[265] Birth control was also said to be the "privilege" and the "democratic right" of the people and a policy that was in accord with their needs and interests. However, even from the evidence in the Chinese press at the time it was very clear that, far from being the demand of the masses, birth control was the demand of the Party Central Committee, to which the masses responded with reluctance.[266]

Little was said about the popular will or about the kinds of promotional tactics that were permissible during the second birth control campaign, but the issue came to the surface again during the third campaign. The statement that birth control is a voluntary matter in China was seldom found in domestic sources during the 1970s, but appeared rather frequently in communications addressed to foreign audiences. Speeches given at international conferences, radio broadcasts beamed overseas, New China News Agency English-language dispatches, and publications for foreign subscribers said again and again that, as a matter of principle, planned parenthood in China was carried out "on a voluntary basis with state guidance."[267] From 1973 to 1979, some domestic sources implied that principle and practice were one, but others indicated that the struggle to win voluntary acceptance of birth control was a gradual process.[268] The claims that birth control was the demand of the masses and in accord with their wishes were also revived during the third campaign.[269]

The central authorities seemed to be firmly convinced that the success of the birth control campaign is essential to China's economic development. They also seemed to believe that if the people could be persuaded that their interests were best served by slowing or stopping population growth, they would practice family planning spontaneously and constant administrative pressures would no longer be necessary. Despite contrary allegations in the mass media and especially to foreigners, they probably have never had any illusions that popular support would come easily. Mao said in 1957 that "the complete realization of family planning in the future will be out of the question without the weight of society behind it, that is, without general consent and joint efforts."[270] Hua said in June 1979 that "measures should be taken to make the people practice family planning willingly, safely, and effectively. . . ."[271] Ch'en Mu-hua declared in August 1979 that "people must be allowed to practice family planning voluntarily."[272] The last two statements seem to admit that ideological education and persuasion have not yet succeeded.

Given the force of traditional values and beliefs, one might not expect to meet targets and quotas by such means alone. Therefore, the central authorities called for stronger measures and the stronger measures were taken. The specific instructions delivered through directives, circulars, and pronouncements at national birth control conferences were never made public, but their general thrust can be inferred from the hardening of hortatory language and from the objectives and methods discussed in news dispatches on family planning work at the local level. The clearest indications that compliance was being secured by means other than persuasion came from criticisms against cadres who carried force too far and prohibitions against the more aggressive forms of compulsion. There were intermittent warnings to birth control cadres that they should refrain from issuing "compulsory orders," from "forcing everyone to do the same thing," from "treating everyone alike," from "pushing the work by force or decree," from enforcing uniform birth control methods, from being "simple-minded and inflexible," and from using "rigid and unsuitable methods,"[273] excesses that undoubtedly were committed in an effort to meet demands from the higher levels that the masses be mobilized to fulfill their birth plans.

Administrative force was an option to which the local cadres were quite prone, as several reported instances attest. A 1973 article in the People's Daily describes how the Party committee in a commune near Wuhsi Municipality had been "at loggerheads" over whether to rely on "meticulous ideological work" or on "administrative orders" to promote family planning, because some commune members who had reached the right conclusions about birth control during public meetings "became muddle-headed again when they returned home." Some of the cadres thereupon lost patience and argued that "it would be better to lay down a few hard and fast regulations, so that time could be saved and quick results produced." This was the wrong approach, the article says, and in due course the errant cadres recognized that "family planning work fundamentally . . . reflects the wishes and interests of the broad masses," hence the masses could be persuaded to conform when properly educated.[274]

From time to time, more candid accounts of coercive measures have been obtained from interviews with refugees, who have been citing specific instances since early in the 1970s. Some involve what foreign commentators call "peer pressure," which can amount to coercion in some circumstances, especially where an entire work group is penalized for the nonconformity of one or a few members. However, in family planning work the use of peer pressure seems to be less frequent than direct pressure by the cadres themselves. Instances of coercion by the latter include denial of maternity leave, refusal of birth registration, withholding of food and cloth rations, and forcible sterilizations.[275]

In 1978 many cases of coercion were described in Chinese news dispatches, most of them in connection with a public campaign against commandism and coercion, which were admittedly widespread and affected many spheres of activity besides birth control. The campaign, which was waged between May and December 1978, was precipitated by a report of "coercion, commandism, and other violations of law and discipline" by some cadres in Hsun-yi County, Shensi Province, that was circulated throughout the country on orders of the Party Central Committee in August 1978.[276] A People's Daily editorial on August 2 asserted that "similar problems varying in degree of seriousness exist in some places throughout the country." The editorial did not go into particulars, but the severity of the problem at its worst could be inferred from the fact that compensation was to be paid to the surviving relatives of those who had died as a result of "coercion and beating."[277]

The provinces responded by publicizing their own campaigns against coercion and commandism, in the course of which much more was revealed about the kinds of offenses the cadres had committed. These included "indiscriminately criticizing and struggling against the masses, parading them through the streets with placards, detaining people under the pretext of running a study course, fining people, making deductions from their grain rations, . . . beating and cursing the masses . . ., giving blind commands and compulsory orders,"[278] arresting and punishing the masses "unscrupulously,"[279] riding "roughshod" over the people, bullying and oppressing them, practicing "class retaliation" and "cruel persecution,"[280] tying people up at will, treating the laboring masses as "class enemies," "adopting arbitrary dictatorial measures,"[281] confining people in cattle sheds,[282] branding them with such "unwarranted" labels as "anti-party" and "counterrevolutionary,"[283] forcing them to make false confessions, and driving them to suicide.[284] Friends and relatives of the victims often suffered with them.[285] The abuses of power were committed by cadres at all levels, from provincial Party secretaries down to commune Party committee members, undermining relations between the cadres and the masses.[286]

A news item from the Kwangsi Region argued that part of the blame for the bad work style of lower level cadres must be shared by higher level cadres:

> The work style problems of some cadres in the lower levels are also caused in part by the fact that the leadership organs do not proceed from reality in arranging work and make arbitrary decisions, and they are also caused by the fact that some leading cadres fail to set a good example and act in a subjective way when they go down to the lower levels to inspect work. For instance, in arranging work some leading comrades set very strict demands without explaining the methods for carrying out the task. As a result, they set working hard in opposition to the policies, to a scientific approach, to a correct work style, and this causes compulsory orders to be issued. Hence, in solving the problem of work style we must not just look at the lower levels. We must start with the leading organs at all levels.[287]

A Szechwan newspaper saw a direct connection between coercion and the assignment of arduous tasks:

> There are many cadres who have created problems in the course of doing hard work. Some resort to coercion and commandism because the assigned tasks are arduous and urgent. Some cadres blindly order others about. In dealing with these problems, the authorities at higher levels must shoulder responsibilities.[288]

The People's Daily added that, faced with arduous tasks and the demand from higher levels to "carry out instructions from the top whether you understand them or not," some cadres

> . . . do not dare seek truth from facts, [but] they dare to resort to deception, coercion, and commandism and to beat and scold people and violate law and discipline. . . . They are not afraid to harm the interests of the people, encroach upon the interests of the people, and violate Party discipline and state laws. They are only afraid of not being able to win the trust of their superiors.[289]

In short, coercion is inevitable when the top leadership of an authoritarian administrative system demands results that cannot be obtained by other means.

While the anticoercion campaign was in progress, coercion in birth control work was also interdicted. In July a meeting of the State Council's new "family planning leading group" was apparently told that "coercion in any form is forbidden."[290] In September K'ang K'o-ch'ing told the Fourth National Women's Congress that "meticulous ideological and educational work" should be used to "raise the consciousness of the masses in family planning" and that "we oppose coercion and authoritarianism."[291] Later in the year, an item in the journal China Youth reported an instance in which women who would not take contraceptive pills had their basic food rations reduced.[292] An article in a leading Peking newspaper discussing unauthorized actions by local officials gave the following two examples:

> Some rural production brigades and teams have casually deducted the grain ration issued to commune members with a variety of excuses. Some localities popularizing birth control have dispatched "militia propaganda teams" to those households that did not practice birth control to "propagandize" and exercise control over their food, drinking water, and workpoints. These local laws have caused a great dissatisfaction among the people.[293]

The local laws, which took many other forms not related to birth control, were regulations arbitrarily decreed by local officials, sometimes on the verbal fiat of a single leader, without higher level authorization. It was said that they were prevalent, had resulted in a "chaotic phenomenon," and had "seriously infringed on the people's democratic rights and interests."[294] They may have included or been similar to what were called "indigenous policies" in birth control work, which were apparently prohibited some time during 1978 in a directive that has not been made public. In January 1979 an American newsman in Peking learned that officials in Szechwan, China's model province in birth control work, had recently been told that "coercion in family matters must stop immediately," and that a provincial official in Kirin had said that "great popular indignation has been aroused by these attempts to dictate what must remain personal decisions." The reporter added that new instructions had been sent to family planning workers across the country that couples must not be coerced into using contraceptives or having abortions by reducing their food rations or threatening political measures against them.[295]

One consequence of the anticoercion campaign was to weaken the authority of the local cadres, with the result that the cadres stopped implementing unpopular policies. The relaxation of family planning efforts reported from many areas during 1978 was probably also due in part to the cadre reforms prompted by this campaign. Having reminded the cadres that they "manage the affairs of state on a mandate from the people," that they must "place their work under constant, direct supervision by the masses" and "humbly listen to their opinions," that "the people have the right to remove cadres they consider unqualified," and that "those [cadres] who violate the law [must be] firmly punished,"[296] the authorities soon discovered that many cadres had become demoralized and had lapsed into apathy. In May 1978 a report from Kirin Province said that "a number of cadres" were confused and could not "distinguish clearly between giving commands blindly and giving commands correctly" because of the directives demanding that they stop acting arbitrarily and respect the "free will of production teams." They were "afraid of committing new mistakes" and were "timid in their work." They had to be told that opposing the "arbitrary issuing of commands does not mean there is no need to direct production. . . ."[297] Even after the surfacing of the Hsun-yi County derelictions, the People's Daily editorial of August 2 wanted more lenient treatment for "those cadres who had accidentally made mistakes of coercion, commandism, and abusing the masses" than for "those bad elements who lorded it over and always bullied the people,"[298] which suggests at least an inclination to overlook quite a bit of cadre misconduct. In Shensi Province, home of the most celebrated bad examples, the errant cadres were assured that "if mistakes have been made, it is all right as long as they are corrected."[299] The Szechwan Daily, while maintaining that problems in cadre work style must not be tolerated or covered up, also took a benign attitude toward the offenders:

> Mistakes are inevitable in doing work but everything is all right as long as mistakes are corrected. The worst mistake is doing no work at all.[300]

After the confusion in signals during 1978 had subsided, the final message seemed to be: avoid coercion if possible but get the job done. Certainly this has been the attitude subsequently toward work in family planning. In September 1979 a Peking paper printed an article about Szechwan's success in family planning work in which it was noted that

> During 1978 some people criticized our birth control planning work, raising such charges as "too many bumpkin policies," "coercive orders," "imposition of undue burdens on the communes and brigades," "overdoing things," "radical pursuits," etc., etc., so that some cadres and active elements were discouraged from grasping birth control planning work on the basis of their own rationale and initiative.[301]

The provincial Party committee conducted an investigation in Szechwan's model county, Shih-fang, which, the authorities said, showed that they had not been "overdoing things" but instead had "not done enough."[302] A little later in the same month, a dispatch from a county in Honan Province described local measures in regard to sterilization that betrayed no concern about coercion or "democratic rights." The item is worth quoting in full:

> Comrade Yen Ch'eng-chien of the Propaganda Department of the Heng-yang County CCP Committee has written to the Hunan Radio Station saying: When certain comrades in the rural areas are mobilized to carry out sterilization measures, they run off to the urban office, factory, mine, or unit where their spouses work. Their communes and brigades then send telegrams, make phone calls, and dispatch people to the units concerned to contact the responsible comrades and request them to assist in conducting ideological education for those comrades and mobilize them to return to their production teams for sterilization measures.
>
> Some units are very cooperative in doing this. However, the leading comrades of other units do not concern themselves with it. Some of them express support at the time but afterwards take no action. As a result, sterilization measures cannot be carried out on these comrades. According to investigations, there are over 800 persons who should be sterilized in the 82 communes of the Heng-yang County. Their actions have a very bad influence among the masses.
>
> A station editor says in a comment on the problem: Our information shows that the problem reported by

> Comrade Yen Ch'eng-chien exists in other places besides Heng-yang County. At a time when we are launching planned parenthood work in depth, it is necessary to block this air raid shelter. We hope that the leading comrades of organs, factories, mines, and other units and the comrades specifically responsible for planned parenthood work will carry out investigations to determine whether this air raid shelter exists in their units. If it does, they must conduct patient and meticulous ideological work for the workers in their own units, organize them to clearly understand the situation and return to the rural areas in a happy frame of mind. Units which can should mobilize them to implement the sterilization measures on the spot.[303]

Although the measures described in this item apparently apply only to Party cadres, from whom much more is demanded than from the masses, there is no mistaking the intent to make sterilization compulsory; the role of ideological work is to make a virtue of the necessity. Finally, it should be noted that none of the family planning regulations adopted in 1979 that have been quoted in detail contain stipulations prohibiting "indigenous policies," commandism, or coercion.

The current evidence suggests that the central authorities believe the reduction of population growth rate is so urgent that they cannot wait until the family planning program can meet its goals on a purely voluntary basis. They seem to expect that education and propaganda can in time win acceptance for the program, particularly if the economic advantages they ascribe to it result in improvements in living standards in both urban and rural areas. But for the time being, at least, the family planning program in China appears to be compulsory.

CONCLUSIONS

Despite many ambiguities, the quantitative and descriptive evidence from China leaves little doubt that fertility remained high in most of the country until the early 1970s, but has declined rapidly since about 1972. A demographic change that is without precedent in human experience has apparently taken place within the past decade. But from the limited information available, it is impossible to trace its course, identify its causes, or reach firm conclusions about its significance.

There are no reliable data on the levels and trends of China's vital rates at any time in the last 50 years. Vital registration has never worked well. From the 1930s to the present, the evidence suggests that underregistration has been a persistent problem. The more complete the data reported, the more anomalies are apparent. Underregistration has characterized the tentative attempts at vital registration in various localities prior to 1949, the experimental registration efforts of the early 1950s, and the universal population registers that have operated since the middle 1950s. Because the data available are few and unreliable, the trends in vital rates over the years remain obscure.

Traditional fertility levels in China seem to have been somewhere in the forties per thousand, but there were apparently regional variations. It is likely that civil war, floods, famines, and other major upheavals and catastrophes had a limited and temporary depressing effect on the national birth rate both before and after 1949. From the 1950s onward, changing age composition should have been a significant factor also. The birth control campaigns of the 1950s and 1960s seem to have been generally unsuccessful and probably had no overall impact. The third birth control campaign has evidently been much more effective and is undoubtedly the main cause of the recent decline in birth and natural increase rates.

Yet the third campaign has also had its difficulties. The official natural increase rates for the country as a whole have shown little or no reduction since 1977. A number of provinces and municipalities have recently been reporting rising growth rates, and these have apparently offset the continuing declines reported by other areas. As a result, the national growth rate targets have not been attained, and this undoubtedly accounts for the extreme intensification of family planning efforts since the end of 1978.

There are four possible explanations for the slowing of the downward trend in population growth rates, and they are not mutually exclusive. One is that age composition in China at the present time is distinctly unfavorable for a reduction in rates of natural increase. As the Chinese authorities themselves are very much aware, sharply rising cohorts of young people are entering the ages for marriage and childbearing. This upsurge may continue until well into the 1990s. Since Chinese youth probably cannot be denied the opportunity to marry and have at least one child, population growth rate targets may soon strike a bedrock below which they cannot penetrate.

A second explanation is that the enforcement of late marriage stipulations in the middle 1970s created a temporary lull in marriages, and therefore in first births, which could not be sustained without continual further postponements of marriage. There are reports that it has been necessary to ease somewhat the restrictions on marriage age, which were probably in danger of alienating a whole generation of youths already suffering acutely from the social and economic maladies brought on by the Cultural Revolution. Even without the easing of restrictions, a wave of first births would have followed inevitably once the enforcement of the higher age limits was substantially complete.

A third explanation is that the setbacks in family planning work in 1976 and 1978 and the growing problems of civil order and Party discipline that continued at least up to the end of 1979 have led to rising birth rates in many areas. Given the fact that progress in birth control work is almost entirely dependent upon the initiative of the Party cadres at all levels, any sign of conflict or indecision among the top leadership will instantly weaken the pressure for unpopular policies and programs at the grass-roots levels. The uncertainty about succession following the disability and death of Mao in 1976 and the confusion about the limits of local authority during the cadre work style reforms of 1978 caused a paralysis in birth control work in some areas, as will any future political disturbance within the central leadership, regardless of what is at issue.

Finally, it is likely that some of the local and provincial figures showing success in reducing population growth that were put forward during the middle 1970s were falsified or based on optimistic estimates or atypical samples rather than on complete and accurate records. As the system of family planning recordkeeping, inspections by higher levels, and regular progress reports has developed, it may have necessitated some upward adjustments in birth and natural increase rates.

More adjustments of that kind may be required in the future. If the 1981 census of China is successful in improving the quality of population data in general and vital data in particular, it could deal a further setback to the drive for lower natural increase rates by showing higher vital rates for 1981 than the trend of current figures would suggest. But accurate new census data on age composition may also permit a more realistic assessment of vital rates during the past decade, leading to retrospective upward revisions of earlier data. However, it is unlikely that new data, new analyses, or adjustment of previous figures would contradict the indications of a marked decline in fertility between 1972 and 1977.

The means by which this transition from high to low fertility was accomplished are much more difficult to assess. The issue is inherently sensitive, and the descriptive reports from various localities in China are often vague and euphemistic and seem to leave a great deal unsaid. The uncertainty of the evidence undeniably allows considerable latitude for varying interpretations, but no responsible reading will sustain the notion that family planning in China is voluntary. The observed conformity can only be a largely involuntary compliance under pressures that range from exhortation to compulsion.

Some foreign observers are reluctant to apply the word "coercive" to the current promotional tactics and will concede only that strong pressures are used. The Chinese themselves do not shrink from the word, though they define it narrowly and limit its scope to officially disapproved measures. But some of the tactics that have been mandated by law or otherwise authorized and encouraged, including the "mobilizations" for "remedial measures" and "on-the-spot" sterilizations, go far beyond what would be called "pressure" in other parts of the world. Even more forceful expedients may be required hereafter if the goal of over 90 percent one-child families is to be attained.

Regardless of the terms employed, it is obvious that if government and Party cadres were to relinquish their grasp of family planning work, the birth rate in China would rebound immediately. How high it would go cannot even be surmised. There is no way of knowing what proportions of Chinese couples in the younger childbearing ages today would stop at various parity levels if the choice were theirs alone. Some may be fully in sympathy with the one-child family ideal and others may be prepared to accommodate without feeling much deprivation. But the impression gained from the evidence is that, in the country as a whole, the numbers of those who conform readily are far from a majority. Family planning is not yet, at any rate, "the will of the people."

It is obvious that the Chinese authorities believe that the reduction of population growth rates is an urgent necessity, and they seem to be convinced that in mandating family planning they are acting in the best interests of the Chinese people. Even if food problems are solved and the economy is spared further crises of the kind that reportedly twice brought it to the brink of collapse in the past 20 years, a failure to improve living standards soon and to contain the inescapable social and economic dislocations of modernization could generate a level of popular frustration and civil unrest that might, under certain circumstances, have equally adverse consequences. The unplanned reduction of population growth through hunger, mass poverty, or civil violence is hardly preferable on moral or any other grounds to a planned reduction accomplished by coercive means. Western countries, which were able to achieve their demographic transitions through spontaneous popular action, can include decisions about childbearing among their basic human rights, but China may not be able to afford such fine scruples. A purely voluntary family planning program could not hold China's population growth rate at whatever its present level, let alone reduce it further.

Nevertheless, such considerations do not entirely obviate the moral questions raised by the current birth control campaign in China. All of the major domestic programs of the last 30 years that have been advanced without regard to popular consent have been justified at the time as in the public interest, including the Big Leap Forward and the Cultural Revolution, which have since been repudiated on the same grounds. In most cases it was political precepts rather than objective analyses of needs and circumstances that determined both the policies and the methods of implementation. The current arguments for family planning seem to have a much sounder basis of economic and social realities; still, given the present state of knowledge about economic and demographic conditions in China, it cannot be shown that certain tactics must be used to reach a certain natural increase rate by a certain year in order to achieve certain economic and social outcomes. Do the current targets really rest on economic necessity, or are they only another example of the arbitrariness with which administrative authority is exercised when there are few constraints? Without reliable data objectively analyzed, it is impossible to reach even an informed judgment as to whether or not human needs in China justify the encroachments on individual privacy and other human rights that the birth control campaign demands. Steps are now being taken to restore and develop the national statistical system and collect the economic and demographic data that may make such analyses possible in the future, but the process will take some time.

Meanwhile, the intensive measures adopted to speed the family planning program involve risks both to the individual families who comply, willingly or otherwise, and to the political leaders. For the couples who have one child, there is always the risk that illness or an accident will deprive them at one blow of what for many will be the main object of their affections and the focus of their lives. The blow may come when it is too late for them to have another child or when it is impossible because of an irreversible sterilization. If living standards rise perceptibly in the next 20 years, some of the couples who unwillingly surrendered a portion of their parenthood may be partially mollified after the fact. But if the economic benefits that are supposed to follow the lowering of population growth rates do not materialize or are too slow in arriving, a massive upsurge of popular resentment could cause serious political instability or even precipitate a change of leadership. Given the animus shown toward former leaders fallen from grace during the past 30 years, those identified with unpopular policies are vulnerable to extreme recriminations if the policies are altered by the new leadership. The heavy-handed approach to family planning is a gamble with high stakes all around.

Whatever the final outcome may be, it is advisable in the meantime to avoid overconfident conclusions about the current levels and trends in fertility in China, the effectiveness of the family planning program, or its long-range prospects. The relevant evidence is still too tentative to support categorical assertions about the implications of the Chinese family planning experience. Certainly it would be unwise at this point to commend the Chinese example for emulation by other developing countries. The resumption of statistical accountability in China seems to hold forth the welcome prospect that more statistical data and more analytical studies will be forthcoming in the future. Until these resources are available, careful assessments of the limited evidence at hand, circumspect interpretation, and caution in rendering judgments will continue to be the minimum requirements for responsible scholarship in studying demographic change in China.

NOTES

1. George W. Barclay, Ansley J. Coale, Michael A. Stoto, and T. James Trussell, "A Reassessment of the Demography of Traditional Rural China," Population Index (October 1976): 607.

2. Ch'iao Ch'i-ming, "Rural Population and Vital Statistics for Selected Areas of China," Chinese Economic Journal (March 1934).

3. John Lossing Buck, Chinese Farm Economy, Miscellaneous Series in Agriculture, no. 13, University of Nanking, Nanking.

4. Ch'en Ta, Population in Modern China (Chicago: University of Chicago Press, 1946).

5. Ibid., pp. 27-28.

6. Ch'iao Ch'i-ming, Warren S. Thompson, and D. T. Chen, An Experiment in the Registration of Vital Statistics (Oxford, Ohio: Scripps Foundation for Research in Population Problems, 1938), pp. 9-10.

7. Ibid., p. 1.

8. For example, see Marshall C. Balfour, Roger F. Evans, Frank W. Notestein, and Irene B. Taeuber, Public Health and Demography in the Far East, report of a survey trip, September 13-December 13, 1948 (New York: Rockefeller Foundation, 1950), pp. 2-3, 111.

9. Irene B. Taeuber, "The Data and the Dynamics of the Chinese Populations," Population Index (April 1973).

10. Barclay et al., "A Reassessment."

11. The scale of the executions is a debatable question. PRC sources are understandably evasive when it comes to numbers. One of the more explicit says that in the Central-South region the People's Liberation Army "inactivated" 1,150,000 "native bandits" between the winter of 1949 and December 1951, of which "only 28 percent" were executed. See Teng Tzu-hui, "Report on the Work of the Central-South Military and Administrative Commission," Ch'ang-chiang jih-pao (CCJP) (Yangtse Daily), Hankow, December 13, 1951, American Consulate General, Hong Kong, Current Background (CB), no. 157,

February 8, 1952, pp. 11-12. In September 1951 it was said that more than one million "bandits" had been "wiped out" in the previous two years. See Liao Kai-lung and Wang Tsung-yi, "Great Achievements of the People's Republic of China during the Past Two Years," New China News Agency (NCNA), Peking, September 24, 1951, CB, no. 120, October 3, 1951, p. 7. A year later the total had been raised to "over 2,000,000." One text says they were "put out of action" and another that they were "eradicated." See Yu Kan, "Great Achievements of the People's Republic of China in Past 3 Years," Nan-fang jih-pao (NFJP) (Southern Daily), Canton, September 23, 1952, CB, no. 218, November 5, 1952, p. 9; Po I-po, "Chung-hua jen-min kung-ho-kuo san nien lai ti ch'eng-chiu" ("The Achievements of the People's Republic of China in the Last Three Years"), Hsin Hua Yueh-pao (New China Monthly), no. 10, October 25, 1952, p. 11. Other categories of the population were also subject to liquidation. The numbers of landlords killed during the land reform movement have been estimated variously but always in the millions. Other categories subject to suppression or other punitive actions included war criminals, collaborators, bureaucratic capitalists, secret agents, despots, and counterrevolutionaries sentenced to death at some 3 million in 1951. See Jacques Marcuse, "How to Talk to the Chinese in Peking," New York Times Magazine, May 23, 1965, p. 82. The proportion of the population liquidated in all of these purges may not have amounted to more than 1 or 2 percent, but many other persons were placed under investigation and surveillance, and the political climate created by these activities undoubtedly affected many people not directly threatened.

12. Between 70,000 and 80,000 deaths were reported as due to these causes in 1952. See "Outline of Propaganda on the Thorough Implementation of the Marriage Law," NCNA, Peking, February 25, 1953, translated in CB, no. 236, March 10, 1953, p. 27.

13. For example, see the following: "Tientsin Population Over 3 Million," Kung-jen pao (Workers' Daily), Tientsin, March 8, 1957, American Consulate General, Hong Kong, Survey of China Mainland Press (SCMP), no. 1,513, April 18, 1957, p. 25; "Nanking Gets One Child Every Ten Minutes; Appropriate Contraception Should Be Promoted," Nan-ching jih-pao (Nanking Daily), Nanking, March 19, 1957, SCMP, no. 1,519, April 30, 1957, p. 13; "Kwangtung Population Up by Over 8,000,000 in Past 7 Years," Wen-hui pao (WHP) (Wen-hui Daily), Hong Kong, April 4, 1957, SCMP, no. 1,507, April 9, 1957, p. 24; Sun Kuang, "Urban Population Must Be Controlled," Jen-min jih-pao (JMJP) (People's Daily), Peking, November 27, 1957, SCMP, no. 1,668, December 10, 1957, p. 4; "Planned Birth and Birth Control in Amoy," Hsia-men jih-pao (Amoy Daily), February 26, 1958, SCMP, no. 1,759, April 28, 1958, p. 27.

14. Roland Pressat, "La Population de la Chine et son Economie," Population (October-December 1958): 572-73.

15. As late as 1953 urban census cadres were directed to supply the urban security police, who were responsible for registration in the cities, with copies of the census returns in those cities where household registration was "not yet well implemented." See "Measures for National Census and Registration of the Population," NCNA, Peking, CB, no. 241, May 5, 1953, p. 35. For further discussion of the early problems of urban population registration see Aird, "Population Growth," in Alexander Eckstein, Walter Galenson, and Ta-chung Liu, Economic Trends in Communist China (Chicago: Aldine Publishing Co., 1968), pp. 218-23, 236.

16. K'ang Chi-ch'in, "Fen-hsi jen-k'ou ch'u-cheng-lü pien-tung ch'ing-k'uang te chien-li ho ching-yen" ("Sample Analysis of Changes in the Birth Rate and the Lessons of Experience"), T'ung-chi kung-tso (Statistical Work), 1957, no. 6, pp. 25-27.

17. State Statistical Bureau, "Chung-hua Jen-min Kung-ho-kuo kuo-chia t'ung-chi-chü t'ing-pan sheng-ming t'ung-chi shih-pan kung-tso te i-chien" ("Opinion of the State Statistical Bureau of the People's Republic of China Concerning the Termination of Vital Statistics Experimental Work"), November 1954, in State Statistical Bureau, T'ung-chi kung-tso chung-yao wen-chien hui-pien (A Compilation of Important Documents on Statistical Work), vol. 1 (Peking: T'ung-chi ch'u-pan-she, 1955), p. 592.

18. Pai Chien-hua, "600 Million People—A Great Strength for Socialist Construction of China," JMJP, November 1, 1954, SCMP, no. 926, November 11-12, 1954, p. 33.

19. All urban places with 100,000 population or more at the time of the census were considered to be municipalities and therefore were probably counted among the large and medium cities in China. Not including Pressat's seven major municipalities, there were at least 94 cities with populations in excess of 100,000 in China in 1953 according to the census. Their population size averaged almost 340,000. Together with Pressat's seven, they could have accounted for 77.5 percent of the 30,180,000. The census figures for all 101 municipalities are given in Morris B. Ullman, Cities of Mainland China: 1953 and 1958, Foreign Manpower Research Office, Bureau of the Census, International Population Reports, Series P-95, no. 59, August 1961, table 1, pp. 18-27.

20. Pressat, "La Population de la Chine," p. 570.

21. Sripati Chandrasekhar, China's Population: Census and Vital Statistics (Hong Kong: Hong Kong University Press, 1959), p. 49.

22. For a detailed summary of the relevant evidence, see John S. Aird, "Population Policy and Demographic Prospects in the

People's Republic of China," in People's Republic of China: An Economic Assessment, Joint Economic Committee, Congress of the United States, May 18, 1972, pp. 244-72.

23. "Birth Control Exhibition Opens," NCNA, Peking, March 8, 1957, SCMP, no. 1,488, March 13, 1957, p. 10.

24. "Pen-shih chieh-yü kung-tso ch'u-te cheng-hsiao" ("Birth Control Work in This City Achieves Results"), Ch'ung-ch'ing jih-pao (Chungking Daily), October 30, 1957.

25. Mothers and Children's Health Section, Sian Municipal Health Bureau, "Wei-sheng-pu-men ta-li k'ai-chan pi-yün shuan-ch'uan chih-tao" ("Public Health Departments Carry Out Contraceptive Propaganda and Guidance with Great Efforts"), Hsi-an jih-pao (Sian Daily) (HAJP), Sian, August 8, 1957.

26. The reasons for suspecting that the atlas figures were 1964 census data were set forth in John S. Aird, "Recent Provincial Population Figures," China Quarterly (March 1978): 14-18.

27. Pi-chao Chen, "China's Population Program at the Grass Roots Level," Studies in Family Planning (SFP) 4 (August 1973): 222.

28. Carl Djerassi, "Fertility Limitation through Contraceptive Steroids in the People's Republic of China," SFP (January 1974): 28.

29. Tameyoshi Katagiri, "A Report on the Family Planning Program in the People's Republic of China," SFP (August 1973): 216.

30. Margaret S. Wolfson, Serving the People: Some Impressions of Social Development in China, report of a study mission to the PRC, Organization for Economic Cooperation and Development, Development Center (Paris: OECD, November 1975), p. 17.

31. Pi-chao Chen, "China's Population Program," p. 220.

32. Han Suyin, "Population Growth and Birth Control in China," Eastern Horizon (EH) (1973): 11.

33. Ronald Freedman, "Some Figures and Observations on Vital Rates and on Birth Planning, Obtained in China on Visit, February 10-27, 1976," unpublished paper, p. 1.

34. Obtained by Pi-chao Chen during his 1978 visit to China.

35. Pi-chao Chen, "Population and Health Policy in the People's Republic of China," Interdisciplinary Communications System, Smithsonian Institution (Washington, D.C.: 1976), p. 79.

36. "When Leaderships Attaches Importance to the Matter, Things Can Be Done Easily," NFJP, July 10, 1973.

37. Ibid.

38. The series is given in Table 4.4.

39. Nanking radio, Kiangsu Provincial Service, December 14, 1975, Foreign Broadcast Information Service (FBIS), no. 242, December 16, 1975, p. G4; "Family Planning," Peking Review (PR), No. 13, March 25, 1977, p. 29.

40. For a summary of these figures and their sources, see the notes to table 4 in Aird, "Recent Provincial Population Figures," p. 40.

41. Data Office, "Jen-k'ou liang-shih hsiao t'ung-chi" ("Statistics on Population and Food Grain"), Ch'i-shih nien-tai (The Seventies), August 1, 1977, p. 31; Wang Chien-min, "K'ung-chih jen-k'ou tseng-chang yü chia-su shih-hsien ssu-hua" ("Control Population Growth and Expedite the Realization of the Four Modernizations"), Chieh-fang jih-pao (Liberation Daily) (CFJP), May 16, 1979, p. 4; Liu Cheng and Wu Ts'ang-p'ing, "Jen-k'ou fei k'ung-chin pu-hsing" ("It Is Imperative that Population Growth Be Brought under Control"), JMJP, May 15, 1979, p. 3.

42. The urban population figure was reported in NCNA-English, Peking, August 21, 1979, FBIS, no. 163, August 21, 1979, p. L10. The national population total was obtained by subtracting the yearend 1978 population total for Taiwan, 17,136,000 given in Directorate-General of Budget, Accounting and Statistics, Executive Yuan, Republic of China, Monthly Statistics of the Republic of China, April 1979, p. 17, from the official yearend total for China including Taiwan, 975,230,000, given in State Statistical Bureau, Communique on Fulfillment of China's 1978 National Economic Plan, Peking, June 27, 1979, p. 10.

43. The Chinese Communist Party Committee of Nankung County, Hopeh, "Conscientiously Study the Theory of the Dictatorship of the Proletariat to Promote the Work in Family Planning," CMJ 2 (May 1976): 166; William L. Parish, "Birth Planning in the Chinese Countryside," paper presented at the annual meetings of the American Sociological Association, August 1976.

44. The Chinese Communist Party Committee of Nankung County, "Conscientiously Study Theory," p. 167; Tsinian radio, Shantung Provincial Service, March 25, 1975, FBIS, no. 64, April 2, 1975, p. G8; Hangchow radio, Chekian Provincial Service, April 9, 1979, JPRS, no. 73,545, May 1979, p. 42; Virgil A. Johnson and Halsey L. Beemer, Jr., Wheat in the People's Republic of China, CSC PRC Report no. 6, National Academy of Sciences, Washington, D.C., 1979; figure obtained by Pi-chao Chen during his 1978 visit.

45. Peking radio, Domestic Service, November 24, 1975, FBIS, no. 228, November 25, 1975, p. L7; Peking radio, Domestic Service, February 6, 1975, FBIS, no. 29, February 11, 1975, p. K1; NCNA, Peking, February 15, 1977, FBIS, no. 37, February 24, 1977, p. G5; "K'ung-chih jen-k'ou ti chan-lüeh jen-wu i-ting yao wan-ch'eng" ("The Strategic Task of Population Control Must Be Accomplished"), KMJP, June 30, 1979, p. 1; "Ssu-ch'uan sheng jen-k'ou tzu-jan tseng-chang-lu ta-chiang" ("Drastic Decline in Natural Population Increase Rate of Szechwan Province"), JMJP,

June 9, 1979, p. 1. The latter unit reportedly has a population of 1.4 million.

46. Kweiyang radio, Kweichow Provincial Service, July 21, 1979, FBIS, no. 153, August 1979, p. Q1.

47. The cities for which rates this high have been cited include Haikow in Kwangtung Province, Loyang and Anyang in Honan, Sian in Shensi, and Lanchow in Kansu. For Lanchow the figures for 1970-72 were 29.41, 26.43, and 23.47, respectively. Haikow radio, Hainan Island Regional Service, February 15, 1977, FBIS, no. 35, February 17, 1977, p. H5; Pi-chao Chen and Ann Elizabeth Miller, "Lessons from the Chinese Experience: China's Planned Birth Program and Its Transferability," SFP (October 1975): 360; Ch'en's figures obtained during 1978 visit; Rewi Alley, "Northwest Return," EH (1974): 26.

48. Freedman, "Some Figures and Observations."

49. James F. Leonard, China Notes, World Affairs Delegation Trip, October 1975, Population Data.

50. Peking radio, Domestic Service, September 10, 1973, Daily Report, People's Republic of China, FBIS, no. 176, September 11, 1973, p. C2; Nicholas R. Lardy, "China Trip Notes: 1978," (undated), p. 30; Peking radio, Domestic Service, January 26, 1974, FBIS, no. 21, January 30, 1974, p. B10.

51. Ch'en and Miller, "Lessons."

52. "Piao-chang chih sheng i-ke hai-tzu ti yü-ling fu-fu" ("In Praise of Those Couples of Childbearing Age Who Pledge to Have Only One Child"), JMJP, June 22, 1979, p. 4; "Pen-shih chi-hua sheng-yü kung-tso ts'o-shih yu-li ch'eng-hsiao hsien-chu" ("Our City's Planned Parenthood Work Achieved Remarkable Success with Effective Measures"), WHP, Shanghai, May 20, 1979, p. 3.

53. The six in 1977 were Hopeh with a rate of 8.75, Kiangsu with 9.97, Szechwan with 8.67, Shantung and Hupeh with "less than one percent," and Liaoning with 8.87. See Shihchiachuang radio, Hopeh Provincial Service, October 10, 1978, FBIS, no. 202, October 18, 1978, p. K1; Nanking radio, Kiangsu Provincial Service, April 10, 1978, FBIS, no. 72, April 13, 1978, p. G5; NCNA, Peking, May 28, 1978, JPRS, no. 71,519, July 21, 1978, p. 60; NCNA, Peking, July 1, 1978, FBIS, no. 128, July 3, 1978, p. E16; Shenyang radio, Liaoning Provincial Service, February 13, 1979, FBIS, no. 50, March 13, 1973, p. L3.

The eight in 1978 were Hopeh, Kiangsu, Shantung, Hupeh, Chekiang, Shensi, and Shansi with rates of "under one percent" and Szechwan with its celebrated 6.06. See NCNA, Peking, January 21, 1979, FBIS, no. 16, January 23, 1979, p. E15; NCNA, Chengtu, March 14, 1979, FBIS, no. 51, March 14, 1979, p. J1.

54. The source gives the figure of 19.7 for 1978 and indicates

that this is 1.88 per thousand less than the 1977 figure. See Nanchang radio, Kiangsi Provincial Service, May 18, 1979, FBIS, no. 103, May 25, 1979, p. 05.

55. Kweiyang radio, Kweichow Provincial Service, December 9, 1978, FBIS, no. 242, December 15, 1978, p. J5.

56. Information provided by Courtenay Slater. The natural increase rate is obtained by dividing the absolute surplus of births over deaths during the year by the average population during the year. The population growth rate is obtained by dividing the net population increment during the year by the population at the beginning of the year. Natural increase rates are usually given per thousand population; growth rates are usually given in percentages. The population growth rate is slightly higher than the natural increase rate because the denominator is slightly smaller.

57. State Statistical Bureau, Compilation of Important Documents; Ch'en Mu-hua, "Shih-hsien ssu-ko hsien-tai-hua, pi-hsü yu chi-hua-ti k'ung-chih jen-k'ou tseng-chang" ("For the Realization of the Four Modernizations, There Must Be Planned Control of Population Growth"), JMJP, August 11, 1979, p. 2.

58. Wang Chien-min, "Control Population Growth."

59. Peking radio, July 21, 1979, FBIS, no. 143, July 24, 1979, p. L9.

60. Wang Chien-min, "Control Population Growth"; Wang Chien-min, "Ch'ieh-shih k'ung-chih jen-k'ou tseng-chang" ("Seriously Control the Growth of Population"), WHP, Shanghai, July 12, 1979, p. 3.

61. An "authoritative Chinese source" was quoted by the Japanese economy and trade delegation in June 1979 as saying that the yearend 1977 population total for China was 962,050,000. See KYODO News Agency, Tokyo, June 1, 1979, FBIS, no. 109, June 5, 1979, p. L11. Given the yearend 1978 figure of 975,230,000, this implies an increase during 1978 of 1.37 percent. If the official totals for Taiwan are subtracted, the implied growth rate is reduced to 1.36 percent (see note 43).

62. NCNA-English, Peking, June 29, 1979, JPRS, no. 73,857, July 18, 1979, p. 3.

63. Tsinan radio, Shantung Provincial Service, March 25, 1975, FBIS, April 2, 1975, p. G8; Peking radio, Domestic Service, February 6, 1975, FBIS, February 11, 1975, p. K1; Kweiyang radio, Kweichow Provincial Service, March 19, 1977, FBIS, March 21, 1977, p. J1; Nanking radio, Kiangsu Provincial Service, December 14, 1975, FBIS, December 16, 1974, p. G4; "Chiang-chin ti-ch'ü chia-ch'iang hsüan-ch'uan chiao-ts'ai-ch'ü yu-hsiao ts'o-shih hen-chua chih sheng i-ko hai-tsu ti kung-tso ch'eng-chi hsien-chu" ("Chiang-chin Prefecture Strengthens Propaganda and Education,

Adopts Effective Measures to Obtain Tight Control of the Work of Having Only One Child, and Achieves Outstanding Success"), KMJP, September 7, 1979, p. 2.

64. Shihchiachuang radio, Hopeh Provincial Service, October 10, 1978, FBIS, no. 202, October 18, 1978, p. K1.

65. "Speech of the Chinese Delegation," International Conference on Population Planning for National Welfare and Development, Lahore, Pakistan, September 25, 1973, p. 7; Nanking radio, Kiangsu Provincial Service, April 10, 1978, FBIS, April 13, 1978, p. G4.

66. Liu Hai-ch'üan, "Yung chua sheng-ch'an chien-she ti chin-t'ou lai k'ung-chih jen-k'ou tseng-chang" ("Show the Same Zeal in Controlling Population Growth as in Grasping Production"), KMJP, September 13, 1979, pp. 1-2; NCNA, Peking, May 28, 1978, JPRS, July 21, 1978, p. 60.

67. The average of the figures for ten provinces for either 1970 or 1971 (taking the later figure where both are available) is 24.76; the average for 16 provinces for 1977 or 1978 is 12.53. The national figures are 23.4 for 1971 and 12.05 for 1978.

68. NCNA-English, Peking, May 21, 1979, FBIS, May 22, 1979, p. O4, table 6; and Tientsin Daily, "To Further Grasp the Work of Family Planning," Tien-chin jih-pao (Tientsin Daily) (TCJP), July 22, 1979, JPRS, October 2, 1979, p. 40.

69. Shenyang radio, Liaoning Provincial Service, February 13, 1979, FBIS, March 13, 1979, p. L3; Shenyang radio, Liaoning Provincial Service, September 15, 1959, FBIS, September 17, 1979, p. S2; Changsha radio, Hunan Provincial Service, November 16, 1978, FBIS, November 29, 1978, p. H6; NCNA-English, Peking, August 13, 1979, FBIS, August 14, 1979, p. 14, table 6; Canton radio, Kwangtung Provincial Service, July 3, 1979, JPRS, July 25, 1979, pp. 135-36; Chengchow radio, Honan Provincial Service, March 29, 1979, FBIS, April 4, 1979, p. P6.

70. For example, see "Shih-ting kuo-chia chien-she ti Hsü-yao, pi-hsü" pa t'ung-chi kung-tso tso-tao yu to, yu k'uai, yu hao, yu sheng" ("To Meet the Needs of National Construction, More, Faster, Better, and More Economical Statistical Work Must Be Done"), editorial, T'ung-chi kung-tso t'ung-hsin (Statistical Work Bulletin), January 29, 1956, p. 3.

71. Edgar Snow, "Interview with Mao," New Republic, February 27, 1965, p. 20.

72. Hua Hsiang, "Confessions of Power Pragmatists—Criticizing Chiang Ch'ing's Confidential Remarks to Lian Hsiao," KMJP, May 2, 1978, JPRS, June 27, 1978, p. 64. The source interprets the remark as an open invitation to fabrication.

73. See Aird, "Population Policy and Demographic Prospects in the People's Republic of China," pp. 279-80.

74. Sian radio, Shensi Provincial Service, May 6, 1978, FBIS, May 9, 1978, p. M2.

75. Nanking radio, Kwangsi Chuang Regional Service, January 12, 1978, FBIS, January 16, 1978, pp. H15-16.

76. In April 1959 the State Statistical Bureau released a 1958 grain production total of 375 million metric tons, more than 100 percent above the 1957 figure of 185 million metric tons. See State Statistical Bureau, "Communique on Fulfillment and Overfulfillment of China's First Five-Year Plan," NCNA-English, Peking, April 13, 1959, CB, April 15, 1959, p. 6; State Statistical Bureau, "Communique on China's Economic Growth in 1958," NCNA-English, Peking, April 14, 1959, CB, April 20, 1959, p. 5.

77. "Communique of the 8th Plenary Session of the 8th Central Committee of the Chinese Communist Party," NCNA-English, Peking, August 26, 1959, CB, September 1, 1979, pp. 2-3. By the end of the year, food shortages were again reported in parts of China, implying that a large part of the claimed 35 percent was also illusory, but, so far as is known, this figure has not yet been repudiated.

78. NCNA, Peking, September 16, 1978, FBIS, September 18, 1978, p. E20.

79. Ch'ien Hsüeh-sen and Wu Chia-p'ei, "Tsu-chih Kuan-li she-hui chu-i chien-she ti chi-shu she-hui kung-ch'eng" ("The Technology of Organizational Management in Social Construction—Social Engineering"), Ching-chi kuan-li (Economic Management), January 15, 1979, p. 7.

80. Sian radio, Shensi Provincial Service, January 23, 1979, FBIS, January 25, 1979, p. M1.

81. Hsüeh Mu-ch'iao, "How Can We Effect Planned Management of the National Economy?," JMJP, June 15, 1979, FBIS, June 20, 1979, p. L11.

82. Statement attributed to Li Hsien-nien during a work conference in April 1979. See "The Economy of the Whole Country Is Seriously Out of Balance," Ming pao, Hong Kong, June 14, 1979, FBIS, June 19, 1979, p. L12.

83. JMJP editorial, September 27, 1978, NCNA, Peking, September 27, 1978, FBIS, October 4, 1978, p. E19.

84. KMJP, October 14, 1978, FBIS, October 31, 1978, pp. E18-19.

85. JMJP, July 5, 1978, NCNA, Peking, July 4, 1978, FBIS, July 7, 1978, pp. E1-5. Provincial news items that provide further details on specific burdens include Hofei radio, Anhwei Provincial Service, July 21, 1978, FBIS, July 24, 1978, p. G6; Haikow radio, Hainan Island Regional Service, August 26, 1978, FBIS, August 30, 1978, pp. H5-6; Changchun radio, Kirin Provincial Service, July 18, 1978, FBIS, July 27, 1978, p. L7; Kunming radio, Yunnan Provincial

Service, July 31, 1978, FBIS, August 4, 1978, pp. J2-6; Nanning radio, Kwangsi Chuang Regional Service, September 17, 1978, FBIS, September 19, 1978, pp. H9-11.

86. "After Wages Went Up," PR, May 5, 1978, pp. 13-14.

87. Ch'üan-kuo pai-fen-chin-liu-shih ti chih-kung tseng-chia kung-tzu" ("Sixty Percent of Workers and Employees in the Country Receive Wage Increases"), JMJP, January 2, 1978, p. 1.

88. "The Economy of the Whole Country is Seriously Out of Balance"; "A Discussion of Unemployment," Ch'i-ming (Enlightenment) (undated), JPRS, August 9, 1978, p. 69; "Vigorously Develop the Collective Economy in the Cities and Townships and Organize Youth Awaiting Employment to Make Contributions to the Four Modernizations," Pei-ching jih-pao (Peking Daily) (PCJP), July 25, 1979, FBIS, August 9, 1979, p. R2; Changsha radio, Hunan Provincial Service, September 16, 1979, FBIS, September 19, 1979, p. P2; Hua Kuo-feng, "Report on the Work of the Government," NCNA-English, Peking, June 25, 1979, FBIS, July 2, 1979, p. 18; Sining radio, Tsinghai Provincial Service, June 28, 1979, FBIS, July 6, 1979, p. T2.

89. Ross H. Munro, "China's Rigid Rationing," Washington Post, November 27, 1977, pp. C1, C5.

90. "Communique of Results of Census and Registration of China's Population," NCNA, Peking, November 1, 1954, CB, no. 301, November 1, 1954, p. 2.

91. Marina Thorborg, "Chinese Employment Policy in 1949-78, with Special Emphasis on Women in Rural Production," in Joint Economic Committee, Congress of the United States, Chinese Economy Post-Mao (Washington, D.C.: U.S. Government Printing Office, November 9, 1978), p. 585.

92. K'ang K'o-ch'ing, "Lofty Tasks of the Women's Movement in China in the New Period" (work report to the Fourth National Women's Congress, September 9, 1978), NCNA, Peking, September 13, 1978, FBIS, no. 181, September 18, 1978, p. E4.

93. Thorborg, "Chinese Employment Policy," pp. 540, 550.

94. K'ang, "Lofty Tasks," p. E6.

95. Thorborg, "Chinese Employment Policy," pp. 563-64.

96. K'ang, "Lofty Tasks."

97. JMJP, September 18, 1978, NCNA, Peking, September 17, 1978, FBIS, September 19, 1978, p. E2. The editorial advised Party organs that they should "honestly believe the female comrades can do whatever male comrades can do."

98. "Resolutely Overcome Egalitarianism and Seriously Implement the Policy of Pay According to Work—Seminar on Pay According to Work Held in Peking," KMJP, October 14, 1978, FBIS, October 13, 1978, pp. E14-16.

99. Ibid.

100. For example, see Women Workers Department, Wuhan Federation of Trade Unions, "Educate Workers and Employees in Birth Control," Kung-jen jih-pao (Daily Worker) (KJJP), Peking, December 30, 1957, SCMP, January 17, 1958, p. 5.

101. For a discussion of the economics of production teams, see Frederick W. Crook, "The Commune System in the People's Republic of China, 1963-74," in China: A Reassessment of the Economy, Joint Economic Committee, Congress of the United States (Washington, D.C.: U.S. Government Printing Office, July 1975), pp. 394-405.

102. T'ao Yuan, "Shih-hsing lao yu so yang kao hao nung-ts'un chi-hua sheng-yü" ("Set Up Retirement Systems for the Aged to Do Family Planning Work Well in Rural Areas"), PCJP, July 18, 1979, p. 3.

103. "Basically Eliminate Illiteracy among the Country's Youth within Seven Years," JMJP (editorial), December 6, 1955, SCMP, December 14, 1955, pp. 5-6.

104. "Elimination of Illiteracy among Youths in Rural Areas throughout Country in 7 Years" (Text of Decision of Central Committee, New Democratic Youth League of China), JMJP, December 6, 1955, SCMP, December 14, 1955.

105. "Actively and Steadily Eliminate Illiteracy," JMJP (editorial), November 25, 1965, SCMP, March 18, 1957, p. 19.

106. "22 Million Former Illiterates Now Read," NCNA-English, Peking, September 21, 1957, SCMP, September 25, 1957, p. 2.

107. "Eliminate Illiteracy with the Revolutionary Spirit," JMJP (editorial), May 20, 1958, SCMP, June 9, 1958, pp. 22-25.

108. "China's Achievements in Literacy Campaign," NCNA-English, Peking, November 12, 1958, SCMP, November 17, 1958, p. 21.

109. Enquiry Subcommittee of the Department of Education of All-China Federation of Trade Unions, "Prevention of Inclination toward Laxity through Obliteration of Illiteracy," KJJP, July 10, 1960, SCMP, August 11, 1960, pp. 20-21.

110. NCNA-English, Peking, July 19, 1978, FBIS, 140, July 20, 1978, p. E14; Li Mei-lin, "K'ung jen-k'ou tseng-chang chia-su ssu-hua chin-she" ("Control the Growth of the Population to Expedite the Construction of the Four Modernizations"), NFJP, October 8, 1979, p. 3.

111. "Vicissitudes of Primary Schools," CNA, August 6, 1954, p. 1.

112. The figure for early 1956 is given in Li Ping-chieh, "Strive to Bring the Universalization of Obligatory Primary School Education into Realization at an Early Date," KMJP, February 22,

1956, p. 3. Other enrollment figures in this section are from John Philip Emerson, Administrative and Technical Manpower in the People's Republic of China, International Population Reports, Series P-95, no. 72, April 1973, Bureau of Economic Analysis, Department of Commerce, appendix table A-6, p. 95.

113. Liu Lin, "Firmly Adhere to the Guiding Principle of Walking on Two Legs, Actively Develop and Consolidate People-Operated Primary Schools," KMJP, February 4, 1962, SCMP, February 27, 1962, p. 8.

114. NCNA, Peking, June 10, 1978, FBIS, June 15, 1978, p. E11.

115. "Primary Schools in China," PR, September 8, 1978, p. 15.

116. "Teng Ying-chao on Campaign to Publicize Marriage Law," NCNA, Peking, March 4, 1953, p. 9.

117. Shih Liang, "Attend Seriously to the Thorough Implementation of the Marriage Law," JMJP, October 13, 1951, CB, November 10, 1951, pp. 23-25; "Supreme Court, Ministry of Justice Issue Directive on Interference with Freedom of Marriage," JMJP, October 15, 1951, CB, November 10, 1951, pp. 26-27; "Outline of Propaganda on the Thorough Implementation of the Marriage Law," pp. 27-28; Liu Ching-fan, "The Thorough Implementation of the Marriage Law," NCNA, Peking, March 19, 1953, CB, May 20, 1953, p. 5; Ku Chou, "Principles for Handling Divorce Cases during the Years since Promulgation of Marriage Law" Cheng-fa yen-chiu (Political and Legal Studies), October 1956, American Consulate General, Hong Kong, Extracts from China Mainland Magazines (ECMM), November 19, 1957, p. 17; Yu T'ung, "T'ui-yü tang-chien li-hun wen-t'i te fen-hsi ho i-chien" ("An Analysis and Views on the Problem of Divorce at Present"), JMJP, April 13, 1957, p. 7.

118. Occasionally complaints about enforced separations were permitted in the media. See, for example, Hsiao Liu, "When Can We Young Couples Have Our Reunion?," Chung-kuo ch'ing-nien (China Youth) (CKCN), May 1, 1958, ECMM, June 25, 1956, pp. 30-31.

119. "What Do Women Live For?," CKFN, no. 7, July 1, 1963, SCMM, August 26, 1963, pp. 21-22; Chu Shao-chun, "The Small Family Is Inferior to the Big Family," NFJP, October 27, 1963, SCMP, March 23, 1963, pp. 17-18; "Treat the Relationship between Work, Children, and Household Chores in a Revolutionary Spirit," CKFN, November 1, 1963, SCMM, December 9, 1963, pp. 23-27.

120. Chai Shang-tung, "How Should We Regard Communist Family Life?," CKCN, November 16, 1958, ECMM, January 23, 1959, pp. 6-11; Hu Sheng, "Concerning the Family," CKFN,

December 22, 1958, ECMM, March 2, 1959, pp. 14-18; Tu Ko-fu, "On the Question of Family," Chi-lin jih-pao (Kirin Daily), Changchun, January 10, 1959, SCMP, February 26, 1959, pp. 1-3; Ch'en Chien-wei, "The Breaking Down of the System of Feudal Patriarch," Ho-pei jih-pao (Hopeh Daily), Tientsin, April 8, 1959, SCMP, June 22, 1959, pp. 1-5.

121. In July 1978, for example, Shantung reported a case of forced marriage and Chekiang a traditional marriage negotiation. That these were not isolated cases is apparent from a criticism of "venal marriage in some places" voiced at the National Women's Congress in September 1978. See Tsinan radio, Shantung Provincial Service, July 24, 1978, FBIS, July 28, pp. G3-4; NCNA, Peking, July 24, 1978, FBIS, August 17, 1978, pp. E8-9; NCNA-English, Peking, September 11, 1978, FBIS, September 12, 1978, p. E10.

122. Leo A. Orleans, "China's Population: Some Confirmations and Estimates," Current Scene (March 1974): 13. Chandrasekhar obtained infant mortality rates for an unidentified sample of urban and rural areas for several years during the middle 1950s and a series of rates for nine specific cities for 1952-56, the latter provided by the Ministry of Health. Pressat was also given figures for the nine cities that differ only slightly from those provided to Chandrasekhar. Both rural and urban rates show a marked downward trend. However, all of these rates undoubtedly suffer from underregistration and are lower than the actual level of infant mortality in the units represented. See Chandrasekhar, China's Population, pp. 52-54; Pressat, "La Population de la Chine," p. 573.

123. Soong Ching-ling, "Women's Liberation in China," PR, February 11, 1972, p. 7.

124. For examples see Jay Mathews, "Chinese Farmers Protest Hunger, Cite Low Income," Washington Post, January 11, 1979, pp. A1, A20; Agence France Presse, Peking, January 21, 1979, FBIS, January 22, 1979, p. E1.

125. NCNA-English, Peking, January 24, 1978, FBIS, January 24, 1978, p. E18. The transfers were meant to be permanent, as many earlier sources indicate, but this source reveals that about 40 percent of the 16 million have returned to the urban areas. It is not clear whether the indicated cumulative backflow rate includes an estimate of the numbers of unregistered returnees.

126. For example, "Fa-yang sheng-yü i-t'ai hsin-feng yen-ko k'ung-chih jen-k'ou tseng-chang" ("Develop the New Fashion of Having One Child; Strictly Control Population Growth"), WHP, Shanghai, April 21, 1979, p. 2.

127. "Revolutionary Youths Should Care for the Affairs of State and Oppose Early Marriage; Revolutionary Cadres Should Boldly Guide Youths to Attain Health Growth," WHP, Shanghai, April 23,

1968, SCMP, May 20, 1968, p. 17; Shanghai radio, Shanghai City Service, December 27, 1969, FBIS, January 7, 1970, pp. C12-13.

128. For example, see Shanghai radio, Shanghai City Service, December 29, 1969, FBIS, no. 3, January 6, 1970, p. C23.

129. Liu Jo-ching, "Planned Control of Population Growth," Hung ch'i (Red Flag) (HC), June 3, 1978, JPRS, August 7, 1978, p. 106.

130. Mao Tse-tung, "Be Activists in Promoting the Revolution," October 9, 1957, Selected Works of Mao Tse-tung, vol. V (Peking: Foreign Languages Press, April 1977), pp. 487-88.

131. In 1949 Mao had said that China's large population was "a very good thing," that the fear that population growth could cause food shortages was utterly groundless, and that rapid population growth was no deterrent to rapid economic development. See "The Bankruptcy of the Idealist Conception of History," Selected Works of Mao Tse-tung, vol. IV (Peking: Foreign Languages Press, 1961), pp. 453-54. In the revised version of Mao's speech of February 27, 1957, he insisted that a large population, despite its difficulties, was an asset and criticized other people who went around "grumbling that there are too many people." See Mao Tse-tung, "On the Correct Handling of Contradictions among the People," NCNA-English, Peking, June 18, 1957, CB, June 20, 1957, p. 16. In 1958 Mao insisted that both the size and the poverty of China's population were advantages to national economic development.

132. W. R. Geddes, Peasant Life in Communist China, Monograph no. 6, Society for Applied Anthropology (Ithaca, N.Y.: Cornell University, 1963), p. 16; Chou En-lai, "Report on the Second Five-Year Plan" (Presented to the Eighth National Congress of the Chinese Communist Party on September 16, 1956), NCNA, Peking, September 20, 1956, CB, October 5, 1956, p. 30.

133. For example, in 1964 Chou expressed approval of China's birth control program and talked of the need to reduce population growth rates in an interview with Edgar Snow. See "Edgar Snow's 5-Hour Interview with Chou En-lai," Washington Post, February 3, 1964. In an interview taped for the Canadian Broadcasting Corporation in May 1971, Chou spoke of a plan to reduce China's natural increase rate to 1 percent in the 1970s and to less than 1 percent during the 1980s. See "A Conversation with Chou En-lai," produced by the Canadian Broadcasting Corporation, July 28, 1971, National Public Radio, Washington, D.C., no date. Only one instance is known in which Chou's interest in birth control was conveyed to people in China through the press. A 1963 article in a youth journal told how Chou had praised a factory worker who had voluntarily had himself sterilized. See Wang Po-ch'ing, "Ch'in-ch'ieh te kuan-huai yeh-ch'ing te ku-li" ("Intimate Concern and Warm-Hearted Encouragement"), CKCN, September 1, 1963, p. 15.

134. Canton radio, Kwangtung Provincial Service, December 12, 1976, FBIS, no. 242, December 15, 1976, p. H16.

135. NCNA-English, Peking, March 6, 1978, FBIS, March 7, 1978, p. D25. Hua's speech had been delivered on February 26. The State Council's decision was reported in NCNA-English, Peking, July 1, 1978, FBIS, July 3, 1978, p. E15.

136. Kirin Medical College Revolutionary Committee, "Ch'ih-chiao i-sheng" 'ei-shun chiao-tsi'ai (Teaching Materials on the Fostering and Training of "Barefoot Doctors") (Peking: Jen-min wei-sheng ch'u-pan-she, 1971), p. 352.

137. For example, see Huhehot radio, Inner Mongolia Regional Service, July 24, 1978, FBIS, July 27, 1978, p. K1; Shihchiachuang radio, Hopeh Provincial Service, July 25, 1978, FBIS, August 2, 1978, p. K2; Foochow radio, Fukien Provincial Service, August 5, 1978, FBIS, August 7, 1978, p. G3.

138. "China Achieves Initial Success in Planned Population Growth," NCNA-English, Peking, August 23, 1974, SPRCP, September 5, 1974, p. 103; Changchun radio, Kirin Provincial Service, January 6, 1975, FBIS, January 7, 1975, p. L1; "Family Planning and Emancipation of Women in China," NCNA-English, Peking, June 27, 1975, SPRCP, July 9, 1975, p. 116.

139. NCNA-English, Peking, March 7, 1978, FBIS, March 16, 1978, p. 69.

140. "The Work Relating to Birth Control Must Be Done Carefully," WHP, Shanghai, January 28, 1973; Chengtu radio, Szechwan Provincial Service, February 28, 1973, British Broadcasting Corporation, Summary of World Broadcasts (SWB), part 3, The Far East, Weekly Economic Report, March 7, 1973, p. FE/W714/A/8-9; NCNA-English, Peking, March 5, 1973, SWB, March 14, 1973, p. FE/W715/A/1.

141. NCNA-English, Peking, April 16, 1973, FBIS, no. 74, April 17, 1973, pp. A8-9.

142. "China's Views on Major Issues of World Population," PR, August 30, 1974, pp. 6-9.

143. NCNA-English, Peking, May 13, 1977, FBIS, May 13, 1977, p. E3.

144. Changchun radio, Kirin Provincial Service, February 16, 1978, FBIS, no. 37, February 23, 1978, pp. L1-2.

145. Canton radio, Kwangtung Provincial Service, April 10, 1978, FBIS, April 12, 1978, p. H1.

146. Peking radio, Domestic Service, July 25, 1978, FBIS, July 28, 1978, p. G1.

147. Chengtu radio, Szechwan Provincial Service, September 2, 1978, FBIS, September 7, 1978, p. J2.

148. Foochow radio, Fukien Provincial Service, September 3, 1978, FBIS, September 7, 1978, p. G3.

149. Nanking radio, Kwangsi Chuang Regional Service, September 17, 1978, FBIS, September 19, 1978, p. H17.

150. Li Tzu-li and Yu Lin, "Cheng-chih t'ung-shuai ching-chi chiu-shih cheng-chih wei ching-chi fu-wu" ("Politics in Command Over the Economy Is Having Politics Serving the Economy"), KMJP, May 22, 1978, p. 4.

151. NCNA-English, Peking, June 14, 1978, FBIS, June 14, 1978, p. E9.

152. Hu Ch'iao-mu, "Act in Accordance with Economic Laws; Step Up the Four Modernizations," JMJP, October 6, 1978, NCNA, Peking, October 5, 1978, FBIS, October 11, 1978, p. E17.

153. Le Wei-hsiung, "The Current State of Chinese Agriculture and Our Historical Experience in Developing Agriculture," Peking radio, Peking Domestic Service, February 14, 1979, FBIS, February 16, 1979, p. E12.

154. Chang Pi-chung, "We Must Start from China's Special Characteristics in Carrying Out the Modernization Program," KJJP, May 3, 1979, FBIS, May 21, 1979, p. L6; JMJP Reporter, "It Is Still Necessary to Grasp Firmly the Buying and Selling of Grain," JMJP, June 25, 1979, FBIS, July 10, 1979, p. L18.

155. Declining per capita food grain allotments were reported in Szechwan, Yunnan, and Kwangtun. See Chengtu radio, Szechwan Provincial Service, February 15, 1979, March 12, 1979, FBIS, March 15, 1979, p. J3; Canton radio, Kwangtung Provincial Service, August 1, 1979, FBIS, August 1, 1979, FBIS, August 10, 1979, p. P2. The last source said that "quite a large number of people in the rural areas [of Kwangtung] still do not have enough grain to eat." Chekiang foresaw the possibility of declining per capita grain in the future if family planning were neglected. See Hangchow radio, Chekiang Provincial Service, April 27, 1979, FBIS, April 30, 1979, p. O6.

156. It is reported that prior to 1949 cultivated land in China amounted to approximately 1.5 billion mou. See Wang Chien-min, "K'ung-chih jen-k'ou tseng-chang yü chia-ssu shih-hsien ssu-hua" ("Control Population Growth and Expedite the Realization of the Four Modernizations"), Chieh-fang jih-pao (Liberation Daily) (CFJP), May 16, 1979, p. 4. As has already been mentioned, there has been a decline of 100 million mou under cultivation since that time (see note 152).

157. Liu Cheng and Wu Ts'ang-p'ing, "Jen-k'ou fei k'ung-chin pu-hsing" ("It Is Imperative that Population Growth Be Brought under Control"), JMJP, May 15, 1979, p. 3.

158. Yu Chin-shun, "Examine the Socialist Theory of Population from the Economic Angle," Ching-chi yen-chiu (Economic Research), May 20, 1979, JPRS, September 7, 1979, p. 54.

159. Peking radio, Domestic Service, July 5, 1979, FBIS, July 11, 1979, p. L24; NCNA-English, Peking, July 15, 1979, FBIS, July 16, 1979, p. L10; Ch'en Mu-hua, "Shih-hsien ssu-ko hsien-tai-hua, pi-hsü yu cha-hua-ti k'ung-chih jen-k'ou tseng-chang" ("For the Realization of the Four Modernizations, There Must Be Planned Control of Population Growth"), JMJP, August 11, 1979, p. 2.

160. Wang Chien-min, "K'ung-chih jen-k'ou tseng-chang yu chia-su shih-hsien ssu-hua" ("Realization of the Four Modernizations").

161. Chang Ch'ing-wu, "K'ung-chih ch'eng-shih jen-k'ou ti tseng-chang" ("Control the Growth of the Urban Population"), JMJP, August 21, 1979, p. 3.

162. Yu Ch'uan-yu, "It Is Necessary to Comprehensively Develop Agriculture, Sideline Occupations, and Industry," NCNA, Peking, March 25, 1979, FBIS, no. 63, March 30, 1979, pp. L1-2.

163, Liu and Wu, "It is Imperative."

164. Chang Shu-kuang and Sun Yün-p'eng, "K'ung-chih jen-k'ou pi-hsu ts'ai-ch'ü ching-chi ts'o-shih" ("It is Necessary to Control Population Growth with Economic Measures"), KMJP, June 17, 1979, p. 3.

165. NCNA, Peking, June 28, 1979, FBIS, no. 127, June 29, 1979, p. L5.

166. For example, Harbin radio, Heilungkiang Provincial Service, April 28, 1979, FBIS, April 30, 1979, p. S1.

167. Wang Chien-min, "K'ung-chih jen-k'ou tseng-chang yü chia-su shih-hsien ssu-hua."

168. NCNA, Peking, June 8, 1979, FBIS, no. 115, June 13, 1979, p. L16; Wen Ying-kan, "To Do Well in Controlling Population Growth Is an Important Item of Work," NFJP, August 1, 1979, FBIS, no. 156, August 10, 1979, p. P3.

169. Wang Chien-min, "Chieh-shih k'ung-chih jen-k'ou tseng-chang."

170. T'ao Yüan, "Shih-hsing lao yu so yang kao hao nung-ts'un chi-hua sheng-yü" ("Set Up Retirement Systems for the Aged to Do Family Planning Work Well in Rural Areas"), PCJP, July 18, 1979, p. 3.

171. "Wu erh wu nü yu i-k'ao" ("The Childless Are Taken Care Of"), JMJP, August 11, 1979, p. 2.

172. Kuei Shih-hsun, "'To tzu to fu' yü ching-chi cheng-ts'e" ("'The More Sons, the More Blessings' and Economic Policy"), CFJP, August 29, 1979, p. 4.

173. NCNA, Peking, July 8, 1978, FBIS, July 11, 1978, p. E20; Foochow radio, Fukien Provincial Service, August 5, 1978, FBIS, August 7, 1978, p. G3; Foochow radio, Fukien Provincial Service, September 3, 1978, FBIS, September 7, 1978, p. G3; Canton radio, Kwangtung Provincial Service, September 26, 1978, FBIS, September 28, 1978, p. H1; Chengchow radio, Honan Provincial Service, March 29, 1979, FBIS, April 4, 1979, p. P6; "Heng-mien Kung-she tang-wei ch'ieh-shih chua-hao chi-hua sheng-yü" ("Party Committee of Heng-mien Commune Earnestly Carried Out Planned Parenthood"), WHP, May 30, 1979, p. 1; "P'o-ch'u sheng-yü wen-t'i chang ti feng-chien tao-te kuan-nien" ("Destroy the Feudal Moral Ideas about the Problem of Childbirth"), CFJP, August 5, 1979, p. 2.

174. For example, see CCP Committee of Ch'ü-hsi Commune, Chieh-yang County, Kwangtung Province, "Vigorously Criticize the Concept of 'Inferiority of Women to Men' and Do a Good Job in Planned Parenthood," NFJP, February 14, 1975.

175. Nanking radio, Kiangsu Provincial Service, March 27, 1978, FBIS, no. 61, March 29, 1978, p. G5.

176. Tso An-hua, "Family Planning in Jutung County (I): Declining Population Growth," PR, April 7, 1978, pp. 18-20; "Family Planning in Jutung County (II): Of the Masses' Own Will," PR, April 14, 1978, pp. 26-27; "Family Planning in Jutung County (III): Measures and Results," PR, April 21, 1978, pp. 23-25.

177. "Contraception and Planned Birth Must Be Practiced," WHP, Shanghai, January 23, 1958, SCMP, February 28, 1958, p. 7.

178. Ch'en and Miller, "Lessons," p. 354; "Han Su-yin Returns to Her Home Province of Szechwan," Ta-kung pao (Impartial Daily), Hong Kong, November 25, 1975, JPRS, February 13, 1976, p. 2; Fox Butterfield, "Family Ties in Rural China Seem More Binding than Peking's Rule," New York Times, December 19, 1977, p. 18.

179. Wuhan radio, Hupeh Provincial Service, December 20, 1977, JPRS, January 24, 1978, p. 87.

180. Kunming radio, Yunnan Provincial Service, December 5, 1978, FBIS, December 7, 1978, p. J2.

181. Peking Economic Institute, Population Research Office, Jen-k'ou li-lun (Population Theory) (Peking: Commercial Press, December 1977), pp. 140-41.

182. Nanchang radio, Kiangsi Provincial Service, August 4, 1978, FBIS, August 7, 1978, p. G4.

183. For example, Hopeh called on local units to help hold the provincial rate below 7 per thousand in 1978; Hunan called for 8 per

thousand in 1978, 7 by 1980, and 6 by the middle of the Sixth Five-Year Plan period; Shantung called for 7 per thousand in 1980, 6 in 1981, and 4 in 1985. See Shihchiachuang radio, Hopeh Provincial Service, April 19, 1978, FBIS, May 1, 1978, p. K3; Changsha radio, Hunan Provincial Service, November 11, 1978, FBIS, November 15, 1978, p. H1; Tsinan radio, Shantung Provincial Service, February 3, 1980, FBIS, February 7, 1980, p. O3.

184. Foochow radio, Fukien Provincial Service, September 3, 1978, FBIS, no. 174, September 7, 1978, p. G4; Ho Yün-t'eng, "Wo-sheng yu i-wan-to-tui fu-fu chih cheng i-ke hai-tzu" ("Kwangtung Province Has Over 10,000 Couples Who Will Have Only One Child"), NFJP, June 14, 1979, p. 1; Shenyang radio, Liaoning Provincial Service, September 15, 1979, FBIS, no. 181, September 17, 1978, p. S2; Chengchow radio, Honan Provincial Service, March 29, 1979, FBIS, no. 66, April 4, 1979, p. P6; Tientsin radio, Tientsin City Service, August 4, 1979, FBIS, no. 153, August 7, 1979, p. R3; information obtained in Shanghai by the writer during a visit in November 1979; Lin Hu-chia, "Cheng-fu kung-tso pao-kao" ("Government Work Report"), PCJP, December 16, 1979, p. 3; Canton radio, Canton City Service, January 19, 1980, FBIS, no. 16, January 25, 1980, p. P2. Canton reported that its birth rate had risen for four consecutive years since 1976.

185. Shihchiachuang radio, Hopeh Provincial Service, December 27, 1975, FBIS, January 6, 1975, p. K2; Chengchow radio, Honan Provincial Service, December 29, 1977, FBIS, January 9, 1978, p. H1; Kunming radio, Yunnan Provincial Service, December 5, 1978, FBIS, December 7, 1978, p. J1; Kweiyang radio, Kweichow Provincial Service, November 24, 1978, FBIS, November 29, 1978, p. J1; Peking radio, Domestic Service, September 10, 1979, FBIS, September 20, 1979, p. R2; Nanning radio, Kwangsi Regional Service, February 25, 1979, JPRS, March 25, 1979, p. 70; Peking radio, Peking City Service, March 4, 1979, FBIS, March 22, 1979, p. R2; "Do Effective Family Planning, Control Population Increase," PCJP, July 12, 1979, JPRS, August 29, 1979, p. 72.

186. Wuhan radio, Hupeh Provincial Service, December 20, 1977, JPRS, January 24, 1978, p. 88; Foochow radio, Fukien Provincial Service, May 2, 1979, FBIS, May 3, 1979, p. O3; Kunming radio, Yunnan Provincial Service, November 14, 1978, FBIS, November 20, 1978, p. J3; NCNA, Peking, July 8, 1978, FBIS, July 11, 1978, p. E20; Changsha radio, Hunan Provincial Service, June 22, 1979, FBIS, June 26, 1979, p. P2.

187. Chengchow radio, Honan Provincial Service, July 16, 1978, FBIS, July 21, 1978, p. H1.

188. Birth Control Office, Wen-tung County, Shantung Province, "Party Committee Should Seriously Grasp Family Planning Work," NFSP, May 18, 1973.

189. CCP Committee of Ch'ü-hsi Commune, "Vigorously Criticize."

190. Hsiao Hung, "Kan-pu tai-t'ou tso-ch'u yng-tzu she-yüan keng-shang shih-hsing chieh-yü" ("Cadres Take the Lead and Set Up Models, Members Follow Suit and Practice Birth Control"), WHP, June 5, 1979, p. 2.

191. "Heng-mien kung-she tang-wei ch'ieh-shih chua-hao chi-hua sheng-yü."

192. NCNA-English, Peking, January 21, 1979, FBIS, January 23, 1979, p. E15.

193. Hofei radio, Anhwei Provincial Service, April 18, 1979, FBIS, April 20, 1979, p. O1; Nanchang radio, Kiangsi Provincial Service, May 18, 1979, FBIS, May 1979, p. O5.

194. Shanghai radio, Shanghai City Service, August 28, 1979, JPRS, September 18, 1979, p. 60; Harbin radio, Heilungkiang Provincial Service, September 4, 1979, FBIS, September 11, 1979, p. S3; Lanchow radio, Kansu Provincial Service, August 11, 1979, FBIS, August 22, 1979, p. T7; Tientsin radio, Tientsin City Service, August 4, 1979, FBIS, August 7, 1979, p. R4; Commentator, "Each Couple Had Better Have Only One Child," Kuei-chou jih-pao (Kweichow Daily), December 24, 1979, JPRS, January 14, 1980, p. 64.

195. Sian radio, Shensi Provincial Service, February 13, 1979, FBIS, February 15, 1979, p. M3; Hofei radio, Anhwei Provincial Service, April 18, 1979, FBIS, April 20, 1979, p. O1.

196. Peking radio, Domestic Service, July 5, 1979, FBIS, no. 134, July 11, 1979, p. L25.

197. "K'ung-chih jen-k'ou shih i-hsiang chung-yao ti chan-lüeh jen-wu."

198. Canton radio, Kwangtung Provincial Service, January 6, 1979, FBIS, January 9, 1979, p. H3.

199. Chengtu radio, Szechwan Provincial Service, February 27, 1979, FBIS, no. 47, March 8, 1979, p. J4.

200. Hofei radio, Anhwei Provincial Service, April 18, 1979, complete translation provided by FBIS on request of the writer.

201. Ibid.

202. Kuei Shih-hsun, "'The More Sons, the More Blessings.'"

203. "Chi-hua sheng-yü hao-ti ying-tang yü-i ku-li" ("Those Who Practice Family Planning Well Should Be Encouraged"), CFJP, June 13, 1979, p. 2.

204. For further information on abortion and sterilization during the first birth control campaign, see Aird, "Population Policy and Demographic Prospects in the People's Republic of China," pp. 261-68.

205. Ibid., pp. 297-98, 299-301.

206. NCNA-English, Peking, January 27, 1980, FBIS, January 29, 1980, p. L16. It is not clear whether the figures were meant to include abortions as well.

207. Kweiyang radio, Kweichow Provincial Service, December 9, 1978, FBIS, December 15, 1978, p. J5.

208. "Birth Control Operation Teams Organized to Visit Rural Districts of Kao-chou Hsien," NJFP, May 18, 1973; Hofei radio, Anhwei Provincial Service, January 26, 1978, FBIS, January 30, 1978, p. G2; Canton radio, Kwangtung Provincial Service, February 1, 1978, JPRS, March 17, 1978, p. 54; Sian radio, Shensi Provincial Service, September 11, 1979, JPRS, October 17, 1979, p. 142.

209. "New Achievements in Family Planning in Kwangtung"; NCNA, Peking, January 26, 1974, FBIS, January 30, 1974, p. B10. NCNA, Peking, June 30, 1976, FBIS, July 1, 1976, p. G2; Kunming radio, Yunnan Provincial Service, November 6, 1979, JPRS, December 11, 1979, p. 112.

210. Tso An-hua, "Family Planning in Jutung County (III): Measures and Results," p. 24; "Family Planning Work Effectively Grasped in K'ai-p'ing County," NFJP, February 3, 1977; Hofei radio, Anhwei Provincial Service, February 1, 1978, JPRS, March 17, 1978, pp. 53-54.

211. "Family Planning Work Effectively Grasped in K'ai-p'ing County"; "Do Our Work Well in Publicizing the Idea That It Is Most Advisable for Each Family to Have Only One Child," Chien-k'ang (Health) (editorial), July 21, 1979, FBIS, July 24, 1979, p. L10.

212. NCNA-English, Peking, February 27, 1979, FBIS, no. 43, March 2, 1979, pp. E12-13. Some men taking the drug were found to have a low level of potassium in the blood.

213. NCNA-English, Peking, August 14, 1979, FBIS, August 15, 1979, p. Q1; NCNA-English, Peking, August 25, 1979, FBIS, August 31, 1979, p. Q2.

214. Foochow radio, Fukien Provincial Service, August 18, 1979, FBIS, August 21, 1979, p. O4; Chenchow radio, Honan Provincial Service, August 25, 1979, FBIS, August 29, 1979, p. P1.

215. Ch'en, "Shih-hsien ssu-ko hsien-tai-hua, pi-hsü yu chi-hua-ti k'ung-chih jen-k'ou tseng-chang" ("For the Realization of the Four Modernizations, There Must Be Planned Control of Population Growth"), JMJP, August 11, 1979, p. 2.

216. Canton radio, Canton City Service, November 10, 1979, FBIS, November 16, 1979, p. P15.

217. Hsin-hua Daily Commentator, "Correct Attitude and Eliminating Chaos and Restoring Order—On the Question of Having a Correct Attitude toward the Great Proletarian Cultural Revolution,"

Nanking radio, Kiangsu Provincial Service, September 15, 1978, FBIS, September 20, 1978, p. G3.

218. "Criticize the Sixth Brigade of Tung-wan Commune for Its Thwarting the Implementation of the Policy Governing Private Plots," JMJP, October 14, 1979, JPRS, December 20, 1979, pp. 51-53. A peasant who resisted was "approached and worked on repeatedly by the commune secretaries and the brigade cadres" until he was "finally persuaded" to submit his document.

219. "Practice of Planned Birth and Late Marriage is Found at State Cotton Mill," Kung-jen tsao-fan pao (Workers' Rebel Paper), Shanghai, February 1, 1970; Birth Control Office, Wen-tung County, Shantung Province, "Party Committee Should Seriously Grasp Family Planning Work"; Foochow radio, Fukien Provincial Service, October 27, 1975, FBIS, November 7, 1975, p. G3; "Under the Guidance of Chairman Mao's Brilliant Thoughts, Great Achievements Were Accomplished in National Birth Control," NCNA, Peking, February 21, 1977, Chung-kuo hsin-wen (China News) (CKHW), Hong Kong, February 22, 1977, JPRS, September 14, 1977, p. 4.

220. "Liu-hang kung-she ta-p'o ssu-chiu t'i-ch'ang wan-hun" ("Liu-hang Commune Extensively Destroyed the 'Four Olds' and Promoted Late Marriage"), WHP, January 22, 1968, p. 3; Party Branch, no. 15 Production Brigade, Ying-hsiung Commune, Nan-t'ung County, Kiangsu Province, "Educate the Young People to Practice Lar Marriage and Family Planning," JMJP, November 20, 1972, SCMP, December 4, 1972, p. 14; CCP Committee, Ch'ü-hsi Commune, Chien-yang County, Kwangtung Province, "Vigorously Criticize"; Nanning radio, Kwangsi Regional Service, February 22, 1977, FBIS, no. 23, February 23, 1977, p. H9; Canton radio, Kwangtung Provincial Service, January 21, 1978, FBIS, January 25, 1978, p. H4.

221. "The New Custom of Marrying Late," JMJP, June 12, 1973, SCMP, June 22, 1973, p. 226; "Do a Good Job in Family Planning and Liberate the Labor Force of Women," JMJP, April 14, 1975, SCMP, April 29, 1975, p. 40; NCNA-English, Peking, June 27, 1975, FBIS, June 27, 1975, p. E3.

222. Tsinan radio, Shantung Provincial Service, February 27, 1976, FBIS, March 1, 1976, p. G9; Kunming radio, Yunnan Provincial Service, November 26, 1976, FBIS, November 30, 1976, p. J3; Sian radio, Shensi Provincial Service, November 23, 1977, FBIS, November 28, 1977, p. M4; NCNA, Peking, February 6, 1975, FBIS, February 11, 1975, p. K1.

223. Fox Butterfield, "Chinese Area Claims It Curbs Population," New York Times, January 29, 1980, p. A6.

224. Commentator, "T'i-ch'ang wan hun"; Liang Yu-ken, "Business Type Marriages Should Cease," NFJP, February 6, 1970, p. 3;

"Provincial and Municipal Revolutionary Committees Call a General Meeting for Family Planning Work."

225. Ch'en Mu-hua, "Four Modernizations."

226. "Party Secretaries Take Command in Mobilizing the Whole Party in Doing a Still Better Job in Planned Parenthood"; Chengchow radio, Honan Provincial Service, July 16, 1978, FBIS, July 21, 1978, p. H1; Changsha radio, Hunan Provincial Service, November 11, 1978, FBIS, November 15, 1978, p. H1.

227. Shanghai radio, Shanghai City Service, December 27, 1969, FBIS, January 7, 1970, p. C12; Hung Sung, "Marry Late in Life, Continue the Revolution," Ch'e-ti p'i-p'an K'ung Meng Chih-tao (Thoroughly Criticize the Teachings of Confucius and Mencius), Shanghai, February 1971; "Leadership Should Be Fully Strengthened," NFJP, January 18, 1975, Foochow radio, Fukien Provincial Service, October 27, 1975, FBIS, November 7, 1975, p. G2; "It is Necessary to Pay Serious and Proper Attention to Propaganda Work on Family Planning," KMJP, February 12, 1977, SPRCP, March 22, 1977, p. 51.

228. Changchun radio, Kirin Provincial Service, January 6, 1975, FBIS, January 7, 1975, p. L2; NCNA, Peking, February 21, 1977, CKHW, February 22, 1977, JPRS, September 14, 1977, p. 42; Kunming radio, Yunnan Provincial Service, December 5, 1978, FBIS, December 7, 1978, p. J2.

229. In June 1976 Changsha radio reported a Hunan provincial telephone conference on birth control work that concluded among other things that "to do a good job of birth control we must seriously study Chairman Mao's important instructions, criticize Teng Hsiao-p'ing's revisionist line, in depth firmly grasp the class struggle concerning marriage and parenthood and resolutely act contrary to Teng Hsiao-p'ing's revisionist line." See Changsha radio, Hunan Provincial Service, June 18, 1976, FBIS, June 18, 1976, p. H2.

230. Canton radio, Kwangtung Provincial Service, December 12, 1976, FBIS, December 15, 1976, p. H16; Chengtu radio, Szechwan Provincial Service, December 21, 1976, FBIS, December 23, 1976, p. J1; Huhehot radio, Inner Mongolia Regional Service, February 14, 1977, FBIS, February 9, 1977, p. K; NCNA, Peking, July 5, 1977, FBIS, July 12, 1977, p. G10; Sian radio, Shensi Provincial Service, November 22, 1977, FBIS, November 28, 1977, p. M3; Hofei radio, Anhwei Provincial Service, February 4, 1978, FBIS, February 7, 1978, pp. G1-2; Kunming radio, Yunnan Provincial Service, December 5, 1978, FBIS, December 7, 1978, p. J2; "Public Health Work Must Serve to Quicken the Pace of Realizing the Four Modernizations," HAJP (editorial), Sian radio, Sian Provincial Service, December 20, 1978, JPRS, January 10, 1979, p. 78; "Heng-mien kung-she tang-wei ch'ieh-shih chua-hao chi-hua sheng-yü"; Wang Chien-min, "Ch'ieh-shih k'ung-chih jen-k'ou tseng-chang."

231. Shanghai radio, Shanghai City Service, December 8, 1968, FBIS, December 9, 1968, p. C11; Tung Yin-ti, "For Revolution's Sake Insist on Late Marriages," NFJP, February 6, 1970, p. 3; League Branch, Pai-ts'un Brigade, An-p'ing Commune, Hsi-yang County, Shansi Province, "Changing Customs and Traditions in Marriage," JMJP, November 20, 1972, SCMP, December 4, 1972, p. 13; "Do a Serious Job in the Work of Family Planning," NFJP (editorial), December 7, 1973; Nanking radio, Kiangsu Provincial Service, December 14, 1975, FBIS, December 16, 1974, p. G5; Tsinan radio, Shantung Provincial Service, February 27, 1976, FBIS, March 1, 1976, p. G9; Nanchang radio, Kiangsi Provincial Service, August 4, 1978, FBIS, August 7, 1978, p. G4; Kweiyang radio, Kewichow Provincial Service, July 21, 1979, FBIS, August 7, 1979, p. Q1.

232. "Lien-hsi shih-chi wen-t'i t'an-t'ao jen-k'ou kuei-lü" ("Associate Real Problems with the Study of Population Law"), KMJP, November 28, 1978, p. 3.

233. Michael Parks, "Sex Is High on List of New Chinese Freedoms," Baltimore Sun, January 25, 1979.

234. "A Simple Discussion of the People's Democratic Rights," Szu-wu lun-t'an (April 5th Forum), no. 7, March 11, 1979, JPRS, July 27, 1979, p. 14.

235. Ch'en Mu-hua, "Four Modernizations." Ch'en, of course, rejects this argument. However, it was part of the official line during the Big Leap Forward. See, for example, Jo Shui, "Mouths and Hands," JMJP, April 15, 1959, SCMP, June 1, 1959, pp. 9-12.

236. NCNA, Peking, December 22, 1979, FBIS, December 28, 1979, pp. L8-9. Ch'en also answers this argument: China need have no fears about an insufficient labor force.

237. Kuei Shih-hsun, "Chi-hua sheng-yü shih i-hsiang chan-lüeh-hsing ts'o-shih" ("Family Planning Is a Strategic Measure"), WHP, August 23, 1979, p. 1. Other sources have cited figures to show that the savings to the state resulting from prevented childbirths are greater than the costs of the rewards. See, for example, NCNA Reporter, "K'ung-chih jen-k'ou ti chan-lüeh jen-su i-ting yao wan-ch'eng" ("The Strategic Task of Population Control Must Be Accomplished"), KMJP, June 30, 1979, p. 3.

238. Chang Shu-kang and Sun Yün-p'eng, "K'ung-chih jen-k'ou pi-hsu ts'ai-ch'ü ching-chi ts'o-shih" ("It Is Necessary to Control Population Growth with Economic Measures"), KMJP, June 17, 1979, p. 3.

239. NCNA, Peking, July 8, 1978, FBIS, July 11, 1978, p. E20; Foochow radio, Fukien Provincial Service, September 3, 1978, FBIS, September 7, 1978, p. G3; Shihchiachuang radio, Hopeh Provincial Service, October 10, 1978, FBIS, October 18, 1978, p. K1; Canton

radio, Kwangtung Provincial Service, December 3, 1978, FBIS, December 3, 1978, FBIS, December 5, 1978, p. H5; Ho Yun-t'eng, "10,000 Couples"; Canton radio, Kwangtung Provincial Service, July 3, 1979, JPRS, July 25, 1979, p. 135; "Shih-ke-wei-hui fa-pu 'kuan-yü t'u-hsing chi-hau sheng-yü ti jo-kan kuei-ting' ke-chi ling-tao yao ch'ing-tzu tung-shou k'ung-shou k'ung-chih jen-k'ou tseng-chang" ("The Shanghai Municipal Revolutionary Committee Promulgated 'Several Regulations Concerning the Promotion of Family Planning'; Leadership at All Levels Must Personally Take Charge of Controlling Population Growth"), WHP, August 20, 1979, p. 1.

240. Party Committee of the T'ai-hu Fishery Commune, Wuhsi Municipality, Kiangsu Province, "Effectively Strengthen the Party's Leadership Over the Family Planning Work," JMJP, July 30, 1979, SCMP, no. 5,435, August 14, 1973, p. 59; Foochow radio, Fukien Provincial Service, September 3, 1978, FBIS, no. 174, September 7, 1978, p. G4; "Heng-mien kung-she tang-wei ch'ieh-shih chua-hua chi-hua sheng-yü."

241. Kweiyang radio, Kweichow Provincial Service, August 10, 1978, FBIS, August 11, 1976, p. J1.

242. NCNA, Peking, July 5, 1977, FBIS, July 12, 1977, p. G9.

243. For example, see Shenyang radio, Liaoning Provincial Service, September 8, 1979, FBIS, September 11, 1979, p. S4.

244. "It Is Necessary to Pay Serious and Proper Attention to Propaganda Work in Family Planning," p. 50; Canton radio, Kwangtung Provincial Service, May 9, 1979, FBIS, no. 92, May 10, 1979, p. P1; Nanchang radio, Kiangsi Provincial Service, May 18, 1979, JPRS, no. 73,646, June 8, 1979, p. 33; "Heng-mien kung-she tang-wei ch'ieh-shih chua-hao chi-hua sheng-yü."

245. Shenyang radio, Liaoning Provincial Service, July 20, 1979, JPRS, August 29, 1979, p. 79; "Kweichow Provincial CCP Issues Circulars on Disciplinary Action against Two Leading Cadres at Prefectural and County Levels for Failure to Practice Birth Control," KMJP, September 7, 1979, FBIS, September 19, 1979, p. Q1; Hangchow radio, Chekiang Provincial Service, November 5, 1979, JPRS, November 27, 1979, FBIS, no. 241, December 13, 1979, p. P6; Changsa radio, Hunan Provincial Service, December 8, 1979, FBIS, December 13, 1979, p. P6; "Ouyang Duang wei-k'ang chi-hua sheng-yü kui-ting shen ch'e-chih ch'u-fen" ("Oyuang Duang, Who Violates and Resists Regulations on Family Planning, Is Dismissed from His Posts"), NFJP, December 10, 1979, p. 3.

246. "Party Secretaries Take Command in Mobilizing the Whole Party in Doing a Still Better Job in Planned Parenthood."

247. K'ang K'o-ch'ing, "Lofty Tasks," p. 57.

248. "Ku-sung kung-she tang-wei wu-shih chi-hua sheng-yü."

249. Ch'en Mu-hua, "Four Modernizations."

250. Canton radio, Kwangtung Provincial Service, January 21, 1978, FBIS, January 25, 1978, p. H4.

251. Canton radio, Kwangtung Provincial Service, July 15, 1978, FBIS, no. 141, July 21, 1978, p. H6.

252. Canton radio, Kwangtung Provincial Service, September 26, 1978, FBIS, September 28, 1978, p. H1.

253. Canton radio, Kwangtung Provincial Service, December 3, 1978, FBIS, December 5, 1978, pp. H4-5.

254. "Need for Planned Parenthood Work in Kwangtung Province Outlined," NFJP, January 6, 1979, JPRS, February 6, 1979, p. 27.

255. Hu-Gu-ch'iang and Ho Yün-t'eng, "Chi-hsü tso-hao chi-hua sheng-yü kung-tso shih-ying ssu-hua hsü-yao" ("Continue to Do Planned Parenthood Work Well to Meet the Needs of the Four Modernizations"), NFJP, May 1, 1979, p. 1.

256. Commentator, "Chien-chüeh pa jen-k'ou tseng-chang-lü ching-hsia-lai" ("Resolutely Reduce the Population Increase Rate"), NFJP, June 14, 1979, p. 1; Ho Yün-t'eng, "10,000 Couples."

257. Canton radio, Kwangtung Provincial Service, July 3, 1979, JPRS, July 25, 1979, pp. 135-36.

258. "Entire Party Mobilizes All People to Start to Develop Planned Parenthood Work—Provincial Revolutionary Committee Calls Telephone Conference; An Immediate New High Tide of Planned Parenthood Activities throughout Kwangtung Province Demanded; Strive to Lower This Year's Natural Population Growth Rate to 10 per 1,000," NFJP, July 4, 1979, JPRS, September 7, 1979, pp. 33-34; "Ch'üan-tang tung-yüan ch'uan-min tung-shou kao-hao chi-hua sheng-yü kung-tso" ("Let the Entire People Take Action to Do Family Planning Work Well"), NFJP, July 4, 1979, p. 1.

259. "Chung-kung Kuang-tung sheng-wei fa-ch'u chin-chi t'ung-chih li-chi hsing-tung chua hao chi-hua sheng-yü kung-tso" ("The Chinese Communist Party Kwangtung Provincial Committee Issues an Urgent Notice for Immediate Action to Carry Out Family Planning Work Well"), NFJP, July 22, 1979, p. 1.

260. The official population total for Kwangtung as of yearend 1978 was 55,900,000, which means an annual average population of well over 56 million in 1979. If the death rate in Kwangtung in 1979 was between 5 and 6 per thousand, as previous official death rates would suggest, the birth rate implied by a natural increase rate of 16 per thousand would be between 21 and 22 per thousand, which means about 1.2 million births during the year. If half that total had already been born during the first half of the year, a roughly equal number must have been pregnant more than three months on July 1 and expecting to deliver during the second half of the year. To get the natural increase rate for the whole year down to 10 per thousand would mean aborting the pregnancies of some 340,000 of the 600,000 women in their second or third trimester as of July 1.

261. Canton radio, Kwangtung Provincial Service, August 24, 1979, JPRS, September 18, 1979, p. 59.

262. "Sheng-ke-ei-hui chao-k'ai chi-hua sheng-yü kung-tso tien-hua hui-i" ("Kwangtung Provincial Revolutionary Committee Holds Telephone Conference on Family Planning Work"), NFJP, November 11, 1979, p. 1. This article was still calling for "remedial measures" to lower the birth rate for the year. This would have meant abortions to women in the eighth or ninth month of pregnancy!

263. Canton radio, Kwangtung Provincial Service, January 2, 1980, FBIS, January 4, 1980, p. P2.

264. Shao Li-tzu, "Concerning the Problem of Knowledge about Contraception," KMJP, December 19, 1954, SCMP, January 28, 1955, p. 29; Chou O-fen, "How to Treat the Question of Contraception," CKCN, February 16, 1955, SCMP, March 29, 1955, p. 32; "How to Approach the Problem of Birth Control," Hsin Chung-kuo fu-nü (New China's Women), April 28, 1955, ECMM, August 22, 1955, p. 2.

265. Chou O-fen, "The Question of Contraception"; "How to Approach the Problem of Birth Control"; "Shao Li-tzu on Contraception at Hangchow," Hang-chow Jih-pao (Hangchow Daily), December 21, 1956, SCMP, January 25, 1957, p. 7; "Exercise Appropriate Birth Control"; Yuan An-chüan and Yang Chen-uo, "To fang-mien lu-li ta tao chih-chih sheng-yü ti mu-ti" ("Many-Sided Efforts to Achieve the Objective of Birth Control"), JMJP, March 24, 1957; Wang Tso and Tai Yuan-chen, "Criticism and Appraisal of the 'New Theory of Population,'" Ching-chi yen-chiu (Economic Research), February 17, 1958, ECMM, May 12, 1958, p. 7.

266. See Aird, "Population Policy and Demographic Prospects in the People's Republic of China," pp. 248-53.

267. See the statement by Chi Lung, Chinese representative to the Twenty-ninth ECAFE session in Tokyo as reported by NCNA-English, Peking, April 16, 1978, FBIS, April 17, 1973, p. A9; Peking radio, French language broadcast to Africa, June 5, 1973, SWB, June 13, 1973, p. FE/W728/A/1; NCNA-English, Peking, September 23, 1973, FBIS, September 24, 1973, p. B2; "Speech of the Chinese Delegation at the International Conference on Population Planning for National Welfare and Development," p. 6; NCNA-English, Peking, August 23, 1974, FBIS, August 26, 1974, p. E4; Huang Shu-tse (leader of the Chinese delegation to the United Nations World Population Conference, Bucharest), August 21, 1974, "China's Views on Major Issues of World Population," p. 9; "Family Planning Gains Popularity," PR, September 20, 1974, p. 18; Nanchang radio, Kiangsi Provincial Service, November 20, 1974, FBIS, November 21, 1974, p. G4.

268. NCNA, Peking, September 10, 1973, FBIS, September 11, 1973, p. C3; NCNA-English, Geneva, November 9, 1973, CB, July 8, 1974, p. 64; Kwei-yang radio, Kweichow Provincial Service, December 21, 1973, FBIS, January 8, 1974, p. E3; Shihchiachuang radio, Hopeh Provincial Service, October 23, 1974, FBIS, October 24, 1974, p. K2; "China on the Population Question," China Reconstructs (CR), 23 (November 1974): 13; Nanking radio, Kiangsu Provincial Service, December 14, 1975, FBIS, December 16, 1975, p. G4; Hofei radio, Anhwei Provincial Service, December 22, 1977, JPRS, January 24, 1978, p. 86; "Pen-shih chi-hua sheng-yü kung-tso ts'o-shih yu-li ch'eng-hsiao hsien-chu."

269. Party Committee of the T'ai-hu Fishery Commune, "Do a Serious, Good Job in the Work of Family Planning," KCJP, December 12, 1973, p. 61; Kweiyang radio, Kweichow Provincial Service, December 21, 1973, FBIS, January 8, 1974, p. E3; Kunming radio, Yunnan Provincial Service, January 25, 1976, FBIS, January 27, 1976, p. J3; Ch'en Mu-hua, "Four Modernizations."

270. Mao Tse-tung, "Be Activists in Promoting the Revolution," p. 488.

271. NCNA-English, Peking, June 20, 1979, FBIS, June 21, 1979, p. L11.

272. Ch'en Mu-hua, "Four Modernizations."

273. NFJP Commentator, "Seriously Do a Good Job of Family Planning Work," NFJP, July 10, 1973, Nanchang radio, Kiangsi Provincial Service, August 4, 1978, FBIS, August 7, 1978, p. G4. Kunming radio, Yunnan Provincial Service, January 25, 1976, FBIS, January 27, 1976, p. J3; Kweiyang radio, Kweichow Provincial Service, March 19, 1977, FBIS, March 21, 1977, p. J2; "Party Secretaries Take Command in Mobilizing the Whole Party in Doing a Still Better Job in Planned Parenthood," p. E11; Ch'en Mu-hua, "Four Modernizations"; "Ching-kung chung-yang kuan-yü chia-k'uai nung-yeh fa-chan jo-kan wen-t'i ti chüeh-ting" ("Decision of the CCP Central Committee on Problems Concerning the Expediting of the Development of Agriculture"), NCNA, Peking, October 5, 1979. Some of these warnings seem intended not to prohibit the use of force but the forcible imposition of uniformity in birth control methods.

274. Party Committee of the T'ai-hu Fishery Commune, "Do a Serious Good Job," pp. 60-61.

275. "Notes on Discussions with Mrs. Lyou," Department of Defense Unclassified Intelligence Report, no. 6 842 0544 76; Parish, "Birth Planning in the Chinese Countryside"; "Tutu's Village," CNA, March 19, 1976, p. 4.

276. NCNA-English, Peking, August 2, 1978, FBIS, no. 151, August 4, 1978, p. M5. This was not the beginning of the campaign.

Instances of "commandism" had been reported since May 1978, and leading cadres in another Shensi county had been found guilty of "issuing compulsory orders and violating law and discipline" in June 1978. See Sian radio, Shensi Provincial Service, June 25, 1978, FBIS, no. 124, June 27, 1978, pp. K1-2.

277. "A Big Change in Cadres' Work Style Is Demanded," MJMP, August 2, 1978, NCNA, Peking, August 2, 1978, FBIS, no. 151, August 4, 1978, pp. E2-5.

278. Canton radio, Kwangtung Provincial Service, August 4, 1978, FBIS, August 7, 1978, p. H3.

279. Changsha radio, Hunan Provincial Service, August 5, 1978, FBIS, August 10, 1978, p. H1.

280. Shenyang radio, Liaoning Provincial Service, August 8, 1978, FBIS, August 11, 1978, p. L7.

281. Haikow radio, Hainan Island Regional Service, August 9, 1978, FBIS, August 11, 1978, p. H7.

282. Tientsin radio, Tientsin City Service, August 5, 1978, FBIS, August 16, 1978, p. K7.

283. "Forget Not the Relationship which Is as Close as Fish to Water," JMJP, August 19, 1978, NCNA, Peking, August 19, 1978, FBIS, August 24, 1978, p. E2.

284. "Get a Good Grasp on Implementing the Party's Cadre Policy," Fu-chien jih-pao (Fukien Daily), August 20, 1978, Foochow Rad Fukien Provincial Service, August 20, 1978, FBIS, August 22, 1978, p. G2.

285. "Forget Not the Relationship which Is as Close as Fish to Water"; Shenyang radio, Liaoning Provincial Service, September 4, 1978, FBIS, September 8, 1978, p. L10.

286. Haikow radio, Hainan Island Regional Service, August 9, 1978, FBIS, August 11, 1978, p. H7; "Forget Not the Relationship which Is as Close as Fish to Water."

287. Nanning radio, Kwangsi Chuang Regional Service, August 12, 1978, FBIS, no. 159, August 16, 1978, p. H3.

288. "All-Out Effort, Policy, and Work Style," Ssu-ch'uan jih-pao (Szechwan Daily), September 26, 1978, NCNA, Peking, September 26, 1978, FBIS, September 29, 1978, p. J1.

289. "We Should Have a Large Number of Cadres Who Dare to Study, Single Out, and Solve Problems," JMJP, December 7, 1978, NCNA, Peking, December 7, 1978, FBIS, December 12, 1978, p. E15.

290. "Meeting on Family Planning." It is not altogether clear from the source, an English-language magazine for foreign consumption, that this warning was included in the instructions to the State Council group. It appears in several paragraphs that seem to be intended as an explanation to foreign readers of the rationale for

China's birth control campaign, and its style and content resemble earlier statements for foreign audiences more than they do discussions for domestic consumption.

291. K'ang K'o-ch'ing, "Lofty Tasks."

292. Cited in "The Minister and the Academy," CNA, December 22, 1978, p. 6.

293. "Some Current Problems in Drafting Laws," KMJP, December 22, 1978, FBIS, no. 3, January 4, 1979, p. E7.

294. Ibid.

295. Parks, "Sex is High on List."

296. "Stick to the Principles of Socialist Democracy," JMJP, September 28, 1978, NCNA-English, Peking, September 28, 1978, FBIS, September 29, 1978, p. E1; "Our Current Pressing Task Is to Improve Cadres' Work Style," JMJP, October 30, 1978, Peking radio, Domestic Service, October 29, 1978, FBIS, October 31, 1978, p. E20.

297. "Conduct Correct Leadership and Boldly Give Commands," Chi-lin jih-pao (Kirin Daily), May 9, 1978, Changchun radio, Kirin Provincial Service, May 9, 1978, FBIS, May 10, 1978, p. L4.

298. "A Big Change in Cadres' Work Style is Demanded," p. E2.

299. Sian radio, Shensi Provincial Service, August 6, 1978, FBIS, August 10, 1978, p. M1.

300. "All-Out Effort, Policy, and Work Style."

301. Liu Hai-ch'uan, "Control Population Growth with the Same Drive Used in Grasping Production and Construction," KMJP, September 13, 1979, JPRS, no. 74,694, December 3, 1979, p. 68.

302. Ibid.

303. Changsha radio, Hunan Provincial Service, September 23, 1979, FBIS, no. 188, September 26, 1979, pp. P2-3.

5

THE FERTILITY DECLINE IN THE WEST AS A MODEL FOR DEVELOPING COUNTRIES TODAY: THE CASE OF NINETEENTH-CENTURY AMERICA

Maris A. Vinovskis

During the 1950s and 1960s population policymakers were not particularly interested in the relationship between socioeconomic factors and fertility. They assumed that most women in the developing countries already wanted to limit their fertility but simply lacked the knowledge and means to do so. The major task of family planning programs was to provide modern contraceptive knowledge and techniques rather than to alter the attitudes of women about the ideal size of their families. Thus the United States Agency for International Development (AID), the largest supporter of family planning programs, summarized its mission in 1969 as:

> Regardless of what special social measures may ultimately be needed for optimal regulation of fertility, it is clear that the main element initially in any population planning and control program should be the extension of family planning information and means to all elements in the population. It seems reasonable to believe that when women throughout the world need reproduce only if and when they choose, then the many intense family and social problems generated by unplanned, unwanted, and poorly cared for children will be greatly ameliorated

---

This chapter is an expansion and a revision of my earlier essay on this subject in Maris A. Vinovskis, Demographic History and the World Population Crisis (Worcester, Mass.: Chester Bland—Dwight E. Lee Lectures in History, 1976), pp. 39-94.

> and the now acute problem of too rapid population growth will be reduced to manageable proportions.[1]

Although many family planning programs are successful in helping to reduce birth rates in countries such as Taiwan and Indonesia, others have failed to reduce the high levels of fertility in the developing countries. Despite the presence of programs that make it easier and less expensive to control the size of families, the vast majority of poeple in the developing countries still continue to have more children than can be economically absorbed in their societies.[2] As a result, population policymakers as well as scholars are becoming increasingly concerned about family planning programs that only provide contraceptive knowledge and devices without trying to interact with the rest of that society.

The growing skepticism about the efficacy and desirability of family planning programs by themselves received strong reinforcement in the resolutions of the Bucharest World Population Conference in 1974. The confrontation at Bucharest between the rich nations of the industrial world and the poor nations of the third world revealed that governments in the developing countries attached a low priority to population matters compared to economic development issues. Thus the World Population Plan of Action adopted at Bucharest states:

> The basis for an effective solution of population problems is, above all, socio-economic transformation. A population policy may have a certain success if it constitutes an integral part of socio-economic development; its contribution to the solution of world development problems is hence only partial, as is the case with other sectoral strategies.[3]

The debate about the relative importance of socioeconomic development in reducing fertility is continuing since Bucharest, partly because of political considerations and partly due to recent academic developments.[4] Thus the relationship between fertility and the social structure has become important not only as a scholarly question, but also as a major issue in the efforts of nations to control the world population explosion today.

To seek answers to these questions, scholars are trying to explain the causes of the decline in fertility in the West during the nineteenth century. Although the situation and experience of Europe and the United States during their period of demographic transition are by no means identical to the problems facing the developing countries today, they do provide us with reasonably good time-series data on the relationship between fertility and shifts in the social structure. In fact, the example of the decline in fertility in the West was cited by several delegates to the Bucharest Conference as an example of the paramount importance of socioeconomic development for initiating a demographic transition. By understanding the determinants of fertility decline in the past, we may gain a better idea of the type and extent of changes required today to reduce the high birth rates in the less developed countries.

THE STUDY OF FERTILITY DIFFERENTIALS AND TRENDS IN NINETEENTH-CENTURY AMERICA

Studies of fertility in the West have focused most of their attention on developments in Western Europe, particularly England and France, where demographic data were available for much earlier periods than in most other countries.[5] Although these studies have been of great significance in ascertaining the relationship between fertility and social structure historically, an analysis of demographic changes in the United States may be of particular importance for understanding the dilemmas facing many less developed countries. This is true because the birth rate in early America was much higher than in Western Europe at that time. Thus in this crucial aspect the historical situation in the United States more closely approximates that of the developing countries today. Furthermore, by the beginning of the nineteenth century in America, the birth rate had begun a steady decline—even though modern contraceptive techniques were not yet available. Reductions in the birth rate reflected shifts in attitudes and circumstances favoring smaller families rather than changes in the availability of contraceptive devices. Finally, industrialization in America in the first half of the nineteenth century occurred in the countryside rather than in existing urban centers, thus permitting us to separate analytically the effects of urbanization and industrialization on fertility differentials and trends.

Although the demographic situation in the United States in the late eighteenth and early nineteenth centuries was similar in many ways to the pattern found in the less developed countries today, the two cases are by no means identical. Most nineteenth-century Americans, for example, benefitted from greater economic abundance and opportunities than are available to the peoples of the third world today. Therefore, one should not expect that an analysis of the determinants of fertility differentials and trends in early America would necessarily predict the pattern of demographic changes in the less developed countries. Nevertheless, the study of the interaction of demographic and socioeconomic factors in early America may yield certain useful insights into the relationship between changes in the social structure and the decline in the birth rates.

Most of the recent work in American historical demography has dealt with the colonial era. But because of the difficulty in obtaining data to carry out the process of family reconstitution, few of these studies have been completed, and most of them provide little detailed information on fertility differentials.[6] Moreover, nearly all of these studies have concentrated on small agricultural communities; little is known about the demographic history of larger commercial centers.[7] As a result, there have been no analyses of rural-urban differences in colonial fertility. Since most reconstitution studies end before 1800, they are unable to produce any information regarding fertility differentials between the industrialized and nonindustrialized segments of society. Finally, most of these studies have collected data only on demographic variables and failed to assemble information on other socioeconomic characteristics of the population.[8]

Because of these and other methodological limitations, most current studies based on family reconstitution have been unable to furnish us with adequate data on or analyses of fertility differentials.[9] Indeed, by its very nature, micro-level analysis of fertility differentials based on family reconstitution makes any interpretation of the influence of the social structure on fertility difficult. A more appropriate place at which to analyze fertility differentials is at the national level, or, even better, among the subunits within the country.[10] The major works along such lines in the United States have been investigations of the differentials in fertility in the nineteenth century based on federal census data.[11]

The pattern of fertility in the United States during the first half of the nineteenth century was distinctly different from the pattern of fertility observed for other countries during the same period. In 1800 birth rates in the United States were much higher than in the countries of Western Europe. Yet by 1800 fertility had already begun a steady decline in America. Most Western European countries did not experience a sustained fertility decline for another 50 or 60 years.

Data documenting these changes in American fertility are based on an index of fertility derived from United States censuses rather than on direct measures of births because such information is not available for the nineteenth century. The index of fertility used is the white refined fertility ratio under ten.[12] As can be seen in Figure 5.1, the white refined fertility ratio dropped from a high of 1,844 (1,844 white children under ten years per thousand white women aged 16 to 44 years) in 1800 to 1,308 in 1860—a decline of 29.1 percent during these six decades. Figure 5.1 also shows that this decline occurred at a fairly uniform pace throughout this period.

FIGURE 5.1

Trend in White Refined Fertility Ratios in the United States, 1800-60

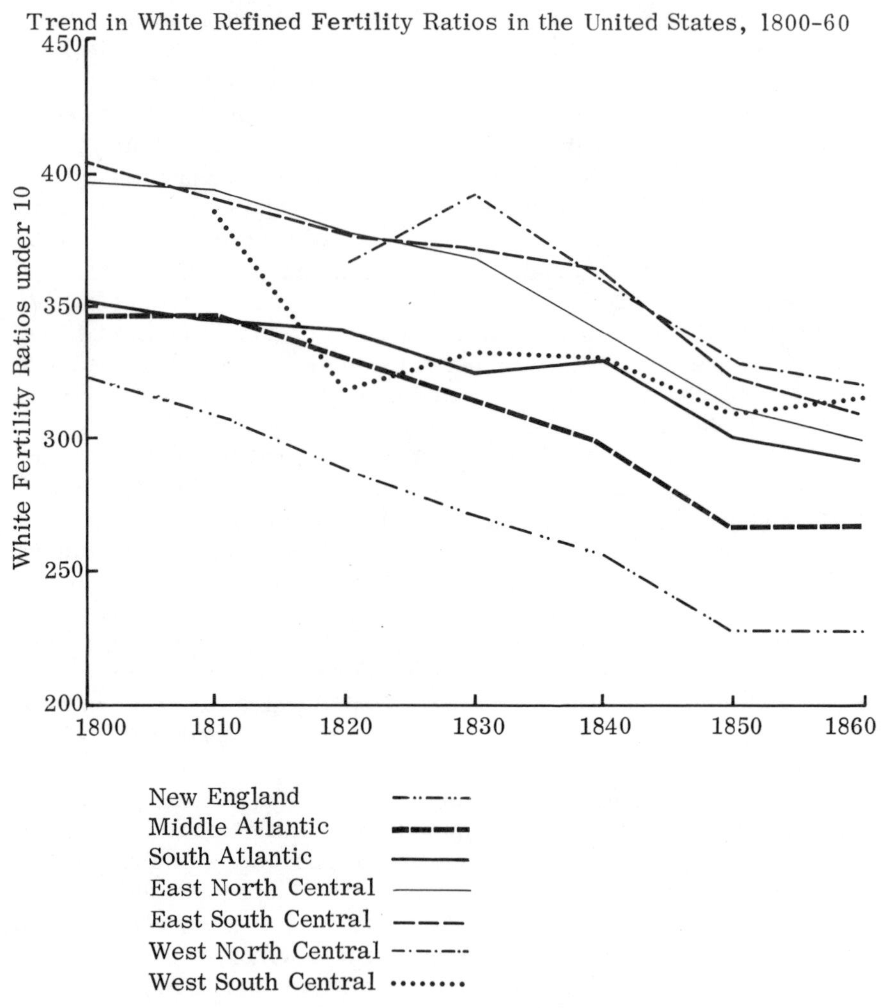

Source:

The contribution to this overall decline made by the various geographic regions within the United States can be seen in Figure 5.2 where the white crude fertility ratios for six regions of the United States are plotted against time. Some interesting information emerges from Figure 5.2. In general, older regions had lower fertility ratios than the newly settled areas. There was a gradual decline in the white crude fertility ratios in all regions from 1800 to 1860 and, with the exception of West North Central and West South Central, the rate of

FIGURE 5.2

Trends in White Crude Fertility Ratios under Ten Among United States Regions, 1800-60

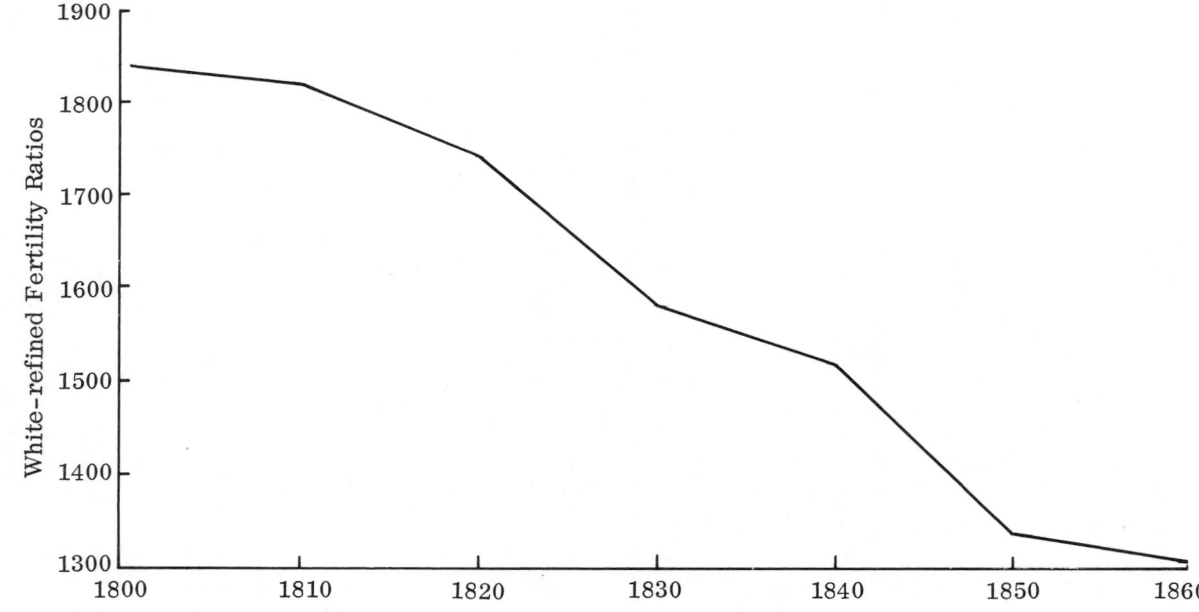

Source:

change was very similar for most regions. Therefore, the regional differences apparent in 1800 are still evident in 1860.

Various hypotheses have been offered to explain these fertility differentials and trends in antebellum America. In this chapter I will examine six of the leading explanations: urban and industrial development, availability of farmland, marriage patterns, changes in mortality, ethnic differences, and modernization. Though no one has proposed an overall demographic model for antebellum America that incorporates all six factors, various scholars have analyzed them either individually or in some combination.

Urban and Industrial Development

One of the most common explanations for the decline of fertility in the West is the supposed impact of urbanization and industrialization. J. Potter has argued, for example, that urbanization and industrialization played a key role in the decline in fertility in the United States:

> The findings have to remain inconclusive. But the evidence still seems to support the view that industrialization and urbanization with the accompaniment of higher living standards and greater social expectations (but possibly also higher infant mortality), were the main reasons for the declining rate of population growth either through the postponement of marriage or the restriction of family size.[13]

This explanation for the decreased rate of population growth in the West has been a persistent theme in demographic literature. It has led some demographers to suggest that urbanization and industrialization are necessary preconditions for effectively reducing fertility levels in today's less developed countries.[14] This emphasis on the importance of urban and industrial development was reinforced by the discovery that fertility is usually lower in urban than in rural areas. It is more expensive to raise a large family in an urban area than in a rural one because food and housing costs are higher, and the value derived from child labor tends to be less off the farm. Since employment opportunities outside the home for women are greater in urban areas, many families, it would seem, decide to limit the number of children they have in order to permit the mother to supplement the family's income by working. Moreover, urban populations are often better educated than their rural counterparts, and are more likely to be employed in white-collar occupations. Since fertility levels are usually inversely related to the amount of education and occupational status, both of these factors contribute to rural-urban differences in birth rates. Finally, cities are often viewed as areas where populations have higher expectations of social achievement. Urban dwellers therefore are more likely to limit their family size to enhance their prospects of upward mobility.

Many of the findings and hypotheses about the relationship between urbanization-industrialization and fertility are correct. Several studies of American demographic development have documented that fertility levels are lower in urban and industrial areas than in the countryside. But there are still serious problems with an interpretation that stresses the importance of urbanization and industrialization in accounting for fertility declines in America in the first half of the nineteenth century. It is difficult to attribute the declining birth rate to these factors when we realize that only a small percentage of the population was living in towns of over 2,500 persons or working in industry. Although the percentage of the population living in urban areas did increase from 5.1 percent in 1790 to 19.8 percent in 1860, the fact remains that a large majority of the population still lived in a rural setting during this period. From the federal censuses it is possible to estimate the percentage of workers employed in nonagricultural pursuits from 1820 to 1860. The results indicate a sizable increase in the number of nonagricultural workers—from 28.1 percent in 1820 to 41.0 percent in 1860—but they also reinforce the conclusion that the United States remained primarily a rural, agricultural nation as late as 1860.[15] Thus it would be impossible to account for the overall decline in fertility in America by any urban-industrial explanation. In fact, Forster and Tucker have estimated that of the absolute decline in fertility ratios for the period 1810-40, 78 percent was due to a decline in rural birth rates, 11 percent to a decline in urban birth rates, and another 11 percent to a population shift from rural to urban areas.[16]

Availability of Farmland

Among economic historians the most common explanation of fertility differentials and trends in the late eighteenth and early nineteenth centuries is the availability of readily accessible farmland. Since the United States was predominantly an agricultural society during these years, access to land constituted a major source of economic opportunity. Any decrease in the availability of farmland might lead to lower fertility through higher ages at first marriage or a decline in marital fertility. As marriages were closely tied to the ability to support a family, a decrease in the availability of farmland would increase the difficulty of establishing a new household and discourage early marriages. In addition, marital fertility would decrease as parents reacted to the decrease in the value of their children's labor, the dangers of the fragmentation of the family farm, and the increased cost of eventually providing their children with sufficient land to establish their own households. The overall result of the increase in the age at first marriage and the decline in marital fertility would be a sizable drop in the total fertility rate of that population.

Much of the current debate about the decline in rural fertility centers around the definition of land availability. Modell used population density as a measure of agricultural opportunity.[17] Population density, however, does not take into consideration the quality of the land or the degree of agricultural settlement of the area. Furthermore, population density not only measures the number of farmers in a given locality, but also the number of persons living in villages and towns.

Yasuba tried to avoid these problems by defining agricultural opportunity as the number of persons per 1,000 arable acres.[18] The population estimates were obtained from the nineteenth-century federal censuses, while the data on arable acres came from 1949 figures on cropland. Yasuba used the latter data because he wanted some measure of the potentially arable land rather than the amount of land actually being cultivated in the antebellum period. Because twentieth-century farming technology and practices are considerably different from those in the nineteenth century, other analysts believe the cropland figures from 1949 are not likely to reflect actual or even relative levels of potential farming areas in the nineteenth century.

A more recent effort by Forster and Tucker relied on the number of white adults per farm, using the white adult population in the census year under investigation and the number of farms in 1850, 1860, or 1880.[19] Their index has the advantage of reflecting nineteenth-century farming conditions and practices more accurately than either Modell's or Yasuba's measures. However, even Forster and Tucker's index of land availability leaves much to be desired. At the state level, an index of white adults per farm is highly correlated with the percentage of the population engaged in nonagricultural occupations and with the percentage of the population in urban areas.[20] Therefore, we cannot be sure whether the high correlation between the white adult-farm ratio and the white refined fertility ratio is due to the availability of farms, the percentage of the population in nonagricultural occupations, or the percentage of the population living in urban areas.

When economists speak of the availability of farms, they are in effect considering the relative costs of establishing a farm. Ideally, we would like to have information on the cost of establishing new farm households. Unfortunately, that information is not available for the nineteenth century. Instead, we must rely on a crude approximation—the average value of a farm. Using this measure, it becomes evident that there was wide geographic variation in the costs of farming in antebellum America. To take an extreme example, in 1860 the average value of a farm in Kansas was $1,179, whereas the average value of a farm in Louisiana was $11,818.[21]

Many of the earlier studies analyzing land availability also had statistical and methodological shortcomings. When appropriate corrections are made in Yasuba's or Forster and Tucker's analysis, a very different picture emerges. The availability of land (as measured by the average value of a farm) is still strongly negatively related to the white refined fertility ratio in 1850, but it is less important than the percentage of the population in urban areas or the percentage of white adults who are illiterate. In 1860 the value of the average farm remains negatively related to fertility, but it becomes quite unimportant in terms of strength.[22]

At the aggregate level, this debate will undoubtedly continue. Some studies continue to show the importance of land availability in explaining fertility differentials at the county level, while others at the county and township levels do not. However, the entire debate is quickly shifting away from aggregate studies to those at the household level. Here again the results to date are mixed. The results from an extensive analysis of northern farm households in 1860 suggest the importance of land availability, while the results from an analysis of households in early nineteenth-century Weston, Massachusetts, or households in Washtenaw County, Michigan in 1850, do not find a strong relationship between fertility and the availability of farmland.[23]

The entire debate about the relationship of land availability to fertility still needs to be clarified conceptually. The model in its present form is quite crude and does not pursue all of the ramifications of a decrease in farmland. For example, though the decreasing availability of farmland makes it more expensive for sons to acquire farm households, it also raises the value of their father's farm, thus giving him more capital with which to assist his children. The entire debate has been focused so much on the contradictory empirical results from these various studies that relatively little effort has been made to think through the implications of this model for farm life and behavior in nineteenth-century America.[24]

In view of the contradictory findings about the relationship between land availability and fertility in nineteenth-century America, it is difficult to make any definitive conclusions on this matter at this time. It does appear that in some cases there is an inverse relationship between the availability of farmland and the fertility of farmers. But that relationship is less consistent and much weaker than scholars such as Yasuba or Forster and Tucker have asserted. Though this chapter does not permit me to go into more depth on this issue, it is unlikely that we will be able to account for the overall dramatic decline in rural fertility by relying mainly on the land availability model. There were many other important changes in nineteenth-century rural America besides the decreasing availability of farmland that need to be considered in any overall explanation of the fertility decline. At the present time the proponents of the land availability model have been too narrowly focused on this factor at the expense of adequately considering other social and economic changes in the countryside.

Marriage Patterns

Birth rates in human societies can be reduced in a number of ways. One method is to delay the age at first marriage and to increase the proportion of persons remaining single. This process operated to reduce the birth rates in Western Europe in the sixteenth and seventeenth centuries. Another method is to control fertility within marriage while maintaining an early age at first marriage and a high proportion of the population married. This process seems to be the pattern of fertility control in many of the developing countries today.

Analyzing the levels and trends in the ages at marriage in nineteenth-century America is difficult because of the lack of accurate marriage data. It was not until the twentieth century that most states adopted comprehensive marriage registration systems, and the federal censuses did not report information on the proportion of women ever married until 1890. Though there is scattered data on the age at marriage in states after 1860, very little information is available for the earlier period.

Some scholars have tried to ascertain the importance of marriage patterns on American fertility by using indirect measures such as the sex ratio of the population. The sex ratio is presumed to be an important determinant of fertility differentials and trends because it reflects the availability of marriage partners in a given area. T'ien asserted that the sex ratio of the population at the state level was very important for explaining fertility differentials and trends in the first half of the nineteenth century.[25] Yasuba, on the other hand, minimized the importance of the sex ratio:

> In conclusion we might say that, although it is reasonable to assume that the sex ratio affected fertility through marriage customs, it is doubtful that it was an important factor in causing interstate differentials in fertility and in reducing fertility over time. Significant positive correlations between the sex ratio and fertility are likely to

> have been chiefly the result of correlations between these two variables, on the one hand, and one or more other variables, say interstate migration, the degree of urbanization, or the availability of land, on the other.[26]

Yasuba was correct in that the change in the sex ratio in antebellum America was not sufficiently large to account for the decline in fertility. He was wrong, however, to argue that the sex ratio would not be an important predictor of fertility differentials after the influence of other variables such as urbanization, land availability, or industrialization was controlled. In most of the studies that analyzed fertility differentials using multiple regression analysis, the sex ratio remained an important predictor variable.[27] Furthermore, in a detailed analysis of the relationship between the sex ratio and the percentage of the population that is married, it does appear that the two items are strongly related—just as T'ien had suggested.[28]

Unfortunately, very little attention has been paid to the entire issue of marriage in the nineteenth century, especially from the perspective of fertility levels. A recent effort to relate the changes in fertility to changes in marriage patterns and the control of fertility within marriages is the analysis of the decline in fertility in Sturbridge, Massachusetts from 1730 to 1850. The authors found that the

> Change in the mean age of women at first marriage was a powerful factor in determining change in the mean number of children ever born. The increase in female age at marriage accounts for about half of the decrease in completed family size over the period.[29]

Other studies of marriage patterns in colonial and nineteenth-century America suggest a significant rise in the age of first marriage for women in the eighteenth century, but no large increases in the first half of the nineteenth century.[30] Since we have so few adequate studies of the changes in the age of first marriage for women during these years, it is impossible to arrive at a conclusion at this point. It does appear, however, that there were increases in the age at marriage for women in some communities, but that the overall decline in nineteenth-century fertility cannot be explained by a rise in the age at first marriage.

Changes in Mortality

One of the fundamental tenets of the demographic transition model is that the decline in birth rates was preceded by a drop in mortality rates. Though demographers have expressed serious reservations about the utility or accuracy of the demographic transition model, most of them still accept the necessity for a drop in mortality rates prior to a sustained decline in fertility.

At first glance, the case of the United States would appear to support such an interpretation. The standard interpretation of mortality levels and trends in antebellum America was set forth by Thompson and Whelpton and recently reaffirmed by Easterlin—there was a steady improvement in life expectancy during the first half of the nineteenth century.[31] Thus there was a decrease in death rates at the same time or prior to the decline in fertility.

Easterlin argues that there was a significant increase in life expectancy in the first half of the nineteenth century.[32] His argument, however, rests very heavily on two life tables that have been thoroughly discredited—the Wigglesworth life table of 1789 and the Jacobson life table of 1850.

The debate on whether conditions of life improved in the first half of the nineteenth century continues. We do not have enough national or even regional mortality data to be reasonably certain of mortality trends. The bulk of the existing evidence for the New England area, however, does not point to any dramatic increases in life expectancy during that period, particularly in the rural areas.[33] Perhaps there were major improvements in nineteenth-century life expectancy in the South, especially since that area was so unhealthy in the seventeenth and eighteenth centuries.[34]

Since the major decline in fertility in early nineteenth-century America occurred in the Northeast where mortality rates, particularly in the countryside, were relatively stable, it is unlikely that the decline in fertility was precipitated by a drop in death rates. Furthermore, a study of the relationship between fertility levels and mortality at the township level in Massachusetts in 1860 failed to produce a strong positive relationship.[35] As a result, it appears that the strong connection between changes in fertility and mortality predicted by most demographers may not have existed in antebellum America—at least not in the Northeast.

Ethnic Differences

Ethnicity has often been cited as a major determinant of fertility differentials in nineteenth-century America. Almost everyone has assumed that the foreign-born population had a higher birth rate than the native population. Since foreigners tended to concentrate in urban areas, they helped to reduce the rural-urban differences in fertility. Furthermore, as large waves of immigrants started to come to this country in the 1840s and 1850s, they may have slowed the overall decline in fertility in the United States.

Recent studies, however, have challenged this interpretation of fertility differentials among ethnic groups. Both Katz's analysis of Hamilton, Ontario and Blumin's study of Kingston, New York found little difference in fertility among women of different ethnic or religious backgrounds. Though these two studies are among the best nineteenth-century community analyses we have, their treatment of fertility differentials is weakened by the indexes they constructed. Katz calculated the number of children under age 15 years to women ages 15-45 years without adjusting his data for differences in the age distribution of the women in the different ethnic groups. Blumin estimated the number of all children in the household per married woman (calculated separately for the different age groups of the women), but did not consider the possibility that his index would be affected by the selective out-migration of young children.[36] The authors should have calculated the age-specific child-woman ratios for the married women and then standardized the results for the differences in the age distribution of the women from the different ethnic groups. Studies employing such techniques have continued to find large ethnic differences in fertility.[37] Thus one of the apparent new discoveries of nineteenth-century demographic history may have been only the result of errors in the way fertility levels were computed.

Modernization

Finally, several scholars studying nineteenth-century fertility differentials and trends in the United States have felt that the demographic and socioeconomic variables that have been surveyed above are inadequate by themselves to explain the demographic changes occurring during this period. They have noted that the parallel decline in fertility ratios in both rural and urban areas suggests the possibility that both areas may have been affected by other broad social changes—commonly categorized by scholars today as modernization. Several demographic studies support this view, finding an inverse relationship between modernization and fertility in the developing countries today.[38] Some scholars, moreover, are now arguing that American society was undergoing the process of modernization during the late eighteenth and early nineteenth centuries.[39] As a result, it is not surprising that modernization has been evoked as an explanation for the decline in fertility in antebellum America.[40]

The concept of modernization is not without its critics. In fact, use of the term in the other social sciences has been severely criticized. The chief complaint, perhaps, has been the lack of a precise definition. Modernization as a term has been used so loosely as to become meaningless from an analytical point of view. Furthermore, modernization is so often identified with urbanization and industrialization that many demographers and sociologists find it difficult to believe that any preindustrial society could have been very modern. Finally, modernization has often been confused with the value-laden notion of progress. Although modernization may produce improvements in the lives of some individuals, it creates hardships and turmoil in the lives of others.[41]

Considerations of space necessarily limit our discussion of the role of modernization in American society during the nineteenth century. But we can conclude that in terms of many of the attitudinal and structural characteristics often associated with modern societies, the United States in the first half of the nineteenth century probably was becoming a much more modern society. There were major changes in the extent and quality of education available to both men and women in antebellum America. During these same years, there was a major change in the amount and type of information available to the public. American society, in addition, was becoming more commercially oriented in its agricultural as well as its industrial sector. More and more workers were brought into a market economy that transcended local interests and considerations. There was also a fundamental change in American attitudes; individuals now became convinced that they could alter and improve not only their own lives, but also those of others as well. The reform spirit that swept through the nation in the early nineteenth century encouraged people to seek more control and direction over their own destinies. Finally, the role and situation of women in nineteenth-century America changed rapidly, and they began to play a larger and more active part in deciding matters within the home. These developments merely illustrate a few of the changes that were occurring and that might be considered as part of the modernization of American society.[42]

Careless use of modernization theory among sociologists has been properly discredited, and modernization theory can be effectively utilized as a research tool. Historians are relative latecomers to the use of modernization theory, and they have avoided some of the simplistic notions of the earlier sociological literature. However, one of the continued weaknesses in the use of modernization theory by historians is that most of them are simply unaware of the recent sociological writings in this area. As a result, historians tend to debate the modernization issue in terms of the sociological literature of the 1950s and 1960s rather than in terms of the recent refinements by sociologists.

Though demographers and economists have been very reluctant to look beyond socioeconomic explanations of the fertility decline in nineteenth-century America, it is important that we also consider some of the broader attitudinal and cultural shifts that were occurring in that society. The fact that the concept of modernization had been badly misused by some scholars in the past should not deter us from analyzing the possibility that American society in the late eighteenth and early nineteenth centuries experienced major changes that could be appropriately summarized under the caption of modernization. Though it is impossible to prove or even to demonstrate convincingly at this time, it is very likely that the broad attitudinal and cultural shifts in American society played a key role in the decline in fertility.

LESSONS FROM NINETEENTH-CENTURY AMERICA

Having surveyed the various explanations for fertility differentials and trends in nineteenth-century America, we should not be surprised by the complex, and sometimes confused, picture that emerges. It should be expected that the determinants of fertility differentials and trends will be quite complicated and may vary in their direction and explanatory strength from one area to the next, depending on the particular circumstances in those locations. Much more research is needed before we can establish any conclusive links between the decline in fertility and changes in the social structure. Nevertheless, we can hazard some preliminary comments on the implications of America's experience for the developing countries today.

First, it is important to note that the decline in fertility in America began well before the nation was highly urbanized or industrialized. In fact, the major portion of the sharp drop in births occurred in the countryside. The early theorists of the demographic transition model, Notestein and Thompson, assumed that industrialization and urbanization were necessary preconditions for a decline in fertility.[43] Yet recent studies of the historical demography of the West have certainly disproved that assertion. Urbanization and industrialization were not necessary preconditions for a sustained decline in fertility in either the United States or France.

Second, those family planning advocates who stress the importance of modern birth control technology should realize that the initial decline in fertility in the United States occurred without the benefit of improved contraceptive devices. Relying heavily on primitive techniques of birth control such as coitus interruptus, American parents in the eighteenth and nineteenth centuries began to reduce the number of children they produced.[44] This is not to imply that improved contraceptive devices are not useful or desirable, but only that they are not a necessary precondition for a decline in fertility.

Third, contrary to the experiences of some Western European

countries, the decline in fertility in the United States occurred without a major drop in mortality. In fact, in the Northeast, which had the lowest fertility in the nineteenth century, death rates were quite low even in the seventeenth and eighteenth centuries—particularly for the adult population in rural areas. Thus, at least in one section of the country, there was a sustained decline in birth rates while mortality remained fairly constant. In this sense the United States, unlike parts of Western Europe, did not experience a true demographic transition.

Fourth, once the fertility decline began in the United States, there was a tendency for areas with the highest levels of fertility to experience a faster rate of decline than those areas with lower levels. As a result, there was a convergence of fertility rates in the United States in the nineteenth century. This suggests that once countries begin to experience sustained falling birth rates in the more developed sectors, the more backward areas may experience an even more rapid rate of fertility decline. Over time, then, the gap between these sectors will narrow. In fact, this is apparently already occurring in the developing countries today.

Fifth, studies of the decline in fertility in the United States and Western Europe suggest that this process can occur within a wide variety of socioeconomic settings.[45] As a result, it is probably unrealistic to expect that we will ever find a simple socioeconomic explanation of the causes of the decline in fertility in the West. Rather, these findings suggest that the less developed countries may also experience their demographic transitions in a wide variety of socioeconomic settings. Even though it is true that highly developed areas of the West almost always experience a decline in fertility, the same situation applied in other areas of the West that were backward in social and economic terms. For example, it is possible to explain much of the decline in fertility in England or Germany in terms of their socioeconomic development, but it is much more difficult to account for a similar decline in an economically backward area such as Bulgaria.[46] On the other hand, some areas with relatively high levels of development, such as a number of Moslem Asian Soviet republics, continue to have high fertility.[47]

Finally, the results of my investigations of the United States, as well as those of Coale and his coworkers on Western Europe, suggest that cultural differences are crucial factors in determining fertility levels and trends. Researchers have focused too narrowly on the socioeconomic determinants of population trends without really testing the possible importance of changing ideas and values upon the general population. This line of reasoning suggests that there may be a connection between modernization and the decline of fertility in the West—a possibility that reinforces many of the recent studies of the less developed countries that argue that modern attitudes and values are an essential part of reducing fertility. The question, then, is this: What factors were responsible for the modernization of American society well before it became heavily urbanized and industrialized? Although the issues surrounding the role of cultural factors and modernization are among the most interesting and promising areas for future research, unfortunately little systematic work has been done on these pressing questions.

In this regard, I would like to draw attention to one particular aspect of development in nineteenth-century America that may have had an important impact on the decline in fertility—the changes in the lives of women. Whereas most women were illiterate in the seventeenth and early eighteenth centuries, by the mid-nineteenth century the vast majority of them were literate. Whereas most women worked only within their own households in colonial America, a large percentage of women, particularly in the Northeast, worked for an outside employer at some point in their lives in nineteenth-century America. Whereas a woman's social role was quite confined in the seventeenth and eighteenth centuries, her sphere of activity was considerably enlarged in the nineteenth century. These are only some of the many changes that women experienced in nineteenth-century America, changes that probably encouraged many of them to begin to control their fertility. Unfortunately, most scholars, particularly economic historians, have not even bothered to consider the impact of these changes on nineteenth-century fertility levels. Yet I suspect that future work will confirm my hypothesis that changes in women's roles were an important factor in producing an early decline in fertility in the United States.[48]

These generalizations may be of some use in formulating policies for current population problems. But there are many other questions—perhaps even more important from a policy point of view—that cannot be answered by our present knowledge of American demographic development.[49] Very little effort, for example, has been made to detect and to try to understand the factors within American society that initiated the decline in fertility in the eighteenth century. Similarly, little research has been done to ascertain the reasons why some regions experienced a more rapid decline than others once the process of general fertility decline was under way. Finally, we have been unable to define modernization, those ideas and attitudes that encouraged couples to restrict their fertility.

Given the wide variety of demographic experiences in the West during its period of fertility decline and social development, it seems unlikely that the developing countries today will follow any single pattern. In that sense, the experiences of the West do not provide any set of coherent guidelines for the less developed countries today. But detailed analyses of the relationship between fertility decline and social development in the West should provide useful insights for designing more effective programs to curb population growth in the future. Only through a better understanding of the personal motivations and societal influences that precipitated declines in fertility in the past can we hope to develop family planning programs that will prove more effective in the future.

NOTES

1. R. T. Ravenholt, "AID's Family Planning Strategy," Science, January 10, 1969, p. 126. Though most population policymakers no longer focus almost exclusively on the distribution of contraceptives, Ravenholt continues to advocate such a mission for AID. In recent testimony before the Congress, he stated that "our experience is that right now there is tremendous unmet demand in the developing countries for which we haven't enough money nor enough contraceptives to meet at the present time." U.S. Congress, House, Select Committee on Population, Hearings, Population and Development: Status and Trends of Family Planning/Population Programs in Developing Countries, 95th Congress, 2d Sess., 1978, p. 9.

2. There is a vast literature on the effectiveness of family planning programs in the developing countries today. For example, see Bernard Berelson et al., Family Planning and Population Programs (Chicago: 1966); Ronald Freedman and John Y. Takeshita, Family Planning in Taiwan: An Experiment in Social Change (Princeton: Princeton University Press, 1969); R. Hill, J. M. Stycos, and K. Back, The Family and Population Control: Family, Caste, and Class in an Indian Village (New York: 1972); Roger Revelle, Ashok Khosla, and Maris A. Vinovskis, eds., The Survival Equation: Man, Resources, and His Environment (Boston: Houghton Mifflin, 1971), pp. 124-76; Paul Demeny, "Observations on Population Policy and Population Programs in Bangladesh," Population and Development Review 1 (December 1975): 307-21; Terence H. Hull, Valerie J. Hull, and Masri Singarimbun, "Indonesia's Family Planning Story: Success and Challenge," Population Bulletin 32, no. 6, 1-53; Bruce Stokes, "Filling the Family Planning Gap," WorldWatch, paper no. 12 (May 1977): 1-54; Timothy King, Population Policies and Economic Development (Baltimore: Johns Hopkins University Press, 1974).

3. World Population Conference, "World Population Plan of Action," Population and Development Review 1 (September 1975): 164.

4. For discussions of the proceedings of the Bucharest World Population Conference in 1974 and the reactions to it, see Jason L. Finkle and Barbara B. Crane, "The Politics of Bucharest: Population,

Development, and the New International Economic Order," Population and Development Review 1 (September 1975): 87-114; Carmen A. Miro, "The World Population Plan of Action: A Political Instrument Whose Potential Has Not Been Realized," Population and Development Review 3 (December 1977): 421-42.

5. For a useful introduction to the current research in the demographic history of Western Europe, see the collection of essays by D. V. Glass and D. E. C. Eversley, eds., Population in History (Chicago: Aldine Publishing Co., 1967).

6. For a review of the recent work in American historical demography, see Philip J. Greven, Jr., "Historical Demography and Colonial America," William and Mary Quarterly, 3d Series, 24 (1967): 438-54; Maris A. Vinovskis, "Recent Trends in American Historical Demography: Some Methodological and Conceptual Considerations," Annual Review of Sociology 4 (1978): 603-27. For a critical survey of the sources of historical demography, see T. H. Hollingsworth, Historical Demography (Ithaca, N.Y.: Cornell University Press, 1969).

7. John Demos, A Little Commonwealth: Family Life in Plymouth Colony (New York: Academic Press, 1970); Philip J. Greven, Jr., Four Generations: Land and Family in Colonial Andover, Massachusetts (Ithaca, N.Y.: Cornell University Press, 1970); Kenneth A. Lockridge, A New England Town—The First Hundred Years: Dedham, Massachusetts, 1636-1736 (New York: 1970). For a collection of the recent work in American historical demography, see Maris A. Vinovskis, ed., Studies in American Historical Demography (New York: Academic Press, 1979).

8. On the problems of generalizing about demographic characteristics of a large population on the basis of family reconstitution data without taking into account the socioeconomic level of the population under investigation, see Maris A. Vinovskis, "American Historical Demography: A Review Essay," Historical Methods Newsletter 4 (1971): 141-48; Maris A. Vinovskis, "The Field of Early American Family History: A Methodological Critique," The Family in Historical Perspective 7 (Winter 1974): 2-8.

9. For an interesting attempt to speculate on the general outlines of early New England demographic history on the basis of these earlier studies, see Daniel Scott Smith, "The Demographic History of New England," Journal of Economic History 32 (1972): 165-83.

10. It is difficult to study the effects of variations in the social structure on fertility when the focus is on the individual or the family. To analyze the determinants and consequences of the social structure on fertility, it is necessary to analyze aggregate social units rather than individuals. See Peter Blau, "Objectives of Sociology," in A Design for Sociology: Scope, Objectives, and Methods, ed. Robert

Bierstedt (Philadelphia: University of Pennsylvania Press, 1969), pp. 51-52; Calvin Goldscheider, Population, Modernization, and Social Structure (Boston: Little, Brown, 1971), pp. 21-47.

11. For example, see Yasukichi Yasuba, Birth Rates of the White Population in the United States, 1800-1860: An Economic Study (Johns Hopkins University Studies in History and Political Science, 79, no. 2; Baltimore, 1962); Colin Forster and G. S. L. Tucker, Economic Opportunity and White American Fertility Ratios: 1800-1860 (New Haven: 1972); John Modell, "Family and Fertility on the Indiana Frontier, 1820," American Quarterly 23 (1971): 615-34; Maris A. Vinovskis, "A Multivariate Regression Analysis of Fertility Differentials among Massachusetts Towns and Regions in 1860," in Historical Studies of Changing Fertility, ed. Charles Tilly (Princeton, N.J.: Princeton University Press, 1978), pp. 225-56; Maris A. Vinovskis, "Socio-Economic Determinants of Interstate Fertility Differentials in the United States in 1850 and 1860," Journal of Interdisciplinary History 6 (Winter 1976): 375-96; Don R. Leet, "Human Fertility and Agricultural Opportunities in Ohio Counties: From Frontier to Maturity, 1810-60," in Essays in Nineteenth-Century Economic History: The Old Northwest, eds. David C. Klingaman and Richard K. Vedder (Athens, Ohio: Ohio University Press, 1975), pp. 138-58; Maris A. Vinovskis, Demographic History and the World Population Crisis (Worcester, Mass.: Chester Bland—Dwight E. Lee Lectures in History, Clark Press, 1976).

12. The child-woman ratio (more commonly referred to as the fertility ratio) does not measure actual fertility levels, but the number of surviving young children per woman in the childbearing ages. Though the child-woman ratio is not an ideal measure of fertility, it is a useful approximation of actual fertility levels, especially for the white population in areas where mortality differentials are not particularly great. Several studies have already considered the methodological problems of using child-woman ratios, but more work still needs to be done on this matter. Maris A. Vinovskis, Demographic Changes in America from the Revolution to the Civil War: An Analysis of the Socio-Economic Determinants of Fertility Differentials and Trends in Massachusetts from 1765 to 1860 (New York: Academic Press, forthcoming); Tamara K. Hareven and Maris A. Vinovskis, "Marital Fertility, Ethnicity, and Occupation in Urban Families: An Analysis of South Boston and the South End in 1880," Journal of Social History 9 (1975): 69-93; Yasuba, Birth Rates of the White Population.

For a critical assessment of the use of child-woman ratios in American historical demography, see Allan N. Sharlin, "Historical Demography as History and Demography," American Behavioral Scientist 21 (November/December 1977): 245-62. Though Sharlin's points are well taken, he is too pessimistic and appears to be unaware that various American historical demographers have considered the biases in the use of child-woman ratios as an index of fertility.

13. J. Potter, "The Growth of Population in America, 1700-1860," in Population in History: Essays in Historical Demography, p. 678.

14. There is an extensive literature on the impact of urbanization and industrialization on fertility levels. For example, see Goldscheider, Population, Modernization, and Social Structure; A. J. Jaffee, "Urbanization and Fertility," American Journal of Sociology 48 (1942): 48-60; Warren C. Robinson, "Urbanization and Fertility: The Non-Western Experience," Milbank Memorial Fund Quarterly 41 (1963): 291-308; Warren C. Robinson, "Urban-Rural Differences in Indian Fertility," Population Studies 14 (1961): 218-34; Robert Michielutte et al., "Residence and Fertility in Costa Rica," Rural Sociology 40 (Fall 1975): 319-31.

15. One must be very cautious in making comparisons about occupational distributions over time from the early federal censuses. For two very helpful discussions of the problems of using census data for the analysis of occupations, see Solomon Fabricant, "The Changing Industrial Distribution of Gainful Workers: Comments on the Decennial Statistics, 1820-1940," Studies in Income and Wealth 11 (New York: 1949), pp. 1-150; P. K. Whelpton, "Occupational Groups in the United States, 1820-1920," Journal of American Statistical Association 31 (1926): 335-43.

16. Forster and Tucker, Economic Opportunity and White American Fertility Ratios.

17. Modell, "Family and Fertility on the Indiana Frontier, 1820."

18. Yasuba, Birth Rates of the White Population, pp. 158-69.

19. Forster and Tucker, Economic Opportunity and White American Fertility Ratios, pp. 19-42.

20. For example, in 1850 the correlation between the white adult-farm ratio and the percentage of the population in urban areas was .615, and with the percentage of persons in nonagricultural occupations it was .815. Similarly, the correlation between the white adult-farm ratio and the percentage of the population urban in 1860 was .886.

21. Vinovskis, "Socio-Economic Determinants of Fertility."

22. Ibid.

23. Richard A. Easterlin, George Alter, and Gretchen A. Condran, "Farms and Farm Families in Old and New Areas: The Northern States in 1860," in Family and Population in Nineteenth-Century America, eds. Tamara K. Hareven and Maris A. Vinovskis (Princeton, N.J.: Princeton University Press, 1978), pp. 22-84;

Sam L. Notzon, "Fertility and Farmland in Weston, Massachusetts, 1800-1820" (M.A. thesis, Department of Sociology, University of Wisconsin, 1971); William C. Trierweiler, "The Differential Child-Woman Ratios in Washtenaw County, Michigan in 1850: An Investigation into the Patterns of Fertility Decline in Ante-Bellum America" (Honors thesis, Department of History, University of Michigan, 1976).

24. For a more detailed critique of the entire land availability thesis, see Vinovskis, Demographic Changes in America from the Revolution to the Civil War.

25. H. Yuan T'ien, "A Demographic Aspect of Interstate Variation in American Fertility, 1800-1860," Milbank Memorial Fund Quarterly 37 (1959): 49-59.

26. Yasuba, Birth Rates of the White Population, pp. 126-27.

27. Vinovskis, "Socio-Economic Determinants of Fertility."

28. Maris A. Vinovskis, "Marriage Patterns in Mid-Nineteenth-Century New York State: A Multivariate Analysis," Journal of Family History 3 (Spring 1978): 51-61.

29. Nancy Osterud and John Fulton, "Family Limitation and Age at Marriage: Fertility Decline in Sturbridge, Massachusetts, 1730-1850," Population Studies 30 (November 1976): 481-94.

30. Vinovskis, Demographic Changes in America from the Revolution to the Civil War.

31. W. S. Thompson and P. K. Whelpton, Population Trends in the United States (New York: McGraw-Hill, 1933); Richard A. Easterlin, "Population Issues in American Economic History: A Survey and Critique," in Research in Economic History, ed. P. J. Uselding, supplement no. 1 (Greenwich, Conn.: JAI Press, 1977), pp. 133-58.

32. Easterlin, "Population Issues in American Economic History."

33. Maris A. Vinovskis, "The 1789 Life Table of Edward Wigglesworth," Journal of Economic History 31 (September 1971): 570-90; Maris A. Vinovskis, "Mortality Rates and Trends in Massachusetts before 1860," Journal of Economic History 32 (March 1972): 184-213; Maris A. Vinovskis, "The Jacobson Life Table of 1850: A Critical Re-Examination from a Massachusetts Perspective," Journal of Interdisciplinary History 8 (Spring 1978): 703-24.

34. Mortality rates were significantly lower in colonial New England than in the South. The South was characterized by very high mortality in the seventeenth and eighteenth centuries and an apparent decline in death rates in the nineteenth century. W. F. Craven, White, Red, and Black (Charlottesville, Va.: University of Virginia Press, 1971); Irene Hecht, "The Virginia Muster of 1624-25 as a Source for Demographic History," William and Mary Quarterly, 3d Series, 30 (1973): 65-92; Edmund Morgan, American Slavery, American Freedom: The Ordeal of Colonial Virginia (New York: 1975); D. B. Rutman

and A. H. Rutman, "Of Agues and Fevers: Malaria in the Early Chesapeake," William and Mary Quarterly, 3d Series, 33 (1976): 31-60; L. S. Walsh and R. R. Menard, "Death in the Chesapeake: Two Life Tables for Men in Early Colonial Maryland," Maryland Historical Magazine 69 (1974): 211-17.

35. Vinovskis, "A Multivariate Regression Analysis of Fertility Differentials."

36. Michael B. Katz, The People of Hamilton West: Family and Class in a Mid-Nineteenth-Century City (Cambridge, Mass.: Harvard University Press, 1975), pp. 32-35; Stuart M. Blumin, "Rip Van Winkle's Grandchildren: Family and Household in the Hudson Valley, 1800-1860," in Family and Kin in Urban Communities, 1700-1930, ed. Tamara K. Hareven (New York: Academic Press, 1977), pp. 100-21.

37. Hareven and Vinovskis, "Marital Fertility, Ethnicity, and Occupation in Urban Families"; Trierweiler, "The Differential Child-Woman Ratios in Washtenaw County, Michigan"; Tamara K. Hareven and Maris A. Vinovskis, "Patterns of Childbearing in Late Nineteenth-Century America: The Determinants of Marital Fertility in Five Massachusetts Towns in 1880," in Family and Population in Nineteenth-Century America, pp. 85-125.

38. For a good introduction to this issue, see W. B. Clifford, "Modern and Traditional Value Orientations and Fertility Behavior: A Social-Demographic Study," Demography 8 (1971): 37-48; J. T. Fawcett and M. H. Bornstein, "Modernization, Individual Modernity, and Fertility," Psychological Perspectives on Population, ed. J. T. Fawcett (New York: 1973), pp. 106-31; J. A. Kahl, The Measurement of Modernism: A Study of Values in Brazil and Mexico (Austin: University of Texas Press, 1968); Karen A. Miller and Alex Inkeles, "Modernity and Acceptance of Family Limitation in Four Developing Countries," Journal of Social Issues 30 (1974): 167-88; B. C. Rosen and A. B. Simons, "Industrialization, Family, and Fertility: A Structural-Psychological Analysis of the Brazilian Case," Demography 8 (1971): 49-69; J. B. Williamson, "Subjective Efficacy and Ideal Family Size as Predictors of Favorability toward Birth Control," Demography 7 (1970): 329-39.

39. For example, see Richard D. Brown, "Modernization and the Modern Personality in Early America, 1600-1865: A Sketch of a Synthesis," Journal of Interdisciplinary History 2 (1972): 201-28; Richard D. Brown, Modernization: The Transformation of American Life, 1600-1865 (New York: Norton, 1976).

40. Vinovskis, "Socio-Economic Determinants of Interstate Fertility Differentials"; Vinovskis, Demographic Changes in America from the Revolution to the Civil War; Robert V. Wells, "Family History and Demographic Transition," Journal of Social History 9 (Fall 1975): 1-20.

41. For some critiques of the modernization approach, see Reinhard Bendix, "The Comparative Analysis of Historical Change," in Social Theory and Economic Change, ed. T. Burns and S. B. Saul (London: Macmillan, 1967), pp. 67-86; Neil J. Smelser, Essays in Sociological Explanation (Englewood Cliffs, N.J.: Prentice-Hall, 1968), pp. 125-46.

42. For the documentation of these changes, see Vinovskis, Demographic Changes in America from the Revolution to the Civil War.

43. Frank W. Notestein, "Population: The Long View," in Food for the World, ed. Theodore W. Schultz (Chicago: University of Chicago Press, 1945), pp. 40-41; Warren S. Thompson, Population and Peace in the Pacific (Chicago: University of Chicago Press, 1946).

44. On the use of birth control and abortions in nineteenth-century America, see James Reed, Birth Control and the Americans (New York: Basic Books, 1977); Wilson Yates, "Birth Control Literature and the Medical Profession in Nineteenth-Century America," Journal of the History of Medicine and Allied Sciences 31 (January 1976): 42-54; James C. Mohr, Abortion in America: The Origins and Evolution of National Policy (New York: Oxford University Press, 1978). One must be very careful, however, with the recent literature on birth control in nineteenth-century America. For instance, Gordon's recent book on this subject is very polemical and misleading in its discussions of the nineteenth century. Linda Gordon, Woman's Body, Woman's Right: A Social History of Birth Control in America (New York: Penguin, 1976).

45. For example, see Massimo Livi-Bacci, A History of Italian Fertility during the Last Two Centuries (Princeton, N.J.: Princeton University Press, 1977); Massimo Livi-Bacci, A Century of Portuguese Fertility (Princeton, N.J.: Princeton University Press, 1971); John E. Knodel, The Decline of Fertility in Germany, 1871-1939 (Princeton, N.J.: Princeton University Press, 1974); Michael S. Teitelbaum, The British Fertility Decline: The Demographic Transition in the Crucible of the Industrial Revolution (Princeton, N.J.: Princeton University Press, forthcoming).

46. Knodel, The Decline of Fertility in Germany; Teitelbaum, The British Fertility Decline.

47. A. J. Coale, B. Anderson, and E. Harm, Human Fertility in Russia since the Nineteenth Century (Princeton, N.J.: Princeton University Press, 1979).

48. There is an extensive literature on the changing role of women in nineteenth-century America. For example, see Ann Douglas, The Feminization of American Culture (New York: Avon, 1977); Keith E. Melder, Beginnings of Sisterhood: The American Woman's Rights Movement, 1800-1850 (New York: Schocken, 1977); Karen

Oppenheim Mason, Maris A. Vinovskis, and Tamara K. Hareven, "Women's Work and the Life Course in Essex County, Massachusetts, 1880," in Transitions: The Family and the Life Course in Historical Perspective, ed. Tamara K. Hareven (New York: Academic Press, 1978), pp. 187-216; Nancy F. Cott, The Bonds of Womanhood: "Woman's Sphere" in New England, 1780-1835 (New Haven, Conn.: Yale University Press, 1977); Maris A. Vinovskis and Richard M. Bernard, "Beyond Catherine Beecher: Female Education in the United States," Signs 3 (Summer 1978): 856-69.

49. For a helpful discussion of the relative usefulness of various theories of fertility change as guidelines for population planning programs today, see Michael S. Teitelbaum, "Relevance of Demographic Transition Theory for Developing Countries," Science 188 (May 1975): 420-25; Thomas K. Burch, "Theories of Fertility as Guides to Population Policy," Social Forces 54 (September 1975): 126-38; Ronald Freedman, "Social Science Research on Population in Asia (with Particular Reference to Fertility)," in U.S. Congress, House, Select Committee on Population, Hearings, Population and Development, pp. 608-29.

6

THE EFFECTS OF INCOME DISTRIBUTION ON FERTILITY IN DEVELOPING COUNTRIES

Robert Repetto

PRELIMINARY CONCEPTS

The influence of income distribution on fertility need not arise, as some sociologists have supposed, from the effect on individuals of perceived inequalities in their societies. It need not depend on envy, emulation, or any other motivation derived from the realization of relative economic status. While the perception of relative economic status may affect fertility, the distribution of income could do so whether such perceptions were important or not.

The influence arises from the fact that the long-term, direct and indirect effect on couples' fertility of changes in their income is not the same for couples at different initial income levels. A maintained rise in annual income level of $500, for example, will not necessarily have the same effect on the fertility of a family with annual income of $5,000 as it will on a family with annual income of $500. Consequently, it matters in determining the number of births per year in the entire population whether additional, or transferable, income goes to the families at $5,000 per year or to those at $500 per year. In other words, the distribution of income matters in the determination of the population's birth rate.

Nobody would object to the statement that as a population gets richer, its fertility changes. This is just another way of stating that

---

Research for this study was supported in part by Resources for the Future, and by the International Bank for Reconstruction and Development.

fertility is influenced by the first moment of the distribution of income. Why is there so much more resistance to the idea that fertility is influenced by the second moment of the distribution as well? Unless fertility is a linear function of household income, that must be true. Would there be strong feelings about the importance of the third moment? In a commonsense view, what reason is there to suppose that the consequences for fertility of income changes should be the same for rich families and poor families? The question is not whether absolute or relative income affects the birth rate, but rather the form that the relationship takes.

Nonlinearity is not in dispute; rather the full implications of non-linearity have not been considered. That the relationship between household fertility and income and other economic status variables is nonlinear is common knowledge.[1] The search for "thresholds" of fertility decline, for instance, exemplifies an interest in these nonlinearities that goes back at least 25 years.[2] Recently an increasing number of studies have explored these non-linearities, and numerous hypotheses regarding interactions among economic variables have been advanced to account for them.[3] While it is probably too early to discriminate definitively among the possible modes of interaction that have been hypothesized, it is important to understand that, insofar as these theories all imply nonlinearity in the household income-household fertility relation and a causal ordering in which income directly or indirectly affects fertility, they all imply the proposition that population birth rates will depend on the higher moments of the distribution of income. In this sense, the income distribution hypothesis is robust: it is a property of many proposed models of household fertility behavior.

Long-term consequences of changes in income should be emphasized because short-term transient fluctuations in household income, those arising from business cycles or harvest fluctuations for example, tend to affect fertility mainly through induced shifts in the timing of births rather than through changes in lifetime fertility. (Of course, there is no reason to suppose that people in all economic strata should alter the timing and spacing of births in the same way in response to given economic fluctuations.)

Direct and indirect consequences should be emphasized because the immediate consequences of changes in income, before everything else has had a chance to adjust, are just not very interesting to anybody but the economist involved in testing propositions from consumer-demand theory. When household permanent income changes, there are a multitude of responses. Aspirations change, work patterns change, the health status of household members changes (at least in poor households); all of these changes affect the allocation of household resources. What is more relevant is the effect of income changes not with health, education, employment status, and all preferences conceptually or statistically held constant, but rather the effect of income changes with all these responding as they do to improvements in economic welfare.

An analytical framework that implies one plausible source of linearity is a stock-adjustment model of fertility, which has been recently explored by several economists.[4] It is derived from the simple proposition that couples desire children, not births per se, and that having babies is just the way in which couples try to get the number of children they want, or close to it. The analogy is to the theory of investment behavior, which depicts current investment as the attempt to reconcile the existing stock of durable assets with that currently desired.

In these terms, current fertility depends on three elements: the number of children currently desired, as well as the sensitivity of parents to shortfall or excess fertility; the number of children the couple already has, which may be more or less than the number desired; and the efficacy of current control over fertility in helping couples adjust to discrepancies between actual and desired family size. A simple stock-adjustment model is presented in the following paragraphs.

The model of current fertility presented below is intended only to illustrate the diverse ways in which household income may affect household fertility when the latter is subject to imperfect and costly control, and to show how nonlinearities are likely to arise in the influence of income on fertility.

At a particular age t, an individual married woman could be assumed to have a desired family size N_t^* if there were no costs to fertility control. This number can be regarded as a demand jointly determined with the demands for other goods and services, and with the allocation of the time through a process of constrained welfare maximization. Welfare maximization models of this type, constrained by the wealth and time resources of the household, have been presented by many economists[5] and need not be reconstructed here. The demand for children in such a process depends upon household wealth, the price of children, and the price of close substitutes, usually assumed to be children of greater resource intensity (that is, of quality).

The price of children is determined largely by the opportunity costs of the mother's time and by the infant mortality rate. The price of more resource-intensive children depends mainly on the direct and opportunity costs of schooling, which include the foregone reward to child labor attributable to school attendance. Therefore,

$$N_t^* = N^*(Y_t, p_{nt}, p_{st}, T)$$

where Y represents household nonlabor income, T represents the total time resources of the household, p_n represents a vector of variables outside the range of household control determining the price of a child, and p_s another set of exogenous factors determining the total price of schooling and other investments in the child's well-being.

Current fertility is a random variable, however. The natural fertility of a woman P_t, measured in terms of the probability of conception within a given time interval, can be modified through application of some technique of birth control with a contraceptive efficiency e. Associated with each contraceptive efficiency e, there is a certain minimum cost, including both psychic and material disadvantages. These costs can be represented by a schedule in which marginal costs are near zero for no birth control and rise rapidly as efficiency approaches unity.

$$C(e) = C_0 + ae^2 \qquad 0 < e < 1$$

The benefits from birth control are derived from the welfare losses of departures from the ideal family size,[6] augmented by the advantages of child spacing. The first can be described by a function that rises rapidly as actual family size exceeds the ideal, and falls as the actual family size falls short of the ideal. The second can be represented by a function that rises with the probability of conceiving in the current period. These components are multiplicative. The desirability of wide spacing is lower the further actual family size is beneath the ideal; the desirability of wide spacing is higher the more the actual exceeds the ideal. Thus a suitable cost function from which the benefits of fertility control can be desired is shown in this equation:

$$B(e) = A - m[P(1 - e)]^2(k) \exp[r(N - N^*)]$$

The parameters have clear-cut interpretations, as is illustrated in Figure 6.1. When actual family size equals the ideal, k is the welfare cost of an additional child, apart from spacing considerations. The parameter r determines the pace at which these welfare costs change from deviations from the ideal, while A is simply a scalar that transforms costs to benefits at some small family size below the ideal. The spacing parameter m measures the welfare costs of a higher probability of conception within the current period. This cost is conditioned by the woman's position of excess or deficit fertility.

Clearly, the welfare-maximizing household will minimize the sum of the welfare costs of contraception and the welfare costs of excessive and too rapid fertility. This implies setting the marginal costs of contraception equal to the marginal costs of childbearing,

FIGURE 6.1

Welfare Losses of Departures from Ideal Family Size

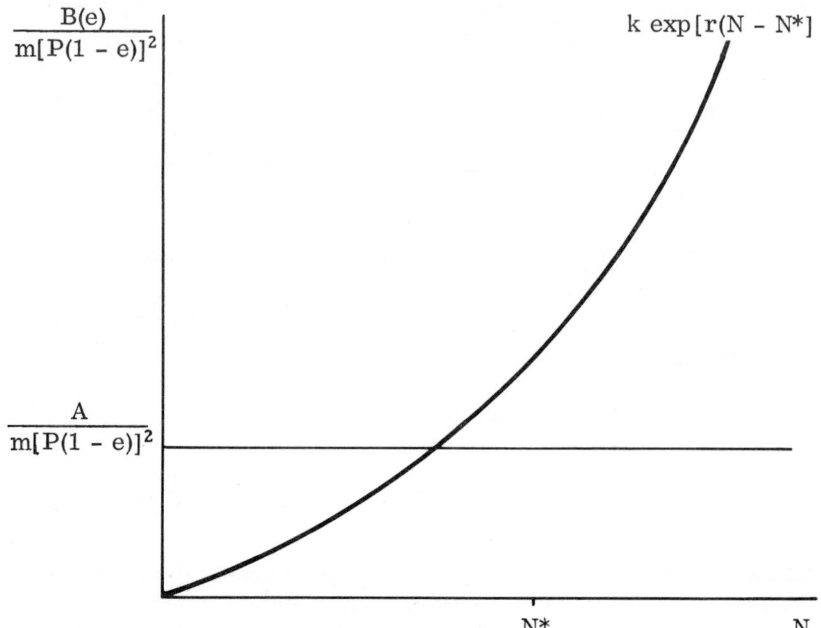

Source: Constructed by the author.

where both are expressed in terms of the probabilities of conceiving. This condition amounts to the stipulation that for the optimal degree of fertility control e*,

$$ae^* = kmP(1 - e^*) \exp[r(N - N^*)]$$

It is helpful to define a new parameter b as the ratio of costs to benefits from a marginal change in contraceptive efficiency at the ideal family size.

$$b = a/kmP$$

Then,

$$(1 - e^*)/e^* = b \exp[r(N^* - N)]$$

$$e^* = \frac{1}{1 + b \exp[r(N^* - N)]}$$

A woman with N children who desires N* would choose a contraceptive technique with efficiency e*. The behavior of e* is depicted in Figure 6.2. Birth control would be near zero at family sizes well below the ideal, and rise to nearly complete efficiency as family size exceeds that desired. Typically, a woman with the ideal number of children would not optimally use contraception with perfect efficiency unless the marginal cost of contraception were zero. Consequently, the expected completed family size would be greater than what would be ideal with costless fertility control.

The optimal degree of fertility control is related in predictable ways to the underlying parameters of the model. It will be higher the lower the marginal costs of contraception, the higher the natural fertility of the woman, and the higher the welfare costs of excess fertility and close birth spacing. Other things being equal, it will be higher the higher the actual stock of children is relative to that currently desired.

This optimal degree of contraception gives rise to a conditional birth probability for the individual woman in each time period:

$$P_t^* = P^*(N/t\ N_t^*,\ N_t,\ b,\ r) = P_t(1 - e_t^*)$$

This, aside from gestation lags, is her fertility rate for the current

FIGURE 6.2

Desired Family Size, Actual Size, and the Choice of Contraceptive Efficacy (stylized)

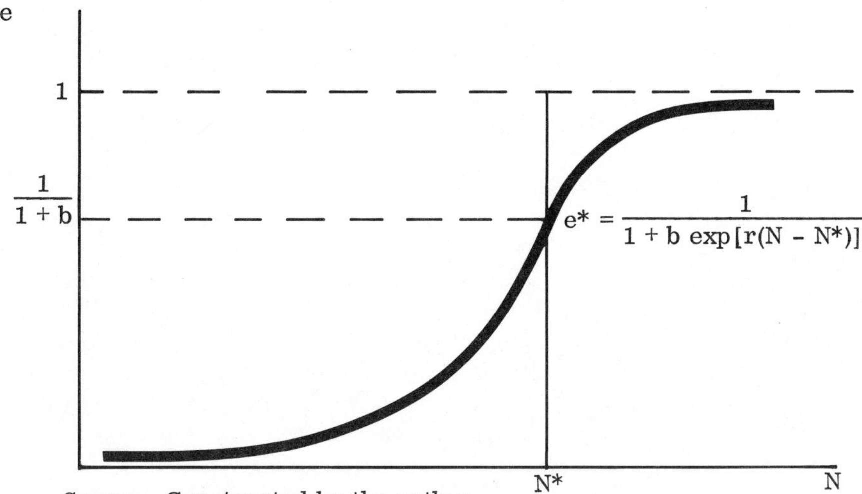

Source: Constructed by the author.

period. To complete the process, expected family size in any interval is generated by the following recursive process:

$$E(N_{t+1}) = N_t(1 - w_t) + P^*_t \qquad N_0 = 0$$

where w_t is the expected infant mortality rate applicable to the household in the period t.

The conditional birth probability P* represents a simple stock-adjustment process; that is, the greater the existing stock of children, the lower the current fertility rate. Within this framework the diverse influences of income can be distinguished. Income might be expected to influence not only ideal family size, but also, through the infant mortality rate, the existing stock of children. The influence of income might also extend to the perceived costs of departures from ideal family size and to the desirability attached to child spacing. Finally, the economic status of the household could influence the natural fertility of the woman and the perceived costs of fertility control. It is clear that whatever restrictions there are on the sign of $\delta N^*/\delta Y$ through the formation of consumer demands, there are no restrictions on the sign of $\delta P^*/\delta Y$. Moreover, under only the remotest of circumstances could P* be represented as a linear function of Y. In general, $\delta P^*/\delta Y$ will be a complicated function of Y itself.

While this representation is at best a model of marital fertility and ignores socioeconomic influences on nuptiality, it does integrate a number of previously unrelated explanations. The determinants of family size norms include both the budgetary constraints on household time and money expenditures that create income and price effects on desired family size, and the influences on attitudes, values, and norms that determine household preferences. The former set of factors has drawn the attention of economists, the latter of sociologists. Both schools agree, however, that it is mainly desired family size that determines actual family size, and individual or societal controls are adequate to ensure rapid adjustment of one to the other.

An earlier generation of demographers, along with biologists and public health specialists, have tended to place their emphasis on factors affecting the probable surviving stock of children of couples for any marriage duration. Of these, the most important for developing countries has been the infant mortality rate: traditional demographic transition theory postulates that fertility after some lag declines to adjust to declining infant mortality rates, to keep expected family size or number of surviving sons stable. In addition, biologists have pointed out possible impairment of fecundity from poor health and nutritional status, changes in which would result in independent shifts in natural fertility.

Family planning specialists, together with many psychologists, have contested whether couples, at least in conditions of underdevelopment, have adequate control over their current fertility to avoid unwanted children in rapidly changing circumstances. On the one hand, they emphasize lack of access to satisfactory contraceptive knowledge and methods; on the other hand, they point to the lack of sufficient personal control over reproduction on the part of female partners. Underlying reasons include lack of marital communication and male dominance, the strength of kin and community pressure, or more general traits of fatalism and passivity stemming from low socioeconomic and political status.

All these influences conjoin in determining current fertility. Since all are, directly or indirectly, affected by the level of household income, the resultant is an extremely complex relation between income and fertility. That this relation should be linear over the range of household incomes represented in the population is most unlikely.

THE INFLUENCE OF INCOME INEQUALITY ON FERTILITY: RECENT AGGREGATIVE EVIDENCE

At the simplest level of observation, it has been recognized that those developing countries that earliest entered into a phase of sustained fertility decline at low levels of average per capita income and other development indexes, were precisely those that were typified by a relatively equal distribution of income and a relatively widespread participation in the benefits of growth. These forerunners include Sri Lanka, which stands in suggestive contrast to India and Pakistan in South Asia, Costa Rica, a similarly striking anomaly in Central America, Mauritius, Korea, Taiwan, and the People's Republic of China.[7] It is the relative equality of the development pattern that these have in common, rather than rapid growth, a high initial level of development, or a particular political system or cultural heritage.

Kerala, among the states of India, has provided an equally suggestive observation.[8] Despite the relatively low ranking of Kerala among the Indian states with respect to average income, Kerala has achieved the most far-reaching and rapid fertility decline. What distinguishes Kerala is the relatively equal distribution of income, the broad popular access to public services and political organizations, and the near universality of basic education.

More formal statistical analysis of cross-national variations in fertility rates and socioeconomic variables has substantiated these observations. It has been found that the income levels of the poorest 40 percent of households are more closely related to fertility rates of the entire population than are average income levels, which include the high incomes of the elite.[9] Direct testing of the hypothesis that income distribution and fertility interact, using the best available comparative data for individual nations, has yielded estimates implying a strong impact of income inequality on fertility.[10] Likely errors of measurement in these data only strengthen confidence in the estimates, because such errors of measurement tend to bias observed correlations toward zero. Difficulties in distinguishing the direction of causality underlying the association, when in fact income distribution and fertility interact, have been addressed in specifying larger models admitting possible direct and indirect feedbacks from fertility to income distribution. Analysis of these larger models by appropriate statistical techniques has resulted in estimates of the effect of income inequality that are indeed larger than those obtained through more simple methods. Consequently, the possibility can be ruled out that observed associations between these two variables are merely the effect of sustained high fertility on measured income inequality.

The elasticity of response in these studies of the population fertility rate of changes in the Gini coefficient is of the order of 0.3, which exceeds the estimated impacts of changes in infant mortality, female literacy, or increases in average income levels without changes in distribution. Despite the strong measured association, these results do not imply that nations with equal income distributions must have low fertility, or that fertility cannot decline without a prior improvement in income distribution. The distribution of income is just one factor, although an important one, which affects a population's fertility rate. Sufficiently advanced and widespread modernization, even with an unequal distribution of income, can result in fertility decline. Sufficiently retarded and restricted modernization, even in the presence of equal income distribution, can result in sustained high fertility.

These results do imply, however, that efforts to explain fertility rates of population without taking into consideration variations in income distribution can create misleading results. If other explanatory factors, like infant mortality rates or literacy rates, vary at least partially in harmony with variations in income distribution, effects on fertility will be ascribed to those that actually could be attributed to income distribution. For this reason there may be large numbers of studies of fertility rates, in which either nations or smaller population aggregates were the units of observation, which have yielded biased estimates of socioeconomic determinants of fertility.

HISTORICAL EVIDENCE: THE RELEVANCE OF THE DEVELOPING COUNTRIES TO DEMOGRAPHIC TRANSITION THEORY

Detailed examination of the pattern of fertility and mortality change in over 700 subnational administrative areas in Europe during the period of transition, organized by the Office of Population Research at Princeton University, has resulted in a number of papers and monographs demonstrating the complexity of the process of change. The results of this research have blurred the simple generalizations regarding the roles of mortality decline, urbanization, and industrialization previously identified with the theory of the demographic transition. Among the findings has been the observation that measures of economic advancement have been only unreliably associated with fertility change in the European transition. While correlations have been found, they are unstable from region to region and period to period.[11] Economic factors in general have been found to be less closely associated with patterns of fertility transition than cultural, linguistic, and historical variations among regions.

Ongoing research into nineteenth-century fertility transition in Hungary by Maria Sophia Lengyel, a graduate student at Harvard, has shed light on the reasons for this. In the reconsideration of the European demographic transition, the experience of the Hungarian provinces was used to demonstrate that early fertility decline had taken place in rural areas, in advance of any significant urbanization or industrialization, thus undermining one main pillar of the conventional explanation.[12] The reasons for the early rural fertility transition remained unclear, and subsequent research[13] failed to uncover any close association of regional or temporal fertility variations with economic conditions in the rural provinces.

A good part of the reason why these relationships have remained obscure seems to be that in the reconsideration of the demographic transition, the distribution of economic welfare has been ignored. Although considerable effort has gone into disaggregation of overall patterns by region and administrative division, little has been done to distinguish changes in economic conditions by socioeconomic strata. Implicitly, each province has been treated as an economically homogeneous unit. Thus, for example, economic variables have been introduced as averages or overall rates for entire districts or provinces. In the analysis of the transition in rural Hungary, variations in economic welfare have been measured primarily by the average value of agricultural output per person employed in agriculture for each province. Similar measures have been used in studies of the demographic transition in other European countries also.[14]

However, Europe in the nineteenth century was anything but homogeneous socially and economically. Rural Hungary in that time was barely removed from feudalism. A traditional aristocracy held vast estates in mortmain. The largest 1 percent of holdings contained half the arable land. Most of the rural population worked inadequate holdings until forced by debt and poverty to migrate, their farms to be taken over by other land-hungry peasants. To average the income from the 50 percent of agricultural land held by the wealthiest 1 percent of the population with that from the 50 percent held by the remaining 99 percent of the population could not but obscure the factors responsible for demographic change.

While Hungary was perhaps an extreme case, the degree of inequality in rural areas was not markedly less in other European countries. Given these huge disparities, one would expect that the insight derived from the study of present-day developing countries, that the economic welfare of the lower income households is more closely related to demographic conditions than is the overall average level of output per household, would also be applicable to nineteenth-century Europe.

Preliminary findings indicate that this expectation is correct. Estimates have been constructed for each of 48 Hungarian provinces at the end of the nineteenth century of output per holding on holdings of less than 100 holds, which accounts for less than half of total acreage but 99 percent of all farms, and of average income per capita among landless workers. There is little correlation across provinces between the income of large landowners and those of smaller holders or of landless workers. The trickle-down effect was evidently not pronounced in nineteenth-century Hungary either. Moreover, regional variations in fertility and fertility decline were significantly correlated with both measures of popular economic welfare, while there was not correlation between the demographic variables and average output per household on all holdings, large and small combined. These findings underscore the fact that the effects of income on fertility differ among households at different income levels. They confirm the influence of income distribution on fertility and shed additional light on factors underlying the demographic transition in Europe. Insofar as studies of that process have not adequately distinguished between average condition and those pertaining to the mass of the people, they have run the risk of mistaking determinants of demographic change.

Even stronger evidence has been produced that the omission of relevant economic variables, and of measures of income inequality in particular, in the study of the Hungarian demographic transition has led previous investigators to mistake the forces at work. Formal statistical analyses of socioeconomic and demographic data for 48 provinces in four census years 1880-1910 support three main conclusions: first, the relationship between fertility rates on the one hand, and the socioeconomic variables conventionally associated with the theory of demographic tradition (such as the infant mortality rate, the degree of literacy, and the degree of urbanization) and those emphasized by more recent research on the European demographic transition (such as the linguistic, ethnic, and religious composition of the population) on the other hand is weak, unstable from period to period, and gives evidence that important explanatory factors have been left out of consideration; second, transient economic forces, such as those arising from harvest fluctuations or financial disturbances, are associated with fertility rates and explain much of the fluctuation of demographic variables over time around trend values; and third, differences among provinces in the welfare of low income households and the degree of economic inequality can be associated with much of the interregional variation in fertility rates not explained by the factors traditionally invoked in demographic transition theory. These findings provide evidence that differences in income distribution have affected fertility rates in the earlier demographic transition, as they have in the demographic transition now taking place in developing countries.

INEQUALITY AND THE PERSISTENCE OF FERTILITY DIFFERENTIALS

Additional light might be shed on the process of transition, both in Europe and in the currently developing nations, were the focus of attention not so narrowly on the socioeconomic correlates of fertility differentials. These differentials have virtually disappeared in the economically advanced countries, yet more and more research has been directed toward their correlates. It would be useful if more attention were paid to the causes and the pace of their disappearance.

Since low fertility patterns typically appear first among a modernizing elite of society, and are then diffused among the subgroups, the extent and persistence of fertility differentials largely determine the overall pace of fertility decline. It is not sufficient to know the characteristics of the relatively low fertility subgroups within the whole population. It is also important to know how much higher is the fertility of high fertility subgroups, how long before they also achieve low fertility, and the factors influencing the length of this lag.

In the European transition increase, socioeconomic fertility differentials widened for 50 years or more in some areas, and persisted for a century or more. Correspondingly, the rate of change in overall fertility was slow by comparison with the rate of change experienced by societies entering the transition at a later date. In countries still manifesting high fertility at the present time, it is common to find modernized elites with low fertility. In many such countries, this has been so for a generation or more without much diffusion to larger subgroups within the total population. Such societies have developed wide, and often widening, socioeconomic fertility differentials, and the overall rate of fertility change has been slow.

By contrast, developing countries that have experienced rapid fertility decline have typically experienced only a relatively short period of widening differentials, and then a rapid convergence, as traditionally high fertility groups that include the majority of the population also experience fertility decline. The experiences of Korea and Taiwan aptly illustrate this process.[15] Both have displayed a high rate of fertility decline, and both have experienced the start of a narrowing of fertility differentials within a decade after the beginning of the period of decline. Diffusion of new demographic behavior has been rapid.

Emphasis on the socioeconomic correlates of current fertility differentials directs attention to status changes within the population as the source of fertility decline, and most theories are couched largely in these terms. They state that as women change status from uneducated to educated, from rural to urban, from housewife to employee, from noncontraceptor to contraceptor, their fertility declines. While this is true (and in countries like Korea and Taiwan in which the fertility decline has been fast, economic development has brought status changes to a large proportion of households), this is by no means the entire story. There have been substantial declines of fertility within all status groups, and especially in traditionally high fertility groups. In decomposition analysis, it is not uncommon to find that half of the total decline must be attributed to declines within rather than among whatever categories the analysis distinguishes between.[16]

It is tempting to ascribe this phenomenon to the diffusion of contraceptive means and knowledge. However, this in part begs the question since it leaves unspecified the factors determining the pace of diffusion of birth control techniques. It is also inaccurate. In Korea, for example, it is clear that changes in marriage age, reduction in desired family size, more widespread recourse to abortion, and reliance on nonclinical, nonprogram means of contraception together made the greatest contribution to the decline. Further, the same range of modern contraceptive methods is potentially available in societies in which socioeconomic fertility differentials are still widening as in those in which they are rapidly converging.[17]

At this point, because the data available on the evolution of fertility differentials are scattered and incomplete, only clues are available about the nature of the forces at work. One would expect that the more homogeneous the socioeconomic characteristics of the population, the less class stratification, and the fewer the barriers to diffusion of social change, the more rapid would be the process of convergence. For the demographic transition in Europe, it was pointed out over a decade ago that fertility differentials narrowed fastest in countries with the least stratification (the Scandinavian countries, in particular).[18] This clue has apparently not been followed up. Impressionistically, however, for the presently developing countries, it seems that in homogeneous countries with relatively equal patterns of income distribution and substantial socioeconomic mobility, fertility declines have been widely spread. Korea is an obvious example. In countries with sharp inequalities and barriers to vertical interchange, wide differentials have persisted and fertility declines have been confined for long periods to small elites. Many Latin American countries provide examples. This may prove to be a partial explanation of the timing of general fertility declines. In some countries, like Mexico, rapid economic growth continued for a substantial period before fertility began to fall significantly. At the time, that economic advance was not widely shared. This inequality and the high degree of stratification may have been barriers to the diffusion of new fertility patterns as well as other kinds of social change.

CROSS-SECTIONAL EVIDENCE

Research into socioeconomic correlates of differential fertility has, despite the reservations expressed above, provided insights into the role of income distribution. The ubiquity of nonlinearities in the relation between household fertility and measures of household economic status has been recognized for a long time, although de-emphasized until quite recently. Economists, in the course of exploring the demand for children (that is, in terms of the stock-adjustment model, N^*), have been intent on establishing that the pure income effect on desired fertility is positive, in accordance with the predictions of consumer demand theory, and on differentiating the effects of income from sources that do and from those that do not affect the relative opportunity costs of having children. In recent years, by recognizing a more varied role for changes in income in affecting fertility, as implied, for example, by the stock-adjustment model presented above, economists have allowed other concerns a more prominent place.

Among the recent contributions in which household fertility has been specified and analyzed as a stock-adjustment process, the investigation of Puerto Rican fertility in 1970 emphasized the implication of the findings with regard to the importance of income distribution.[19]

Puerto Rican couple fertility is nonlinearly related to family income. Increases in income are associated with declines in fertility, but more so at low income than at high. Consequently, given increases in income will result in greater declines in fertility if the recipients are low income families rather than high income families. This is implied by the research findings within age, educational, occupational, and residence groupings, and also across those categories.

The Puerto Rican study also distinguished between the effects on fertility of variations in both the family's own income and the family's economic status relative to that typical of its community. This distinction was possible because the available data included information about the community in which each household lived, as well as information about the household itself. There has been a widespread misconception that the impact of income distribution on fertility stems only from the household's perception of its relative deprivation or advantage rather than from the varying effects of economic changes on the fertility of households at different income levels.[20] The findings regarding Puerto Rican fertility were unambiguous: income distribution strongly affected birth rates through the varying effect of income changes on fertility, and not from the perception of relative economic status.

Further explorations of cross-sectional data generated in the Korean segment of the World Fertility Survey provided greater insight into the mechanisms underlying these findings. Short-run, ceteris paribus treatment of household income changes are unsatisfactory for reasons already mentioned: maintained improvements in living standards influence aspirations and values, the allocation of household resources, and the nature of contacts the household establishes with the environment. It is misleading to treat all these as independent of one another. In the analysis of recent Korean fertility, the influence of income and other socioeconomic variables on the mechanisms of fertility decline—nuptiality, contraceptive use, and desired family size—was investigated. Similarly, the influence of economic status on crucial parental attitudes—aspirations for children, and the expectation of security and support from children—was explored. It was found that household fertility was the more strongly and the more nonlinearly related to income, the more the indirect influences of income changes were taken into consideration. The nature of the relationship was such that the more equal the distribution of income over the population studies, the lower the population birth rate.

Analyses of this sort can be readily extended to other populations, and there could be considerable gains from doing so. Common sense suggests that at very low levels of income, household formation and fertility must be impaired. Consequently, the response of fertility to income increases can scarcely be a declining function of income over the whole range of incomes to be found in the developing world. Data from some very low income populations corroborate this reasoning.[21] Moreover, there seem to be populations, such as the Philippines, in which the curvature of the nonlinearity is reversed.[22] Investigation of such apparently discrepant observations, and of the applicable range of the hypothesis, would be worthwhile.*

Finally, although this is a limitation of most research in economic demography, the restriction of analyses at the household level to cross-sectional samples is restrictive. It would be desirable to follow households over time to investigate economic demographic interactions through panel studies and resurveys. Interest is rising in this kind of research.

POLICY IMPLICATIONS

Despite the range and consistency of the empirical evidence, there have been reservations about whether any policy implications can be drawn from these findings.[23] Doubt has been expressed whether observed correlations reflect any causal relation. Both the cross-sectional research and historical studies bear on this doubt. In econometric analysis in which simultaneous interactions among fertility, income concentration, and other economic variables were admitted, strong influences leading from the degree of inequality to the level of fertility were discovered. Also, in an historical study of Korea's experience, the change in income distribution preceded and was independent of subsequent rapid fertility decline. The change in the degree of income inequality came about through war, hyperinflation, land reforms, and educational reforms triggered by foreign influences. They were not determined by demographic conditions, but the evidence strongly suggests that demographic changes were greatly influenced by the changes in the distribution of income.

---

*Some apparently discrepant observations are attributable to the use of an inappropriate measure of household income. In particular, the use of total household income without standardization for the number of household members is inappropriate, especially in communities in which extended families are common. Under these circumstances, total income may be a very misleading indication of the resources available per household member. It is like comparing the economic status of India and Denmark by comparing their GNPs, with no correction for their population sizes.

It has also been suggested that different means of redistributing income would have different demographic consequences, some pronatalist and others antinatalist.[24] One can imagine benefits provided to low income households entirely through family allowances in one scheme and entirely through incentives for fertility reductions or contraceptive use in another. One would expect the demographic consequences to differ in the two schemes. While this is theoretically unassailable, it is largely beside the point. The main avenues for the reduction of inequality at the lower end of the income scale in the developing countries would involve stimulation of additional employment, redistribution of productive assets (mainly land and basic education), and the plentiful supply of goods consumed heavily by the poor. While several of these are theoretically pronatalist, like land reform and subsidized basic education in that they reduce the opportunity cost of children, there is no evidence that these economic measures have resulted in higher fertility. Indeed, in countries in which they have been carried out, the consequence has been accelerated fertility decline.

If from this evidence it can be concluded that patterns of development that provide more rapid improvements in living standards to low income households result in faster rates of fertility decline, the consequences are important. It follows that there exists a positive reinforcement between greater equality and lower birth rates, because it has also been established that lower birth rates and slower population growth produce lesser distribution of income in the long run. Therefore, the adoption of development policies that distribute benefits widely tends to create a self-sustained and self-reinforcing process.

A second important consequence of the evidence is the further refutation of the idea of a growth-equity tradeoff in economic development. This idea rested precariously on the contention that greater income inequality resulted in higher overall savings rates. Neither the evidence of the socialist countries, which managed both high rates of capital accumulation and equal income distributions, nor the fact that household savings, to which the argument applies, are only one component of total savings has completely eliminated belief in this tradeoff.

However, the association of greater income equality with lower rates of population growth should do so. A slower rate of population growth would result in faster accumulation of capital per worker and a faster growth of output per worker. In the past two decades the difference in the growth of output per capita between LDCs and advanced countries as groups can be entirely associated with differences in population growth rates. The faster growth of output per worker and the reduced dependency burden would tend to raise the savings rate out of household income, promoting faster capital accumulation.

The slower growth of the labor force would reduce dualism in the economic structure and increase the chances for adoption of more appropriate advanced technologies. At the same time, less stress would be placed on fixed environmental resources. Through these mechanisms, economists would expect greater income equality to result in faster rates of economic growth. Instead of a growth-equity tradeoff, once demographic consequences are considered, there is growth-equity reinforcement.

NOTES

1. Donald Bogue, Principles of Demography (Chicago: 1969).

2. U.N. Dept. of Social Affairs, Population Division, Determinants and Consequences of Population Trends, Population Studies no. 17 (New York: 1953).

3. Y. Ben-Porath, "Fertility in Israel: Point and Counterpoint," Journal of Political Economy, supplement (March-April 1973); P. R. Gregory and J. M. Cambell, Jr., "Fertility Interactions and Modernization Turning Points," Journal of Political Economy 84, part I (August 1976): 835-49; J. Simon, The Effects of Income on Fertility (Chapel Hill, N.C.: Carolina Population Center, 1974); B. Boulier and M. Rosenzweig, "Age, Biological Factors and Socioeconomic Determinants of Fertility (Yale University, Economic Growth Center, 1977, mimeo); B. Turchi, The Demand for Children (Ballinger, 1975); R. Willis, "A New Approach to the Economic Theory of Fertility," Journal of Political Economy, supplement (March-April 1973); R. D. Lee, "Target Fertility, Contraception and Aggregate Rates: Toward a Formal Synthesis" (Population Studies Center, University of Michigan, May 1977, mimeo).

4. R. Anker, "An Analysis of Fertility Differentials at the Household Level: Births in the Last Two Years" (I.L.O. World Employment Program, Geneva, April 1977, mimeo); T. P. Schultz, "An Economic Interpretation of the Decline in Fertility in a Rapidly Developing Country" (Yale University Economic Growth Center, March 1977, mimeo); R. Repetto, "Inequality and the Birth Rate in Puerto Rico: Evidence from Household Census Data," paper presented to the Annual Population Association of America meeting, St. Louis, April 1977.

5. Gary Becker, "An Economic Theory of Fertility," in Demographic and Economic Change in Developed Countries, Universities-National Bureau Conference Series (Princeton, N.J.: Princeton University Press, 1960); Willis, "A New Approach."

6. Robert Michael and Robert Willis, "Contraception and Fertility: Household Production under Uncertainty," in N. E. Terlechyj,

ed., *Household Production and Consumption*, National Bureau of Economic Research, Studies in Income and Wealth, vol. 40 (New York: Columbia University Press, 1975).

7. W. Rich, *Smaller Families through Social and Economic Progress* (Washington, D.C.: Overseas Development Council, 1973).

8. J. W. Ratcliffe, "Poverty, Politics and Fertility: The Anomaly of Kerala," *Hastings Center Report* 7 (February 1977): 34-42.

9. J. Kocher, *Rural Development, Equity and Fertility Decline* (New York: Population Council, 1974).

10. T. King et al., *Population Policies and Economic Development: The World Bank Staff Report* (Washington, D.C.: 1974); R. Repetto, "The Interaction of Fertility and the Size Distribution of Income," *Journal of Development Studies* (June 1978).

11. M. Teitelbaum, "Relevance of Demographic Transition Theory for Developing Countries," *Science*, May 2, 1975, pp. 420-25.

12. P. Demeny, "Early Fertility Decline in Austria-Hungary: A Lesson in Demographic Transition," *Daedalus* 97 (Spring 1968): 502-22.

13. E. Szababy, "Economic Factors in the Decline of Fertility in Hungary in the 19th and Early 20th Century," in A. Coale, ed., *Economic Factors in Population Growth* (New York: 1976).

14. R. Lesthaeghe and E. van de Walle, "Economic Factors and Fertility Decline in France and Belgium," in Coale, *Economic Factors in Population Growth*.

15. R. Freedman et al., "Trends in Fertility and in the Effects of Education on Fertility in Taiwan, 1961-74," *Studies in Family Planning* 8 (January 1977): 11-18.

16. R. Retherford and N. Ogawa, "Decomposition of the Change in the Total Fertility Rate in the Republic of Korea, 1966-70," paper presented at the Seventh Summer Seminar on Population, East West Center, Honolulu, June 1976.

17. R. Repetto, Kwon Tai Hwan, Kim Son Ung, Peter Donaldson, and Kim Dae Young, *Economic Development and the Demographic Development in the Republic of Korea* (Cambridge, Mass.: Harvard Institute for International Development, 1978).

18. D. H. Wrong, "Trends in Class Fertility in Western Nations," in W. Bendix and S. Lipset, eds., *Class, Status and Power* (London: 1966).

19. R. Repetto, *Economic Equality and Fertility in Developing Countries* (Baltimore: Johns Hopkins Press for Resources for the Future, forthcoming).

20. N. Birdsall, "Analytic Approaches to the Relationship of Population Growth and Development," *Population and Development Review* (March, June 1977): 63-102.

21. T. Hull and V. Hull, "The Relation of Economic Class and Fertility: An Analysis of Some Indonesian Data," Population Studies 31 (March 1977): 43-58.

22. Boulier and Rosenzweig, "Age, Biological Factors."

23. W. McGreevey et al., The Policy Relevance of Recent Social Science Research on Fertility (Washington, D.C.: Smithsonian Institution, 1975).

24. Simon, Effects of Income on Fertility.

7

ECONOMIC VALUE AND COSTS OF CHILDREN IN RELATION TO HUMAN FERTILITY

Moni Nag

While people in all societies at all times have wanted children, cross-cultural ethnographic evidence suggests that in every society some individuals have tried to prevent births. The desire to prevent births is an indication that children are not always an unmixed blessing to all parents, even in societies whose culture and institutions are strongly oriented toward high fertility. In other words, children are valued by parents and societies, but there are also recognized costs associated with them. There are various dimensions of the value and costs of children to parents. The underlying hypothesis of this chapter is that fertility decline is caused primarily by a decrease in the economic value and an increase in the economic costs of children to their respective parents—in terms of both the perception of parents and actual reality. The emphasis of the chapter is on less developed countries.

CONCEPTS OF VALUE AND COSTS

Attempts to estimate the economic costs of children in developed countries have a long history (Espenshade 1977), but the value and costs of children gained recognition as concepts worthy of investigation in less developed countries only recently when social scientists started seriously to ponder the question: Why do people want children? An understanding of the complex motivations for childbearing has its own merits, but the actual impetus for investigation came from the realization that it might yield results useful to the policymakers interested in changing the childbearing motivations of couples in conformity with national fertility goals.

The concept of the value of children, when applied to parents, is often expressed by various other terms, such as satisfaction, benefit, utility, reward, and advantage. The Value of Children (VOC) project of the East-West Center defines the value of children as a "hypothetical net worth of children, with positive values (satisfactions) balanced against negative values (costs)" (Arnold et al. 1975: pp. 2-10). The findings of the project led to the identification of five positive general values of children to their parents: emotional benefits; economic benefits and security; self-enrichment and development; identification with child; and family cohesiveness and continuity. There were also five negative general values: emotional costs; economic costs; restrictions or opportunity costs; physical demands; and family costs.

In the microeconomic theory of fertility (Becker 1960; Demeny 1972; Easterlin 1975; Leibenstein 1957, 1974; Robinson and Horlacher 1971; Schultz 1974), primary attention is given to economic aspects of the value of children, while social and psychological aspects, labeled as tastes, preferences, or consumption value, are often assumed to be constant or ignored. Leibenstein (1957: p. 161) distinguished three types of value of children: work or income value, old-age security value, and consumption value; and two types of economic costs: direct and indirect. In a later version of his theory of the relationship of economic development and fertility, Leibenstein (1976) identified six types of value of children: consumption value; work-economic value; economic risk-education value; old-age security value; long-run family status maintenance; and contribution to the extended family. Mueller (1972a: p. 182) identifies three categories of indirect economic or opportunity costs: opportunities of (usually) wife foregone for labor force participation; opportunities foregone for saving and investing; and consumption expenditures foregone in order to be able to afford children.

DEVELOPED COUNTRIES

The fertility decline that has occurred in developed countries is associated generally with the processes of industrialization, urbanization, rising level of education, female labor force participation, and so forth. One common mechanism by which these processes might have generated a preference for smaller families is the consequent reduction in the value of children and increase in the costs of children to their respective parents.

One reason why fertility declined earliest and most drastically among the new professional and business classes is that the decreased value and increased costs of children impinged first on these groups. The shift of the productive function from the household to the market in the process of industrialization reduced the economic value of children. Their economic value was also reduced by the institution of child labor laws and by compulsory education, both of which gradually removed children from the labor force. Their noneconomic value also decreased because of changes in the social support for familial roles—in particular, motherhood. Some noneconomic values retained their importance, but they could be achieved without bearing a large number of children.

The direct economic costs of children in terms of education, housing, food, and many other items increased with industrialization and urbanization. There was also an enormous increase in indirect costs of both an economic and noneconomic nature because of a change in tastes or consumption standards. The increased opportunities for social mobility gave rise to a competitive system in which the consumption of goods and services (other than children) was used as a symbol of newly achieved status (Banks 1954; Blake 1972: pp. 286-87).

Among all items of costs of children, perhaps the greatest increase associated with industrialization was in the educational costs. The demand for skilled labor increased tremendously as the industrial revolution passed from its early textile phase to its later phase of the manufacture of chemicals and steel. Although the benefit of education was perceived quickly by middle-class industrialists, the working class was also not too late in recognizing the need for education in its political fight against exploitation (Simon 1960: pp. 17, 180). There was a rapid increase not only in the number of children attending school in all industrial countries, but also in the number of years of schooling and the cost of education per child. For example, by analyzing the U.S. data from 1900 to 1956, T. W. Schultz (1974: p. 25) estimated that "The percentage rise in educational costs were about three and a half times as large as in consumer income." The available data from industrial countries reviewed by Espenshade (1977) and Minge-Kalman (1977) demonstrate clearly the increase in the cost for education of children to their parents as a direct and indirect consequence of the industrialization process. In a thorough analysis of the demographic transition in Australia, Caldwell and Ruzicka (1978: pp. 88-90) attribute the increasing costs for education of children as the primary factor in the rapid decline of fertility during the last quarter of the nineteenth century.

The fertility decline in the developed countries occurred mainly through two mechanisms: delayed age at marriage and increasing use of contraceptives by married couples. While the value and costs of children to their parents are generally regarded as important factors in motivating the latter to use contraceptives, there is not enough knowledge regarding their importance in delaying the age at marriage. Although Malthus advocated postponement of marriage as a means of fertility regulation, how true is it to say that the main reason for postponement of marriage in industrial societies was to regulate fertility? If not, the costs and value of children were not an important factor. Caldwell and Ruzicka (1978: pp. 84-88) found that the postponement of marriage was responsible for three-fifths of the total fall in fertility in Australia during the second half of the nineteenth century, but the major reasons for the postponement were the great shortage of marriageable women and the high costs inherent in marriage itself. Since fertility regulation was not a reason for postponement of marriage, the latter was not a response to any change in value and costs of children.

LESS DEVELOPED COUNTRIES

The results of the VOC project referred to above lend support to the notion that changes in the economic value and costs of children, which are associated with modernization and urbanization, are a major cause of demographic transition. Some consistent differences were found among the perception of the parents of the three socioeconomic groups studied: urban middle class, urban lower class, and rural (Arnold et al. 1975: pp. 131-43). There was a contrast in attitudes between the urban middle class, which emphasized the psychological or emotional benefits of children, and the rural group, which emphasized the economic benefits. The urban lower class shared the values of the other two groups. For the rural parents, the economic benefits of children were paramount both with respect to their current work value and their security value in parents' old age. The direct economic costs of children were emphasized more by the urban lower class than by the other two groups. The opportunity costs of children were more important to the urban middle-class parents than others, which is presumably an indication of the greater range of alternative satisfactions available to that group.

The VOC results show that, for rural and lower-class urban parents, expected economic benefits were a relatively strong reason for wanting an additional child. The old-age security value of children, rather than their current work value, appears to be more important to the parents. In every country in the study, more than 70 percent of rural respondents expected to rely at least somewhat on their children for financial support in old age. Measures of expected economic benefits from children were related positively to ideal, actual, and wanted family sizes. These measures were negatively related to the knowledge, attitude, and use of contraception. Since the study was cross-sectional, the findings do not demonstrate cause-and-effect relationships.

A survey conducted in Taiwan in 1969 had as one of its major objectives an examination of the perceived economic value and costs of children and how these concepts were related to fertility (Mueller 1972a, 1972b). Two attitudinal measures were constructed: Perceived-Utility Index, designed to capture the perceived benefit of children as a source of securing in old age or in emergencies; Cost-Sensitivity Index, designed to gauge the subjective burden of direct maintenance costs. Both indexes were found to have a significant effect on preferred family size. The analysis also reveals that preferred family size is more likely to be affected by parents' sensitivity to costs than by their perceptions of the utility of children.

Economists concerned with the actual economic value of children to society as a whole rather than to parents have generally concluded that large families are economically disadvantageous in contemporary less developed countries (Coale and Hoover 1958; Enke 1966; G. B. Simmons 1971). These studies do not deal explicitly with the agricultural sector and do not analyze the actual economic value of children in particular. There are others (Boserup 1965; Clark 1967; Mamdani 1972) who claim that a large family is economically advantageous to parents in peasant societies, but their studies are also not based on systematically collected empirical data on the actual economic value of children. For example, Mamdani cites a few persons in an Indian village who want a large number of sons to enhance their economic condition, but the village studied seems to be in a transitional stage of development when demand for labor is high, and the persons cited by him do not include any who had a relatively large number of daughters.

In an evaluation of the above two contrasting views, Mueller (1977: p. 145) concludes:

> In sum, the aggregate and the life cycle model agree in showing that children have negative economic value in peasant agriculture. Up to the time when they become parents themselves, children consume more than they produce. Surveys conducted in LDCs support this conclusion. They find many rural respondents of the opinion—"Children are expensive." However, the individual point of view would seem to lead to a lower estimate of the net cost of children than the social point of view.

It is true that in her Taiwan survey Mueller found the rural respondents to be quite sensitive to the high costs of children, but can this finding be generalized for less developed countries? In the VOC study the perceptions of the rural respondents were found to be quite different. The majority of rural respondents in Taiwan, Japan,

Philippines, and Thailand did not consider as many as three children a heavy financial burden (Arnold et al. 1975: pp. 43-44). Several studies in African societies have shown that children do not seem to be considered by parents as a burden on their resources (Caldwell 1977a). The hypothetical model constructed by Lorimer (1967: p. 93) on the economics of family formation in agrarian societies with high fertility and high mortality suggests that "the economic stress [during the years after several children are present and before any have achieved significant productivity] is not very intense."

Mueller's definition of economic activities as only those "activities which contribute to GNP" seems inappropriate for the study of peasant households, which are economic units of production, and for whose existence a certain amount of household maintenance work has to be performed. One of the main difficulties faced by Mueller in making estimates of the relative total productivity by age and sex is the lack of reliable time allocation data by age and sex in peasant societies. Her estimates are partly based on labor force participation data, which are particularly unreliable for women and children, and partly on a time allocation study carried out in Egypt, which admits underreporting of work done by women and children (ILO 1969: p. 39). The results of other studies, discussed below, indicate that Mueller's conclusion about the negative economic value of children in peasant agricultural societies is not likely to be valid in general.

The labor force participation data collected in national censuses tend to underestimate the proposition of economically active children in agricultural societies (Nag 1972: pp. 62-67). However, a comparative analysis of such data (1946-58) relating to percentages of those considered economically active among boys and girls of 10 to 14 years in countries with different degrees of industrialization show that the economic contribution of children is considerably higher in agricultural societies than in industrial societies. The differences can be observed clearly in Table 7.1.

Sudan is one of the few less developed countries with good statistics on children's participation in the labor force. Table 7.2, prepared from the 1964 Census of Agriculture, shows clearly the value of children as productive workers.

In a recent systematic study of the allocation of children's time among activities in a Javanese and a Nepalese village, it was found that both boys and girls spend a considerable amount of time in work activities (Nag, White, and Pett 1978). For example, both boys and girls aged 15 to 19 in these two villages were working an average of more than 55 hours per week on different types of directly productive and household maintenance activities. The results indicate that children in large families tend to be not less but more productive than those in small families. The residential pattern of men and women

TABLE 7.1

Percentages of Economically Active among Boys and Girls Aged 10 to 14 in Countries with Different Degrees of Industrialization, 1946-58

Degree of Industrialization	Percent of Active Males Engaged in Agricultural and Related Activities	Number of Countries	Percent Active among Children Aged 10 to 14	
			Boys	Girls
Industrial	Less than 35	18	4.1	2.4
Semi-industrial	35-59	28	13.2	—
Agricultural	60 or more	18	23.9	10.2

Source: United Nations 1962: pp. 12-22.

61 years and over and the nature of their interaction with others indicate that they depend heavily on their children, particularly sons, for old-age security.

The results obtained in the study of the Javanese village indicate that even in a peasant village of high population density, households with a relatively large number of surviving children may be economically more successful than those with a relatively small number of

TABLE 7.2

Percentages of Economically Active among Boys and Girls of Various Age Groups in Sudan, 1964

Age	Boys	Girls	Total
0-5	4.7	4.9	4.8
6-11	34.2	28.6	31.6
12-14	59.3	45.3	53.2
15-19	92.7	62.5	77.1

Source: ILO 1976: Table 60.

surviving children. In contrast to the generally accepted view of widespread unemployment and underemployment in densely populated rural Java, the study has identified a large number of occupations (most of them with lower economic return than rice cultivation) in which access is virtually unlimited; hence the number of potential producers does not significantly reduce each individual's opportunity to engage in these occupations. It appears that each individual household, by increasing its size (through recruitment or, more commonly, through reproduction), obtains not less but more available opportunities for productive labor, even though the aggregate result of such behavior among the whole population may be an overall decline in job availability.

This, however, requires an explanation of why the fertility level of peasant villagers such as those in Java is not higher than it is. The explanation seems to lie in the difficulties experienced by households in their early phase of expansion if there is a large number of young children whose productive input does not yet exceed their costs. Since for many activities the economic returns of labor are quite low, it is difficult for a household at its early phase to bear the burden of a high consumer-producer ratio resulting from a rapid succession of closely spaced births. The reproductive strategy (conscious or unconscious) of the Javanese villagers, perhaps in common with couples in many other contemporary peasant societies, may be characterized as "having as many children as they can afford and find useful."

The above findings regarding the Javanese village are based mainly on a small sample of relatively poor households of the village. Another study done subsequently in a Javanese village (Maguwoharjo), with more diverse socioeconomic classes, provides useful data regarding the value of children in various social classes (Hull and Hull 1977). In Maguwoharjo, the relative economic standing of households is found to be related to differences in family structure, economic needs, and social role expectations that influence the value of children. The value of children as instruments of accumulating and exercising personal power by parents is true only for the village elites. The children of the upper socioeconomic classes attend school for longer periods of their childhood. They are also "less likely to participate in serious productive work, confining themselves instead to the sorts of tasks which they are told to do around the house while avoiding as much as possible involvement in agricultural or trading activities." The value of children as sources of security is important to all classes of parents, not so much as sources of livelihood as the sources of emotional security.

In a recent study of a relatively poor village in Bangladesh, Cain (1977) found that the children of both sexes put in quite long hours of work at young ages and that, from the perspective of parents, high fertility and a large number of surviving children are economically "rational" propositions. Children's work time is approximately one-half an adult workday by ages 7 to 9, increases to three-quarters by ages 10 to 12, and at ages 13 and above children work, on the average, as long as or longer than adults.

There are some interesting differences and similarities among the economic classes of the Bangladeshi village studies by Cain. For example, among males aged 10 and older, those from the landless households do considerably more work than those from the landed classes; but below age 10, boys from landless households work fewer hours overall than boys from landed households. This is consistent with the unequal control of productive assets, which limits early productive employment of the poor. However, despite the absolute differences between classes in terms of work time by males, hours worked by children within each class approach the adult equivalent workday at similar rates for all classes, indicating that male children are of equal work value within each class with respect to their time inputs relative to adults. Females over age 10 in economically better-off households spend as much or more time working than females in poorer households. The children of the well-to-do do not do any wage work, but otherwise both rich and poor children engage in the same type of activities. Boys in well-to-do households spend considerable time in animal care and crop production and girls in housework.

On the basis of some quite conservative assumptions regarding the economic costs and productivity per unit of time, Cain estimates that rural Bangladeshi male children appear to become net producers at least by age 12, compensate for their cumulative consumption by age 15, and compensate for their own and one sister's cumulative consumption by age 22. Whether this is a sufficient reason for parents' desire for a large number of sons depends on the degree to which the parents value the future economic welfare of their children. In this matter, parents' perceptions as well as the actual realities are unknown and indeed very difficult to assess. Under the current Bangladeshi inheritance laws, for property owners the future welfare of any one child is expected to decline, other things being equal, with the increasing number of siblings; however, Cain draws attention to the real possibility that sons born at the appropriate time may be, for many, instrumental in both preventing the loss of land and accumulating more land.

Recent field investigations directed by Caldwell in a number of African countries have demonstrated that children are of great value, both economic and otherwise, to their parents. A survey among a sample of old men and women in Ghana showed that parents believed they had received a net lifetime return on expenditure on children, especially on educated ones, although children cost more once schooling was available (Caldwell 1966). A detailed analysis of various tasks performed by the Yoruba children in Nigeria showed that "housework and carrying were the work of the young, and that, with increasing age, carrying declined among both sexes and housework among boys, while sons did more farming and daughters more marketing as adulthood approached" (Caldwell 1976a). About 70 percent of Yoruba respondents over 40 years reported to get real assistance from one or more of their adult children. Such assistance in the form of money and goods was not associated with the age or health conditions of the parent and was given by children of all ages and marital conditions.

The economic value of children to their parents as a factor in the persistence of high fertility in African countries has been emphasized by the researchers who collaborated in the Changing African Family Project (Caldwell 1977a). Quantitative analysis is rather rare. Ware (1977: pp. 498-99) cites the results of a recent nutritional survey in Zaire in which the productivity of a girl of 10 to 14 is estimated to be twice that of an adult man. It has been concluded from seven intensive field studies of African food production systems that large families are essential to meet seasonal peaks in labor demand (McLoughlin 1970: p. 312). The powerful control of elderly parents over their adult son's labor or earned wages is well-documented in African ethnographies (Ware 1977: pp. 488-96).

Relatively fewer studies have been done in Latin American countries compared to Asian and African countries. The studies done so far have been limited to the perceived value and costs of children through survey interview techniques (Hollerbach 1976). They indicate that low-income respondents see the value and costs of children much more in economic terms than in sociological and emotional terms, a characteristic more typical of middle-income respondents (A. B. Simmons 1971, 1974; J. T. Simmons 1976). A study in Mexico showed that women cited more the emotional benefits of children while men cited more the economic benefits (Elu de Lenero 1973: pp. 83-89). The degree of rural development seems to have an effect on the perceived economic value of children. For example, in Peru, where rural development is less advanced, 83 percent of respondents felt that a disadvantage of a small family was loss of help from the children, in comparison to 54 percent in Costa Rica where rural development is more advanced (Micklin and Marnane 1975).

Some less developed countries or areas within them recently have been going through a process of rapid or moderate fertility decline. The analysis of such decline is usually done in terms of aggregate behavior regarding marriage and fertility regulation, but hardly includes the changes in value and costs of children as a factor affecting them. In an analysis of the recent spectacular decline in Kerala state of India, Ratcliffe (1977) makes an attempt to include value and costs of children as an intermediate factor. He thinks that the decline was due to a decrease in the value of children as social security in the old age of parents and also in the opportunities for child labor. Relatively successful implementation of land reform legislation, legislation providing security of employment and pension to agricultural laborers (a first in India), and a few other special measures have diminished the need for parents in Kerala to rely upon their children for security (Pathak, Gunapathy, and Sarma 1977; Ratcliffe 1977: p. 127). The long tradition of free primary schooling in Kerala has been supplemented by a few policy measures, such as extension of free schooling facilities on the high school level, provision of free lunch at the primary level, and greater emphasis on primary and secondary school education compared to higher education. These measures have contributed toward highest percentage of school enrollment and lowest percentage of school dropouts in Kerala when compared to other states of India (United Nations 1975: pp. 122-25). The decrease in the opportunities for child labor may have been partially due to high enrollment of children in schools. An effective enforcement of minimum wage and child labor laws may also be partially responsible for such a decrease. Intensive investigation at the community level is needed for a better understanding of the process.

THEORIES OF FERTILITY INVOLVING VALUE AND COSTS OF CHILDREN

The theory of demographic transition refers to the decline in the economic value of children as one of the mechanisms by which modernization and industrialization bring about fertility decline (Notestein 1953: pp. 15-18). According to this theory, the fertility level is high in poor, traditional agrarian societies because of high mortality, the lack of opportunities for social mobility, and the economic contributions of children early in life. All these things are assumed to change with modernization and industrialization.

Leibenstein (1957) was one of the pioneer economic theorists who was not satisfied with the imprecise nature of the theory of demographic transition, and worked toward a more formal explanation of fertility decline in the last stage of demographic transition. He developed a theory on the presumption that couples would balance the value and costs they ascribed to an nth child in order to determine whether they wanted that child. The emphasis was on the higher birth orders. Leibenstein assumed that the consumption value of a child is constant with respect to household income, while work and old-age security values decline with income. The direct costs rise with income level, but "the disutility of bearing these costs in terms of the costs [out of a higher income] need not rise." Indirect (opportunity) costs may or may not rise with income. It is not possible to deduce from the theory that parents should necessarily desire fewer children as income grows, but it can be used to explain the reduction of high parity children as per capita income grows.

Becker's 1960 article, "An Economic Analysis of Fertility," initiated an approach that is now known as the New Home Economics. Applying the Hicksian version of microconsumption theory to household fertility behavior, he argued that children should be "viewed as a durable good, primarily a consumer's durable, which yields income, primarily psychic income, to parents." It was assumed that the household makes a calculated decision whether to have a child on the basis of its income and expected value costs (price) over time. Becker's emphasis on psychic income to parents rather than economic value of children implies that he was primarily concerned with developed countries.

Becker hypothesized that with rise of income people would want more children. The empirical evidence to the contrary was explained by him with the argument that those with higher income are likely to want "higher quality" children, which would make the cost (price) effect more important than the income effect. His hypothesis stimulated a good deal of theoretical and empirical research among a group of economists, sometimes referred to as the Chicago School. Mincer (1963) shifted the emphasis of Becker's approach from income effects to the effects on fertility of variation in the costs of children, by showing that the opportunity costs of the wife's time, as measured by the wife's educational wage rate, was negatively related to fertility. Empirical tests in developed countries tend to support Mincer's viewpoint (T. P. Schultz 1969; Nerlove and Schultz 1970; Sanderson and Willis 1971).

The approaches of the Chicago School have been questioned by a number of sociologists and economists. Sociologists generally hold the view that given the educational level, occupation, income and a few other factors related to reference or influence groups, most couples would consider that they have a very narrow range of choice regarding childbearing and the expenditures on children (Banks 1954; Blake 1968; Duesenberry and Okun 1960). Easterlin (1969) has argued that increased income raises the relative desire for material goods.

Leibenstein (1974, 1976) has refuted some of the basic premises of the New Home Economics and has modified his earlier theory of fertility decline (1957) by incorporating the element of social group influences stressed by sociologists. On the assumption that every population is divided into a hierarchy of socioeconomic statuses (SES), he has formulated the following three hypotheses: the higher the SES, the lower the nonconsumption value of a prospective birth of a given order; the higher the SES, the higher the share of average income spent on status goods, including the position of direct economic costs of children that represent status expenditures; the higher the SES, the higher the proportional indirect costs of children, especially the income and time foregone by mothers. The general implication of these hypotheses is that, for higher SES, the lower economic value and higher economic costs of a marginal birth are likely to influence their desired number of children negatively. They also imply that in the course of economic development, as more and more households are incorporated into higher SES groups, there would be an overall trend toward a reduction in fertility despite behavioral deviations of individual households, particularly in the extreme SES groups.

The economic value of children to their parents is an important element in the demand for labor theory developed by Coontz (1957), as an elaboration of Adam Smith's idea that the demand for men regulates the production of men. The demographic transition theory attributes rapid growth of population in less developed countries only to the decline of mortality. Coontz's theory states that population growth is also attributable to an increase in fertility or maintenance of high fertility induced by an increased demand for labor. A few anthropologists have provided empirical support for Coontz's theory at the household level. Polgar (1972) observes that the demand for labor in colonial countries induced the peasants to have large families. The costs of children in peasant households were offset by their work contribution during seasonal peaks of high labor demand. White (1973) argues that Dutch colonial policies in Java—demanding taxes and rent from the peasants—served to discourage them from using their traditional forms of birth control to reduce fertility when public health and other measures reduced the mortality rate. In order to meet the demands for taxes and rent, the peasants depended on the labor of their children, who probably became net producers at very young ages. The increase in the demand for children's labor is not a characteristic of colonial situations only. For example, it is not uncommon to find in contemporary less developed countries that the need to travel greater distances to gather firewood as the number of trees declines increases the demand for child labor.

In a recent article entitled, "Toward a Restatement of Demographic Transition Theory," Caldwell (1976b) introduced the concept of the intergenerational flow of wealth (money, goods, services, guarantees) to explain the transition of societies from high to low fertility. The changes in the value and costs of children to parents are implicit in the changes in the magnitude and direction of the intergenerational wealth flow. There are three main propositions in Caldwell's theory: the direction of the wealth flow is from children (younger generation) to parents (older generation) in all traditional societies with high fertility levels, and it is reversed in all developed countries with low fertility levels; a reversal of flow can occur only when there is a transformation of familial relationships from the extended to the nuclear system, both economically and emotionally; and the nucleation of the family in less developed countries is not dependent on the spread of industrialization but on the process of social westernization.

Caldwell's contention of social westernization as a major force of change in fertility decline has been challenged by two of his collaborators in the Changing African Family Project (Oppong 1977; Faulkingham 1977). It cannot be generalized for less developed countries. Caldwell himself has mentioned China as an example where the extent of the system of extended family obligations and the flow of wealth from younger to older generations has been disrupted by political means but, all the same, with the effect of reducing fertility (Caldwell 1976b: p. 357). It is not possible to associate the recent substantial decline in fertility in Bali and East Java with any process of social westernization (Hull, Hull, and Singarimbun 1977). But there is no doubt that the concept of the intergenerational flow of wealth as defined by Caldwell opens a new research strategy for exploring fertility decline in less developed countries, namely, in terms of value and costs of children to their parents.

CONCLUSION

Research regarding the value and costs of children to their parents is of very recent origin. We are still far away from a theory of the change in value and costs of children and its relationship to fertility. Concepts and measurements of various dimensions of such value and costs have to be refined. We are aware of some of the factors that affect children's value and costs in developed and less developed countries, but what is needed is a comprehensive framework including all the factors that can affect them.

It is very difficult to assess the changes in the various dimensions of the value and costs of children that were associated with the decline of fertility in the developed countries. The data necessary for the purpose are not available. The existing assessment is based generally on the literature that is not specifically focused on the value and costs of children. The available information is mostly sporadic in nature. More systematic analysis similar to that of the Australian demographic transition (Caldwell and Ruzicka 1978) would be very useful.

At present there is a wide variation of fertility in less developed countries. Empirical investigations regarding actual and perceived value and cost of children in countries with very high fertility (such as Bangladesh and Nigeria) will provide benchmark data for assessing the future trend. The less developed countries or regions in which the fertility has declined appreciably in the recent decades can be classed under two general categories: those that have been experiencing economic development somewhat similar to the Western countries (for example, Taiwan, Korea, Singapore); and those that have not done so (China, Bali, Kerala). Investigations in both these categories of countries should reveal the similarities and differences in the recent changes in the value and costs of children. Since available evidence from developed as well as less developed countries suggests that the changes in economic value and costs of children are more influential than noneconomic value and costs in fertility decline, the emphasis should be on the former.

REFERENCES

Arnold, Fred, et al. 1975. The Value of Children: A Cross-National Study. Volume 1: Introduction and Comparative Analysis. Honolulu: East-West Center.

Banks, J. A. 1954. Prosperity and Parenthood: A Study of Family Planning among the Victorian Middle Class. London: Routledge and Kegan Paul.

Becker, Gary S. 1960. "An Economic Analysis of Fertility." In Demographic and Economic Change in Developed Countries, A Conference of the Universities—National Bureau Committee for Economic Research. Princeton: Princeton University Press.

Blake, Judith. 1968. "Are Babies Consumer Durables? A Critique of the Economic Theory of Reproductive Motivation." Population Studies 22(1): 5-25.

____. 1972. "Fertility Control and the Problem of Voluntarism." In Scientists and World Affairs (Proceedings of the Twenty-Second Pugwash Conference on Science and World Affairs, September 7-12, 1972, London).

Boserup, Ester. 1965. The Conditions of Agricultural Growth. Chicago: Aldine.

Cain, Mead T. 1977. "The Economic Activities of Children in a Village in Bangladesh." Population and Development Review 3(3): 201-28.

Caldwell, John C. 1966. "The Erosion of the Family: A Study of the Family in Ghana." Population Studies 20(1): 5-26.

____. 1976a. "Fertility and the Household Economy in Nigeria." Journal of Comparative Family Studies 7(2): 193-253.

____. 1976b. "Toward a Restatement of Demographic Transition Theory." Population and Development Review 2(3 & 4): 321-66.

____, ed. 1977a. The Persistence of High Fertility: Population Prospects in the Third World. Family and Fertility Change Series, No. 1, Parts 1 and 2. Canberra: Australian National University.

____, ed. 1977b. "Introduction." In The Persistence of High Fertility: Population Prospects in the Third World. Ed. John C. Caldwell. Family and Fertility Change Series, No. 1, Part 1. Canberra: Australian National University.

____ and Lado T. Ruzicka. 1978. "The Australian Fertility Transition: An Analysis." Population and Development Review 4(1): 81-104.

Clark, Colin. 1967. Population Growth and Land Use. New York: St. Martin's Press.

Coale, Ansley J. and Edgar M. Hoover. 1958. Population Growth and Economic Development in Low-Income Countries. Princeton: Princeton University Press.

Coontz, Sidney. 1957. Population Theories and the Economic Interpretation. London: Routledge and Kegan Paul.

Demeny, Paul. 1972. "Economic Approaches to the Value of Children: An Overview." In The Satisfactions and Costs of Children: Theories, Concepts, Methods. Ed. James Fawcett. Honolulu: East-West Center.

Duesenberry, J. S. and B. Okun. 1960. "Comment." In Demographic and Economic Change in Developed Countries, A Conference of the Universities—National Bureau Committee for Economic Research. Princeton: Princeton University Press.

Easterlin, Richard A. 1969. "Towards a Socio-Economic Theory of Fertility: A Survey of Recent Research on Economic Factors in American Fertility." In Fertility and Family Planning: A World

View. Ed. S. J. Behrman, L. Corsa, and R. Freedman. Ann Arbor: University of Michigan Press.

____. 1975. "An Economic Framework for Fertility Analysis." Studies in Family Planning 6(3): 54-63.

Elu de Lenero, Ma del Carmen. 1973. Hacia Donde Va La Mujer Mexicana: Proyecciones a Partir de los Datos de una Encuesta Nacional. Mexico: Instituto de Estudios Sociales, A.C.

Enke, Stephen. 1966. "The Economic Aspects of Slowing Population Growth." Economic Journal 76: 44-56.

Espenshade, Thomas. 1977. The Value and Cost of Children. Population Bulletin 32(1) April. Washington, D.C.: Population Reference Bureau.

Faulkingham, Ralph H. 1977. "Fertility in Tudu: An Analysis of Constraints on Fertility in a Village in Niger." In The Persistence of High Fertility: Population Prospects in the Third World. Ed. John C. Caldwell. Family and Fertility Change Series, No. 1, Part 1.

Hollerbach, Paula. 1976. "Fertility Decision-Making in the Latin American Context." Paper presented at the Conference on Women and Development, cosponsored by the Federation of Organizations for Professional Women and the Center for Research on Women in Higher Education and the Professions, Wellesley College, June.

Hull, Terrence and Valerie Hull. 1977. "Indonesia." In The Persistence of High Fertility: Population Prospects in the Third World. Ed. John C. Caldwell. Family and Fertility Change Series, No. 1, Part 2. Canberra: Australian National University.

____, and Masri Singarimbun. 1977. Indonesia's Family Planning Story: Success and Challenge. Population Bulletin 32(6), November. Washington, D.C.: Population Reference Bureau.

ILO. 1969. Rural Employment Problems in the United Arab Republic. Geneva: ILO.

____. 1976. "Growth, Employment and Equity: A Comprehensive Strategy for Sudan." Vol. II. Technical Paper. Final Report of the ILO/UNDP Employment Mission. Geneva: ILO.

Leibenstein, Harvey. 1957. Economic Backwardness and Economic Growth. New York: John Wiley and Sons.

____. 1974. "An Interpretation of the Economic Theory of Fertility: Promising Path or Blind Alley?" Journal of Economic Literature 12(2): 467-79.

____. 1976. "Relation of Economic Development to Fertility." In Population Growth and Economic Development in the Third World. Volume 2. Ed. Leon Tabah. Dolhain, Belgium: Ordina Editions.

Lorimer, Frank. 1967. "The Economics of Family Formation under Different Conditions." In Proceedings of the World Population Conference, Belgrade. Volume II. New York: United Nations.

McLoughlin, P., ed. 1970. African Food Production Systems: Cases and Theory. Baltimore: Johns Hopkins University Press.

Mamdani, Mahmood. 1972. The Myth of Population Control. New York: Monthly Review Press.

Micklin, Michael and Patrick J. H. Marnane. 1975. "The Differential Evaluation of 'Large' and 'Small' Families in Rural Colombia: Implications for Family Planning." Social Biology 22: 44-59.

Mincer, Jacob. 1963. "Market Prices, Opportunity Costs, and Income Effects." In Measurement in Economics: Studies in Mathematical Economics and Econometrics. Ed. C. F. Christ et al. Stanford: Stanford University Press.

Minge-Kalman, Wanda. 1977. "Family Production and Reproduction in Industrial Society." Ph.D. diss. in Anthropology, Columbia University.

Mueller, Eva. 1972a. "Economic Cost and Value of Children: Conceptualization and Measurement." In The Satisfactions and Costs of Children: Theories, Concepts, Methods. Ed. James T. Fawcett. Honolulu: East-West Center.

____. 1972b. "Economic Motives for Family Limitation: A Study Conducted in Taiwan." Population Studies 26: 383-403.

____. 1977. "The Economic Value of Children in Peasant Agriculture." In Population and Development. Ed. Ronald G. Ridker. Baltimore and London: Johns Hopkins University Press.

Nag, Moni. 1972. "Economic Value of Children in Agricultural Societies: Evaluation of Existing Knowledge and an Anthropological Approach." In The Satisfactions and Costs of Children: Theories, Concepts, Methods. Ed. James T. Fawcett. Honolulu: East-West Center.

____, Benjamin N. F. White, and Robert Creighton Peet. 1978. "An Anthropological Approach to the Study of the Economic Value of Children in Java and Nepal." Current Anthropology 19(2): 293-306.

Nerlove, March and T. Paul Schultz. 1970. Love and Life between the Censuses: A Model of Family Decision Making in Puerto Rico, 1950-1960. RM-6322-AID. Santa Monica, Calif.: Rand Corporation.

Notestein, Frank W. 1953. "Economic Problems of Population Change." In Proceedings of the Eighth International Conference of Agricultural Economics, 1953. London: Oxford University Press.

Oppong, Christine. 1977. "The Crumbling of High Fertility Supports: Data from a Study of Ghanian Primary School Teachers." In The Persistence of High Fertility: Population Prospects in the Third World. Ed. John C. Caldwell. Family and Fertility Change Series, No. 1, Part 1. Canberra: Australian National University.

Pathak, R. P., K. R. Gunapathy, and Y. U. K. Sarma. 1977. "Shifts in Pattern of Asset-Holdings of Rural Households, 1961-62 to 1971-72." Economic and Political Weekly 12(12): 507-17.

Polgar, Steven. 1972. "Population History and Population Policies from an Anthropological Perspective." Current Anthropology 13: 203-11.

Ratcliffe, John. 1977. "Social Justice and the Demographic Transition: Lessons from India's Kerala State." International Journal of Health Services 8(1): 123-44.

Robinson, Warren C. and David E. Horlacher. 1971. "Population Growth and Economic Welfare." Reports on Population/Family Planning, No. 6. New York: Population Council.

Sanderson, Warren and Robert J. Willis. 1971. "Economic Models of Fertility: Some Examples and Implications." National Bureau of Economic Research, 51st Annual Report: New Directions in Economic Research. September.

Schultz, T. Paul. 1969. "An Economic Model of Family Planning and Fertility." Journal of Political Economy 77(2): 163-80.

Schultz, Theodore. 1960. "Capital Formation by Education." Journal of Political Economy 68: 571-83.

____. 1969. "New Evidence on Farmer Responses to Economic Opportunities from the Early Agrarian History of Western Europe." In Subsistence Agriculture and Economic Development. Ed. Clifton R. Wharton. Chicago: Aldine.

____. 1974. "Fertility and Economic Values." In Economics of the Family: Marriage, Children and Human Capital. Ed. Theodore Schultz. Chicago: University of Chicago Press.

Simmons, Alan B. 1971. "Projective Testing for Ideal Family Size." In Ideology, Faith, and Family Planning in Latin America. Ed. J. Mayone Stycos. New York: McGraw-Hill.

____. 1974. "Ambivalence toward Small Families in Rural Latin America." Social Biology 21: 127-43.

Simmons, George B. 1971. The Indian Investment in Family Planning. New York: Population Council.

Simmons, Jean Turner. 1976. "Times Have Changed: Family Formation, Contrasts and Continuities among Mothers and Daughters." Paper presented at the annual meeting of the Population Association of America.

Simon, Brian. 1960. Studies in the History of Education, 1780-1870. London: Lawrence and Wishart.

United Nations, Department of Economic and Social Affairs. 1962. Sex and Age Patterns of Participation in Economic Activities. Demographic Aspect of Manpower, Report 1. Population Studies, No. 33. New York: United Nations.

____. 1975. Poverty, Unemployment, and Development Policy: A Case Study of Selected Issues with Reference to Kerala. New York: United Nations. (ST/ESA/290).

Ware, Helen. 1977. "Economic Strategy and the Number of Children." In The Persistence of High Fertility: Population Prospects in the

Third World. Ed. John C. Caldwell. Family and Fertility Change Series, No. 1, Part 2. Canberra: Australian National University.

White, Benjamin N. F. 1976. "Production and Reproduction in a Javanese Village." Ph.D. diss. in Anthropology, Columbia University.

____. 1973. "Demand for Labor and Population Growth in Colonial Java." Human Ecology 1: 217-36.

8

INFANT MORTALITY AND BEHAVIOR IN THE REGULATION OF FAMILY SIZE

Susan C. M. Scrimshaw

INTRODUCTION

The relationships between infant mortality and fertility have been the subject of debate among population analysts for some time. The prevailing assumption is that high fertility is a necessary biological and behavioral response to high mortality. This assumption is manifested in propositions like the theory of the demographic transition, which states that mortality declines are eventually followed by fertility declines;[1] the child replacement hypothesis, which states that children who die will be replaced as quickly as possible;[2] the child survival hypothesis, which states that couples must produce enough children to ensure the survival of a given number to adulthood;[3] and the health approach, which says that couples will not reduce their fertility until they are convinced infant mortality levels have indeed dropped.[4] As will be demonstrated further on, these hypotheses do not hold consistently for many societies. It is suggested here that these inconsistencies may be partially explained by another factor in the fertility mortality equation that is seldom mentioned. This is the idea that mortality may sometimes be a response to high fertility instead of the reverse. While the biological effects of high fertility on

---

Reprinted with permission from Population and Development, September 1978. I would like to thank Judith Blake, Joe Wray, and Daniel March for careful readings of earlier versions of this chapter and for contributing many helpful suggestions. Any inadequacies in this chapter are my own responsibility.

mortality due to close spacing and related factors have been recognized, there may also be a behavioral response to fertility that results in increased mortality. In some societies, infant mortality may be a completely unconscious or even an overt way of attaining a given family size. Where this occurs, health officials may be puzzled at the underutilization of child health services, often accompanied by an underutilization of family planning services as well. Where a certain level of infant mortality is expected, or when a child is unwanted due to close spacing or high birth order, there may be underinvestment in some children that is manifested in their care, their feeding, and the response to their illnesses. This chapter focuses on this direction in the relationship between fertility and mortality.

A review of theoretical and empirical analyses of the fertility-inflating effects of infant mortality is undertaken to demonstrate that while such effects have been found in some settings, neither the magnitudes of the effects nor their directions can satisfactorily account for fertility-infant mortality relationships. Second, evidence is cited to suggest the presence of deliberate control of both fertility and mortality in primitive and preindustrial societies. Finally, evidence of avoidable infant mortality in contemporary societies is examined for possible linkages to fertility levels.

FERTILITY-INFLATING EFFECTS OF INFANT MORTALITY

The two principal hypotheses in the literature on the fertility-inflating effects of infant mortality are the child survival hypothesis and the child replacement hypothesis. The former relates to parents' perceptions of mortality conditions in their social setting; the belief that children will survive to adulthood is assumed to be a prerequisite for acceptance of fertility regulation.[5] By contrast, the latter relates to parents' responses to mortality incidence in their own family: when a child dies, it is hypothesized, a couple will attempt to replace it as quickly as possible. The two hypotheses are closely related and are frequently discussed with little distinction between them.

Although there is evidence in support of both hypotheses, it is contradictory and on balance suggests that neither hypothesis alone nor the two taken together can satisfactorily describe fertility-mortality relationships. Taylor et al. question the existence of a direct causal link between the decline of child mortality and a decline in fertility as implied by the child survival theory. They point out situations in which reduced child mortality may not always have been a precondition for lower fertility. With regard to replacement theory, they caution that it is difficult to prove that parents replace each child and argue that "No single factor can be expected to explain the totality of complex motivations which lead to or inhibit fertility reduction." They suggest that the balance of factors also varies with the society and its stage in the process of demographic transition. Interestingly, the authors suggest that the relative degree of unwantedness of children is a factor in infant mortality and fertility. The spectrum of infant mortality may range from lower parity children who die, but were wanted, to children at higher parities whose births go beyond family expectations. But they do not elaborate further on the possibility of mortality as a family size control strategy.[6]

Preston also describes the failure of fertility declines to match mortality reduction in many cases. He defines replacement rate as the average ratio of additional births to additional deaths,[7] and points out that in no population are as many as 50 percent of child deaths replaced by additional births. He suggests a variety of reasons for this. There may not be a target number of surviving children, the targets may be so high that fertility could not possibly be any higher, the targets are framed in terms of one sex only, the couple has fecundity problems, the child death results in a downward modification of ideal family size, and child death is anticipated and protected by insurance strategies of "overproduction."[8] Of these explanations, only the one that says targets may be framed for one sex allows for the possibility that every possible effort may not be made to prevent some child deaths.[9,10]

One of the most interesting analyses of child survival and child replacement is provided by Chowdhury et al. for Pakistan and Bangladesh. They assess various complications in assessing the impact of child mortality on fertility, such as the influence of fertility on mortality. As has been discussed by the literature on fertility and health, high fertility can contribute to high mortality.[11] While their data show that women with fewer living children experience shorter birth intervals, they point out the difficulty of attributing causality: Are the shorter intervals due to conscious efforts to replace dead children? Are they the result of shorter lactation amenorrhea following an infant death? Do they contribute to the deaths through shortening lactation, maternal depletion, and so forth? In an attempt to shed light on these relationships, they conducted an analysis of birth intervals according to previous child death, but excluded women who had experienced a child death just prior to the birth interval examined. They found no statistically significant difference in birth intervals between women who had experienced at least one child death and those who had not. They conclude an absence of the child replacement motivation for these two societies as represented by their samples. "In the context of these two South Asian societies with moderately high levels of fertility and mortality there is no evidence that child deaths generate a desire to replace children. . . ."[12]

All this is not to say that the child survival hypothesis and the child replacement hypothesis are not operable in some societies. The literature contains many examples of situations where mortality may have a positive effect on fertility.[13] However, there is clearly a certain amount of infant mortality in many societies that cannot be explained by assuming that it is due purely to factors beyond the control of individuals in that society. The fact that many individuals are not replacing dead children, and that fertility may drop before mortality has dropped drastically or obviously, points to a greater complexity in causes of infant mortality than is often assumed to be the case.

HISTORICAL EVIDENCE OF MORTALITY CONTROL

Many of the theories just outlined that relate infant mortality to fertility assume that individuals and societies have been powerless to prevent such mortality and must reproduce rapidly in order to compensate for it. The assumption that human populations have long found it necessary to maintain high birth rates to compensate for high mortality rates is strongly challenged by the archeological and anthropological evidence. One of the best summaries of this evidence is found in an article by Steven Polgar. Polgar questions the idea that "preindustrial societies were perilously poised on the edge of extinction."[14] The idea that mortality and fertility were extremely high is contradicted by a careful model involving women's reproductive span in preindustrial times, the mean number of births expected, maternal mortality, and infant and child mortality. Using the most conservative estimates, Polgar arrives at a figure of at least six births per woman, of which three children may survive to reproduce. "This gives a possible net reproduction rate on the order of at least 1.5, which means a 50 percent increase each generation—a far cry from constant danger of extinction." Polgar adds to this the fact that contemporary hunting and gathering populations do not live in abject misery, but are relatively well-nourished and healthy. Instead of high mortality, Polgar presents convincing evidence for deliberate human intervention producing a slow rate of population growth. The means he cites include infanticide, abortion, and warfare.[15]

Hassan differs slightly with this interpretation by Polgar, arguing that birth rates may have indeed been that high (he calculates several alternative possibilities), but that if so many offspring had survived, the world's population would have grown much faster than it did. He suggests that an additional 10 to 20 percent of the infants beyond those affected by expected rates of infant mortality would have needed to be "eliminated" (presumably through contraception, abortion, or infanticide).[16] Dumond[17] and Cowgill[18] present similar arguments about the relationships between fertility and mortality in early and contemporary human populations.[19]

Deliberate infanticide has been practiced by human societies for as long as recorded history and doubtless before.[20] In his review of societies where infanticide occurs, Carr-Saunders argues that the practice dates back to the Upper Paleolithic.[21] Mildred Dickman provides a detailed discussion of the existing literature on infanticide. She presents a number of additional examples of societies that use infanticide to control population for ecological or social reasons.[22] Marvin Harris calls infanticide "the most widely used method of population control during much of human history." He also points out that the "psychological costs of killing or starving one's infant daughters can be dulled by culturally defining them as non-persons."[23]

Studies of the Human Relations Area Files[24] reveal that infanticide has been practiced to avoid having too many children, to select the sex of children, in the case of deformities or abnormal births, and in the case of twins.[25] An analysis of these data by Granzberg focuses on twin infanticide. He found that 18 societies out of a sample of 70 did not permit one or both twins to live. Usually, the stronger (larger) twin was the one spared. What is interesting about Granzberg's analysis is that he suggests that the underlying (and usually unconscious) reasons for allowing only one twin to survive (if any) are a response to economic, technological, and ecological pressures. He hypothesizes that twin infanticide will occur in societies where twins are born to women who cannot successfully rear two children at once without neglecting other responsibilities. Also, only one twin will be permitted to live in situations where, if attempts are made to rear both, both may die. He demonstrates support for this hypothesis on the basis of the 70 societies analyzed in his study.[26]

In another example of infanticide as part of an adaptive strategy, the Tapirape of the Amazon jungle had a social structure that prevented the group from splitting into smaller groups when the community became too large for the subsistence base (slash and burn agriculture and some hunting). Instead, infanticide was mandatory to limit each family to three children, who could not all be the same sex. The explicit reason given for this was that otherwise there would not be enough game (protein) to go around and some would sicken and die.[27]

While conscious infanticide has been practiced in a few societies, historians and demographers have documented a more pervasive series of behaviors resulting in high infant mortality. Much of the evidence comes from Western Europe from the Middle Ages up through the nineteenth century. In a paper on the relationships between infant mortality and fertility, Helen Ware presents detailed evidence of extreme child neglect, particularly in Britain and France. She suggests this in part explains the relatively late decline of infant mortality in parts of Europe.[28] Shorter also documents this situation, citing "horror stories of neglect." For example, infants were left alone for long periods of time, and many succumbed to accidents and illness. Infant mortality increased during harvest times when children were left alone while their mothers worked. Shorter points out that mothers "were forced to subordinate infant welfare to other objectives."[29] Braun also records this conflict between the need to work and child care in Zurich in the eighteenth and nineteenth centuries. In his assessment, the bad socioeconomic conditions made a child a liability for too long, since a child could not start to work until age five. At that point, a child had to earn his or her rast, a certain amount of money per day or week to pay for maintenance. Children often left the family at age ten to make their own way. Under these circumstances, it is not surprising that "As hard and 'inhuman' as we may find this today, the parents were also not unhappy to have their children die."[30]

Another common form of neglect was the practice of sending infants to wet nurses in the rural areas. There, the infants were subject to poor environmental sanitation, indifference or neglect by the wet nurse, and access to milk only after the woman's own child had nursed first. These women also took in foundlings and would sometimes be nursing three or more babies at a time, with frequently fatal results.[31] The widespread abandonment of children due to desperate poverty led to large numbers of foundlings who had poor chances of survival. Shorter reports that the mortality of foundlings at Rouen at one point was 90 percent.[32]

MODERN EVIDENCE OF UNDERINVESTMENT IN SOME CHILDREN LEADING TO DIFFERENTIAL MORTALITY

The chances of survival are much better for contemporary infants than for those in past centuries, but there remain some mortality differentials that appear to go beyond what might be expected biologically. As already mentioned, current analyses of infant mortality patterns tend to assume that most of it is due to the biological effects of close spacing, poor nutrition, and infection.[33] In general, there is little attempt to sort out inevitable biological factors (such as the effects of maternal depletion from closely spaced pregnancies on birth weight and quality of lactation)[34] from behavioral factors (such as food distribution within the family, the timing of medical attention for illnesses, and many others).[35] Other behavioral factors, such as those induced by severe economic deprivation, may affect family members with more equal inevitability. In fact, one of the difficulties of sorting out behavioral and biological factors affecting infant mortality is that the two act synergistically. For example, poor diet during an episode of intestinal infection leaves a child more susceptible to the next infection.[36]

Behavioral factors are manifested in practices leading to what might be termed avoidable infant mortality. Avoidable infant mortality is precipitated by behaviors ranging from benign neglect to such customs as improper treatment of the umbilical cord without awareness of the potential danger. The evidence that such practices may be a mechanism for determining family size and structure rests on variations in infant mortality by sex, birth order, spacing, and total family size. Unfortunately, the quality of available data is often poor for this type of analysis. One of the best examples comes from societies that strongly favor children of one sex over the opposite sex.[37] In such societies, differential care leading to differential male-female mortality rates is more common. India provides the example not only in unexpectedly high female infant mortality rates, but also in studies of opposite sex fraternal twins, where the male twin frequently is better nourished and has a higher survival rate. One of the first studies to point out this differential infant mortality in India was the Khanna study, which found that boys receive more food and medical care than girls,[38] and that in the first five years of life the female death rate was 74 per thousand per year, while the male death rate over the same period was 50 per thousand per year.[39] Finis Welch reports a similar finding in Bangladesh, where a girl is more likely to survive if she is born into a family with more boys than girls.[40]

In a study in highland Ecuador, the sex ratios for the first child were unrealistically high in favor of males (68 males to 32 females). Normal ratios at birth are about 51 males to 49 females. The statistical probability of the observed ratio occurring by chance is less than .01, and subsequent births had ratios within the normal range of probability. Thus it seems likely that women were collapsing their first and second pregnancies in their reporting, and that the child born first in these cases was a girl. While people in the village would not overtly discuss this, the results of several in-depth anthropological studies in the same region indicated that female neglect or even infanticide occurred occasionally, and that it was considered very important that the first child be male.[41] Thus it is possible that sex preferences and the sex composition of the "ideal" family can significantly affect mortality within the family.

Differential male and female infant mortality in effect permits sex selection, in that children of the desired sex may receive more attention, food, and other resources that improve their chances for survival. Khan and Sirageldin mention this in an article on son preference in Pakistan, where they note that the negative inducement of the number of living sons on wanting additional children is three times that due to the number of living daughters.[42] The factor of sex selection through differential care, no matter how unconscious, offers the chance to influence the sex composition of the couple's living children as no other currently practiced method can.

Besides children of unwanted sex, other vulnerable children include high birth order children. In this case, however, it becomes more difficult than in the case of sex bias to sort out behavioral and biological factors, since high birth order children are born to older women who also may have been physically depleted by earlier pregnancies. To make matters more difficult, there are few studies that have produced the kind of multivariate analysis needed to ask the correct questions about possible areas of causality in the relationship between high birth order and infant mortality. For example, in a study of a number of Latin American countries, Puffer and Serrano report that infant deaths increase with ascending birth order. In Recife, Brazil, 13.7 percent and 13.9 percent of first and second births respectively died in infancy, with 50.7 percent of fifth or later births dying before age two. In Monterrey, Mexico, the figures are 15 percent and 14.2 percent for first and second births, and 48.6 percent for fifth or higher births.[43] In both Chile and Monterrey, the infant mortality rates were 40 per 1,000 for first births and 90 per 1,000 for fifth or higher birth orders.[44] Unfortunately, Puffer and Serrano's discussion does not relate these data to the total number of live births in the same cities. Also, they tend to discuss their data one variable at a time, so it is impossible, for example, to control for the age of the mother and the interval since the previous birth in looking at higher infant mortality for higher order births.

In addition to children of high birth order, children from large families experience a greater risk of mortality. Wyon and Gordon found that the risk of infection increased with increased family size in the Punjabi population they studied.[45] Similarly, Wray and Aguirre report for Candelaria, Colombia, that the larger the family, the more protein-calorie malnutrition could be found in the children of that family.[46] They also found that malnutrition was worse if the birth interval was less than three years. They noted that abortion had the effect of decreasing malnutrition, and suggested that "If mothers in Candelaria were able to limit their family size, and they have clearly expressed their desire to do so, the evidence suggests unequivocally that the nutritional situation of pre-school children there would improve." While it is again difficult to distinguish biological from behavioral factors, Wray and Aguirre note that some children were relatively neglected.[47]

Obviously, at higher birth orders, higher mortality risk and the higher risk in large families are related. Large families will have more children of high birth order, and children of high birth order will tend to come from large families, although if many previous children have died, the actual number of living children may be smaller.

Another susceptible group of children appears to be members of a closely spaced pair. Kwashiorkor, the synergistic effect of malnutrition and infection, has long been described as the disease that affects the elder child of a pair when it is replaced at the breast by a younger sibling.[48] The Khanna study reported that birth interval is the greatest influence on mortality in the first year of life. In that population both infant mortality and second year mortality go down as the birth interval lengthens.[49] Wray and Aguirre are also among those reporting the effect of birth interval on mortality, although they look only at prospective intervals.[50]

The analysis of urban Ecuadorian data showed that in that population it was the second child of a closely spaced pair who was more likely to die. The analysis of the fertility histories of roughly 2,000 women who had had two or more pregnancies included controlling for many obvious factors such as the economic status of the family, the mother's age at the child's birth, birth order, and sex. Nonetheless, postneonatal and infant mortality was strongly influenced by the interval between the conception of one child and the birth of another. While the survival chances of the first child of a pair was somewhat influenced by interval, the second child was particularly susceptible if the interval was short and the first child was alive at the time of conception of the second child. That is, a family with a closely spaced pair of children appeared to invest more (financially and emotionally) in the care of the first child of the pair, who had already survived that critical first year of life. Neonatal mortality rates and stillbirth rates were also affected, but those rates would tend to reflect the effects of multiple, closely spaced pregnancies on the mother and her offspring even more than mortality after the neonatal period. A portion of these findings are summarized in Table 8.1.

The possibility that maternal depletion is influencing the mortality significantly (a factor that is still poorly understood and under much current investigation) is lessened by the fact that the second child of a closely spaced pair is not at risk of higher mortality if the first child of the pair was not alive when the second child was conceived. In other words, some factors beyond the biological are operating to influence mortality rates when a family has to cope with two closely spaced children.

A further clue to the behavioral component in the relationship between fertility and infant mortality is that in this population, the

TABLE 8.1

Child Mortality Rates by Survivor-Birth Interval Length, 1962-71[51]

	Interval in Months from Birth to Conception		
	0-2	12-14	24-26
Stillbirth rate	11.2	14.3	0.0
Neonatal mortality rate	45.2	19.7	33.1
Infant mortality rate	127.0	35.3	42.4
Post neonatal mortality rate	82.6	29.0	8.4
Death rate, Age 1	61.8	13.4	15.2
Number	179	385	171

proportion of live births decreased from 89 percent in 1942-46 to 82 percent in 1967-71, as infant mortality decreased, presumably due to improvements in health care. The decrease in live births was entirely attributable to an increase in admitted induced abortions and in spontaneous abortions, some of which were clearly not spontaneous. Also, the proportion of spontaneous abortions increases more with birth order than it does with age, and the proportion of admitted induced abortions goes steadily up from .2 percent with the first pregnancy to 6.4 percent with the eleventh or higher pregnancy.[52] While it is impossible to establish a direct cause and effect relationship between these occurrences, it is clear that not all pregnancies, and therefore not all children, were wanted. Data on family size preferences and contraceptive practice for this population are consistent with the above assumption.[53]

Other researchers have also questioned the biological inevitability of some proportion of infant deaths. Omran says, "it is obvious that perinatal mortality is caused at least in part by poor home environment or maternal care."[54] He adds that adequate maternal care is related to the number of children and their spacing. Newcombe also suggests that the increased risk with birth order to infants beyond the neonatal period and to children reflects environmental factors.[55] Taylor et al. mention the relative degree of unwantedness of children as a factor affecting child survival.[56] There is no question that in many societies children are highly valued. It is simply that sometimes, some children are more valued more than others.

It is clear from the above discussion that there are differential mortality rates for infants and children that are not completely explained by biological or environmental factors beyond their parents' control. It is suggested here that at least some of this mortality occurs when an infant is relatively unwanted due to high birth order, close spacing, number of living children already in the family, the sex composition of the family in relation to that child's sex and sex preferences for children, and occasionally, when the infant is "difficult," physically unattractive or otherwise less acceptable. However, it is not suggested that this differential mortality is often due to conscious behavior on the part of the parents. Most of the time, underinvestment or benign neglect is part of an unconscious set of behaviors that nonetheless reflects a family's or a culture's population policy. We shall turn now to some of the forms this underinvestment may take.

BEHAVIOR POSSIBLY AFFECTING MORBIDITY AND MORTALITY IN INFANTS

While aggressive neglect and child abuse occur in many societies, and seem to be the focus of a great deal of attention in the United States in particular, this chapter concentrates on underinvestment in some children, particularly the ones described as vulnerable in the preceding section. Their neglect may be facilitated by cultural norms about child care that reflect subtle responses to population pressures, or by familial desperation with existing conditions. Often, the loss of children is a common enough occurrence that every woman grows up with the certain knowledge that she will lose at least one child. Of necessity, there is an acceptance of high rates of infant mortality and an accompanying lack of a felt need to take desperate measures to save a child's life.[57]

In the affluent, developed countries, with the important exception of the apparently growing problems of child abuse and neglect, the loss of a child is a major tragedy, a rare event that happens only to an unlucky few. In contrast, the mechanism for accepting a child's death may be more salient in a developing area, such as many parts of Latin America. Among the poor in Latin America, "The death of an old person or of an infant causes little disturbance."[58] It is not that families do not grieve at these deaths, they do. But death, especially the death of a child, has a different meaning.

> They [the country people of Ecuador] hold the unshakable belief that when a baby dies, it dies in a state of grace and flies directly to heaven. Within this framework then, death is something to celebrate; he has been released without sin from a life of poverty and suffering to become

> one of God's little angels. . . . I would talk to farmers, who, when I asked them how many children they had, would say sadly and as though cursed "Oh, ten, I think. I've had bad luck; not even one angelito."[59]

The angelito theme is a familiar one to anyone who has worked in Latin America. In Lewis's description of infant and child deaths, he also mentions the Catholic belief that a child's soul goes directly to heaven. Thus in Tepotzlan, a small child's funeral is supposed to be an occasion for rejoicing. Gay music is played for the angelito. Little boys are dressed like St. Joseph, little girls like the Virgin of Guadalupe, with a crown of paper flowers.[60] While I found similar attitudes toward angelitos in Bolivia (1965), Ecuador (1971), and Colombia (1974), the child's age at death is also significant. The younger a child is, the less impact its death has. After about age three, a child has a firmer place in the family and its loss is more keenly felt. As Whitehead reports for Ecuador, Peru, and Bolivia, children often are not really considered people until they have survived the first year or so of life, a factor that partially accounts for underreporting on censuses.[61]

In Latin America, then, high morbidity and mortality are "considered a normal pattern by the people themselves."[62] Thus apathetic response to programs attempting to improve the health of children may have a valid underlying (but unconscious) purpose. Through the management of infant and child illness and nutrition, morbidity and mortality are strongly affected. Clusters of behavior affecting morbidity and mortality in Latin America have become so firmly established that they are reflected even in cultural norms about child behavior. A good child is a quiet child. "An inactive child neither demands nor receives as much attention as an active, inquisitive child."[63] Since apathy and listlessness are often symptoms of malnutrition and infection,[64] these cultural norms about children's activity level work against the early detection of such problems. In the investigation of use patterns of a health program in Colombia, it was found that parental definitions of illness in children differed from those of the health program to the extent that many children were not brought to the clinic at all or were brought much later in the course of an illness than the health care providers would have wished.[65] This is an example of overall cultural norms that impact on infant mortality, as discussed earlier in this chapter. However, the cultural norms also facilitate variable treatment of children within individual families.

There are many specific behaviors that lead to increased morbidity and mortality in infants. One cluster of behaviors revolves around infant feeding. While children can clearly survive on artificial formulas, there is increasing evidence that breast feeding provides the best diet for at least the first four to six months, and also provides protection against infection.[66] Both attributes of breast feeding become particularly important in environments where the probability of infection is high, and where the available food for foods fed to infants are low in nutritive value. Knodel and Kintner, for example, discuss the lower mortality risk of breast-fed infants, and describe a continuum in the mortality that is highest when children are not breast fed at all, lower with partial breast feeding, and lowest with complete breast feeding.[67] For Derby, England, at the turn of the century, Knodel and Van de Walle found that 7 percent of children fed only breast milk died before age one, as compared with 19.8 of never breast-fed children and 9.9 percent of children who had mixed feeding.[68] Whether a child is breast fed at all and the frequency and duration of feedings may depend on the mother's attachment to the child and on her involvement with the child.[69] Thus the desirability of the child may affect breast feeding.

Other feeding patterns may be affected as well. In discussing an Australian aboriginal group, Yengoyam writes that there is no more open infanticide, "but differential care [physical and affective] extended to infants could be interpreted as a means of infanticide." He adds that food and maternal care are withheld, followed by a decrease in the child's weight, and frequently by death from malnutrition. In general, the distribution of food in a household may favor some individuals over others. When scarce resources must be distributed among several children, the more wanted children may receive more and better food than the others. In an article on interrelationships between mortality and fertility, Schultz states:

> It is not unlikely that the desire for offspring continued to have a bearing on its later survival. Infanticide is no longer common throughout the world, but the allocation of limited family resources among members and the mother's time to care for them cannot help but reflect family priorities and influence chances for survival in a statistical sense.[70]

In Candelaria, Wray and Aguirre report more malnutrition if the birth interval between the children studied was less than three years.[71] Infant-feeding patterns may also be an unconscious societal population control measure through many practices that can be negative for some individuals. For example, many foods considered unsuitable for infants in some cultures are the foods richest in protein. Gokulathathn and Verghese calls this "sociocultural malnutrition."[72]

Another cultural mechanism that leads to increased mortality is the diet of ill infants. Often, cultural norms prescribe the withdrawal of nearly all foods when illness occurs. For example, in an urban Ecuadorian community measles, diarrhea, and some other infections were treated by feeding the child only a thin lentil broth.[73] In the case of diet during illness in infants, less wanted children may be treated differently within a given family.

Other behaviors related to illness in infants may be operating both at the societal and familial levels. For example, beliefs at the societal level, such as the idea that ascaris is normal unless a child really has difficulty, such as vomiting worms, will tend to affect childhood morbidity in general. However, at the familial level there may be a great deal of variation in the attention different children receive during illness, and particularly in the use of anything costly or time-consuming, such as health services. The less valued child is more likely to be taken to a health practitioner later in the course of the illness (if at all), is less likely to receive consistent care, and may not receive prescribed medications or food.[74] This is the child who is rehydrated again and again while health officials wonder why the mother "can't follow orders" as to its care. Wray and Aguirre document this problem in Candelaria, calling it maternal competence.[75] The fact that in the population they studied induced abortions are associated with apparent decreases in malnutrition in living children is additional evidence that the factor they call maternal competence is not necessarily a fixed set of behavior primarily related to a woman's intelligence, knowledge, or organizational ability, but may reflect the woman's involvement in a particular child. As has been mentioned earlier, in an Ecuadorian population the rate of induced abortions went up as the infant mortality rate went down. These two instances of relationships between mortality and nutritional status and induced abortions are a further indication of the influence of parental investment in children (which affects morbidity and mortality) as dependent on how badly that child is wanted. While there are variations in maternal management from one woman to another in a given society,[76] some of the variation in a single woman's behavior may reflect differential investment in children. The lack of continuity in health providers may obscure the differences in the way one woman treats different children, and she may be labeled inefficient in general because of her response to problems in one specific child.

Preventive health measures can be discussed in similar terms. At the societal level, there may be many negative measures, such as improper treatment of the umbilical cord. At the individual familial level, some children may be protected more than others, or are more involved in preventive health care programs. In Upper Volta, Retel-Laurentin and Benoit report that child care improves when children are scarce.[77] Omran also discusses variations in care and attention as related to infant mortality patterns.[78]

A final, overall way that parents can affect morbidity and mortality patterns in children is through what might be called nurturing. This involves a sum of the behaviors discussed above, but it also encompasses affection and attention, which appear to be important to normal child development. Its absence has been implicated in the problem of "failure to thrive" children in the U.S. population.[79] An example of this can be found in the case of a Guatemalan woman who had tried unsuccessfully to abort one of her many pregnancies. When a normal, healthy infant was born, she looked at it and said: "That's a sickly baby. It will never live." It didn't.[80]

In an article on subsistence and ecology, James Neel says:

> The relationship between rapid reproduction and high infant mortality has been apparent for centuries. During this time, we have condoned in ourselves a reproductive pattern which (through weanling diarrhea and malnutrition) has contributed, for large numbers of children, to a much more agonizing natural demise than that resulting from infanticide. Moreover, this reproductive pattern has condemned many of the surviving children to a marginal diet inconsistent with full physical and mental development.[81]

While in some societies this situation may be easier to accept than deliberate regulation of fertility, in most cases the relationship between infant mortality and fertility argues for a balance between the regulation of both variables, as discussed by Preston in a recent article.[82] In fact, this balance is often achieved one way or another, as has been discussed throughout this chapter.

CONCLUSIONS AND POLICY IMPLICATIONS

This chapter has argued that population scientists have on the whole overlooked one of the many factors contributing to behavior related to infant mortality: parents will not always go to extremes to save the life of a child, and may in fact invest more time, attention, and resources in some children than in others. Their actions directly influence ultimate family size as some children have a lower probability of surviving when they are relatively unwanted, even subconsciously. As Schultz states, "this evidence should lead one to be cautious in interpreting even child mortality as an exogenous event that parents are unlikely to influence."[83]

The consideration of this factor should help to explain the inability of the child survival hypothesis and the child replacement hypothesis to account for actual fertility behavior in many situations. It may also contribute to the understanding of rapid fertility declines before drops in infant mortality due to health programs have become clearly obvious to a community. Finally, it may help to account for the underutilization of health programs in some cases. In essence, the traditional assumption that high mortality leads to ("causes") high fertility must be questioned. Often, the reverse may be true. High fertility may be accompanied by the acceptance or even the unconscious encouragement of high mortality. The relationship between infant mortality and fertility can thus be described as circular rather than linear.

Clearly, the distinction between biological and behavioral influences on infant mortality needs to be elaborated by careful investigation. Omran mentions the scarcity of studies specifically designed to investigate either direct or indirect effects of child survival on fertility.[84] Similarly, Schultz suggests that research is needed to determine under what conditions a reduction in child mortality induces more than an offsetting decline in fertility, and points to the need to sort out biological and behavioral factors. He states, "No one, to my knowledge, has yet estimated . . . the separate fertility effects of a child's death attributable to behavioral and biological factors while holding constant the more important socioeconomic determinants of reproductive demands."[85] In sum, questions such as the impact of maternal age, weight, health status, and nutritional status on perinatal, infant, and child mortality must be addressed. Differential mortality needs to be assessed while controlling for birth order, number of living children in the family, lactation, and other related variables. On the behavioral side, particular attention needs to be paid to the impact on children of the family's economic situation and the inevitable choices forced by that situation in terms of factors such as food, medical care, and lack of attention (or poorer care) while the mother works. Currently, plans are under way to carry out an investigation that would attempt to answer some of these questions for a Guatemalan population.[86]

Despite the need for additional investigation on the dynamics of the interaction between behavioral and biological factors in influencing infant mortality and fertility, the observations of mortality and fertility interrelationships reported here indicate some policy guidelines. First, health workers may be able to identify more easily children who are potentially more vulnerable to morbidity and mortality and thus may be able to focus more attention on these children. Depending on the culture, these children might be the wrong sex in a family that already had children of that sex, closely spaced, high birth order, come from a very large family, or be difficult or unattractive. In short, it can be useful to look at the family structure and the child's place within it for explanations of a high frequency of medical or nutritional problems, and for the answers to some maternal incompetence or noncompliance. This may help us to understand resistance to health services and to provide more responsive programs. It may also be possible (but not simple) to make connections for program users between underinvestment in some children and the fact that maybe a woman or couple do not want more children or want to space them farther apart. Thus the second implication of the factors discussed here is that the mothers and fathers of these vulnerable children may be prime candidates for effective, acceptable contraceptives. High mortality, when looked at in the context of family formation patterns, may point to readiness for family planning rather than the opposite.

NOTES

1. Kingsley Davis, "The World Demographic Transition," Annals of the American Academy of Political and Social Science 237 (1945): 1-11.

2. Samuel H. Preston, ed., The Effects of Infant and Child Mortality on Fertility (New York: Academic Press, 1978), p. 6.

3. Carl E. Taylor, Jeanne S. Newman, and Narindar U. Kelley, "The Child Survival Hypothesis," Population Studies 30 (1976).

4. Alan Berg, "Toward Survival: Nutrition and the Population Dilemma," Interplay (February 1970): 24-27; Abdel R. Omran, "The Health Theme in Family Planning," Carolina Population Center Monograph 16 (Chapel Hill: University of North Carolina Press, 1971). The discussion of health also includes the idea that the limitation of family size and the greater spacing of births will contribute to improvements in the nutritional and health status of mothers and children. Joe D. Wray, "Population Pressure on Families: Family Size and Child Spacing," Reports on Population/Family Planning, no. 9, 1970.

5. Berg, "Toward Survival"; Omran, "Health Theme." The child survival hypothesis can be summarized in this statement by Omran: "it is unlikely that parents will consider limiting the size of their families if they have become accustomed to high childhood mortality and expect some of their children to die no matter what they do." Often it is not merely the survival of children to adulthood, but the survival of sons that is important. According to an analysis by Heer and Smith, in a society where sons are important, couples will have children until they are 95 percent sure that a son will survive until

the father is 65. David Heer and D. O. Smith, "Mortality Level, Desired Family Size, and Population Increase," Demography 5 (1968): 104-21.

6. Taylor et al., "Child Survival Hypothesis." Alfred Aguirre goes a little further in relating infant mortality to family size. He reports incidents of infants and young children being "allowed to die" when attacked by disease, calling this "masked infanticide." "Colombia: The Family in Candelaria," Studies in Family Planning no. 11 (New York: Population Council, 1966).

7. Preston, Effects of Infant and Child Mortality.

8. Ibid., pp. 12-14.

9. Ibid. The remaining articles in the book provide useful insights on the effects of child mortality on fertility where this can be inferred, although in some instances the case cannot be made. For example, in the chapter by Rutstein and Medica on Latin America, the authors find no increase in births with child deaths in several countries where data are available. In fact, in Colombia and Mexico parity levels may decrease with increased child deaths. They hypothesize that this is due to health problems in the mother related to birth, or to discouragement after a child has died, but do not consider the idea that the child who died may have been a burden.

10. Other studies provide examples of the failure to replace dead children. In Guatemala, Teller and associates conclude that "Women do not seem to be overcompensating for an intra-interval death by hastening the coming of the next conception." C. Teller et al., "Effect of Declines in Infant and Child Mortality on Fertility and Birth-spacing: Preliminary Results from Retrospective Data in Four Villages," in Seminar of Infant Mortality in Relation to the Level of Fertility, Committee for International Coordination of National Research Demography (CICRED) (Bangkok: May 1975), pp. 338-43. Even in a low mortality population such as Canada, Newcombe and Rhynas failed to find evidence for compensation in many cases of infant death. There was some overcompensation in the first year following stillbirths, no difference the second year, and fewer children than expected the third and fourth years. It was a case of either early replacement or none at all. H. B. Newcombe and P. O. W. Rhynas, "Child Spacing following Stillbirth and Infant Death," Eugenics Quarterly 9 (1962): 29.

11. D. Chowdhury et al., "The Effect of Child Mortality Experience on Subsequent Fertility: Pakistan and Bangladesh," Population Studies 30 (1976): 253; Omran, "Health Theme," and Berg, "Toward Survival."

12. Chowdhury et al., "Effect of Child Mortality Experience," pp. 255-58.

13. Donald W. Snyder, "Economic Determinants of Family Size in West Africa," Demography 11 (1974): 613-27; Julie Da Vanzo, "The Determinants of Family Formation in Chile, 1960" (Santa Monica: Rand Corporation, R-830-AID, 1972); Omran, "Health Theme," p. 115; M. Nerlove and P. T. Schultz, Love and Life between the Censuses: A Model of Family Planning Decision-Making in Puerto Rico (Santa Monica: Rand Corporation, 1970); and Heer and Smith, "Mortality Level."

14. Steven Polgar, "Population History and Population Policies from an Anthropological Perspective," Current Anthropology 13 (Chicago: University of Chicago Press, 1972): 203-11.

15. Ibid.

16. Fekri A. Hassan, "On the Mechanisms of Population Growth in the Neolithic," Current Anthropology 14 (1973): 535-42.

17. Don E. Dumond, "The Limitation of Human Population: A Natural History," Science 187 (1975): 713-21.

18. George Cowgill, "On Causes and Consequences of Ancient and Modern Population Changes," American Anthropologist 77 (1975): 505-25.

19. The evidence discussed by these scientists suggests that population has long been regulated in accordance with available resources and norms concerning the quality of life. This view has been widely discussed in the field of ecological anthropology. Anthropological ecologists theorize that "beliefs and behaviors that affect fertility, death and disease rates are major factors in the adaptations of human societies. Over time, every society develops behavioral strategies which maximize gains and minimize losses in its population size relative to particular environments." Good mini-max strategies improve these relations in terms of the number of individuals particular environments can support, and are therefore adaptive in strictly biological terms. For any given biocultural adaptation there is a maximum population level beyond which energy extraction may create irreversible environmental changes inimical to the survival of the group. This level has been called carrying capacity. When a population approaches carrying capacity, Malthusian checks on size may begin to operate and the group may or may not become stabilized and avert environmental degradation by the evolution of more successful strategies. Alexander Alland, Adaptation in Cultural Evolution: An Approach to Medical Anthropology (New York: Columbia University Press, 1970), p. 203. These theories help explain why behavior that is detrimental to individual survival (such as infanticide) may be practiced, since the possibility of survival or the quality of life of the entire group may be enhanced if fewer individuals are present.

According to Josué de Castro in Geography of Hunger (London: Victor Gollancz, Ltd., 1952), pp. 162-63, the Japanese population was kept "practically static" for four centuries from the mid-fifteenth to the mid-nineteenth centuries by means of abortion, female infanticide, the abandonment of the aged, and a ubiquitous death penalty.

20. Clellan Stearns Ford, "A Comparative Study of Human Reproduction," Anthropology, no. 32 (Yale University Publications, 1964, reprinted by Human Relations Area Files Press): 74; de Castro, "Geography of Hunger."

21. A. M. Carr-Saunders, The Population Problem: A Study in Human Evolution (Oxford: Clarendon, 1922), p. 74.

22. Mildred Dickman, "Demographic Consequences of Infanticide in Man," Annual Review of Ecology and Systematics 6 (1975): 100-37.

23. Marvin Harris, Cannibals and Kings: The Origins of Cultures (New York: Random House, 1977), p. 5.

24. The Human Relations Area Files are a pool of data collected by anthropologists in this century, and so represent contemporary or recent societies.

25. Ford, "A Comparative Study of Human Reproduction," p. 73; Gary Granzberg, "Twin Infanticide: A Cross-Cultural Test of a Materialistic Explanation," Ethos 1 (1973): 405.

26. Granzberg, "Twin Infanticide," pp. 406, 411.

27. Charles Wagley, "Cultural Influences on Population: A Comparison of Two Tupi Tribes," in Environment and Cultural Behavior, ed. Andrew P. Vayda (New York: Natural History Press, 1969), pp. 268-80.

28. Helen Ware, "The Relationship between Infant Mortality and Fertility: Replacement and Insurance Effects," IUSSP Proceedings of the International Population Conference 1 (Liege, Belgium: 1977).

29. Edward Shorter, The Making of the Modern Family (New York: Basic Books, 1977), pp. 168-70. This conflict between women's work and child welfare needs to be more closely investigated in modern times. In one Guatemalan case, a young woman left her only child to be nursed by her mother (the child's grandmother), who was also nursing a slightly older infant of her own. Both infants were exhibiting clinical signs of malnutrition after several months of this. Mary Scrimshaw, personal communication, 1978.

30. R. Braun, "Protoindustrialization and Demographic Changes in the Canton of Zurich," in Historical Studies of Changing Fertility, ed. Charles Tilly (Princeton: Princeton University Press, 1978), pp. 318-21. Also see Aguirre, "Colombia: The Family in Candelaria," p. 2.

31. Shorter, Making of the Modern Family, pp. 174-81; Philippe Ariès, Centuries of Childhood (New York: Vintage Books, 1962), p. 374; Joe Wray, "Maternal Nutrition, Breast-Feeding and Infant

Survival," in *Nutrition and Human Reproduction*, ed. Henry Mosley (New York: Plenum Press, 1978), p. 206.

32. Shorter, *Making of the Modern Family*, p. 181.

33. For example, Preston, *The Effects of Infant and Child Mortality on Fertility*; Berg, "Toward Survival"; Omran, "Health Theme."

34. Wray, "Maternal Nutrition."

35. Chowdhury et al., "Effect of Child Mortality Experience"; Ware, "The Relationship between Infant Mortality and Fertility."

36. Nevin S. Scrimshaw, "Synergism of Malnutrition and Infection: Evidence from Field Studies in Guatemala," *Journal of the American Medical Association* 212 (1970): 1,685-91.

37. Ford, "A Comparative Study of Human Reproduction," p. 73; Nancy E. Williamson, "Boys or Girls? Parents' Preferences and Sex Control," *Population Bulletin* 33 (Washington, D.C.: Population Reference Bureau, 1978).

38. Sohan Singh, John E. Gordon, and John B. Wyon, "Causes of Death at Different Ages by Sex, and by Season in a Rural Population of the Punjab, 1957-1959: A Field Study," *Indian Journal of Medical Research* 53 (1965): 906-17.

39. J. Wyon and J. Gordon, *The Khanna Study: Population Problems in Rural Punjab* (Cambridge, Mass.: Harvard University Press, 1971), pp. 193-95.

40. Finis Welch, "Sex of Children: Prior Uncertainty and Subsequent Fertility Behavior" (Santa Monica: Rand Corporation, R-1510-RF, 1974).

41. Susan C. M. Scrimshaw, "Culture, Environment and Family Size: A Study of Urban In-migrants in Guayaquil, Ecuador" (New York: Columbia University, International Institute for the Study of Human Reproduction, 1974, submitted in partial fulfillment of the requirements for the degree of Doctor of Philosophy in the Faculty of Political Science).

42. A. Khan and I. Sirageldin, "Son Preference and the Demand for Additional Children in Pakistan," *Demography* 14 (1977): 493.

43. Wray, "Maternal Nutrition"; Omran, "Health Theme." In an analysis of data from British Columbia, Howard Newcombe finds that the increased risk of infant death at higher birth order is independent of the mother's age at birth. "Environmental versus Genetic Interpretations of Birth Order Effects," *Eugenics Quarterly* 12 (1965): 91-101.

44. R. R. Puffer and C. V. Serrano, "Results of the Inter-American Investigations of Mortality Relating to Reproduction," in *Epdemiology of Abortion and Practices of Fertility Regulation in Latin America: Selected Reports*, no. 306 (Washington, D.C.: PAHO

Scientific Publication, 1975); and R. R. Puffer and C. V. Serrano, "Patterns of Mortality in Childhood," Scientific Publication no. 262 (Washington, D.C.: WHO/Pan American Health Organization, 1973): 248-49. Omran discusses Puffer and Serrano's data for Latin America along with data from other continents that also indicate that infant death rates rise with parity (cited in "Health Theme," pp. 18-34).

45. Wyon and Gordon, The Khanna Study.

46. Joe D. Wray and Alfredo Aguirre, "Protein Calorie Malnutrition in Candelaria, Colombia—I. Prevalence, Social and Demographic Causal Factors," Journal of Tropical Pediatrics 15 (1969): 91.

47. Ibid., pp. 93-97. In discussing differences between the mothers of normal and of malnourished children in India, Graves noted that mothers of malnourished children felt significantly ($p < .01$) more negative about the pregnancy that produced the malnourished child. The index and control children were of similar age, but the index children were of higher parity than the control children. P. L. Graves, "Nutrition, Infant Behavior and Maternal Characteristics: A Pilot Study in West Bengal, India," American Journal of Clinical Nutrition 30 (1972): 242.

48. Cicely D. Williams and Derrick B. Jelliffe, Mother and Child Health: Delivering the Services (London: Oxford University Press, 1972).

49. Wyom and Gordon, The Khanna Study, p. 25.

50. Wray and Aguirre, "Protein Calorie Malnutrition."

51. David Wolfers and Susan Scrimshaw, "Child Survival and Intervals between Pregnancies in Guayaquil, Ecuador," Population Studies 29 (1975): 490.

52. Ibid., pp. 486-87.

53. Susan C. M. Scrimshaw, "Families to the City: A Study of Changing Values, Fertility, and Socioeconomic Status among Urban In-Migrants," in Population and Social Organization, ed. Moni Nag (Paris: Mouton, 1975), pp. 320-24. The classic example of this has been Chile, where in 1965 Armijo and Monreal reported that 41 percent of nearly 4,000 women had spontaneous or induced aborations (23 percent had admitted induced abortions). The women aged 20-34 had 80 percent of the abortions. "The Problems of Induced Abortion in Chile," Milbank Memorial Fund Quarterly 43 (1965): 263-80. Hall also describes high rates of induced abortions for women over 30 in their fourth or subsequent pregnancy. "Family Planning in Lima, Peru," Milbank Memorial Fund Quarterly 43 (1965): 100-16.

54. Omran, "Health Theme," p. 134; Wray, "Population Pressure on Families."

55. Newcombe, "Environmental versus Genetic Interpretations."

56. Taylor et al., "Child Survival Hypothesis."

57. Shorter, Making of the Modern Family, p. 200.

58. Oscar Lewis, "Life in a Mexican Village," in Pregnancy and Birth (Urbana: University of Illinois Press, 1963).

59. Moritz Thompsen, Living Poor: A Peace Corps Chronicle (Seattle: University of Washington Press, 1969), p. 35. Shorter, Making of the Modern Family, also mentions this attitude in Europe, pp. 172-73.

60. Lewis, "Life in a Mexican Village."

61. L. Whitehead, "Altitude, Fertility and Mortality in Andean Countries," Population Studies 22 (1968). Ariés, Centuries of Childhood, describes how children in the Middle Ages were not viewed as real people.

62. N. L. Solien de Gonzales and M. Behar, "Child-rearing Practices, Nutrition and Health Status," Milbank Memorial Fund Quarterly 44 (April 1966): 80.

63. N. S. Scrimshaw, "Food, Health, Family Planning" (Washington, D.C.: WHO, 1974).

64. Williams and Jelliffe, Mother and Child Health.

65. Susan Scrimshaw, Michele Shedlin, Susan Bram, and Maria-Eugenia de Ruales, "Aceptabilidad e impacto: La evaluacion de un programa modelo de prestacion de servicios de salud en Cali, Colombia" (New York: Columbia University, International Institute for the Study of Human Reproduction, 1975).

66. Wray and Aguirre, "Protein Calorie Malnutrition"; D. B. Jelliffe and E. F. Patrice Jelliffe, Human Milk in the Modern World (Oxford: Oxford University Press, 1978); John Knodel, "Breast-Feeding and Population Growth," Science 198 (December 1977).

67. John Knodel and H. Kintner, "The Impact of Breast Feeding Patterns on the Biometric Analysis of Infant Mortality," Demography 14 (1977): 391-93.

68. John Knodel and E. Van de Walle, "Breast Feeding, Fertility and Infant Mortality: An Analysis of Some Early German Data," Population Studies 21 (1967): 115.

69. Marshall H. Klaus and John H. Kennel, Maternal-Infant Bonding (St. Louis: C. V. Mosby, 1976). E. Pollit, "Behavior of Infant in Causation of Infantile Marasmus," American Journal of Clinical Nutrition 26 (1973): 264, deals with the problems of response synchrony in breast feeding. Also, J. Cravioto found that a mother's interest in her child's test performance could discriminate between malnourished and normal children. "Complexity of Factors Involved in Protein-Calorie Malnutrition," Bibliography of Nutritional Diet 14 (1970): 7-22.

70. T. P. Schultz, Interrelationships between Mortality and Fertility in Population and Development: The Search for Selective Interventions, ed. Ronald C. Ridker (Baltimore: Johns Hopkins University Press, 1976).

71. Wray and Aguirre, "Protein Calorie Malnutrition."

72. K. S. Gokulathathn and K. P. Verghese, "Socio-cultural Malnutrition (Growth Failure in Children Due to Socio-cultural Factors)," Journal of Tropical Pediatrics (September 1969): 118-24.

73. Susan C. M. Scrimshaw, "Culture, Environment and Family Size."

74. S. Chandrasekhar, Infant Mortality, Population Growth and Family Planning in India (Chapel Hill: University of North Carolina Press, 1972).

75. Wray and Aguirre, "Protein Calorie Malnutrition."

76. Mary Scrimshaw, "Family Patterns of Nutrition and Health on a Guatemalan Coastal Plantation," paper presented at the 1976 Annual Meeting of the American Anthropological Association, Houston.

77. Anne Retel-Laurentin and D. Benoit, "Infant Mortality and Birth Intervals," Population Studies 30 (1976).

78. Omran, "Health Theme," p. 135.

79. R. Q. Bell, "Contributions of Human Infants to Caregiving and Social Interaction," in The Effect of the Infant on Its Caregiver, eds. Lewis and L. A. Rosenblum (New York: Wiley, 1974).

80. Mary Scrimshaw, personal communication, 1977.

81. James V. Neel, "Lessons from a 'Primitive' People," Science 170.

82. S. Preston, "Health Programs and Population Growth," Population and Development Review 1 (1975).

83. Schultz, Interrelationships between Mortality and Fertility, p. 256.

84. A recent international collaborative study by Omran represents an ambitious and valuable attempt to look at the impact of high parity, large family size, and closely spaced pregnancies on infant and child mortality and development, maternal health, and subsequent fertility. However, the child replacement hypothesis is one of the underlying assumptions of the study, and the possibility that some infant mortality is unconsciously influenced is not taken into account. Family Formation and Health (Geneva: WHO, 1976).

85. Omran, "Health Theme," p. 115.

86. Project IV Behavioral Correlates of Demographic Change (INCAP: Guatemala Program Project on Nutrition, Fecundity, Fertility and Population Growth, 1978).

9

POPULATION, NUTRITION, AND FECUNDITY: SIGNIFICANCE FOR INTERPRETATION OF CHANGES IN FERTILITY

Rose E. Frisch

The number of living births a married couple have in the course of their entire reproductive span (the total fertility rate [TFR]) is a valuable supplement to the crude birth rate because it gives insight into the many biological and social factors that can affect fertility (Figure 9.1). This is particularly so for a developing country, where the total fertility rate would be expected to differ by socioeconomic level. Couples in the high socioeconomic classes may have a TFR of two or three due to the use of efficient methods of contraception, as is found in most developed countries. Couples in the lowest socio-economic classes may have a relatively high TFR, in the range of six or seven live births. However, a total fertility rate of six or seven is still well below the average human maximum of 11 or 12 found in well-nourished, noncontracepting populations such as the Hutterites[1] (Figures 9.1 and 9.2).

BIOLOGICAL AND SOCIAL FACTORS INFLUENCING THE TOTAL FERTILITY RATE

The reasons for a submaximum total fertility rate may be: (1) A submaximum level of reproductive ability of the female and/or male. The level of reproductive ability can vary from zero to 100 percent in response to ordinary environmental factors such as the quality and quantity of food, chronic or acute disease, physical work, and altitude, and by intrinsic factors such as age (Figure 9.1). (2) A small number of children are desired. Differences in the desired number of children may be influenced by the value of children, the cost of children, religious beliefs, the mortality of children from infancy to age

FIGURE 9.1

Biological and Social Factors Influencing Mean Number of Live Births per Couple (Total Fertility Rate)

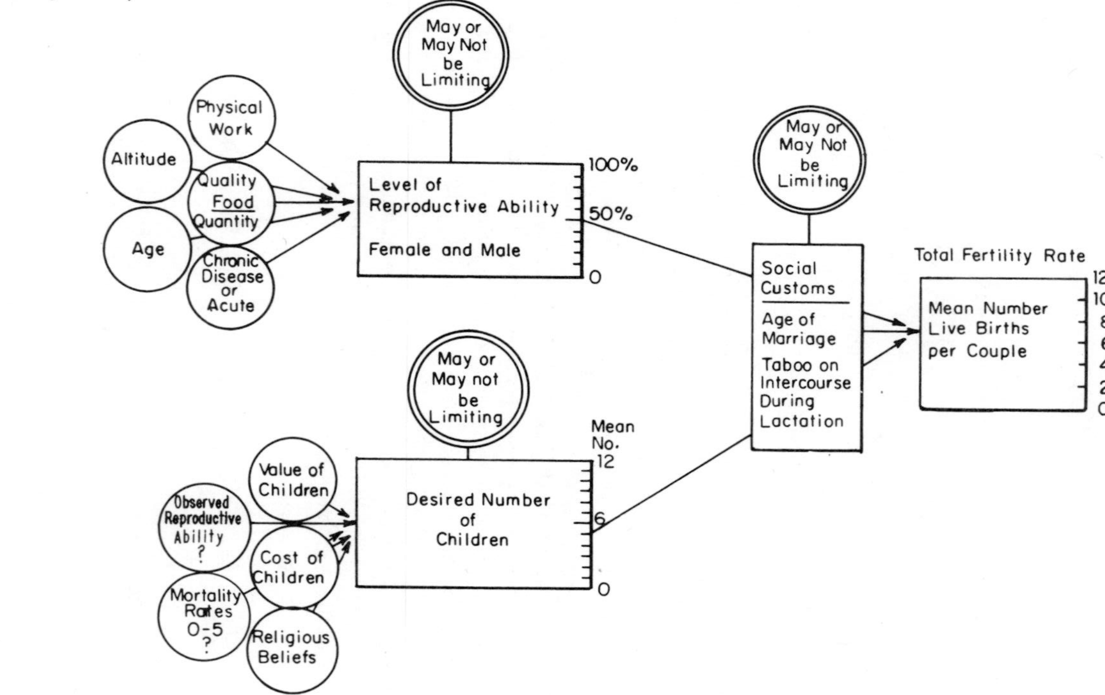

Note: The mean number of live births per couple (total fertility rate) may be influenced by the level of reproductive ability and the desired number of children. Each of these major factors is influenced, in turn, by environmental factors such as nutrition, intrinsic factors such as age, and social factors such as the value of children. Each of the major factors may be limiting alone or together, or in interaction with social customs such as age of marriage. Social customs may or may not be limiting. Well-nourished couples may have a level of reproductive ability of 100 percent and yet have only two children because that is their desired number, and efficient contraception is used. Poorly nourished couples may have a total fertility rate of about five, as is found among Bush people of the Kalahari desert; however, the desired number is apparently greater than five. (The Bush women say "God is stingy with children" [Howell[60]].) The main limiting factor for the Bush women may be a reduced level of reproductive ability due to relative undernutrition and high levels of physical activity.

FIGURE 9.2

The Curve of Procreative Power or Reproductive Efficiency (Maximum Fertility Rate = 100)

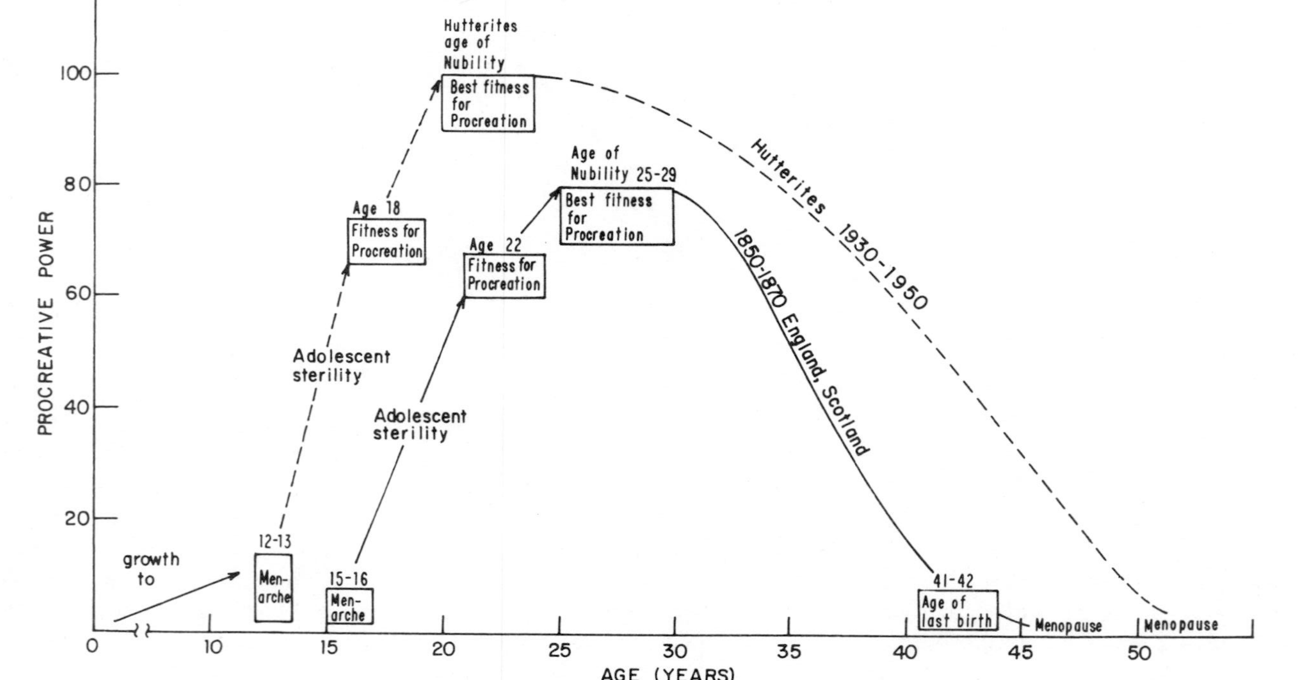

Note: The mid-nineteenth-century curve of female "procreative power" (variation of the rate of childbearing with age) compared to that of the well-nourished, noncontracepting modern Hutterites. The Hutterite fertility curve results in an average of 10 to 12 children; the 1850 to 1870 fertility curve in about six to eight children. Reprinted with permission from Science 199 (1978).

five years, and the perceived reproductive ability (Figure 9.1). (3) Social customs, such as a taboo on intercourse during lactation or customary home visits of the wife, may decrease the risk of conception. Similarly, age of marriage may affect frequency of intercourse, and therefore risk of conception. A late age of marriage is also associated with declining natural fecundity (Figure 9.2). The female age of marriage is relatively young in developing countries, so this factor is not usually limiting at the lower socioeconomic levels.

Each of the many factors listed above, alone or in combination, may be limiting for the total fertility rate (Figure 9.1). The effects of socioeconomic factors on the total fertility rate have been demonstrated and discussed by many authors.[2] This chapter will focus on the possible limiting effects of biological factors on the mean number of live births couples have during their reproductive lives.

Poor couples in many developing countries average about six or seven live births,[3] as did poor couples historically in countries now termed developed.[4,5,6] Because of the decrease in mortality rates subsequent to necessary public health measures introduced by developed countries into the developing countries, six to seven children per couple today results in a very rapid rate of population growth.

NUTRITION AND NATURAL FERTILITY

Differences in natural fertility of populations have long been recognized and explained by differences in length of birth intervals[7] or by variation in general health and food intake without specification of mechanism.[2,8] Mauldin cited data of Mahalanobis and others that suggested that low levels of fertility at certain periods of Indian history may have been due to impaired fecundity because of low levels of consumption.[9] Gopalan and Naidu related malnutrition and relatively low fertility in India.[10] Chen et al. showed from a prospective study that fertility in Bangladesh varied in correlation with the food supply in an essentially noncontracepting population.[11] Similarly, Wilmsen reports seasonal variation in births correlated with seasonal changes in dietary intake among the Kalahari San.[12]

Frisch has suggested a possible mechanism to explain variations in natural fertility through the effects of environmental factors, particularly nutrition, on the timing of the ages of menarche and menopause, and on the efficiency of reproductive events of the life cycle.[13,14,15] Historical data on nutrition, growth, age-specific fertility rates, and the ages of reproductive events show that the slow growth to maturity of women and men due to undernutrition, hard work, and disease is correlated with a reproductive span that is shorter and less efficient than that of a well-nourished population

(Figure 9.2). The submaximally nourished females and males are identifiable by a later age of completion of growth, 20 to 21 years and 23 to 25 years, respectively, compared to that of contemporary, well-nourished females and males who complete their growth by ages 16 to 18 years and 20 to 21 years, respectively.[14,15]

The historical data for these slower growing females show that they subsequently differ reproductively from well-nourished females not only by having a longer birth interval, but also by having a later mean age of menarche, an earlier mean age of menopause, and greater relative and absolute sterility than do well-nourished women.[14] These data suggested that undernutrition and hard living may be the explanation, wholly or in part, of the lower than maximum fertility of mid-nineteenth-century England and Scottish populations.

Such a shortened, less efficient reproductive pattern is observed also among the poor populations of many developing countries today when data on age of menarche,[16] age of menopause,[17] length of birth intervals,[18] and pregnancy wastage[19] are available. Some of the main biological points are considered below without consideration of interaction with social factors or mortality, although the importance of these factors is recognized.

UNDERNUTRITION AND ADULT REPRODUCTIVE FUNCTION

Data from both normal and anorectic women show that a loss of body weight in the range of 10 to 15 percent of normal weight for height, which represents a loss of about one-third body fat, results in cessation of menstrual cycles (amenorrhea).[20,21] Data from obese women show that excessive fatness also causes amenorrhea. Too little fat or too much fat therefore is associated with the cessation of reproductive function in the human female.[22,23]

The weight loss of about 10 to 15 percent, which results in nutritional, secondary amenorrhea in normal women, is not starvation; many ballet dancers, runners, and models maintain themselves at this weight level.[24,25] Fluctuating weight gain and loss around the minimum weight for height results in irregular cycles.[20,21] Nutritional amenorrhea differs from the cessation of cycles that occurs after birth (postpartum amenorrhea), as will be discussed in detail below. It should be noted that other factors (such as emotional stress) can affect the maintenance or onset of menstrual cycles. Therefore menstrual cycles may cease without weight loss and may not resume in some women even though the minimum required weight is attained.

Male reproductive ability is also affected by a decrease in caloric intake and subsequent weight loss. Healthy male volunteers

FIGURE 9.3

The Male Curve of Procreative Power or Reproductive Efficiency

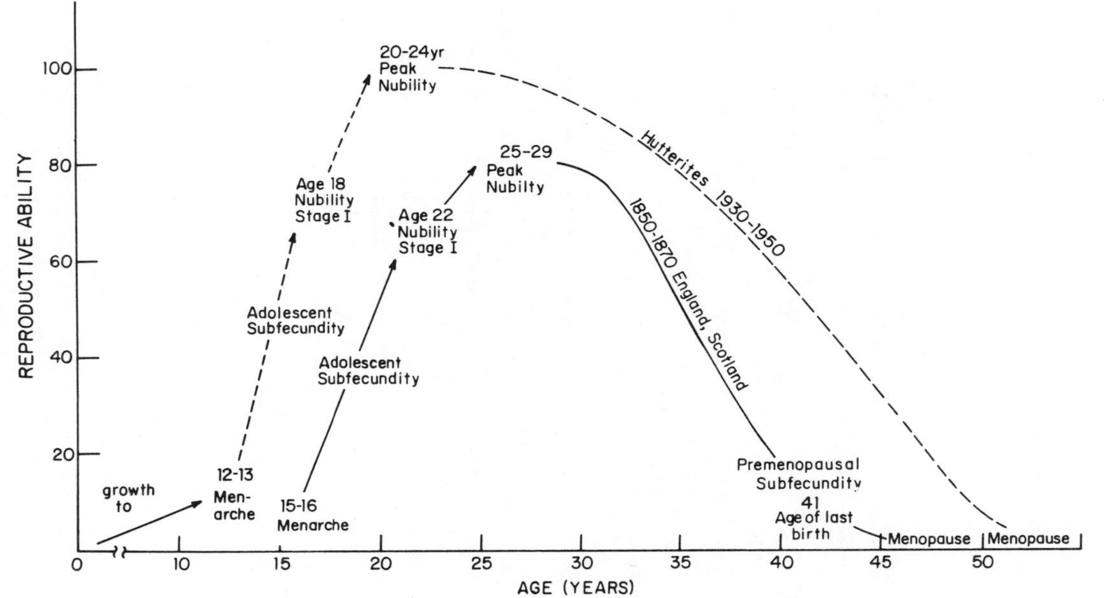

<u>Note</u>: Hypothetical curves of male reproductive ability for modern males and males from 1850 to 1870, based on ages of peak height velocity, completion of height growth, and hormonal data for modern males and the relation to ages of menarche of the female in Figure 9.2. Reprinted with permission from <u>Science</u> 199 (1978).

who reduced their caloric intake by 50 percent over a period of six months, first experienced a loss of libido, then a decrease of prostate fluid, follow by a decrease in sperm mobility, motility, and sperm longevity. The most severe effects were associated with a weight loss in the range of 25 percent of normal weight for height.[26,27] Undernutrition also delays the onset of sexual maturation in boys,[28] as it does in girls.[29]

Both the male and the female show a decline in fecundity with increasing age (Figures 9.2, 9.3). The male decline may be more rapid with undernutrition, as is found for the female.

NUTRITION, AGE OF MENARCHE, AGE OF MENOPAUSE, AND BIOLOGICAL CONSISTENCY

The age of menarche (first menstrual cycle) has become earlier by about three or four months per decade in the last century.[30] The average age of menarche of girls in the United States is now about 12.6 years. In 1900 the age of menarche was about 14 years. In 1850 in Britain, the age of menarche was about 15 to 16 years; the age varied with socioeconomic level, the richer girls having an earlier menarche.[14,29]

Menarche normally takes place after a period of rapid weight gain of the adolescent growth spurt. Since menarche is associated with the attainment of a minimum weight for height, apparently representing a critical fat/lean ratio, factors slowing the rate of growth also delay menarche; for example, undernutrition, high altitude, hard physical work, disease, and twinning (twins usually grow more slowly than singletons) are associated with a delay in the age of menarche.[31] Norwegian data on changes in age at menarche from about 1830 to 1930 show the disappearance of class differences in age of menarche as the average age became earlier, as would be expected with the gradual equalization of diet and mode of living among the social classes.[32]

This well-established relationship of undernutrition, altitude, or disease delaying menarche would have little demographic significance when the age of marriage is at least 16 years or older,[33] if it were an isolated reproductive phenomenon. However, historical data and data from contemporary undernourished populations show that it is not an isolated event. A later age of menarche in a population usually is associated also with a longer period of adolescent sterility, a higher frequency of nutritional amenorrhea when food supplies are marginal, a higher amount of pregnancy wastage,[34] a longer lactation interval, a longer period of premenopausal subfecundity, and an and an earlier age of menopause, for example, 45 to 47 years, as compared to 50 to 51 years for women in well-nourished societies.[14,15,17]

The extent of the secular change in age of menopause (about three years) is approximately the same as the change in age of menarche in the last hundred years. The menopausal change is less marked since it is only about a 6 percent change, compared to the 20 to 25 percent change in age of menarche. In historical populations where this type of biological profile is found, there is also a later peak of age-specific fertility, and the peak is at a lower level compared to that of well-nourished societies[14,15] (Figure 9.2).

POSTPARTUM AMENORRHEA—FACTORS AFFECTING THE RESUMPTION OF MENSTRUAL CYCLES AFTER PARTURITION

When a live infant is born, the postpartum amenorrhea of a lactating, undernourished woman is longer by varying intervals, dependent on other interacting factors, than that of a lactating, well-nourished woman.[11,18,19,35,36] The amenorrhea associated with lactation is endocrinologically and physiologically different from the nutritional amenorrhea due to weight loss described by Frisch and McArthur.[20,21,37] The weight for height of a lactating woman subsequent to parturition is, by the fact of a successful pregnancy, necessarily well above the minimum weight for height necessary for menstrual cycles. In addition, data for American and European women show that there is weight gain during pregnancy that includes an increase in fat deposition[38] (Figure 9.4). The changes in weight for height associated with length of postpartum amenorrhea and resumption of menstrual cycles while lactating, are not as yet known for any racial or ethnic group, nor is the extent of the interaction with the suckling stimulus at differential nutritional levels.

However, it is not necessary, or expected, that lactating women would have to gain weight before resumption of normal ovulatory cycles. Only those women who ate so poorly and/or worked so hard physically while lactating that they lost a great deal of weight would have to gain weight to resume cycles. (Such women might then have a weight for height below the threshold weight for regular cycles.) Preliminary data on weight for height of lactating women in Zaire indicate that heavier women had a return of menstrual cycles sooner than did lighter weight women of the same height.[39]

Differences in amount of suckling undoubtedly contribute to length of amenorrhea.[40] The biological interaction, however, is difficult to unravel. For example, a lighterweight baby may want to

FIGURE 9.4

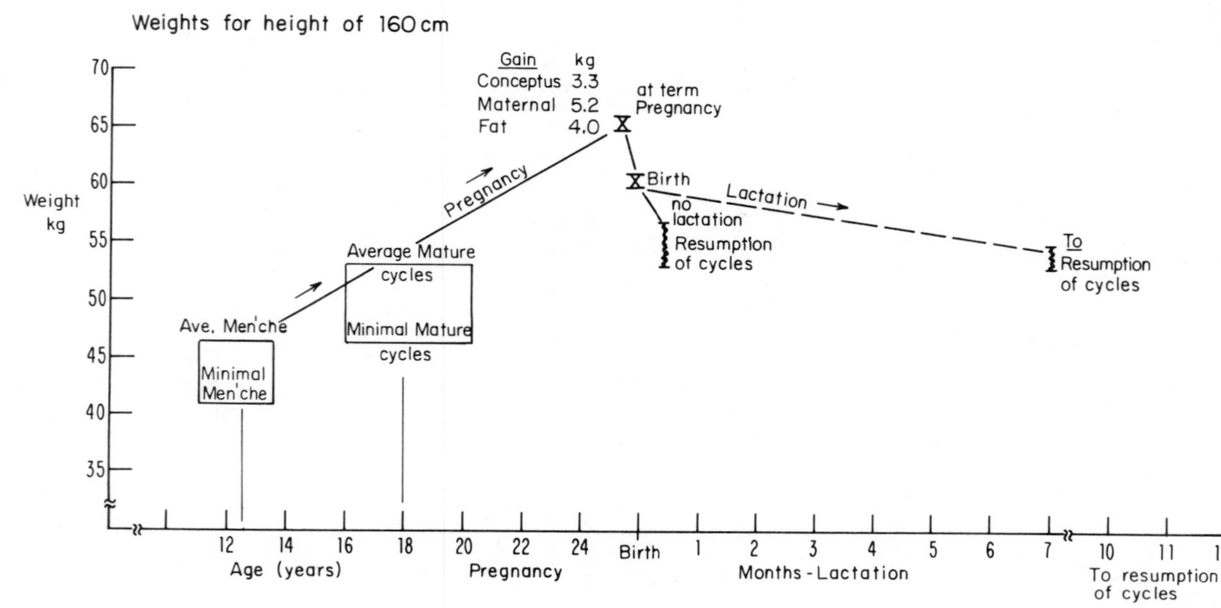

<u>Note</u>: Scheme of changes in weight (approximate) for a woman 160 cm tall from the age of onset of menstrual function to pregnancy and birth of the first child. Little is known about the mechanisms controlling the time of resumption of regular ovulatory cycles of lactating women, particularly in relation to their nutrition.

nurse more often, but a heavier baby also may want to eat more often, depending on the amount of milk available. This in turn can be affected by parity, age, and nutrition.[35]

An explanation of the relatively short interval between the early death of an infant and a new pregnancy, even in the undernourished populations of Bangladesh,[40] may be the increase in body weight and fatness that takes place normally during pregnancy.[38] This increase in fatness, in addition to the increases gained during the adolescent spurt and later maturation,[41] would increase the probability that a second pregnancy will occur in a short interval if the infant dies soon after birth.[42]

POSSIBLE BIOLOGICAL MECHANISMS

The data suggest that physical differences in rate of growth result not only in a displacement of the age-specific fertility curve in time, but in a difference in the ultimate level: the faster the growth of the females (and males), the earlier and more efficient the reproductive ability. A biological mechanism for this interaction is suggested by the data of Frisch, Hegsted, and Yoshinaga from experiments in which rats were fed high-fat and low-fat diets, the fat being substituted isocalorically for carbohydrate. The high-fat diet rats matured sexually (first estrus) significantly earlier than did the low-fat diets rats.[43] Carcass analysis of the rats showed that at maturation the high-fat diet rats were relatively fatter than were the low-fat diet rats.[44]

Conversion of weak androgens to estrogen by aromatization is known to take place in human adipose tissue.[45] Adipose tissue may therefore be a significant, extragonadal source of estrogen. Also, differences in relative fatness affect the pathway of metabolism of estrogen, to more or less potent forms of estrogen.[46,47] Women who are well nourished, particularly on diets containing a high percentage of calories from fat,[43] may have higher levels of the more potent estrogens than do poorly nourished women on a low-fat diet.[44]

HUMAN REPRODUCTION RECONSIDERED?: SIGNIFICANCE

The usual biological explanation given for the relatively low fertility observed historically for the lower socioeconomic classes in mid-nineteenth-century Britain and in poor agricultural societies is the use of "folk contraception," usually coitus interruptus. One cannot disprove the use of this method of contraception. However, the physical and reproductive data suggest an alternate explanation: the effects of undernutrition and hard living on reproductive ability.

Undernutrition, instead of the widespread use of folk contraception, may also partly explain the completed family size of six or seven children found in many developing countries today, as has already been suggested.[9,10,11,13] If so, the need for family planning programs may be much greater than realized heretofore,[14,15] since in some groups of an undernourished population the concept of control of fertility may not be present. The data suggest also that when couples are well fed and their potential fertility is high, while infant mortality is low, then there is interest in and receptivity to the idea of efficient means of contraception.

EVIDENCE FOR THE EFFECTS OF UNDERNUTRITION ON MATERNAL REPRODUCTION

Although it has been suggested by Butz and Habicht that "the reproductive function is well protected from nutritional insults and poor health,"[33,48] a great many biological data are contrary to this conclusion. (In a teleological way the Butz and Habicht statement makes sense, since it is a fact that reproduction turns off completely when undernutrition is severe,[26,49,50] or even with female weight loss in the range of 10 to 15 percent.[20,21] However, this is not the sense of the statement by these authors.)

Two well-documented examples of the negative effect of undernutrition on human reproductive function other than the pregnancy wastage and weight loss effects already discussed above are folate deficiency and undernutrition of the mother. Folate deficiency is associated with major obstetric complications (abruptio placentae and placenta previa), congenital abnormalities, perinatal mortality, premature delivery, and repeated miscarriages. Tropical populations are particularly liable to folate deficiency, which may be due to inadequate dietary folate and/or increased utilization of the vitamin during pregnancy.[51] Undernutrition of the mother, particularly during the third trimester of pregnancy, which includes a critical period of rapid brain growth, results in low birth weight. Low birth weight is associated with a greater incidence of moderate or severe neurological and physical handicaps in the infant than is found at normal birth weights. Low birth weight boys are handicapped more than are low birth weight girls,[52] as would be expected since boys are affected by adverse circumstances more than girls. Babies who are small for their gestational age may be more seriously impaired mentally than chronologically immature babies of the same birth weight.[53]

Maternal conditions that affect the birth weight of the child are thus of major importance. These include maternal stature, pre-pregnancy weight, weight gain during pregnancy, toxemia and infection, age of mother below 19 years or above 35, closely spaced births, excessive work during the last months of pregnancy, and nutrition.[34,52-57] The natural experiments of wartime show that the birth weight of the infant is affected by the nutrition of the mother. Severe malnourishment of the mother during the famine conditions at the siege of Leningrad reduced the birth weight of infants by 400 to 500g. Less severe, but abnormally low, calorie intakes associated with war conditions in Holland resulted in 200 to 300g reductions in average birth weights.[26,50] The reverse effect, a rise in birth weight associated with improved nutrition, has also been shown. In Great Britain the improvement of food quality through wartime rationing caused a decrease in fetal mortality due to prematurity and other causes.[53]

The physiological effects of maternal undernutrition on the birth weight of the infant are a function of the pre-pregnancy weight of the mother and of her weight gain during pregnancy. Each factor acts independently and is additive in its effects.[56]

Thomson and Billewicz[57] found that the percentage of low birth weight babies was highest for mothers who had been stunted in their own physical growth. Eastman and Jackson conclude that the effect of maternal height is produced through its association with maternal weight.[56] Whether the effect on birth weight is mainly through height, weight, or both, it is clear that for successful reproductive ability, good nutrition should begin early in life, not just after pregnancy has begun.

That the condition of the mother is important for successful pregnancy outcome is shown also by a high incidence of low birth weights (birth weights below 2500g; they may be at term) in association with too early childbearing and closely spaced births.[34,55,58,59] Children with intersib intervals of less than 12 months had twice as many neurologically abnormal or suspicious cases at age one year than did children with sibling intervals of 24 to 60 months. The low birth weight of the rapid interval children was the major component in the results.[58]

These data suggest that contrary to the idea that the reproductive ability of undernourished women is protected from nutritional insult and poor health, priority must be given to the nutritional needs of pregnant and of lactating women to ensure the future physical and mental well-being of the child. An efficient and safe method of contraception is an essential component of nutrition programs for these vulnerable women: a longer interval between pregnancies allows nutritional rehabilitation of the mother, thus reducing the incidence of low birth weight infants. A longer interval between pregnancies also prevents the too early cessation of lactation, thus ensuring high quality protein and sufficient calories for the infant in the important early months of life.

REFERENCES

1. J. W. Eaton and A. J. Mayer, "The Social Biology of Very High Fertility among the Hutterites. The Demography of a Unique Population." Human Biology 25 (1953).

2. A. J. Coale, The Growth and Structure of Human Populations: A Mathematical Investigation (Princeton: Princeton University Press, 1972).

3. W. Brass, "Population Size and Complex Communities, with a Consideration of World Population," in Population and Its Problems: A Plain Man's Guide, H. B. Parry, ed. (Oxford: Clarendon Press, 1974).

4. E. A. Wrigley, Population and History (London: Weidenfeld and Nicolson, 1969).

5. D. V. Glass, "Fertility and Population Growth," J. Roy. Stat. Soc. 129 (1966).

6. J. M. Duncan, Fecundity, Fertility, Sterility, and Allied Topics, 2d ed. (Edinburgh: Adam & Charles Black, 1871).

7. L. Henry, "Some Data on Natural Fertility," Eugenics Quarterly 8 (1961).

8. A. J. Coale, "The History of the Human Population," Scientific American 231 (1974).

9. W. P. Mauldin, "The Population of India: Policy, Action and Research," Economic Digest 3 (1960).

10. C. Gopalan and A. N. Naidu, "Nutrition and Fertility," Lancet 2 (1972).

11. L. C. Chen, S. Ahmed, M. Gesche, and W. H. Mosley, "A Prospective Study of Birth Interval Dynamics in Rural Bangladesh," Population Studies 28 (1974).

12. E. N. Wilmsen, "Seasonal Effects of Dietary Intake on Kalahari San," Federation Proc. 37 (1978).

13. R. E. Frisch, "Demographic Implications of the Biological Determinants of Female Fecundity," Social Biology 22 (1975).

14. R. E. Frisch, "Population, Food Intake and Fertility," Science 199 (1978).

15. R. E. Frisch, "Nutrition, Fatness and Fertility," in Nutrition and Human Reproduction, W. H. Mosley, ed. (New York: Plenum Press, 1978).

16. A. K. M. Chowdhury, S. L. Huffman, and G. T. Curlin, "Malnutrition, Menarche and Marriage in Rural Bangladesh," Social Biology 24 (1978).

17. R. H. Gray, "The Menopause, Epdemiological and Demographic Considerations," in The Menopause, R. J. Beard, ed. (Baltimore: University Park Press, 1976).

18. R. G. Potter, J. Wyon, N. New, and J. Gordon, "Lactation and Its Effects upon Birth Intervals in Eleven Punjab Villages," J. Chronic Dis. 18 (1965).

19. C. E. Taylor, J. S. Newman, and N. O. Kelly, "Interactions between Health and Population," Studies in Family Planning 7, no. 3 (1976).

20. R. E. Frisch and J. W. McArthur, "Menstrual Cycles: Fatness as a Determinant of Minimum Weight for Height Necessary for their Maintenance or Onset," Science 185 (1974).

21. J. W. McArthur, B. O'Loughlin, B. Johnson, L. Horihan, and C. Alonso, "Endocrine Studies during the Refeeding of Young Women with Nutritional Amenorrhea and Infertility," Mayo Clinic Proc. 51 (1976).

22. R. E. Frisch, "Food Intake, Fatness and Reproductive Ability," in Anorexia Nervosa, R. Vigersky, ed. (New York: Raven, 1977).

23. R. E. Frisch, "Fatness and the Onset and Maintenance of Menstrual Cycles," Research in Reprod. 9, no. 6 (1977).

24. J. Mayer, personal communication (1974); L. Vincent, personal communication (1978).

25. New York Times, April 17, 1978, "Training Linked to Disruption of Female Reproductive Cycle," p. C 1.

26. A. Keys, J. Brozek, A. Henschel, O. Mickelsen, and H. L. Taylor, The Biology of Human Starvation, vol. 1 (Minneapolis: University of Minnesota Press, 1950).

27. M. W. H. Bishop, "Aging and Reproduction in the Male," J. Reprod. Fert., suppl. 12 (1970).

28. R. E. Frisch and R. Revelle, "Variation in Body Weights and the Age of the Adolescent Growth Spurt among Latin American and Asian Populations in Relation to Calorie Supplies," Human Biol. 41 (1969).

29. R. E. Frisch, "Weight at Menarche: Similarity for Well-nourished and Under-nourished Girls at Differing Ages, and Evidence for Historical Constancy," Pediat. 50 (1972).

30. J. M. Tanner, Growth at Adolescence (Oxford: Blackwell Press, 1962).

31. R. E. Frisch and R. Revelle, "Height and Weight at Menarche and a Hypothesis of Menarche," Arch. Dis. Childh. 46 (1971).

32. V. Kiil, "Stature and Growth of Norwegian Men during the Past Two Hundred Years," Skr. Norske Vidensk Akad. 2 (1939).

33. J. Bongaarts, "A Framework for Analyzing the Proximate Determinants of Fertility," Population and Development Review 4 (1978).

34. E. Siegel and N. Morris, "The Epidemiology of Human Reproductive Casualties with Emphasis on the Role of Nutrition," in Maternal Nutrition and the Course of Pregnancy (Washington, D.C.: National Academy of Sciences, 1970).

35. R. Buchanan, "Breast-Feeding: Aid to Infant Health and Fertility Control," Population Reports, Series J, no. 4 (1975).

36. J. Knodel, "Breast Feeding and Population Growth," Science 198 (1977).

37. R. E. Frisch and J. W. McArthur, "Difference between Postpartum and Nutritional Amenorrhea," Science, in press.

38. F. E. Hytten and A. M. Thomson, "Maternal Physiological Adjustments," in Maternal Nutrition and the Course of Pregnancy (Washington, D.C.: National Academy of Sciences, 1970).

39. M. Carael, "Relations between Birth Intervals and Nutrition in Three Central African Populations (Zaire)," in Mosley, Nutrition and Human Reproduction.

40. H. Mosley, "The Effects of Nutrition on Natural Fertility," Natural Fertility Seminar (Paris: IUSSP, 1977).

41. R. E. Frisch, "Fatness of Girls from Menarche to Age 18 Years, with a Nomogram," Human Biol. 48 (1976).

42. N. Howell, "Toward a Uniform Theory of Human Paleodemography," in The Demographic Evolution of Human Populations, R. J. Ward and K. M. Weiss, eds. (London: Academic Press, 1976).

43. R. E. Frisch, D. M. Hegsted, and K. Yoshinaga, "Body Weight and Food Intake at Early Estrus of Rats on a High-Fat Diet," Proc. Nat. Acad. Sci. U.S.A. 72 (1975).

44. R. E. Frisch and D. M. and K. Yoshinaga, "Carcass Components at First Estrus of Rats on High-Fat and Low-Fat Diets: Body Water, Protein and Fat," Proc. Nat. Acad. Sci. U.S.A. 74 (1977).

45. A. Nimrod and K. J. Ryan, "Aromatization of Androgens by Human Abdominal and Breast Fat Tissue," J. Clin. Endocrin. Metab. 40 (1975).

46. J. B. Brown and J. A. Strong, "Effect of Nutritional Status and Thyroid Function on the Metabolism of Oestradial," J. Endocrinol. 32 (1965).

47. J. Fishman, R. M. Boyar, and L. Hellman, "Influence of Body Weight on Estradiol Metabolism in Young Women," J. Clin. Endocrinol. Metab. 41 (1975).

48. W. Butz and J. P. Habicht, The Effects of Nutrition and Health on Fertility: Hypotheses, Evidence and Interventions (New York: Rand Paper Series, July 1976).

49. Z. Stein and M. Susser, "Fertility, Fecundity, Famine," Hum. Biol. 47 (1975).

50. C. A. Smith, "Effects of Maternal Undernutrition upon the Newborn Infant in Holland (1944-1945)," J. Pediat. 30 (1947).

51. R. F. Branda and J. W. Eaton, "Skin Color and Nutrient Photolysis: An Evolutionary Hypothesis," Science 201 (1978).

52. C. M. Drillien, Growth and Development of the Prematurely Born Infant (Baltimore: Williams and Wilkins, 1964).

53. D. Baird, "The Influence of Social and Economic Factors on Stillbirths and Neonatal Deaths," J. Obstet. Gynaec., Brit. Emp. 52 (1945).

54. B. J. Van den Berg and J. Yerushalmy, "The Relationship of the Rate of Intrauterine Growth of Infants of Low Birth Weight to Mortality, Morbidity and Congenital Anomalies," J. Pediat. 69 (1966).

55. J. W. B. Douglas, "Health and Survival of Infants in Different Social Classes," Lancet 440 (1951).

56. N. J. Eastman and E. Jackson, "Weight Relationships in Pregnancy," Obstet. and Gynec. Survey 23 (1968).

57. A. M. Thomson and W. Z. Billewicz, "Nutritional Status, Maternal Physique and Reproductive Efficiency," Proc. Nutr. Soc. 22 (1963).

58. W. L. Holley, A. L. Rosenbaum, and J. A. Churchill, "Effect of Rapid Succession of Pregnancy," in Perinatal Factors Affecting Human Development (Washington, D.C.: Pan American Health Organization, 1969).

59. "Relation of Nutrition to Pregnancy in Adolescence," Chap. 6 in Maternal Nutrition and the Course of Pregnancy.

60. N. Howell, The Bush People (London: Academic Press, forthcoming).

10

AMERICAN EFFORTS TO REDUCE THE FERTILITY OF LESS DEVELOPED COUNTRIES

William Petersen

Remarkably, population policies in less developed countries have been similar enough to warrant classifying them into a single category, or at most perhaps two or three very closely related subcategories. Differences among antinatalist programs have been insignificant when contrasted with the wide divergence in such key variables as the countries' population size and density, their family types, the cultural practices affecting their fertility, and the level and rate of growth of their economies. The reason for this essential similarity is that typically the programs did not develop separately within each national context but were introduced, sponsored, and largely financed by Western or international institutions, which set a relatively unitary perspective on the problem and the means by which it could be mitigated or solved. Such differences as one notes between, for example, francophone and anglophone countries in Africa, derive from the different sponsorship rather than an on-the-spot appreciation of a variation.

The view dominant in the United States of how to cut the fertility of less developed countries has been challenged by a few dissidents, of whom Kingsley Davis and Edwin Driver are perhaps the most prominent.[1] The perspective of government and foundation officials, however, has generally been echoed in academics' papers and family planning propaganda. The "instructive entertainment" that Bernard Berelson found in the "great debate on population policy"[2] seems to be nearing the final curtain. Is the play really almost over? Is it true, as Donald Bogue asserted in a presidential address to the Population Association of America, that the American birth controllers have hit upon the "necessary and sufficient conditions" to achieve success anywhere in the world?[3]

THE THEORY OF FAMILY PLANNING

What is the picture of the world held by the Americans largely responsible for the U.S.-aided family planning programs in less developed non-Communist countries? How should one select the quotations to illustrate this view? Critical readers of an earlier version of this chapter noted my dependence, for instance, on Dr. Ravenholt, remarking that he is often criticized privately for his reckless statements but that, like most persons seeking public funds, he is more interested in expediency than truth. In other professions such behavior would be the equivalent of malpractice. The fact that publicly he has been virtually unchallenged, though he has controlled some millions of tax dollars, is a comment also on the discipline as a whole.[4] Nor is it irrelevant that the leaflets and pamphlets that every week are stuffed into the mailboxes of American demographers summarize weightier presentations.

The theory of family planning at least implicit in these several places is not one that could be derived from a detailed knowledge either of particular cultures of less developed countries or of the history of how fertility declined in the West. It is summed up in a series of propositions.

> The population growth both of the world as a whole and of almost every country in it is too rapid. Under just about any conditions, to reduce fertility immediately would bring mainly, or only, benefits to everyone.

This stance can be exemplified best by recent policy recommendations concerning the United States itself. The debate over the past generation or two on whether a growing population can ever bring net benefits appears to be over. Catholic spokesmen oppose abortion and occasionally also contraception, but would any repeat today the doctrine that "the family which courageously rears a large number of children in an overpopulated area merits special praise for its virtue"?[5] During the 1930s, the last time that American fertility fell to more or less its current level, almost the entire scholarly community saw this as economically deleterious, if not disastrous. In a presidential address to the American Economic Association, Alvin Hansen spelled out the dire consequences of zero population growth (ZPG).[6] Louis Dublin addressed one women's club after another, personally appealing to the members to have more children.

In the frenetic campaign to effect ZPG today, most of its proponents have simply ignored the Keynesian arguments of the recent past. Their efforts have been a paradoxical counterpoint to the decline of American birth rates to their lowest levels in the country's history.

According to the Report of the quasi-official Rockefeller Commission, "it does not appear, for several reasons, that a lower population growth rate will cause serious problems for any industry or its employees" (emphasis added).[7] While it may be that the disruptions from a lower growth rate and the consequent shift in age structure will be balanced by equal or greater benefits to other sectors of the economy, the assertion that there would be no serious disruption at all brands the authors as ideologues. The Commission was accommodating itself to the doomsday mood set by such works as The Limits of Growth and The Population Bomb, whose totalist position represented a marked deterioration in demographic analysis. Ever since Malthus evaluated the extraordinarily rapid growth of the American colonies to be beneficial, policymakers have typically tried, however difficult the task, to distinguish over- from underpopulation and to set a course accordingly.

> The most important reason for the overrapid population growth, given the reduction in mortality, has been the lack of physical, moral, and financial access to contraceptives.

The proposition is based on the premise that contraception, almost like antibiotics, is an invention of modern Western technology, and thus that other peoples can control their fertility only through the beneficent intervention of those disseminating the techniques. But all primitive cultures include customs with a primary function of restricting family size or population increase, or both.[8] One cannot even say that there has been an overall improvement in efficacy; as a means of controlling the number of one's offspring, nothing works better than either celibacy or infanticide. The decline of the fertility of France and the United States, the two Western countries where natality fell first and fastest, was well under way before any means was available more modernist than withdrawal, douche, or sponge. The Western innovation was the birth-control movement, which in France was under continuous and effective attack, and in the United States was not organized until well into this century. What these two countries had in common was a democratic ideology, with revolutionary slogans repeated so often that their application spread from narrowly political issues to the family.

Less developed countries have varied greatly in both the means by which family size is traditionally controlled and the effect of this control on fertility. But the premodern culture of no single one of them lacks impediments to unrestrained procreation. Even so pronatalist a country as Hindu India forbade the remarriage of widows, many of whom were betrothed in infancy or early childhood and were thus totally excluded from procreation. In Confucian China, the prototype of a familist society, it was crucial to have a male progeny but no less important to avoid conceiving sons at inauspicious times. According to astrological calendars still circulating in Taiwan, only about 100 days a year are suitable for marital intercourse, for the life of a son conceived at any other time would be irremediably unlucky.[9] When the Confucian ethic was transferred to Japan, it adapted marvelously to the more straitened circumstances: the emphasis on continuity of the lineage was undiminished, but the same end was achieved by stressing quality rather than quantity in the male offspring. Throughout the several centuries of Tokugawa Japan, even though the country was artificially isolated from the West and could be designated the very acme of traditionalism, the population remained more or less static. "The necessary conclusion from the Japanese experience," Irene Taeuber remarked, "is that the role of family limitation in premodern societies may have been underestimated and the motivating factors oversimplified."[10]

> Since the fertility of modernist societies is far lower than that of most less developed ones, any shift from traditional to modernist culture is likely to bring about a lower fertility.

This notion is a corollary from the false postulate that no traditional society has any bars to maximum procreation. Since, on the contrary, these bars are often embedded in religious or superstitious beliefs, the first effect of secularization is likely to be their dissipation. One needs only an elementary knowledge of Western social history to be aware of what John Hajnal called the European marriage pattern, distinguished by a high average age at marriage and a large proportion who never married.[11] This custom, which persisted with diminishing effect until around 1900 (or in Ireland and traditional enclaves elsewhere far longer), cut the potential fertility tremendously. One of the most important demographic effects of the industrial revolution was to undermine the social controls needed to inhibit young people from breeding. "The years 1790-1860 were, in virtually every [European] society or community we know about, the peak period of illegitimacy."[12] Those social classes of which a high proportion were indifferent to whether their children were born in or out of wedlock did not worry over much about the number of their offspring. The smaller family size we associate with industrial societies came later, when, for example, the Englishmen seeking to rise to the new positions that were opening up first postponed their marriage to an average age of 30 years and then later achieved the same end by the initially surreptitious use of contraceptives.[13]

In short, even if one accepts the dubious propositions that throughout the underdeveloped world the transition to industrialism will be completed and that the end products will be similar to presently developed societies, the change will take at least several generations, during which the effect of modernization on natality, as determined by the typical attitudes of policymakers, is likely to be ambiguous at best. As a group, the leftist nationalists who control most less developed countries have been among the most persistent opponents of antinatalist programs. From a statement summarizing a Mexican survey, we learn that "there is strength in numbers. True, numbers bring problems, but we are forging these numbers into a great nation." According to N. Viera Altamirano, the influential editor of San Salvador's El Diario de Hoy, "to populate America is to civilize America. To oppose population is to oppose civilization."[14] Yet Mexico and Central America were at that time and continue to be areas where the increase of population has been, according to antinatalist analysts, both unduly rapid and manifestly the cause of serious economic and social problems.

Why should this pronatalist view, so obviously wrong according to present Western standards, have been fostered by so many Westernized statesmen and intellectuals? During the colonies' struggle to achieve independence, one recurrent charge by nationalist leaders, that the imperial rule was inefficient, was typically answered with the assertion that the rate of population increase was so high that no administration could keep up with it. Nehru (who as late as 1948 called India underpopulated), Nasser, and their equivalents elsewhere came to power convinced that the difficulties supposedly associated with high fertility were nothing more than an excuse for imperialists' maladministration. This belief was reinforced by both nationalism and Marxist doctrine. For how could leaders of nascent nations begin their careers with programs based on the idea that their peoples were getting to be too numerous? The Marxist dogma rampant during Stalin's lifetime that a socialist society can cope with any rate of population increase[15] has never quite disappeared in spite of the shift in Communist policy. Birth-control programs in less developed countries have been infused not only with bureaucratic sloth and corruption, but also with some persistent doubts about their necessity or urgency.

> The birth-control programs in less developed countries are most effective if administered under government auspices or by full state agencies.

This premise hardly derives from the history of the West where, without exception, the efforts of private groups to disseminate contraception were fought by officialdom. The postulate is rather a corollary of the previous one: if modernization connotes a turn toward the control of fertility, and if the states of less developed countries generally are seen to be the chief modernizers, then birth control should also be the province of the government.

All societies comprise a mass of undifferentiated individuals among whom ideas and attitudes flow freely, for the benefits that everyone would derive from a smaller progeny are so great that each potential parent needs only a minimum stimulus to curb his or her procreation.

In the West fertility declined first among the middle classes and then, partly because the lower classes followed this lead and partly because the benefits of the small-family system were indeed general, it spread throughout society. When Bogue advocated the use of "influentials" or Stycos of "elites" to disseminate the KAP process, this was rather a large-scale imitation of Planned Parenthood; but the middle-class types who carried the message of birth control to the masses were not markedly successful even in the United States, with its relatively undifferentiated population.[16] Proposing that Westernized elites, hardly less alien than Westerners themselves, be used as missionaries passes over the typical rigid structure by castes (as in India), tribes (as in Africa), or widely divergent social classes. Yet such impediments to diffusion were not mentioned even in a paper specially on the supposed spread of antinatalist practices, which did list ten rediscovered banalities (for example, "family planning is often a taboo topic for discussion").[17]

The Western birth-control programs that were at all successful, moreover, tried to motivate prospective clients by emphasizing such personal factors as the damage to a woman's health from too many pregnancies. In England, for example, the societal rationale of the Neo-Malthusian League under the Drysdale family proved to be very much less appealing than the medical and personal approach started by Marie Stopes. In less developed countries some programs have been associated with medical clinics and some of the advocacy has been addressed to individual needs. However, the supposition remains that protestations about general welfare typically motivate a change in behavior so intimate as childbearing.

Typically prospective parents behave rationally, weighing the advantages of having another child against the disadvantages.

This improbable thesis has become a key to American economists' reentry to demography. Gary Becker's notion that would-be parents consider whether their children will have separate bedrooms, nursey schools and private colleges, dance or music lessons, and so forth is manifestly drawn from only a small sector of even a well-to-do country. Yet hypotheses about even that upper middle class included a largish unanalyzed element, which Becker labeled "tastes."[18] Of those who have done research on attitudes of the American poor, the most prolific has been Lee Rainwater. Why, he asked, are lower-class black women not more motivated to limit their families? "Because they do not believe they have much chance of success; lack of hope reduces the likelihood of making a serious effort, . . . [and] having children without specifically wanting them merely confirms the self-conceptions that they have developed of being . . . hapless creatures."[19]

> Some respondents are quite passive and fatalistic about family planning; they do nothing because they do not think anything will help, or they go through the motions of using a method in which they have little confidence (and therefore do not use it very consistently).[20]

Family planning like planning of any other type, implies an orientation to the future, and those convinced that they have no control over what happens to them do not plan. They live in the present, not happy but content if their level of life does not get even worse.

That this thesis has received so little attention is in one sense amazing, for it applies both to the sector of the American population whose high fertility has at times been accused of generating serious social problems and also, by extension, to a large proportion of the masses in less developed countries. Understandably, would-be policy-makers do not find it an attractive theorem, for except in an outright dictatorship it allows them no leverage. Paradoxically, wholly passive people would be difficult to move, since they would not conduct their lives on the basis of any sort of utilitarian calculus. When someone knows that life brings only misery and that nothing can alter that axiom, what incentive can be offered to make the overprolific change their behavior?

THE "SUCCESS" OF FAMILY PLANNING

The social theory on which family-planning programs are based is dubious or false; the agencies that distribute the contraceptives are very often inappropriate; the belief that the world's peoples lack only IUDs in order to have fewer children is silly. Yet, ostensibly, almost all programs have succeeded. Obviously, if these postulates approximate the premises on which the programs are based, the criteria of success are inadequate.

A representative compilation of the range of data or suppositions that are used to allege the achievement of programs' aims gives criteria that have become standard in more pretentious writings. In Indonesia, we read, "a record high of 1.5 million new acceptors were recorded in 1974." In Bangladesh, "over a six-month period 16 percent of all eligible couples in four test villages were brought into the program." In Colombia, "Profamilia together with the Coffee Growers Association using local volunteers reached 20 percent of all eligible couples." In Egypt, "over a five-month period several rural pilot projects recruited an average 30 percent of the eligible couples." In Brazil, "with six months a community-based project in the Northeast region recruited 12 percent of the fertile couples."[21]

One of the commonest measures of progress is the number of acceptors or even, as in the Colombian example, the number who have been reached. The distributors of contraceptives are the missionaries of our secular age, intent for personal as well as ideological reasons on building up a good record of conversions. Villagers who resist their blandishments are characterized as ignorant and prejudiced; those who accept are bathed in approval. In the most significant independent replication of a major study, the author quotes one of the earlier respondents as follows:

> [The program's field workers] were so nice, you know. And they came from distant lands to be with us. . . . All they wanted was that we accept the [foam] tablets. I lost nothing and probably received their prayers. And they, they must have gotten some promotion.[22]

In "action-research," when an effort to obtain information is combined with proselytizing, the data collected are worthless. If some actually use the contraceptives they accept, they do not necessarily contribute to a reduction in fertility. Some merely shift from less convenient or more expensive methods to the means furnished by Western taxpayers; others soon lapse into recurrent childbearing. In the best case, the acceptors are never typical of the target population. They are the cream skimmed off the top, those most receptive to birth-control propaganda. The implicit snowballing from encouraging beginnings is the opposite of the extrapolation that one should ordinarily assume.

Just as sectors of particular populations are used to indicate the rate of acceptance of whole countries, so those countries in which fertility has declined are used to indicate the supposed trend of the whole world. Consider, for example, Population: Dynamics, Ethics and Policy (published by the American Association for the Advancement of Science), in which a chart is reproduced from an article by R. T. Ravenholt and John Chao, employees respectively of the U.S.

Agency for International Development (AID) and the U.S. Bureau of the Census.[23] The statistics circulated are not only misleading but also—it is impossible to avoid concluding—deliberately so. The chart includes only the 82 countries "with good vital statistics," and in 72 of them the crude birth rate declined over the period from 1960 to 1972—by a full 50 percent in Greenland down to only 0.8 percent in St. Lucia. The rather exotic flavor of these two countries is characteristic of the whole table. It includes, for example, Gibraltar, St. Kitts-Nevis, Cook Island, the Isle of Man, and the Faeroe Islands—whose combined population is well under that of the District of Columbia. It also includes the United States, the United Kingdom, both Germanies, the U.S.S.R., Australia, New Zealand, and so on through all developed countries. Omitted are only less developed countries like Communist China, India, Pakistan, Bangladesh, Nigeria—or more than half the estimated population of the world.

Since the senior author is an officer of AID, it is of some interest to note how American taxpayers affect world fertility. Table 10.1 shows the top ten recipients of U.S. family planning assistance, with the growth rates as estimated by the United Nations.[24] The comparison is crude: a more or less equivalent decline in mortality is assumed, the dates when the programs started might make a difference, and the growth rates reflect the loosest kind of guess. Even so, the tabulation is of some interest. Nine of the ten countries were omitted from the chart noted above. According to Dr. Ravenholt, "The Philippines and Indonesia are examples of countries where effective donor action, mainly by AID, has made a crucial difference in the speed with which these two countries have been able to deal with their serious population and development problems."[25] It is remarkable that he cited the two countries whose data are so poor even by the modest standards and world statistics that a special notation was made to that effect. Of the ten countries, two (Thailand and South Korea) undoubtedly had a real and significant decline in fertility; two (Tunisia and Ghana) were recorded with a marked rise in the estimated growth rate; and the rest reflected only the fact that they, like the others, are terra incognita.

That is not the summary that Dr. Ravenhold offered:

> These fertility patterns document a widespread and substantial though by no means uniform decrease in fertility during the 1960s in many countries of the world. . . . But a much more powerful and concerted worldwide effort is needed during this decade to insure that every person of reproductive age has the information and means for effective fertility control. . . . When that goal is achieved, world fertility will surely decrease rapidly with accel-

TABLE 10.1

The Top Ten Recipients of U.S. Family Planning Assistance

Country	Growth Rate		
	1965-70	1970-75	1976-78
Philippines	3.2	3.3	2.9*
India	2.4	2.4	2.1
Indonesia	2.6	2.6	2.3*
Pakistan	2.9	3.1	3.0
Thailand	3.1	3.3	2.6
Tunisia	2.1	2.3	2.7
South Korea	2.1	2.3	1.8
Afghanistan	2.4	2.5	2.2
Ecuador	3.4	3.2	3.0
Ghana	2.2	2.7	3.3

*With a stipulated probable error of as much as 10 percent.

erating improvement in socio-economic development and individual well-being.[26]

In other words, since the vast sums spent by AID have been used effectively, kindly increase its budget.

If data on a downward trend in fertility can be surmised, a correlational analysis can be used to demonstrate a program's effectiveness.

It would be well to approach such a thesis with the background datum that even in the United States the proportion of contraceptive failures has been far higher than most persons would suppose:

Within one year of exposure	
Failure to prevent a pregnancy	14%
Failure to postpone a pregnancy	26%
Failure to prevent a pregnancy within five years of exposure	
Youngest age category	56%
Oldest age category	16%
All respondents	44%

These figures are derived from a 1970 National Fertility Study, which reflected an improved control over an earlier survey. More than half of this greater efficacy in both preventing and postponing pregnancies, however, was attributable to the substitution of the pill for other contraceptive means,[27] and oral contraceptives, one should emphasize, are hardly available in most less developed countries.

In order to determine the trend of even the crude birth rate, one must have as a minimum reasonably plausible figures at two points in time for the number of births and the size of the population. If only some sectors of a society have good statistics, it is highly improbable that in any of their other characteristics these are typical of the whole; it is quite misleading to extrapolate from advanced regions or social classes or villages to the remainder of the population. If there are censuses but no vital statistics, then one must face the fact that the gaps in the census data are likely to be worst precisely in the components of the child-woman ratio—that is, the number of children aged under five years (including an estimate of those who had died during the period as a possible additional factor) and the number of women in the fecund ages. In fact, we have only partial and unsatisfactory clues to the trend in fertility of some of the largest of the world's countries, which are also often the ones with the heaviest burden of overpopulation.

The efforts of some of the West's best demographers to derive plausible projections from incomplete data, using the method first devised by William Brass and later developed in collaboration with Ansley Coale, can be exemplified by a work on the population of Tropical Africa.[28] As in many other less developed areas, the turmoil during the postcolonial period has hardly been conducive to the collection of good data, and in some instances there has been a decline from even the poor and incomplete coverage of earlier years. The summary appraisal by Etienne van de Walle is realistic:

> The very size of [Nigeria's] population is uncertain after the last censuses, its mortality is unknown, and its fertility can only be guessed. . . . No sophisticated procedure upon which we would base even a mere guess about what this population would be 10, 15, or 25 years ahead is justified. Unfortunately this is still true of a large part of Africa.

If, however, acceptable data do show a definite downward trend in fertility, there is no necessity that such a decline resulted from the government's purposive action rather than any of a dozen factors that typically influence natality. If fertility rises, the contraceptive program may have been successful—in preventing its more rapid rise. If fertility falls, the program may have been a total failure—by impeding its more rapid decline. In other words, in order to evaluate the reasons for a particular trend in fertility one needs much more than bare data on births and population. A successful policy constitutes more than planned change that is congruent with actual change; the analytic question is, can one reasonably substitute the determinant of for congruent with?

Of all non-Western countries with official efforts to reduce fertility, Taiwan has been the subject of the most analysis. For a period it became a showpiece to demonstrate the efficacy of the contraceptive program there and, by implication, elsewhere. Even the first half of this appraisal is not really warranted. Though the island has better statistics than some fully industrial countries, the relation between the government's antinatalist efforts and the decline in fertility is not at all clear-cut. From 1962 to 1970, while the total fertility rate fell by an average of 182 units in all of Taiwan, by 211 units in small towns, and by 156 units in all major cities, in Taichung, where the program was initially concentrated, it fell by only 154 units—less than in any of the other categories. One need not conclude that the special effort in Taichung inhibited the decline that was going on naturally, but one can hardly ascribe to it any reinforcement of that downward trend. The same conclusion comes from a temporal analysis: not only did the downward trend in fertility begin well before the program got under way, but it also continued at the same slope.[29]

More generally, the less developed countries with the earliest demonstrable declines in fertility are mainly what Parker Mauldin has categorized as islands and peninsulas: Hong Kong, Taiwan, Thailand, Mauritius, Costa Rica, Puerto Rico, Trinidad, and so on.[30] These are relatively small countries whose social problems are slight compared to the infinite complexity of India, for example, partly because these are typically developing areas, rather than merely less developed ones. This crucial distinction has become so standard in scholarly writings and even in the extrusions from the United Nations that the acronym LDCs is generally understood. It is a curious reversion to an earlier and less satisfactory terminology to entitle a paper, as Mauldin and Berelson did, "Conditions of Fertility Decline in Developing Countries, 1965-75."[31]

This is a conscientious and useful summary of a large number of studies, and it avoids the most obvious flaws of some earlier prior analyses. With an engaging frankness, the authors note that the initial letters of the "best available data" they have used spell out BAD. But is a joke, even a good one, sufficient to cover the deficiencies in the data from 94 countries ranging from Afghanistan to Bangladesh, from Ethiopia to Laos, from the People's Republic of Yemen to the People's Republic of China? No caveats can cover the irresponsibility of citing crude birth rates in 1965 and 1975 from such an array. These figures on natality, such as they are, are then correlated with seven other variables, of which we can take GNP per capita as representative. For seven countries in the list this is given as less than $100 a year, ranging down to $84 for Mali and $80 for Bhutan. That it is physiologically impossible to subsist at such a level does not seem to disturb analysts who use such figures. The problem is rather how the systematic error is built into them. Gross national product is measured ordinarily from commercial operations, and in countries where much of the countryman's produce is not marketed but consumed directly, comparable to the work of housewives in advanced economies, much of the country's production is either excluded from the GNP by definition or is brought in by the wildest of guesses. Since the extension of the market economy means precisely that a larger and larger proportion of this household production is shifted to cash crops or paid work, a recorded increase in GNP can reflect either that transformation of the distribution system or a higher overall production, or both in an unknowable ratio. As Morgenstern put it, rates of growth in GNP are "worthless in view of the exacting uses to which they are being put"; that is, they provide a loose suggestion of broad distinctions but not an acceptable basis for exact differentiation.[32]

As Mauldin and Berelson point out, only four of the 24 studies they summarized included a consideration of the availability of contraceptive services, and all four were "done with the participation of donor agencies directly concerned with policy issues." It is no reflection on the honesty of every businessman that we expect his books to be audited by someone other than his own bookkeeper, and it is not because we find every scientific researcher suspect that the canon has been enshrined that findings are to be checked independently. In every type of study, the many judgmental decisions to be made can shift the reported results decisively. Of course, not all self-appraisals are positive. In the famous Khanna study, the six target villages were compared with six control villages. The temporary decline in the birth rate began before the program got under way, continued at the same rate for a certain period among both the test and the control populations, and was due to a rise in the age at marriage rather than the increased use of contraception. Yet even this honest admission of failure fell far short of the critique available from a replication by an outsider.[33]

Statements about what has happened to the world's fertility depend largely on guesses about countries of which we know least. What can be reasonably averred concerning the trend in the world's two most populous contries, China and India? Of the United Nations guestimated population of the world in 1978, 4,365 million, Communist China supposedly had 1,004 million and India 657 million.

Between them, thus, they made up almost 38 percent of the whole, hardly a lacuna any researcher could accept comfortably.

CHINA

What can be said about the world's most populous country, Communist China? It has had precisely one officially released census, in 1953, when the count was almost 583 million. According to the official announcement, there was a net underenumeration of only 0.116 percent, thus making this the most accurate large-scale census in world history.[34] Though we can reject this judgment as pure bombast, the figure is not only the best datum we have but the only reliable one. The farther we move from 1953, the wider is the range of estimates, whether by officials of the government or by knowledgeable outsiders. There is a static figure of 800 million, repeated year after year together with statements that the population is growing annually by 1.5 percent or 2.0 percent or whatever. Obviously, the party's leaders are not anxious to draw attention to the country's population size, but they have permitted provinces to make their own estimates, which in 1978 totaled some 916 million.[35] Occasional stories are leaked out of Peking that planners are using a figure in the neighborhood of 950 million. Thus, in his report of a recent trip to China, Norman MacRae noted that

> the director general of the agricultural ministry in Peking rather crossly assured us that the population of China was only 800 million; the day before a member of the Politburo told us the population was really 900 million; and the week after a specialist research team on population growth had been told it was 950 million.

The difference of 150 million amounts to a sixth of China's supposed population, or almost 4 percent of all humankind.

MacRae was one of three journalists associated with the London Economist who traveled around China and wrote three independent reports, which in sum are a fascinating picture of every facet of that society.[36] These were not demographers or sinologists, but intelligent and generally well-informed Westerners, somewhat more skeptical of propagandistic reports than some experts in the U.S. State Department. All three were inclined to accept the claim that life expectancy was raised from around 30 years in 1949 to around 60 years today. Middle-aged Chinese, according to Brian Beedham's report, "unlike their fathers and grandfathers, are in no danger of dying of starvation in a ditch; [and] they are in reach of at least some rudimentary medical help if a sudden pain grips their insides."

But the implication from so large a drop in mortality is that fertility has also declined, and when one notes how this has been effected the reported success is plausible. Almost everyone in China is paid either on the eight-grade wage system in the towns or by one to ten work points in the countryside. Though in general the rating is based on productivity, and less on political attitude than in the recent past, this shift apparently has not carried over to behavior flouting the party's line on family size. "One senior official said that in his province a girl who had an illegitimate baby after being refused permission to marry below the minimum permitted age of 24-25 would have her work points cut." A girl can protect herself against such penalties only by claiming that she was raped, and the penalty for rape is death. Mothers of three children are sometimes threatened that a fourth child will get no ration book. The important degree of control of labor, of rates of pay, of the distribution of food, means that it may well have been possible both to raise the age at marriage with little premarital dalliance and to restrict sharply the number of children per family.

One need not credit the statements of the Communist regime that its antinatalist program has succeeded, partly because in all likelihood no one in China knows what its fertility is, and more fundamentally because during the course of any policy, official pronouncements proclaim its success almost automatically. Curiously, one of the few exceptions one could cite pertains to this question. At the end of 1978 an official radio broadcast noted that the number of births in Kwantung province would be some 100,000 in excess of the planned figure. Since this was the first time such a failure was admitted, analysts in Hong Kong interpreted the statement as a truthful indication of official concern. The change in policy during 1978 increasing the income to peasant families that, as family units, did more work, apparently had the unintended effect of stimulating procreation.[37] Yet from both anecdotal evidence and more detailed reports by Western scholars,[38] one can reasonably suppose that overall fertility has been cut considerably.

One should keep in mind, however, that from 1949 to the mid-1950s China followed the standard Marxist line that with its planned economy and socialist society the country could cope with any growth in numbers. The first antinatalist policy was initiated in a curious fashion: the state continued the traditional Marxist opposition to birth control while inducing couples, ostensibly for their personal welfare rather than for societal reasons, to put off getting married. Moreover, twice during the country's short history—during the Great Leap Forward and again during the Cultural Revolution—the party reverted to the earlier orthodoxy and abandoned its intermittent antinatalist stance. It would seem that the party's leaders have been divided on the population issue, with first one faction and then the other setting policy. Western experts are inclined to accept the present commitment to the so-called planned birth program, which combines postponement of marriage with contraception, as strong and unequivocal. One can cite Party statements to document this view. But, to repeat for emphasis, while any policy is in force, all public statements are likely to endorse it enthusiastically. To take another question altogether: from the beginning of the Communist regime the party's commitment to education has been at the center of its plans to raise the efficiency of the economy. Yet during the Cultural Revolution schools and universities were closed, and the cohorts that would have attended are going through life as what Emily MacFarquhar calls the country's walking wounded.

Like the Soviet Union, Communist China has a totalitarian counterpart to the business cycle: full adherence to dogma is maintained until it chokes the economy and supplants any initiative with fear, and then a relaxation is permitted until its continuation seems to threaten the full and absolute control by the party. That certain elements of the Chinese antinatalist system are transferable—contraception should be provided at low cost or gratis, services should be combined with medical or paramedical ones, and so on[39]—is essentially a foolish notion. Most of these ideas have been tried elsewhere with generally little success, and the crucial element, the totalitarian control of people's lives, is neither easily diffused nor welcome.

INDIA

How difficult it is to apply authoritarian methods in a nontotalitarian state is exemplified by the recent experience of India, the second most populous country in the world. During the quarter century 1951-76, its population increased by an estimated 68 percent, from 361 million to 607 million. According to a set of projections based on three alternative trends in mortality and six in fertility, it is virtually certain that the population will reach 900 million by the end of the century, and possibly over a billion.[40]

Though India reputedly began its antinatalist effort earlier and more energetically than other less developed countries, in fact it started slowly and reluctantly, during Nehru's lifetime never achieving even a minimal success.[41] Under Nehru's first Minister of Health, a devoted disciple of Gandhi, a project to implement the rhythm method by the distribution of colored beads became an international joke. By the end of the second Five-Year Plan in 1961, India was still engaged in what the director of the census termed "a pilot experimentation."[42] When the census of that year recorded a total larger than had been anticipated, efforts to generate a full program really began. In the subsequent period control was decentralized to some degree and experiments were made with various types of motivation and distribution systems, but essentially the administrators engaged in a continual search for the contraceptive means. The large-scale program based on IUDs, for instance, was more or less abandoned when it became evident that the proportion of women who either expelled the device or removed it because of bleeding or pain was excessively large, and that other prospective users were being frightened off.[43]

According to an early analysis of vasectomies in one area, the 3,465 men who had been sterilized averaged 39 to 40 years in age, with an average of 5.33 living children. The author saw "no possibility of vasectomy camps having a significant effect on the birth rate, . . . [but] they have no doubt helped to create a climate favorable for popularizing family planning."[44] In other words, the operation was being used mainly by men who had already fathered more children than the birth controllers set as their upper limit of a desirable family size. Even so, when Sripati Chandrasekhar became Minister of Health and Family Planning in 1967, he shifted the emphasis to male sterilization, which he called "of all the methods tried so far the only one that has yielded significant results." After Chandrasekhar was dropped from the cabinet, the pressure to undergo vasectomies was greatly increased.

> Funds earmarked for drought relief, road building, and Harijan welfare are believed to have been used to mobilize respondents. When villagers applied for loans to buy seeds or fertilizers they were ordered first to undergo a vasectomy. . . . Even Nirman Bhawan [of Indira Gandhi's Health and Family Planning Ministry] cautiously admits that some of the camps may have been counter-productive, leaving family-planning workers little time to propagate conventional contraceptive methods.[45]

Undoubtedly in part as a result of such irregularities, the budget for family planning programs was cut from $101 million in 1972-73 originally to $50 million and then, after a partial restoration, to $68 million in the following year. The cut to well under half of the $149 million that had been requested ostensibly was based on general financial pressure, but it also reflected doubts about both the wisdom and the effectiveness of the government's program. The targets in the fourth Five-Year Plan (1969-74) were 15 million sterilizations (contrasted with 10 million performed), 6.6 million IUD acceptors

(2.4 million actual), and 10 million users of conventional contraceptives (4.1 million actual). Instead of a cumulative total of 28 million couples protected by one means or another, there were only 19 million. The announced goal of reducing the birth rate to 25 per thousand in 1978-79 was put off until 1984—symbolically hardly the most propitious year.[46]

When the Minister for Health and Family Planning was replaced by Karan Singh, until then Minister for Tourism and Civil Aviation, he issued a statement announcing a stepped up program. "Clearly," he stated, "only the fringe of the problem has so far been touched." The minimum age at marriage would be raised to 18 for girls and 21 for boys. The compensation for undergoing a sterilization (either male or female) would be increased to Rs. 150 if performed with two or fewer living children, Rs. 100 with three living children, and Rs. 70 with four or more living children (respectively, $16.67, $11.11, and $7.78). Medical facilities for sterilization and what is termed MTP (medical termination of pregnancy) were being extended to rural areas. "Suitable group incentives" would be introduced for the medical profession, district and block councils, teachers at various levels, cooperative societies, and labor organizations, in order to "make family planning a mass movement with greater community involvement." Compulsory sterilization would not be introduced "at least for the time being," but only because "the administrative and medical infrastructure in many parts of the country is still not adequate to cope with the vast implications."[47] Civil liberties had been suspended for almost a year, and Minister Singh did not think it necessary to respond to moral or libertarian objections to compulsory sterilization. There was supposed to be a new mood of national discipline, and allegedly there was "a substantial increase in political support of the family-planning program," with "an unprecedented interest in promoting family planning to slow down the rate of population growth."[48]

In fact, the sterilization program was an important reason for the downfall of the Gandhi government. Sanjay Gandhi, the Prime Minister's son, took on birth control as his special province and, with no official position, attacked the problem with his characteristic combination of enthusiasm and corruption.[49] India's 17 states were informed that, contrary to the constitution, increases in population would no longer bring them more representatives in Parliament or a larger share of federal revenues. Several states encouraged civil servants and teachers to fill Sanjay's sterilization quotas by denying them raises and transfers (and sometimes even salaries) until they had convinced a specified number of eligible parents to undergo sterilization. Bounty hunters began to offer their services, charging a fee for each subject found. In some cities officials used the licensing of hotels, theaters, banks, airlines, and other businesses to force firms to induce their employees with three or more children to be sterilized.[50]

Opposition to the program was exacerbated by charges, sometimes well based, that the Hindu majority was using it to reduce the proportions of Untouchables and particularly of Moslems. Sheikh Mohammed Abdullah, who had been keeping the state of Kashmir quiet for the Gandhi government, traveled to Delhi to see for himself what was going on. A Moslem slum had been cleared of its inhabitants at gun point and then razed. When the people were allowed back to where their homes had been, they were given ration cards, which would be renewed only if the men underwent an operation forbidden by their religion. Sheikh Abdullah was so mad he demanded an audience with Mrs. Gandhi immediately; one result was that some of those who had complained to him were arrested.[51] Police and family planners were killed, and in one ugly incident, according to seven opposition members of Parliament, several dozen protesters were shot down and 150 wounded in antisterilization riots. As Prime Minister Gandhi was forced to admit, "Some deaths have taken place, due to firing."[52] Her government fell soon thereafter.

In the new government, according to Prime Minister Desai, "there is no room for compulsion, coercion, or pressures of any sort." The new Minister of Health and Family Planning, Raj Narain, recommended abstention from sex as the best means of birth control. "Instead of the barbarous methods of compulsion employed by Mrs. Gandhi, we will draw inspiration from our old epics and traditions of celibacy, self-control, yoga, and self-discipline." The number of sterilizations fell from an estimated 1 million a month to about 50,000 a month, the lowest rate in a decade. True, the Desai government remained committed to reducing India's fertility, but even its reduced goal could hardly be met under the program it initiated. Even if impossible improvements were to be made in the program, "a further downward revision of targets is likely to be necessary in the future."[53] Even a flawed democracy like India under Mrs. Gandhi cannot use totalitarian methods without stimulating a backlash that, in all likelihood, will soon erase whatever reduction in fertility had been effected.

MARX VERSUS MALTHUS

With whatever embellishments one can find here and there, the American efforts to cut the fertility of less developed countries have been based essentially on offering contraceptives to the masses, usually with inducements of some sort to use them. These so-called

Malthusian programs have been attacked by such neo-Marxists as Mamdani as not merely inefficient in detail, but also unsound fundamentally. According to his analysis, the reluctance of most lower-class Indians to accept contraception is due not to ignorance or irrelevant tradition, but to a rational choice between correctly judged alternatives. In India, few smallholders can afford to hire even one farmhand; for the most part they have to depend on family labor. If a smallholder's sons move to the city and manage to get jobs, the pittances they send back might tide the family over a difficult period or even enable it to buy more land. Similarly, the landless farm laborers are typically paid a share of the crop they pick, which the entire family—males and females, adults and children—gather together. The more hands a family can muster, the more land it can contract for from a landowner. Children pay for the cost of their modest upkeep almost as soon as they can toddle.[54] If this analysis is correct, it challenges the very fundament of utilitarianism: If each of the smallholders or landless workers (in sum, the vast majority of the Indian population) rationally chooses to have a large family, the composite of these correct individual decisions builds up to a disaster for the whole country.

This contrast between awaiting the demographic consequences of broad socioeconomic changes and offering contraceptive services has often been interpreted as a continuation of the dispute between Malthus and Marx. No less a theorist than Sauvy entitled one chapter of his best known work, "Les pays sous-développés: Marx ou Malthus?"[55] A compilation of Marx's own writings on Malthus was introduced with the opinion that "if the social struggles of the early nineteenth century were essentially summed up in the controversy between Malthus and Ricardo, those of our own times are perhaps not unfairly summed up in that between Malthusians and Marxists."[56]

This recurrent label, however convenient many have found it, is a strange commentary on the actual theories of both historic figures. Indeed, Marx believed that the built-in contradictions of capitalism would lead (but hardly in places like India) to the institution of a different social system. The few things he had to say about population, however, sum up only to a denial of its long-term importance in any respect. Neo-Malthusianism, on the other hand, inherited its overemphasis on contraceptive means from the nineteenth-century movement. If one restores to this truncated version the portion the Drysdales and others dropped, Malthus's theory of fertility includes some elements of what is now called neo-Marxism, as well as a direct analysis of motivation that is lacking in both of the modern versions.

According to Malthus, wages are determined by the amount of money available for that purpose and by the level of demand workers set, and he held that generally these two factors change together. Workers who move into the middle-class income range would generally come to aspire to a middle-class style of life, including—and this became for him the key to solving the population problem—the smaller number of children associated with that class. This desirable embourgeoisement of the proletariat could be greatly facilitated, Malthus held, by an appropriate political setting.

> Of all the causes which tend to generate prudential habits among the lower classes of society, the most essential is unquestionably civil liberty. No people can be much accustomed to form plans for the future who do not feel assured that their industrious exertions . . . will be allowed free scope. . . . [Moreover,] civil liberty, . . . [which] teach[es] the lower classes of society to respect themselves by obliging the higher classes to respect them.[57]

In line with these ideas, Malthus advocated a system of universal free education, for his time a radical proposal indeed.

> In most countries, among the lower classes of people, there appears to be something like a standard of wretchedness, a point below which they will not continue to marry and propagate their species. . . . The principal circumstances which contribute to raise [this standard] are liberty, security of property, the diffusion of knowledge, and a taste for the comforts of life. Those which contribute principally to lower it are despotism and ignorance.[58]

This social analysis of the determinants of fertility, almost always overlooked when even learned demographers use the label Malthusian, was most succintly summed up in a pair of review essays Malthus wrote criticizing two books on Ireland by Thomas Newenham.[59] These reviews are remarkable, first of all, for their quite anomalous observations on religion. By their "dastardly, servile, and useless" acquiescence in the terms of the union with Britain, Irish Protestants "had sacrificed their own wealth and honor by sacrificing their country." On the other hand, "the humiliated Catholic, with no rank in society to support, had sought only . . . subsistence; and finding, without much difficulty, potatoes, milk, and a hovel, he had vegetated in the country of his ancestors and overspread the land with his descendants." "Let the Irish Catholics have all they have demanded; for they have asked nothing but what strict justice and good policy should concede to them." Even today, the emotional impact of Malthus's language is hardly to be found outside the writings of Irish nationalists. At that time, with Anglicans, Presbyterians, Methodists, and radicals more or less one in their anti-Catholic stance, and with English Catholics somewhat embarrassed by their animalic coreligionists, Malthus's demand for responsible government, free trade, and elementary justice was more exceptional still.

He returned to the topic in his testimony before the 1827 Committee on Emigration. The Irish, he noted, "are inclined to be satisfied with the very lowest degree of comfort, and to marry with little other prospect than that of being able to get potatoes for themselves and their children." What, he was asked, would "produce a taste for comfort and cleanliness?" "Civil and political liberty," he responded, "and education."[60]

If one wants to link Malthus to a single strand of his complex analysis of population, this is the most important one in relation to policy. To reduce the family size of impoverished masses, one should educate them and give them the freedom to use their knowledge to advance themselves.

NOTES

1. Kingsley Davis, "Population Policy: Will Current Programs Succeed?" Science 158 (1967): Edwin Driver, "Social Ideology, Social Organization, and Family Planning: A World View," in his Essays on Population Policy (Lexington, Mass.: Heath, 1972).
2. Bernard Berelson, The Great Debate on Population Policy: An Instructive Entertainment (New York: Population Council, 1975).
3. Donald J. Bogue, "The Demographic Breakthrough: From Projection to Control," Population Index 30 (1964): 449-54.
4. In 1978, in response to the criticims of an interagency panel, AID shifted country programs from Ravenholt's Office of Population to regional bureaus. Reportedly the reason was that he had lost two patrons in the Senate, Hubert Humphrey by his death and Daniel Inouye by his departure from the relevant committee; see Stephen S. Rosenfeld in the Washington Post, April 28, 1978.
5. Anthony F. Zimmerman, Overpopulation (Washington, D.C.: Catholic University of America Press, 1957), p. 103.
6. Alvin H. Hansen, "Economic Progress and Declining Population Growth," American Economic Review 29 (1939): 1-15.
7. Commission on Population Growth and the American Future, Population Growth and the American Future (Washington, D.C.: U.S. Government Printing Office, 1972), p. 40.

8. A. M. Carr-Saunders, *The Population Problem: A Study in Human Evolution* (Oxford: Clarendon, 1922).

9. Wolfram and Alide Eberhard, "Family Planning in a Taiwanese Town," in Wolfram Eberhard, ed., *Settlement and Social Change in Asia* (Hong Kong: Hong Kong University Press, 1967).

10. Irene Taeuber, *The Population of Japan* (Princeton, N.J.: Princeton University Press, 1958), pp. 33.

11. John Hajnal, "European Marriage Patterns in Perspective," in D. V. Glass and D. E. C. Eversley, eds., *Population in History* (Chicago: Aldine, 1965).

12. Edward Shorter, "Illegitimacy, Sexual Revolution, and Social Change in Modern Europe," in Theodore K. Rabb and Robert I. Rotberg, eds., *The Family in History: Interdisciplinary Essays* (New York: Harper Torchbook, 1973). See also Peter Laslett, *Family Life and Illicit Love in Earlier Generations: Essays in Historical Sociology* (Cambridge, England: Cambridge University Press), p. 113.

13. J. A. Banks, *Prosperity and Parenthood: A Study of Family Planning among the Victorian Middle Classes* (London: Routledge & Kegan Paul, 1954).

14. Both are quoted in J. Mayone Stycos, "Opinions of Latin American Intellectuals on Population Problems and Birth Control," *Annals of the American Academy of Political and Social Science* 360 (1965): 11-26. There has been some change in opinion since these statements were made; see, for instance, John S. Nagel, "Mexico's Population Policy Turnaround," *Population Bulletin* 33 (December 1978). In such a so-called turnaround, however, typically some of those with continuing strong doubts about antinatalist policy remain and, in effect, reduce the effectiveness of whatever efforts ensue.

15. William Petersen, "Marx vs. Malthus: The Symbols and the Men," *Population Review* 1 (1957): 21-32.

16. See J. Mayone Stycos, "A Critique of the Traditional Planned Parenthood Approach in Underdeveloped Areas," in Clyde V. Kiser, ed., *Research in Family Planning* (Princeton, N.J.: Princeton University Press, 1962).

17. Nan Lin and Ralph Hingson, "Diffusion of Family Planning Innovations: Theoretical and Practical Issues," *Studies in Family Planning*, no. 5 (1974).

18. Gary S. Becker, "An Economic Analysis of Fertility," in National Bureau of Economic Research, *Demographic and Economic Change in Developed Countries* (Princeton, N.J.: Princeton University Press, 1960).

19. Lee Rainwater, *Family Design: Marital Sexuality, Family Size, and Contraception* (Chicago: Aldine, 1965), p. 233.

20. Ibid., p. 201. See also H. Theodore Groat and Arthur G.

Neal, "Social Psychological Correlates of Urban Fertility," *American Sociological Review* 32 (1967): 945-59; Karl A. Bauman and J. Richard Udry, "Powerlessness and Regularity of Contraception in an Urban Negro Male Sample," *Journal of Marriage and the Family* 34 (1972): 112-14.

21. Population Crisis Committee, *Population*, no. 4 (July 1976).

22. Mahmood Mamdani, *The Myth of Population Control: Family, Caste, and Class in an Indian Village* (New York: Monthly Review Press, 1972), p. 23.

23. R. T. Ravenholt and John Chao, "World Fertility Trends, 1974," *Population Report* (Department of Medical and Public Affairs, George Washington University, Medical Center) series J, no. 2, August 1974.

24. Environmental Fund, "Questioning the Source," *Special Report*, no. 1 (May 1976); Environmental Fund, *World Population Estimates, 1978*, compiled from estimates by the United Nations and other official sources.

25. R. T. Ravenholt, address before an International Population Conference, November 21, 1975, quoted in Environmental Fund, "Questioning the Source."

26. Ravenholt and Chao, "World Fertility Trends."

27. Norman B. Ryder, "Contraceptive Failure in the United States," *Family Planning Perspectives* 5 (1973): 133-42.

28. William Brass et al., *The Demography of Tropical Africa* (Princeton, N.J.: Princeton University Press, 1968).

29. Wen L. Li, "Temporal and Spatial Analysis of Fertility Decline in Taiwan," *Population Studies* 27 (1973): 97-104.

30. W. Parker Mauldin, "Fertility Trends: 1950-75," *Studies in Family Planning* 7 (September 1976).

31. W. Parker Mauldin and Bernard Berelson, "Conditions of Fertility Decline in Developing Countries, 1965-75," *Studies in Family Planning* 9 (May 1978): 89-147.

32. Oskar Morgenstern, *On the Accuracy of Economic Measurement*, 2d ed. (Princeton, N.J.: Princeton University Press, 1963), p. 300.

33. John B. Wyon and John E. Gordon, *The Khanna Study: Population Problems in the Rural Punjab* (Cambridge, Mass.: Harvard University Press, 1971); Mamdani, *The Myth of Population Control*.

34. John S. Aird, "Population Growth and Distribution in Mainland China," in U.S. Congress Joint Economic Committee, *An Economic Profile of Mainland China* (Washington, D.C.: U.S. Government Printing Office, 1967).

35. John S. Aird, "Recent Provincial Population Figures," China Quarterly, no. 73 (1978): 1-44.

36. Norman MacRae, Emily MacFarquhar, and Brian Beedham, Economist, December 31, 1977, pp. 13-42.

37. Jay Mathews, dispatch from Hong Kong to the Washington Post, December 9, 1978.

38. For example, John S. Aird, "Fertility Decline and Birth Control in the People's Republic of China," Population and Development Review 4 (1978): 225-54; Leo F. Goodstadt, "Official Targets, Data, and Policies for China's Population Growth: An Assessment," Population and Development Review 4 (1978): 255-75.

39. Pi-chao Chen, "Lessons from the Chinese Experience: China's Planned Birth Program and Its Transferability," Studies in Family Planning 6 (1975): 354-66; Judith Banister, "International Effects of China's Population Situation," Stanford Journal of International Studies 10 (1975): 83-113.

40. Robert Cassen and Tim Dyson, "New Population Projections for India," Population and Development Review 2 (1976): 101-36.

41. T. J. Samuel, "The Development of India's Policy of Population Control," Milbank Memorial Fund Quarterly 44 (1966): 49-67.

42. R. A. Gopalaswami, "Family Planning: Outlook for Government Action in India," in Research in Family Planning.

43. D. V. R. Murty, "Evaluation of Family Planning Programme in India," and S. N. Agarwala, "The Progress of IUCD in India," in International Union for the Scientific Study of Population, Proceedings, 1967 (Sydney: 1967).

44. Kumudini Dandekar, "Vasectomy Camps in Maharashtra," Population Studies 17 (1963): 147-54.

45. Sunanda Datta-Ray, "Family Planning in India: A Crisis in Confidence," International Planned Parenthood Federation, People (January 1974): 3-7.

46. K. B. Pathak, G. Rama Rao, and C. V. S. Prasad, "A Future Perspective of Family Planning Performance in India (1975-1985)," Journal of Family Welfare 23 (1976): 11-20.

47. Karan Singh, "National Population Policy: A Statement of the Government of India," Population and Development Review 2 (1976): 300-6.

48. Pravin Visaria and Anrudh K. Jain, "India," Population Council's Country Profiles (May 1976).

49. Ved Mehta, The New India (New York: Penguin Books, 1978), chap. 5.

50. Wall Street Journal, February 4, 1977.

51. Mehta, The New India, chap. 7.

52. New York Times, October 28, 1976; Amit Roy, "Too Many Mouths," London Sunday Telegraph, December 12, 1976.

53. Dorothy L. Nortman, "India's New Birth Rate Target: An Analysis," Population and Development Review 4 (1978): 277-312.

54. Mamdani, The Myth of Population Control, chap. 4.

55. Alfred Sauvy, Théorie Générale de la Population, vol. 1 (Paris: Presses Universitaires de France, 1952), chap. 18.

56. Ronald L. Meek, ed., Marx and Engels on Malthus (New York: International Publishers, 1955), p. 47.

57. T. R. Malthus, Principles of Political Economy, Considered with a View to Their Practical Application, 2d ed. (London: William Pickering, 1836; reprinted, Clifton, N.J.: Kelley, 1974), pp. 226-27.

58. T. R. Malthus, An Essay on the Principle of Population, 7th ed. (London: Reeves and Turner, 1872), pp. 436-41.

59. T. R. Malthus, Edinburgh Review 12 (1808): 336-55; 14 (1809): 151-70. Both are reprinted in Bernard Semmel, ed., Occasional Papers of T. R. Malthus (New York: Burt Franklin, 1963).

60. U.K. Select Committee on Emigration from the United Kingdom, Evidence of T. R. Malthus, May 5, 1827.

INDEX

abortion, 54; Africa, 110; China, 175-76
Abu Dhabi, 36
Africa, 9, 39, 46, 73, 94, 97-115, 342; age at marriage, 46; age structure, 86; economic growth, 15; family planning, 110-12; family structure, 112-14; fertility differentials, 107-09; fertility trends, 102-03; mortality rates, 104; pattern of fertility, 98-102; population estimates, 4; socioeconomic factors, 104-07; status of women, 59; sterilization, 53; urbanization; value of children, 57, 279, 283 (see also specific countries)
age: at marriage, 46, 55, 58, 88-89, 323, 340; income distribution and, 52; structure, 45-46, 85-88, 89-93, 94
Agency for International Development, 7, 228, 345, 346
Aguirre, Alfredo, 302, 307, 308
Aird, John, 82
Albania, 97
Algeria, 104, 108, 110, 111, 112
Altamirano, N. Viera, 341
amenorrhea, 324, 327-29
American Economic Association, 338
angelito theme, 305-06
Argentina, 36
Arnold, Fred, 275, 277, 279
Asia, 39, 73, 94; age structure, 86; status of women, 59; value of children, 283 (see also specific countries)
Australia, 48, 59, 387

Bali, 83, 288
Bangladesh, 41, 79, 83; family planning, 344; infant mortality, 297, 301; value of children, 55, 282, 288
Banks, J. A., 276, 285
Bannister, Judith, 82
Barbados, 73, 79
Becker, Gary S., 275, 285, 342-43
Beedham, Brian, 350
Benoit, D., 308-09
Berelson, Bernard, 83, 337, 348, 349
Berliner, David, 133-34
Bhawan, Nirman, 353
Bhutan, 349
Billewicz, W. Z., 331
Biraben, Jean-Noel, 12
birth control (see family planning)
Blake, Judith, 288
Blumin, Stuart M., 241
Bogue, Donald, 337, 342
Bolivia, 104, 306
Bolton, Craig, 21
Boserup, Ester, 278
Botswana, 110
Boulding, Kenneth, 29
Brass, William, 347
Braun, R., 300
Brazil, 52, 79, 83, 344, 382

Brown, Lester R., 82
Buck, John Lossing, 121, 123, 124
Bulgaria, 244
Burma, 52
Burundi, 102
Butz, W., 330
Byrne, Joycelin, 93

Cain, Mead T., 281-82
Caldwell, John C., 16, 59, 276, 277, 279, 282-83, 286-87
Cape Verde, 98
Carr-Saunders, A. M., 299
Caribbean, 39, 53, 93
Castro, Josue de, 49-50
Central America, 261, 341 (see also specific countries)
Chad, 109
Chandrasekhar, Sripati, 129, 353
Changing African Family Project, 283, 287
Chao, John, 344-45
Chen, D. T., 122
Ch'en Hsien, 140
Chen, L. C., 323
Ch'en Mu-hua, 164, 165, 172, 177, 180-81, 184, 187
Ch'en Ta, 121
Chi Lung, 162
Chiang Ch'ing, 145
Ch'iao Ch'i-ming, 121, 122
Chicago school of economics, 285
Chile, 73, 302
children, value of, 55-58, 274-88; Africa, 113; China, 165; Cost-Sensitivity Index, 278; Perceived-Utility Index, 278
China, 36-37, 39, 119-98, 288; abortion, 175-76; collectivization, 151-52; Common Program of 1949, 150; education, 152-55; familism, 155-57; family planning, 79, 82, 120, 131-32, 135, 136, 143, 146, 157, 159-97, 350-52; income distribution, 52, 261; infant mortality, 157-58; literacy, 152-54; living standards, 147-49; Marriage Law of 1950, 155-56; National Symposium on Population Theory, 181; National Women's Federation, 150, 151; population estimates, 33, 36, 79, 349; social and economic change, 147; status of women, 149-51; sterilization, 175-77; urbanization, 149; value of children, 165
China Youth, 190
Chou En-lai, 160, 179, 181
Chowdbury, D., 297
Clark, Colin, 278
Coale, Ansley J., 244, 278, 347
Coffee Growers Association, 344
Colombia, 73, 302, 306, 344
Comoros, 98
Confucian ethics, 181, 339-40
contraception (see family planning)
Coontz, Sidney, 286
Costa Rica, 73, 261
Cowgill, George, 299
Cuba, 73, 88

David, Kingsley, 337
death rates (see mortality rates)
Demeney, Paul, 289
Demographic Institute, University of Indonesia, 83
Desai, Prime Minister, 355
Dickman, Mildred, 299
Dominican Republic, 73
Driver, Edwin, 337
Drysdale family, 342

Dublin, Louis, 338-39
Duesenberry, J. S., 285
Dumond, Don E., 299

East-West Center, Value of Children (VOC) Project, 275, 278
Easterlin, Richard A., 240, 275, 285
Eastman, N. J., 331
economic growth, 51-53 (see also income)
Economist, 350
Ecuador: angelito theme, 305-06; infant mortality, 51, 301, 303
education: Africa, 107-08, 114; China, 152-55; costs of, 48
Egypt, 12, 73, 79, 102-03, 108-09, 110, 111; birth rate, 39; birth registration, 83; family planning, 15, 115
El Salvador, 73, 79
Elu de Lenero, Ma del Carmen, 283
Engerman, Stanley, 57
England, 37, 47-48, 61, 244, 324, 331; family planning, 342; urbanization, 49
Environmental Fund, 7
Espenshade, Thomas, 274, 279
Ethiopia, 32
Europe, 47, 97, 264, 265-66

family planning, 53-55, 228-30, 257-61, 338-58; Africa, 110-12; China, 79, 82, 120, 131-32, 135, 136, 143, 146, 157, 159-97, 350-52; India, 83, 352-55; Mexico, 83
Fiji, 73, 98
filariasis, 109
Fogel, Robert, 57
Forster, Colin, 236, 237
France, 39, 47, 61, 339
Frisch, R. E., 323-24, 327, 329

Gabon, 53, 98, 109
Gandhi, Indira, 31, 354, 355
Gandhi, Sanjay, 354
Germany, 39, 52, 244
Ghana, 103, 104, 107, 108, 110, 345; value of children, 282-83
Gini index, 52, 262
Gokulathathn, K. S., 307
Gopalan, C., 323
Gordon, J., 302
gossypol, 176-77
Granzberg, Gary, 299
Great Britain (see England)
Greenland, 345
Grenada, 93
Guatemala, 310
Guinea, 109
Gunapathy, K. R., 284
Guyana, 93

Habicht, J. P., 330
Hajnal, John, 340
Hansen, Alvin, 338
Harris, Marvin, 299
Hassan, Fekri A., 298-99
Hegsted, D. M., 329
Henry, Louis, 14
Holland, 331
Hollerbach, Paula, 283
Hong Kong, 73, 79, 89
Hoover, Edgar M., 278
Hopeh Daily, 179
Horlacher, David E., 275
Hsueh Mu-ch'iao, 144, 148, 151
Hu Ch'iao-mu, 163
Hua Kuo-feng, 79, 92, 155, 160-61, 170, 183, 187
Hull, Terence H., 83, 281, 287
Hull, Valerie, 83, 281, 287
Human Relations Area Files, 299
Hungary, 48, 52, 263-65
Hutterites, 319

income: Africa, 104-07; distribution, 51-53, 65, 254-71; Puerto Rico, 30
India, 31, 45, 62, 79, 82, 342; family planning, 352-55; income distribution, 261; infant mortality, 50, 51, 301; nutrition and fertility, 323; population estimates, 32, 33; remarriage of widows, 339; value of children, 283-84
Indonesia, 12, 37, 50, 79, 82-83, 229, 344
Indonesia, University of, 83
Indonesian Fertility-Mortality Survey, 1973, 83
infant mortality, 50-51, 295-311; angelito theme, 305-06; child replacement hypothesis, 296-98; child survival hypothesis, 296-98; China, 157-58; control, 298-300; fertility-inflating effects, 296-98
infanticide, 54, 298, 299, 307
inheritance laws, 47, 282
International Labor Office, 62
Ireland, 340
Islam, 107, 113
Italy, 39, 52
Ivory Coast, 104, 107

Jackson, E., 331
Jacobson life table, 240
Jamaica, 73, 79, 88, 93
Japan, 14, 33, 47, 48, 61, 340; family planning, 15; value of children, 278-79
Java, 57, 62, 83, 280-81, 286; value of children, 279
Jones, Gavin, 83

K'ang K'o-ch'ing, 150, 183, 190
Katz, Michael B., 241
Kenya, 104, 107, 110
Keynesian economics, 338
Khan, A., 302
Khanna study, 54, 301, 303, 349
Kintner, H., 317
Knodel, John, 14, 15, 307, 317
Korea, 266, 267, 268, 269, 288; income distribution, 261 (see also South Korea)
Kuznets index, 52
kwashiorkor, 303

land tenure, 48, 63
Latin America, 15, 39, 49, 50, 73, 79, 86, 94, 267; angelito theme, 305-06; infant mortality, 302; status of women, 59; value of children, 283 (see also specific countries)
Leasure, J. William, 21
Lebanon, 102
Lee, Ronald Demos, 14
Leibenstein, Harvey, 284-85, 291
Lengyel, Maria Sophia, 263
Lesotho, 110
Lewis, Oscar, 306
Li Chi, 154
Li Hsein-nien, 157, 161
Libya, 104
life expectancy, 48, 72
Limits of Growth, The, 339
Lin Piao, 154, 181
literacy: Africa, 107; China, 152-54
Liu Hsi-yao, 155
Liu Shao-ch'i, 181
Lorimer, Frank, 279

McArthur, J. W., 327
MacFarquhar, Emily, 352
McLoughlin, P., 283
MacRae, Norman, 350
malaria, 94, 122

Mali, 349
Malthus, 48, 161, 276-77, 339, 355-58
Mamdani, Mahmood, 278, 365
Mao Tse-tung, 145, 151, 155, 157, 160, 162, 180, 183, 187
Marnane, Patrick J. H., 283
marriage: age at, 46, 55-58, 88-89, 323, 340; nineteenth century America, 238-39
Marxism, 48, 49-50, 181, 341, 351, 355-58
Mauldin, W. Parker, 323, 348, 349
Mauritius, 73, 98, 103, 110; income distribution, 261
Melanesia, 104
menarche, 323, 324, 326-27
menopause, 323, 324, 327
Mencius, 181
Mexico, 12, 33, 39, 45, 79, 267, 341; angelito theme, 306; family planning, 83; income distribution, 52; infant mortality, 302; value of children, 283; vital statistics, 33
Micklin, Michael, 283
migration, 93
Minge-Kalman, Wanda, 276
Modell, John, 236
Mohammed Abdullah, Sheikh, 355
Monterey, 302
Morgenstern, Oskar, 349
Morocco, 97, 104, 108, 109, 110, 111, 112
mortality rates, 48, 60, 72; high fertility and, 104; nineteenth century America, 239-40 (see also infant mortality)
Moslem society, 15, 97, 358
Mueller, Eva, 275, 278, 279
Nag, Moni, 279
Naidu, A. N., 323
Nasser, 341
National Fertility Study, 346-47
National Symposium on Population Theory, 1st, Peking, 1978, 181
natural fertility, 14
Nehru, 341, 352
Neel, James, 309
Neo-Malthusian League, 342
Nepal, 279
Nerlove, March, 285
New China News Agency, 147-48, 158, 165, 176, 186
New Home Economics, 285
Newenham, Thomas, 357
Nigeria, 41, 62, 79, 83, 104, 107-08, 115; family planning, 110, 111; intergenerational flow of wealth, 59; population estimates, 32; value of children, 283, 2-8
Notestein, Frank W., 252, 284
nutrition, 49-50; adult reproduction function and, 324-26, 330-32; menarche and, 326-27; menopause and, 327; natural fertility and, 319, 323-24

Office of Population Research, Princeton University, 123, 263
Okun, B., 285
Omran, Abdel R., 304, 309, 310, 316
Orleans, Leo A., 82

Pakistan, 41, 79, 83; income distribution, 261; infant mortality, 51, 297; son preference, 302

Panama, 73
Pathak, R. P., 284
Peet, Robert Breighton, 279
Peking Review, 169
People's Daily (Peking), 127, 148, 151, 165, 179, 180, 187-88, 189-90
Peru, 283, 306
Philippines, 50, 52, 79, 83, 89, 269, 279
Pi-chao Chen, 135
Polgar, Steven, 12, 286, 298
polygyny, 109, 112, 113
Population Association of America, 337
Population Boom, The, 339
Population: Dynamics, Ethics and Policy, 344
Portugal, 97
Potter, J., 234
Pressat, Roland, 125, 127, 128
Preston, Samuel H., 297, 309
Princeton University, Office of Population Research, 123, 263
Puerto Rico, 30, 52, 88, 267-68
Puffer, R. R., 302

Rainwater, Lee, 343
Ratcliffe, John, 283-84
Ravenholt, R. T., 82, 338, 344-45
Red Flag, 163
Retel-Laurentin, Anne, 308-09
Reunion, 103
Rhodesia, 110
Ricardo, David, 356
Rio Muni, 109
Robinson, Warren C., 275
Rockefeller Commission, 339
Russia, 50
Ruzicka, Lado T., 16, 276, 277, 287
Rwanda, 102

St. Kitts, 94
St. Lucia, 345
Sanderson, Warren, 285
Sao Tome, 98
Sarma, Y. U. K., 284
Sauny, Alfred, 356
Saudi Arabia, 32-33
Schultz, T. Paul, 285, 309, 310
Schultz, Theodore W., 276
Scotland, 324
Senegal, 107
Serrano, C. V., 302
sexual abstinence, 54, 108, 109-10, 115
Seychelles, 103
Shorter, Edward, 300
Simmons, A. B., 283
Simmons, G. B., 278
Simmons, J. T., 283
Simon, Brian, 276
Singapore, 79, 89, 288
Singarimbun, Masri, 83, 287
Singh, Karan, 354
Sirageldin, I., 302
Slater, Courtenay, 140
slavery, 57
Smith, Adam, 286
South Africa, 39, 103, 110
South Korea, 41, 73, 79, 83, 89, 345; income distribution, 52
Spain, 97
Sri Lanka, 15, 52, 73, 89, 98; income distribution, 261
sterility, 53, 108, 109
sterilization: China, 175-77; India, 353, 355
Stopes, Marie, 342
Stycos, J. Mayone, 342
Sudan, 109, 279
Sweden, 39, 52
Sweezy, Alan, 14
Szechwan Daily, 163, 191

Taeuber, Irene, 122-23, 340
Taiwan, 73, 79, 266, 288, 348; age structure, 89; astrological calendar, 340; family planning, 229; income distribution, 52, 261; value of children, 278-79
Tanzania, 110
Tapirape, 299
Taylor, Carl E., 304
Teng Hsiao-p'ing, 147, 161
Thailand, 79, 83, 279, 345
Thompson, Warren S., 122, 240, 243
Thomson, A. M., 331
T'ien, H. Yuan, 238, 239
Tobago (see Trinidad and Tobago)
Trinidad and Tobago, 73, 79, 83
Tsinghua University, Institute of Census Research, 121
Tucker, G. S. L., 235, 236, 237
Tunisia, 39, 73, 102, 103, 110, 111, 115, 345
Turkey, 79, 83, 89
twin infanticide, 299

United Nations, 32, 33
United Nations World Population Conference, Bucharest, 1974, 79, 229
United States, 52, 228-46; availability of farmland, 235-38; efforts to reduce fertility in less developed countries, 337-58; ethnic differences, 240-41; marriage patterns, 238-39; modernization, 241-42; mortality changes, 239-40; urban and industrial development, 234-35
United States Agency for International Development, 228, 345, 346
University of Indonesia, 83
urbanization, 49; China, 149; United States, 234-35

Value of Children (VOC) Project, 275, 278
van de Walle, Etienne, 14, 15, 307, 347
venereal disease, 53, 94, 109
Venezuela, 73, 79
Verghese, K. P., 307

Ware, Helen, 283, 300
wealth, intergenerational flow of, 59, 286-87 (see also income)
Welch, Finis, 301
West Germany, 62
West Indies, 98
Wheat Studies Delegation, 1976, 138
Whelpton, P. K., 240
White, Benjamin N. F., 279, 286
Whitehead, L., 306
Wigglesworth life table, 240
Willis, Robert J., 285
Wilmsen, E. N., 323
Wolfson, Margaret, 133-34
women, status of, 58-59, 65; Africa, 111-12; China, 149-51; United States, 245
World Fertility Survey, 1976, 83, 268
World Population Conference, Bucharest, 1974, 79, 229
World Population Plan of Action, 229
Wray, Joe D., 302, 307, 308

Wyon, J., 302

Yasuba, Yasukichi, 236, 237, 238, 240
Yeh Chien-ying, 162
Yen Ch'eng-chien, 192-93
Yengoyam, 307
Yoruba, 107-08
Yoshinaga, 329

Zambia, 107, 110
Zaire, 104, 109, 283
zero population growth (ZPG), 338

ABOUT THE EDITOR AND CONTRIBUTORS

NICHOLAS N. EBERSTADT is visiting research fellow at the Rockefeller Foundation in New York. He is the author of Poverty in China (1979) and the forthcoming volume Ideology and the Food Crisis.

JOHN S. AIRD is chief, foreign demographic analysis division, at the Bureau of the Census in Washington, D.C. Widely regarded to be one of the foremost living authorities on China's population, he has published extensively on the subject.

JOHN C. CALDWELL is professor, department of demography, Australian National University, Canberra, Australia. His many publications on Africa and the demographics of the family include Population Growth and Family Change in Ghana (1968), Population Growth and Socioeconomic Change in West Africa (1975), which he coauthored, and The Persistence of High Fertility: Population Prospects in the Third World (1977), which he edited.

ROSE E. FRISCH is lecturer in population science at the Harvard School of Public Health in Boston and a member of the Harvard Center for Population Studies. Dr. Frisch has published more than 50 papers dealing with various aspects of nutrition.

W. PARKER MAULDIN is senior scientist at the Rockefeller Foundation in New York. Previously he was associated with the Population Council in New York, where among other positions he served as acting President. Dr. Mauldin has written more than 85 articles on various aspects of world fertility trends.

MONI NAG is senior research associate, Center for Policy Studies, The Population Council. Previously he was professor anthropology at Columbia University. He is editor of Population and Social Organization (1976) and is currently preparing a volume on fertility decline in the Kerala and West Bengal provinces of India.

WILLIAM PETERSEN is Robert Lazarus Professor of Social Demography Emeritus at Ohio State University in Columbus. Among his many works are Population (1969), Malthus (1969), and the forthcoming Dictionary of Demography.

ROBERT REPETTO is associate professor at the Harvard School of Public Health in Boston, and is affiliated with the Harvard Center for Population Studies and the Harvard Institute for International Development. He has written widely on development issues, his most recent book being Economic Equality and Fertility in Developing Countries (1979).

SUSAN C. M. SCRIMSHAW is associate professor of public health at the University of California's School of Public Health in Los Angeles. Dr. Scrimshaw has devoted most of her career to applying anthropological techniques to the study of population, and has done fieldwork in Ecuador, Colombia, Guatemala, and other Latin American countries.

MARIS A. VINOVSKIS is associate professor of history at the University of Michigan in Ann Arbor. Until recently, he also served as deputy staff director, U.S. House Select Committee on Population, in Washington, D.C. He has written extensively on American demographic history. Among his most recent works are Education and Social Change in Nineteenth Century Massachusetts, which he wrote in collaboration with C. F. Kaestle, Studies in American Historical Demography (1978), which he edited, and Family and Population in Nineteenth Century America (1978), which he edited in collaboration with Tamara Hareven.